Harry Secombe
—— An ——
Entertaining Life

Also published by Robson Books:

FICTION
Twice Brightly
Welsh Fargo

NON-FICTION
Goon Abroad
The Harry Secombe Diet Book
Harry Secombe's Highway
The Highway Companion
The Zoo Loo Book

FOR CHILDREN
Katy and the Nurgla
The Nurgla's Magic Tear

Harry Secombe
—— An ——
Entertaining Life

HARRY SECOMBE

 Robson Books

This special omnibus edition of Sir Harry Secombe's autobiography first published in 2001 by Robson Books, 10 Blenheim Court, Brewery Road, London N7 9NY

A member of the Chrysalis Group plc

British Library Cataloguing in Publication Data
A catalogue record for this title is available from the British Library.

ISBN 1 86105 471 8

Printed in Great Britain by Butler & Tanner Ltd, London and Frome

Contents

Foreword by The Prince of Wales   vii

Part One: Arias and Raspberries (1921–1951)

Preface	9
Beginnings	11
Schooldays – Could Do Better	29
The Young Tycoon	49
Playing Soldiers	61
The Real Thing	81
Italy – Shells and Showbiz	105
Out of the Frying Pan into the Foyer	129
Learning the Trade	143
New Responsibilities	169
Those Crazy People	197

Part Two: Strawberries and Cheam (1951–1996)

Preface	1
The Goons	5
Radio Days	18
Treading the Boards	25

Hits and Mishaps in Film and TV   46
Life on a Main Road   80
Pickwick and other Musicals   108
A Wanderlust   141
Entertaining the Services   167
On the Highway   181
Pickwick Again   200
Grand Finale   211

Part Three: Family Memories (2001)   217

Foreword

For those of us in my generation – *and* my father's for that matter – who grew up with the sound of Harry Secombe's inimitable voice booming at them from the wireless, this last week has seen the approaching end of an era with the passing of a truly special person and the last but one of the original Goons. After having to endure every kind of appalling suffering and illness in his later years with Job-like fortitude and indomitable faith, one of the great life-enhancers of our age has departed the stage of life, trailing behind him in his wake nothing but memories of laughter, happiness and sheer goodness. A light has, quite literally, gone out in our lives with the removal of such a vital spirit.

In company with many others in our country, Harry made a deep impression on me during that unforgettable period of *The Goon Show* when enormous efforts were made to tune into the BBC each week so as not to miss a single episode. Indeed, such was the impression made upon my young self that, at a later stage, my younger brothers actually believed *I* was the Goons ... But Harry also made a deep impression on so many people for a multitude of other reasons; for his unforgettable singing voice, for his frequent television appearances and, above all, for his countless acts of kindness and irresistibly unstoppable good humour. Not one generation, but two, owe a huge debt to Harry Secombe for quite simply making life infinitely more worthwhile and totally hysterical. When it is increasingly noticeable how cynical, tasteless and devoid of true wit so much of what passes for humour has now become, you begin to realize just how refreshingly, gloriously innocent – and uncomplicated – Harry's approach to life was. No wonder more and more people want to watch, or listen to, the older programmes that bear the elegant hallmark of wit, the subtle play on words, the double intent and the sheer skill of proper farce. Harry exemplified the enduring importance in our lives of those great and timeless traditions that are fast disappearing – unless, perhaps, we mark his departure by rediscovering these vital elements in our battered culture...

I often wonder how much of a role the shared suffering and constant danger of the last war played in helping to bring out the peculiarly zany humour of those former military combatants – Harry Secombe, Spike Milligan, Peter Sellers and Michael Bentine. I suspect that their experiences had a pretty profound effect and, in many ways, we have been fortunate beneficiaries. I remember Harry telling me years ago that some of the characters featured in *The Goons* had been inspired by eccentric figures they had come across during the War and in wonderfully unlikely situations. Major Denis Bloodnok, for instance, must have been partly modelled on a particularly eccentric individual whose encounters with various types of curry have a faint ring of military truth...

Whatever the case, Harry Secombe's unique gift was to have been able to enrich the sum of human happiness; to have become a much-loved household name throughout the length and breadth of a Land that has always thrived on laughter and on seeing the funny side of life – even in the worst possible situations – and to have left so many of us with a genuine feeling of sadness and loss at his departure.

The Prince of Wales
(This foreword first appeared
in the *Observer* on 15 April 2001)

ARIAS

&

RASPBERRIES

The Autobiography

of

HARRY SECOMBE

Vol 1

'THE RASPBERRY YEARS'

For my family – I love them all

Preface   9
 1 Beginnings   11
 2 Schooldays – Could Do Better   29
 3 The Young Tycoon   49
 4 Playing Soldiers   61
 5 The Real Thing   81
 6 Italy – Shells and Showbiz   105
 7 Out of the Frying Pan into the Foyer   129
 8 Learning the Trade   143
 9 New Responsibilities   169
10 Those Crazy People   197

PREFACE

When a man delves into his past he glimpses a stranger who is vaguely familiar. Did I say that? Did I really do that? Only fragments of conversation come to mind and events become kaleidoscopic. One can only hope to reveal the essence of oneself, and embellishment here and there is inevitable.

An entertainer leaves little of himself behind after he has gone. A round of applause cannot be framed and a standing ovation cannot be displayed on a mantelpiece. The best memorial he can hope for is that at some time in the future a man in a bar may say to his companion, 'That Harry Whatsisname was a funny bloke, he always made me laugh.'

This book is for him.

Beginnings

Just as all true cockneys are born within the sound of Bow Bells, so all true Welshmen are presumed to have been born on a hillside.

My parents kept a welcome for me in Dan-y-graig Terrace, which lies along the slope of Kilvey Hill, Swansea. The date was 8 September 1921, and the time was midday. I was the third child, Frederick Thomas having arrived two years and eight months earlier, and my sister, Joan, about a year before I made my squalling entrance.

These facts are indisputable and can be verified, I'm afraid. I say 'I'm afraid', because for quite a while during my childhood I held the romantic notion that I was really a royal prince who had been left on the doorstep, and that one day the arrival at the door of a group of bemedalled important personages would signal the beginning of my reign.

I used to search my person for anything resembling a royal birthmark – a mole, or a wart, even, which would reveal to me my own true identity. The best I could come up with was a blind boil which I discovered on the back of my neck by arranging the mirrors on the dressing table.

When at the age of eight I turned yellow, I thought that my real colour had come through at last and that at any minute Oriental gentlemen in embroidered robes would come along to the council estate and bear me off on a litter to my rightful inheritance. Unfortunately, it turned out that I had jaundice.

After that, I became reconciled to the fact that I really was the son of a commercial traveller and that my mother was who she said she was.

At this distance my recollection of the time spent in Dan-y-graig Terrace is naturally pretty dim. I remember sitting on the back doorstep looking at the funnels of ships, and have a vague memory of wearing a long flannel nightgown and bouncing up and down on a bed with my brother. It is fairly reasonable that this period of my life should be difficult for me to reconstruct because we left the house – in which my parents only rented a couple of rooms from the Roberts family – when I was four years old.

We then went to live on a new council estate which was being built on the lower part of Kilvey Hill, about half a mile away. My memory of the day we moved into the new house is with me still. My mother was carrying my baby sister, Carol, in her arms, and my brother Fred and I ran alongside her. When we came to the top of St Leger Crescent, workmen were still busy on the other houses, and outside number 7 was a huge mound of rubble where the garden was supposed to be. My mother opened the freshly painted green gate and we all proceeded towards the equally freshly painted green front door with its new brass knocker. Mam opened it with her shiny new key and in we went. I remember looking with awe at all the space inside. There was a front room downstairs and beyond that a kitchen and a bathroom. A flight of stairs faced the front door and I climbed them timidly. At the top were three more rooms and a toilet. The immensity of the place intimidated me. I ran downstairs to my mother and asked her if I could go in all the rooms, because back in Dan-y-graig Terrace my brother and I were constantly being told not to open doors other than ours in the house, as we were 'not allowed in there'.

'Yes,' said Mam. 'You can go where you like here. This is our home.'

And my brother and I ran, whooping like Red Indians, through the house and up and down the stairs and out into the back garden until we were exhausted.

It was a particular relief for my mother to leave Dan-y-graig Terrace, because my elder sister, Joan, had died at the age of four during the time she had lived there. She fell victim to peritonitis, the result of a badly diagnosed appendicitis. I cannot remember her at all, but my mother constantly talked about her and her big dark violet blue eyes stared solemnly down on us from the enlarged photograph in its oval brown frame which hung on the wall in the front room. She was an almost tangible presence in the house until my sister Carol started to grow from a baby into a self-assertive little girl and gradually dissipated the hold that my dead sister had over my mother's mind.

It was a happy place to live in and as we were surrounded by neighbours equally new to the estate, there was no feeling of having to keep up with the Joneses – most of the families were called Jones anyway. There was a family on either side of us; the Foulkses on the left and the Johnses on the right, and we were soon borrowing from each other – a cup of sugar, 'a piece of cheese for our Joe's box'.

The geography of the estate was peculiar, to say the least. Grenfell Park House, after which the estate was named, had been demolished just after the First World War, and the council houses built on the land upon which it had stood. Grenfell Park Road ran along the side of Kilvey Hill forming the north side of the recreation ground, and St Leger Crescent swept down the hill in a slow curve, skirting St Thomas Church and meeting up with Port Tennant Road at the bottom. Pen-ys-acoed Avenue led down from Grenfell Park Road in an 'L' shape, joining up with St Leger Crescent and leaving, in the space between, a piece of spare ground which became known as 'the patch' and which was the arena for all our childhood games. We fought the Great War all over again on it, played mothers and fathers and doctors and nurses – monitored by our parents, who could look down on our activities from their bedroom windows, and hurl admonishments if and when the occasion demanded.

We were a close family, and although as we grew up Fred, Carol and I quarrelled quite a lot over trivial things, Mam and Dad never seemed to do so, and whatever happened we felt secure in the knowledge that they were always there to console us in our darkest moments and exult with us in our times of success.

My father was a dapper little man who had worked his way up from lathering customers – having to stand on an orange box to do so – in his uncle's barber shop when he was only twelve, to become a commercial traveller in the wholesale grocery firm of Walters and Batchelors in St Mary's Street, off Swansea's High Street.

He was never very well paid – I think thirty shillings a week was his salary when we were kids – so he supplemented his income by entering cartoon competitions in the *South Wales Evening Post*. These were open to all comers and had to be of a sporting nature. When he was young he had shown exceptional talent as an artist and was admitted to Swansea Art School. However, he was forced to leave after a short while because his mother wanted him to go to work to help support the family. He was so disappointed that he left all his paints and pencils behind in his desk.

He was one of seven children. Will was the eldest of the boys, then came Dad (Frederick Ernest), then Stanley, Harry and Cyril. The two girls were Josie – the eldest child – and Margery, a beautiful redhead who played the piano in Woolworth's for years, demonstrating sheet music. Everybody knew Aunty Marge – she was a stunner.

Stanley, Harry and Cyril all worked for South Wales Transport as conductors when I was a lad, their fingers stained green through handling all the coppers in those leather bags they wore across their shoulders. When they worked the

St Thomas train route I was always pleased to see them –
I'd get a big wink, a joke and a free ride.

Uncle Cyril went on to be an inspector on the buses, and
when I was a schoolboy he was my idol. He was always telling
funny stories and was a great favourite in concerts around the
town. His speciality was playing an ordinary household saw.
He would place it between his legs, then, by striking the
surface with a drumstick, he was able to manipulate it into
making music. The sound he produced was like a high-pitched
soprano – which was what he might have become had he not
been careful with the lethal teeth of his instrument.

Margery's husband, George Charles, was another character
who influenced me a lot in my impressionable years. He had
dabbled in show business when he was a youth, and was
quite a good tap dancer. Thanks to him I was able to learn
a few steps myself – the result of a handful of lessons on
odd Saturday mornings. However, his main claim to fame
was the fact that he was the drummer with the Keskersays
Dance Band which played every week at the Langland Bay
Hotel. Uncle George was known to everyone locally and he
and Aunty Marge were a very glamorous pair in my eyes.

Dad's mother, Nana – as we called her – was also quite
'card'. She was the life and soul of many a social gathering
when she put on my grandfather's working clothes and sang
the old music hall songs.

Bampa Secombe, as long as I could remember, always sat
in an old upright wooden armchair near the fire, puffing away
under his thick grey moustache on a smelly old pipe, with a
spittoon at his feet. In his day he had been a stonemason, a
trade only Will, his eldest son, had taken up after him. The
poor old fellow's chest was forever rattling and I can rarely
recall him standing up. He was a pretty good shot with the
tobacco juice, though – something I always envied him. My
juvenile attempts at emulating him at home with an improvised spittoon were strenuously suppressed.

George and Margery lived with my grandparents at number
38 William Street, along with their son, Freddie. He was an

extremely mischievous boy who always made me laugh. He still does.

The house backed on to the Vetch Field, the home of Swansea's Football Club, and in order to watch the games the family erected a wooden stand which could only be reached by a ladder. On Saturdays the Secombe males would turn up in force for their free entertainment, and the platform would rock to and fro in rhythm with the ebb and flow of the match. It was strange to see how these gentle little men turned into red-faced militants as they yelled abuse at the referee.

As the years went by, the Swansea FC built higher and higher fences around the ground, and our family responded by increasing the height of the stand, until it got so precarious that my mother forbade me to go to William Street on a Saturday. Dad and Fred still went, but I was secretly glad not to go. Soccer never held much fascination for me, and to be perfectly honest I found the transformation of my uncles and their friends from kindly men into roaring loonies a bit frightening.

But I still remember with nostalgia the smoke-filled kitchen at number 38 after the match, where Dad and his brothers would play crib; the cries of 'fifteen one, fifteen two, fifteen four and one for his nob', and the odd juicy plop as another of Bampa's well-aimed shots found its mark.

That, very briefly, sums up my father's side of the family – and, on reflection, it seems pretty obvious how my theatrical ambitions began to take shape.

Another factor in the formation of my desire to become involved in the theatre was the time I spent as a choirboy. From the age of seven, when I first donned a cassock and surplice much too big for my diminutive size, I was hooked on the church. But although I loved the hymns and the ritual I wasn't so keen on the sermons.

St Stephen's Church in Dan-y-graig was the first church I attended as a choirboy. It was the church which my parents belonged to and was just a few yards along from where we used to live in Dan-y-graig Terrace. A small Gothic building, it stood next to the red corrugated iron Church Hall where I gave my first-ever performance. I was a cat in the Sunday School concert and wore a white cat suit with a long tail and a face mask which my father had decorated rather handsomely with whiskers and a little black nose. For the life of me I cannot remember what the play was all about, but I do know that I was the cause of tears among other members of the cast for being too hearty in my interpretation of the part – something I was to be accused of at various times in my future career. I also held up the curtain for some minutes due to the fact that I had dropped one of my cat paw gloves down the toilet, and I refused to go on until it had been dried out. It was put on a radiator – and the smell of that steaming, pee-soaked object remains with me to this day.

My tenure with the St Stephen's choir was fairly short-lived as my folks thought it was too far for Fred and me to have to walk from our house in St Leger Crescent. We transferred our allegiance to St Thomas Church, a larger building which was at the foot of our street. It was the parish church of St Thomas and could be seen for miles – a greyhound of a church looking haughtily down on the mongrel Nonconformist chapels of Port Tennant, its chimes both a reproach and a summons.

On a Sunday those bells controlled my life and Fred's. Eight o'clock communion, then eleven o'clock for the first service, Sunday School at three and six o'clock for evensong. We were up and down St Leger like little yo-yos.

The church played a vital part in Fred's life, because at the age of about twelve, after hearing one particular sermon by a missionary, he made up his mind to become a clergyman and he never at any time wavered from that decision. There was a faint hope in my mother's breast that I would feel a similar call, but after I read the lesson one Sunday morning in the distinctive tones of Sandy Powell, my favourite comedian, she abandoned the idea.

Yet I liked going to church. I would seek the mote-filled shafts of light coming through the stained-glass windows, imagining that they were spotlights and I was a tragic actor. I could hold on to an 'Amen' longer than anybody except the vicar's wife, who had a ship's siren-like quality to her voice. She was referred to rather unkindly within our family as the 'fog-horn conclusion'. The only time I would switch off the dramatic effect was during the sermon when I would surreptitiously unwrap a toffee, avoiding the watchful eye of the choirmaster, who had a mirror above the keyboard of the organ so that he could keep control of his charges. He knew better than anyone that butter would melt in my mouth – especially butterscotch. It was often a race to finish the sweet before the end of the sermon, but occasionally it was possible to get through two toffees before the sermon finished. I became rather expert at judging whether a visiting preacher would deliver a one- or two-toffee sermon, although I was once badly caught out by a missionary from Uganda who finished so abruptly I inhaled a pear drop – an event which brought a gleam of satisfaction to the reflected eye of our choirmaster.

Despite my theatrical aspirations I was really terribly shy and whenever I had a solo to sing it felt like torture. My mouth would go dry and my voice would take on a wobble which threatened to burst the seams of my mother's gloves as she gripped the back of the pew in front of her.

This shyness attacked me even when I was invited to sing within the family circle. Every Sunday after church we all went along to my mother's parents in Jersey Terrace, which was off Dan-y-graig Road, opposite the cemetery. Aunty Doris, who was married to Mam's brother Tom, would bang away on the battered old upright piano and various members of the family would do their party pieces. My father was always called upon to do 'The Wreck of the 11.69', a parody of 'The Wreck of the Hesperus', which he could only perform if he had a chair to hold on to. Mam would sing something in her contralto and Grandad

Davies, who had been a bass soloist in Anglesey Cathedral, would contribute 'Heigh-ho said Anthony Rowley' or something from Gilbert and Sullivan. My sister, Carol, who was the star of the Secombe family, would do some acrobatics or a comedy monologue – and then it would be my turn.

Because I was so shy, it became standard procedure for me to go to the outside toilet and leave the door open to allow my audience to listen from inside the kitchen. I would perch on the wooden seat, my trousers around my ankles – the squares of newspaper hanging from a nail on the wall my only set decoration – and launch into 'Rock of Ages' or 'Abide with Me', accompanied fitfully by the odd tomcat. It was fine in the summer evenings, but the wind off the sea in the winter was pretty cruel, and sometimes even today when I sing those hymns goose-pimples form in the most odd places.

My grandfather on Mam's side, Thomas Arthur Davies, was a very interesting character. He was born out of wedlock to a young lady in the village of Clun in Shropshire. She refused to marry his father, the son of a local landowner. His education was taken over by the village parson, and my grandfather turned out to be a very bright pupil, but owing to his illegitimacy he was denied entry to the professions. Eventually he became a teacher on board the *Clio*, a training ship for young delinquents which was permanently anchored in the Conway Strait.

He met my grandmother, Caroline, when she was sixteen, and they eloped. She was the daughter of a yeoman farmer called Edwards who had been killed in a hunting accident, leaving his children £2,000 each in his will. With her endowment they bought a small hotel near Bristol on a bank of the River Severn. Unfortunately he was not properly insured, and one day the Severn Bore, the tidal wave which sweeps periodically up the estuary, was higher than usual and the

> Life is mostly froth stubble.
> Two things stand like stone.
> Kindness in another's trouble
> Courage in one's own.
>
> Money lost, much lost;
> Honour lost, most lost;
> Courage lost, all lost.
>
> Grandpa
> Aug 16 1935

hotel was flooded. They lost everything and had to be rescued by rowing boat from the bedroom.

After that he had a variety of jobs, none of which were commensurate with his intelligence and he took to drinking heavily. By the time I became aware of his history he was working as a tallyman on the docks, credited with having the finest copperplate handwriting anyone had ever seen in that particular job.

Like Bampa Secombe, he too sat for hours in his wooden chair by the fire in the living-room of the terraced house in Jersey Terrace. He had an uncertain temper, but he was good company for Fred and myself when he'd had a flagon or two. He encouraged us to read good books, and by the time my brother was about ten, Grandpa Davies had taken him through Gibbon's *Decline and Fall of the Roman Empire*. Fred was the apple of his eye because he could see his potential. He wasn't so sure about me. I was never still long enough for him to get to know me properly. Then, when I was seven, both Fred and I contracted scarlet fever and were taken to the Isolation Hospital. Life was very restricted in there and I was forced to lie in my bed and read. Grandad sent me all of Sir Walter Scott's 'Waverley' novels as a present, and I devoured them eagerly. The print was very small, and by the time I was released from hospital I was permanently short-sighted – but I could recite Sir Walter's prose by the yard.

My grandmother suffered from an extreme case of rheumatoid arthritis and was bent like a bow from the waist. In spite of this she was always busy around the house. I can see her now in her black buttoned boots and black bombazine dress and white apron, her hair – of which she was very proud – piled high in a bun, as she whistled away. She had no teeth, but she could whistle like a man. The big copper in which she did the washing was, in season, the vat in which she made her elderberry or parsnip wine, and many a Pearl Insurance man or rent collector would reel down the steps after a couple of glasses of her brew.

There was always a copy of *The Tatler* on the oil-clothed table, and Gran knew the names of all the royalty in Europe and all the spicier bits of gossip about the elegant folk who always seemed to be photographed opened-mouthed with forks of food poised for ingestion. She would grin wickedly as she tapped her crooked finger at a photograph of some high-born lady and say "Er was a proper little tart in 'er time.' And she could quell her husband into submission with a stern 'Tom, behave yourself.'

Mam had two sisters and two brothers – Doll and May, and Harry and Tom. Tom was married to Aunty Doris, whom I have already mentioned, and Harry was married to Essie – more of them later. Aunty Doll was the youngest of the Davies children and my mother, Nellie Jane Gladys, was the eldest. Aunty May was the manageress of Peacock's Bazaar in

Swansea Market (a position once held by my mother) until, after a long engagement, she married Maudsley Adams.

They conducted their courtship in the front parlour in Jersey Terrace – a room which was always tidy and smelt of mothballs. It was only used on Sundays because the piano was in there, otherwise it was reserved for receiving the insurance man on paying out days and for May and Maudsley's lengthy wooing. Maudsley had an artificial leg and when we saw his stick in the hallway we kids would tiptoe past the parlour down to the kitchen, trying to suppress our giggles.

Saturdays were special days for me because I was allowed to go with my mother into town on the tram to do the shopping in Swansea. My task was to help carry home the carrier bags up the steep hill from the tram stop. My reward for doing this was a fish and chip supper at the Dolphin behind the market, or faggots and peas in the market itself.

It was like Aladdin's cave in the Market for a young boy. Football boots hung from the canopies of leather-wear stalls and the confectionery stalls held veritable mountains of pear drops, boiled sweets in the shape of goldfish – which if put in your mouth sideways gave you a sticky grin from ear to ear – coconut mushrooms, liquorice allsorts of every conceivable hue, and trays of toffee which had to be broken with a silver hammer. There were bookstalls, which were always a great attraction for me, especially at Christmas time when all the boys' annuals came out. *The Wizard, The Rover, The Magnet, The Champion* – all these comics had a hardback edition published in time for the festive season. There was the stall where Mam would buy laverbread for our regular Sunday breakfast of laverbread, bacon and fried bread. Lots of people knew my mother, and she loved a good gossip. I would hop from foot to foot as I waited for her to move on to the next piece of scandal, the string handles of the carrier bags beginning to dig into my fingers.

'Come on, Mam,' I'd wheedle. But she was never one to be hurried along.

'I waited nine months for you, so you can wait five minutes for me,' was her standard reply.

But there was never anything to compare with the utter bliss and contentment I felt sitting with her at a table in the crowded Dolphin, the fruits of our shopping resting against our chairs, and the steam from a fourpenny hake cutlet and threepenny-worth of lovely fat chips clouding my spectacles.

'There's a good boy, now, eat up tidy.'

And I would, oh I would.

My father seldom came shopping with us because he couldn't stand the crowds. During the First World War he had been blown up by a shell in the Battle of Neuve Chapelle and he was the recipient of a war pension, which I always collected for him from the post office in Port Tennant Road. I usually did the messages for the household, a chore I was quite happy with because it gave me a legitimate reason for running.

I ran everywhere. I ran to school, I ran to choir practice, I ran to Sunday School, I ran to the grocer's, the butcher's, the post office, and I ran into Swansea to my father's place of work, Walters and Batchelors, with my father's 'book'. This last trip was always worth threepence because it entailed a long jog and was pretty important. The 'book' was a black, ruled notebook containing the orders, written in beautiful copperplate, that my father had taken on his perambulations around the little grocery shops in the Swansea Valleys. It also contained the money he had collected, all wrapped around with rubber bands. My job was to take the 'book' and post it in the letter-box, make sure it dropped, and then come home. The money made it a pretty dangerous operation in my young mind, and I used to see myself as a Pony Express rider taking the US Mail through Indian territory.

Down St Leger Crescent I would lope, my gym shoes squeaking on the pavements; past the church, down on to

Port Tennant Road – head moving from side to side for signs of trouble – skipping the piles of dog turds, skidding around the corner by East Dock station; and if by some mischance the New Cut Bridge had opened to allow a ship to go through, I'd mark time on the spot until it closed, then off I'd go again, a horseless Buffalo Bill carrying at least eight pounds in notes and silver.

After the long pull up Wind Street it was only a few yards down the narrow St Mary's Street to my destination. Once the 'book' had thudded safely through the brass letter-box I would turn around and head for home, still running, but this time I would be the Last of the Mohicans – fleet of foot, looking for tracks in the snow. Once, running in the gutter, eagle-eyed for any signs of grizzly bears, I came across a threepenny bit outside a pub at the bottom of Wind Street. Immediately I became a hazard to trams and cyclists as I ran, head down, looking for loose change. I picked up about three more coins that evening, and, though from that day on I never found any more money, it took innumerable collisions with lamp-posts and prostrate drunken seamen before I could persuade myself to leave the gutter to those who lived there and get back to running on the pavement. I suppose you could say that I had a good run for my father's money.

My constant companion, from the time I was about five or six right up to the time I passed the scholarship and went to Dynevor Secondary School, was Ronnie Jones. His house was a few doors away in Grenfell Park Road and he lived there with his mother and father. Mr Jones was the captain of a tug boat and was the image of Spencer Tracy – or he would have been if he'd had any teeth. Ronnie's mother was a small lady who always smelt of apples with a slight hint of gin.

Ronnie had been born with a cleft palate which made his speech difficult to understand when he was young, and I was the only one who could make out what he was saying. So when he was sent on an errand I used to go with him as a sort of interpreter. It worked pretty well as a rule, although things went rather badly wrong one Saturday lunchtime. Mrs Jones sent us to the butcher's to get half a pound of steak and a pound of sausages, and we were given twopence each for going. Unfortunately, on the way to the shop we got so involved in trying to decide what to do with our money that we arrived before Mr Allchurch, the straw-boatered butcher, uncertain whether it was a pound of steak and a half a pound of sausages or vice versa. Eventually we decided on the former, not realizing that the difference in price was considerable in those days, and anyway it was to be charged.

When we got back to Mrs Jones, we found her half-way up the stairs. Ronnie handed her his purchases through the banisters. She opened the parcel containing the pound of steak, and saw the cost of her house-keeping soaring. A lady with a volatile temper, she proceeded to lose it at once, and with an ear-splitting screech she hurled the steak at Ronnie, who ducked, and the man from the Pearl – who had followed us over the threshold – took it full in the face. The steak fell to the floor, where the next-door neighbour's cat, which had been sunning itself on the back doorstep, smartly fielded it and, unable to believe its luck, promptly disappeared into the wilderness which was the Bayless's garden.

Ronnie and I went our separate ways when we reached the age of twelve or thereabouts, but we always remained good chums. It was part of our childhood dreams together that we would one day go hunting lions in Africa. Many years later, when the news came out in the *South Wales Evening Post* that my regiment, the Swansea TA Artillery, had participated in the North African landings, Ronnie met my mother at a bus stop in town. He tapped her on the shoulder with his paper and said, 'He's gone to Africa without me, after all.' And his eyes were bright with tears.

Some of the happiest days of my childhood were spent with my Uncle Harry and Aunty Essie in Llangyfelach. Harry

Davies was my mother's brother and I was named after him. He came to see my mother just after I was born and said, 'If that little bugger is not christened Harry after me, I'll never talk to you again.'

And Harry I became – Harry Donald Secombe. The 'Donald' was my father's idea. He firmly believed that his ancestors came from Scotland – although subsequently we discovered that his family originated from Cornwall. So much for ancestry.

Uncle Harry was an indomitable character. He had lost an eye in the First World War and wore a glass replica with which he played stomach-churning practical jokes. When he played cricket with us he would take off his coat to serve as a wicket, and put his glass eye on it, saying, 'Now, keep your eye on the ball.' He was not averse to dropping it in the fruit salad at tea-time and serving it up to a visitor if he thought he or she needed a laugh.

Aunty Essie was very jolly, very fat and always laughing. She spoiled Carol and Fred and me whenever we stayed there for weekends. The rivalry between us used to be intense, and it was always a matter for tears for the two who were left behind – only one of us could be accommodated at a time. Margaret was their only child, and she was always looked upon by us as a sister. We were all envious of her in a way. She could swim extremely well, ride like a cowboy and outrun us all.

They lived on Llangyfelach Common, a few miles from Morriston, and to me it was Shangri-La. I would get the bus from Christina Street after school on Friday and sit on the top deck, nursing my school satchel which contained a change of clothes for the weekend, and urging the driver to go faster. When the bus stopped at the Plough and Harrow in Llangyfelach, Uncle Harry and Margaret would be there to meet me and away we'd go, whooping and yelling across the common.

There was no electricity in the house for the first years I can remember, and I used to love the smell of the paraffin lamps which provided illumination for each room. The house was redolent with good smells – pipe smoke, bacon frying in the morning, machine oil from Uncle Harry's motorbike and sidecar, and the sweet scent of hay from the stable where Grandpa Cranfield, Aunty Essie's father, kept his horse and cart. There was also the smell of horse manure, which was not all that pleasant and which I invariably brought in on my shoes from the yard.

'Take those bloody shoes off before you come in here, you little bugger, you!' Uncle Harry never minced his words, but he never meant anything unkindly.

Saturday was the day Margaret and I would go out with Grandpa Cranfield in his horse-drawn cart delivering blocks of fuel. I loved that – a good excuse for getting absolutely black without fear of recrimination. The old man was quite a character. He came from Oxfordshire and looked the proper countryman with his knee-high leggings and stout boots, and the eternal hand-rolled cigarette dyeing his straggly grey moustache with nicotine. I used to watch him groom Amy the horse, named after Amy Johnson the celebrated flier. He would hiss away between his teeth as he curry-combed her till she shone. I was allowed to sit on her back and trot around the yard, but I never really got the hang of it – not like Margaret, who could ride bareback like an Apache.

Llangyfelach was where I learned to do important things, like how to tie my shoe laces properly, how to get a proper knot in my school tie, and how to ride a bike. There was love in abundance in that little house on the common, and I always shed a tear when the time came to leave. But life had to go on and school loomed large on Monday mornings.

Schooldays – Could Do Better

The first school the three of us attended was St Thomas' Infants. It was part of a large, red-brick, educational sandwich – Infants at the bottom, Boys in the middle and Girls on the top floor. I took to school very well in the beginning. My mother had taken me along with her for company when Fred was enrolled, and to her surprise I didn't want to go home. Carol, though, after her first day at school refused to go back on the second day, saying firmly, 'I've left.'

Playtime was my favourite subject, although the hard asphalt of the playground made contact sports hazardous. I fell down one day and cut my knee rather badly. Miss Leonard, the headmistress, carried me into her office and gave me a glass of pop and a biscuit with an iced butterfly on top. For several weeks after that incident I kept falling down outside her office, but I never got another biscuit.

The games we enjoyed in those days seem all to have disappeared. We played marbles – where you placed a number of marbles inside a chalked circle and then in turn tried to knock them out of the ring with a glass alley from the top of a lemonade bottle, or a steel ball if you were lucky enough to have one. The horse chestnut season brought with it the game of conkers, in which you threaded a piece of string through a conker and set out in search of someone else with a similar weapon. You would then hold your conker still on the end of

The Angel

An angel came to me
at night.
He was clad in a robe of
shimmering white;
The plaited locks hung
down his back:
His handsome face did
nothing lack:

He carried in his hand
a book of gold,
With the names of persons,
young and old,
Who were to go to realms
above
Where angels call
good Lord "Love."

By Harry Secombe. Aged 11.
7 St. Leger Crescent,
St. Thomas,
Swansea.
Glamorgan

its string so that your opponent could take a whack at it. If it survived, you then had a turn at demolishing his conker. Each conker you destroyed was then added to your score, provided yours stayed intact. 'Conker six', for example, meant that your conker had seen off six others. I was never very good at that game – either my chestnut shattered at the first go or it flew off the string when I aimed it at an adversary.

I could whip a pretty good top, though. These were wooden mushroom-shaped pegs, gaily striped, which you spun on the ground with the aid of a string whip. Great stuff.

As the years went by I progressed from the Infants' School and into the Boys' section. I was a dunce in anything to do with mathematics, but I did rather well in English composition and drawing.

There was a temporary set-back in my education when I contracted scarlet fever, because, as I related earlier, my eyesight had been affected by an overdose of Sir Walter Scott. I was not aware of how bad my eyes were until I returned to Mr Minty's class following my illness. I was placed at the back of the classroom and found that I was unable to read what he wrote on the blackboard, with the result that I got caned for being stupid. After this had happened a couple of times I came home crying one lunchtime and complained to my father, who happened to be home that day. He was furious – something that rarely happened, in my experience – and insisted on coming back to see 'Mr McGinty', as he called him. I don't know what he said to him, but Mr Minty put me in the front row that afternoon and never again laid a hand on me.

The result of the confrontation was that my parents realized something had to be done about my eyesight, and I went along to the clinic for a test. I was found to be extremely myopic and, in due course, I was given a pair of glasses. The difference was literally staggering. I could see so much more with them on that I almost fell down when I left the optician's. I could read the names of the shops, I could see Kilvey Hill clearly and not as a grey blur, and I didn't care if the whole world called me 'old four-eyes'– I could see!

The next milestone of my school days came when I reached the scholarship class. This was taught by Mr Corfield, a fine teacher in his late forties who knew how to encourage boys to do their best. Mr Corfield took a liking to the way I wrote my essays and showed me how to construct a sentence properly, but he realized, along with every other teacher I had, that maths was a closed book to me.

'Never mind, Secombe,' he'd say. 'One day you'll be a writer.'

Years later when I was topping the bill at the Palladium, I was visiting my folks in Swansea when I heard that Mr Corfield was not too well. I went along to see him, exhibiting all the trappings of showbiz success – the Rolex watch, the snappy suit and the big car. He was well wrapped up and sitting by the fire when I entered his house.

'Hello, Mr Corfield,' I bellowed over-heartily.

He looked at me for some thirty seconds and then said, 'Harry, what went wrong?'

A preliminary examination was held each year before the scholarship proper, and the first time I sat it I passed, much to everyone's surprise, as I was really too young for the main exam, which I failed.

The next year I passed both examinations and elected to go to Dynevor Secondary School, principally because my brother, Fred, was already there and I would have company on the way to school. I don't think Fred was all that keen on the idea, because I was getting to be a bit of a handful. He was also nearly three years older than me, a huge gap when you're young. However, I was very proud of my school cap and tie which I wore with an ordinary jacket; Mam's budget didn't allow for a blazer. 'Nihil sine labore' was the motto emblazoned on the cap – 'Nothing without work' – ominous words, I thought.

Dynevor was a school where the emphasis was on learning, and it provided a good pre-university education for boys like Fred, who was clearly destined for an academic career. For me, it was like stepping into the world of *The Magnet* with Harry Wharton and his pals. The masters wore gowns, and we had a school orchestra, cricket nets, a fives court – all brand new experiences for me. Chaps played pranks on the masters just as the Greyfriars boys did in my favourite comic.

I chose to take French and German rather than Welsh and German, and was put in the 'A' stream. This turned out to be somewhat unfortunate for me because my brother was also an 'A' pupil, and every master reminded me of how well he had done before me.

'Hope you're as good as your brother,' they'd say, patting me heavily on the head with some weighty tome.

But, of course, I never was – except in English and art. When the exam results came out I would be 29th in arithmetic,

REPORT for...... *Easter* ......Term ending...... *2ap* 19 36

Name...... *Secombe H. D.* ......Form...... *4a* ......

Age... *14* ...yrs... *6* ...mths. Height... *5* ...ft... *0* ...ins. Weight... *6* ...st... *11½* ...lbs.

Average Age of Form... *14 7* ... No. of Boys in Form... *32* ... Position... *27* ...

Subject.	Maximum	Marks	Position	Remarks	Subject.	Maximum	Marks	Position	Remarks
ENGLISH Comp	50	30	4	S	ARITHMETIC	50	3	31	P. X
Gram	100	50	15	S	ALGEBRA	100	41	25	V.7
do. Literature	100	44	11	75	GEOMETRY	100	0	31	V.P. X
GEOGRAPHY I.	200	58	21	Wk X	MATHEMATICS I.				
do. II.				V.7	do. II.				
HISTORY	200	92	14	V.7	CHEMISTRY I.	150	17	31	P X
do. European					do. II.	50	40	14	S.
FRENCH	200	91	23	V.7	PHYSICS I.	150	34	30	V.P
do. Literature					do. II.	50	38	21	S.
GERMAN	200	66	19	P. X	ART	100	68	9	Vg
do. Literature					WOODWORK	100	—	—	—
WELSH					METAL WORK	100	30	11	Wk. X
do. Literature	(37%)				MUSIC	100	—	—	—
LATIN									
do. Literature									
GREEK									

Absent... *8* ...half-days. Late... *0* ...times. House Marks : Gained... *O* ...Lost... *1* ...

School Activities ...... *School Choir. 1st Prize Short Story.* ......

Conduct... *G.* ...

Remarks: ...... *A very disappointing result from a capable* ...
lad. There must be a greater striving for accuracy ...

Form Master... *G. Birrell* ......
Determined effort is necessary. This report shows a "falling off" in his work

Head Master, *Llewelyn John* A.R.C.S., B.Sc.

Parent or Guardian...... *F. E. Secombe* ......(Signed)

Remark ......

Next Term begins on......

31st in algebra and 1st in English and art. 'Could do better' was the theme of every housemaster's end-of-term summary of my efforts.

Every year we had a school Eisteddfod, and for some reason I decided in my first term in school to enter in the poetry recitation section. The poem we all had to learn was W H Davies's 'Can I forget the sweet days that have been?' I declaimed the damned thing all over the house – I even recited it to the milkman one morning.

'Very nice,' he said, with an utter lack of conviction. Behind him his horse removed three feet of privet from the hedge next door.

I must have bored half the street with my treble-registered interpretation of the Welsh tramp poet's masterpiece.

Then came the day of the eisteddfod and the moment I had been looking forward to. The whole school was assembled in the Hall, and when my name was announced I stood up to begin the walk up on to the platform where the judges sat awaiting my efforts. Suddenly I realized what I had let myself in for, and my knees began to do castanet impressions. My glasses misted over and I stumbled up the steps, vaguely aware of the forbidding presence of Mr 'Beak' John, the headmaster (so-called because of his large nose), sitting in his chair drumming his fingers impatiently.

'Can I forget the sweet days that have been,' I began, dry-mouthed and even higher-pitched than usual. Then the words flew from my mind and I stood, petrified, looking at the mass of faces before me. I tried again. 'Can I forget the sweet days that have been,' and still nothing came. I repeated the line three more times and then, mercifully, my brother Fred, who was near the front as an on-duty prefect, came up on to the rostrum and led me off, still babbling that traumatic first line.

That experience has never left me, and sometimes on first nights it comes into the back of my mind and a little *frisson* of fear starts up the spine.

*

Despite this débâcle I still had a vague desire to do something in the theatre. I had become a rabid wireless fanatic; indeed the whole family had become 'hooked'. Dad had hired a Rediffusion set with that familiar rising sun motif on the loudspeaker and three stations to choose from – BBC Home, BBC Light and Radio Luxembourg, which was the commercial station with all the advertising jingles. 'We are the Ovaltinies', 'Hurrah for Beetox, what a delightful smell, the stuff that every self-respecting grocer has to sell,' etc. These were tunes that we kids sang ad nauseam. Pre-Rediffusion, Dad had been given an old crystal set which seemed to work very fitfully.

'I've got it!' he would cry as he twiddled the crystal, then 'Damn and blast!' He'd lost it again.

Now we had the world at our command. I don't think we ever missed 'Saturday Night Music Hall' and 'In Town Tonight'. The comedians were my favourites – Rob Wilton, Stanley Holloway with his monologues about 'The Lion and Albert' and 'Sam, Pick Oop Tha' Musket', Sandy Powell, Tommy Handley, Suzette Tarry with her signature tune, 'Red Sails in the Sunset', and – everybody's favourite – Gracie Fields. I loved them all. Billy Bennett, Scott and Waley, Bennett and Williams with their 'phono-fiddles', Clapham and Dwyer, Max Miller and Flanagan and Allen were like intimate friends.

On the way to school I used to pass the poster on the wall of Weaver's Flour Mills, which revealed who was appearing at the Swansea Empire each week, and I would almost swoon with the knowledge that one of my favourites was actually in the same town as me, breathing the same air. I would haunt the back of the Empire hoping for just a glimpse of one of my heroes. George Charles, who knew the stage door-keeper, used to leave my autograph book with him for the stars to sign, and I would pore for hours over the famous names. That's the reason why I never mind signing autographs today – they mean such a lot to some kids. One of my great disappointments was to discover that Roy Fox, the bandleader, had not really signed my book at all, but had used a rubber stamp. That shook my faith in human nature.

My daily intake of radio comedy began to manifest itself in impersonations of my idols, until eventually I had a whole repertoire which I used to trot out on family get-togethers.

Another influence on me was the local cinema, which went through various transformations in my boyhood. At first it was called the Pictorium, or the 'Pic', and then it was refurbished and became the Scala, a name we kids could never pronounce properly. It was the dream factory for the neighbourhood and stood at the confluence of two roads, Foxhole and Morris Lane, a very steep hill which led to the council estate. We would come roaring down the lane on a Saturday afternoon, Ronnie Jones and I, to join the queue for the 'twopenny rush'. The first task was to buy sweets to take in with us from the little sweet shop at the bottom of Morris Lane. There we were faced with an agonizing choice. A sherbet dab? A lucky packet? (This usually contained fibrous twigs of raw liquorice and tiger nuts.) Or a pennorth of unshelled peanuts? I usually plumped for a bullseye, which would at least last most of the main feature, although there would not be the satisfaction of watching it change colour when the lights went out.

Inside the cinema the smell of wet knickers, orange peel and carbolic flowed over us like a warm, sticky bath and the ravaged plush seats held all sorts of perils – old chewing gum underneath, and the odd stain from a previous tenant's over-excitement. The din before the lights went out was indescribable, and sometimes the manager in his boiled shirt and dickie bow would come out in front of the curtains and threaten us with mass expulsion if we didn't calm down. This normally did the trick, and the curtains would eventually jerk back and the projectors would clatter into life, and a collective sigh would go up as the titles appeared on the screen.

Cowboy films and African jungle epics were my favourites when I was very small, and then I progressed to a fondness for 'Andy Hardy' and gangster films. When the exit doors were flung open – always before the end of the serial, so that the screen became blank – I would emerge from the cinema as James Cagney or Mickey Rooney. All the way back up the hill I'd be reliving the film, firing imaginary bullets at unheeding old ladies behind their lace curtains in Morris Lane, or swinging precariously from the lower limb of the dead tree at the end of Grenfell Park Road. My parents never knew who would come home from the pictures on a Saturday afternoon.

Sometimes at the evening performances children were allowed in with an adult, because in those days there were no 'X' rated films. Mam and Dad rarely went to the the 'Pic'; Dad because he'd have to leave half-way through the performance with an attack of hyperventilation, and Mam because she preferred going to the Plaza on a Wednesday afternoon with her friend, Mrs Beynon, who live opposite us in Pen-ys-acoed Avenue.

However, there was one person who was always good-natured enough to take other people's children with her on these occasions. Her name was Mrs Bayless, and she lived a couple of doors up from our house at the top of St Leger Crescent. She came from the Midlands and had about six children of her own. Thus, when we all trooped up the step behind her, she would demand one ticket for herself and sometimes as many as twelve half-price tickets would spew out of the machine in the booth for the rest of us. The manager, unable to do anything about it, would tear the stubs in half with controlled fury and pass us through into the cinema. In the evenings it was a completely different place from the scene of the 'twopenny rush' – discreet organ music would be playing and an overpowering perfumed disinfectant concealed the unspeakable odours of the matinée.

Mrs Bayless also exchanged ladies' magazines with my mother – publications like *True Story* and *Confessions* which Mam used to hide from us. I found the hiding-place one day on top of the wardrobe in her bedroom and became hooked on the delicious dots which always came at the end of a steamy passage, where the reader was left to his or her imagination – a quality I had in abundance. The readers' page always intrigued me – even though the problems that 'Worried of Walthamstow' or 'Distraught of Denbigh' were seeking advice about were beyond the experience of a spotty, bespectacled twelve-year-old. A bucket of cold water would have done us all the world of good.

This was the time when I was becoming aware of girls, although I was pretty shy in their company. There was one particular girl I took a tongue-tied fancy to, by the name of Enid Passmore. Her parents kept a fruiterer's shop near the cinema and I used to see her on the way home from school. She went to Delabeche, which was the sister school to Dynevor, and I was sometimes allowed to carry her books home. She was a strapping brunette with a ready grin which revealed one slightly chipped front tooth. She treated me with a teasing condescension and I never at any time spent even five minutes alone in her company. But her black wool stockings and her toothy smile haunted my boyhood dreams for many a month.

The first romance I ever had was with a very pretty little girl called Mildred O'Malley. She lived in Pen-ys-acoed with her brothers and parents, and her father was the proud owner of a three-wheel Morgan runabout. I must have been about ten when we got married.

The event took place on 'the patch', the piece of waste ground on the estate which looked as if it was the result of the architect having left a packet of cigarettes on the blueprint and absent-mindedly drawn around it.

It was a warm Saturday afternoon and a tent had been set up for the wedding. Joyce Griffiths, who was a bit older than me, was the parson, wearing one of her father's collars back to front and armed, for some reason, with an umbrella. The bride was all ready with her white dress, a lace doily as a veil and a bunch of buttercups and dandelions as a bouquet.

Unfortunately, the bridegroom, Billy Beynon, had been hauled off to go shopping with his mother and so, until I happened to pass by – on the way to Mrs Gorman's sweet shop, which she had set up illegally in her front room – the wedding had come to a standstill.

'Come on, you'll do,' cried Joyce good-naturedly, and in no time I found myself standing alongside Mildred, whom I had always worshipped from a discreet distance.

Joyce rammed an old trilby on my head, reducing my vision considerably. 'Do you take this woman to be your lawful wedded wife?' she asked, pretending to read from a railway timetable.

I nodded nervously, causing the trilby to slip further down over my nose.

'Say "yes", mun,' hissed the parson.

'Yes,' I croaked.

Mildred's reply to her question was firm. 'Yeth,' she declared, bending down to pick at a scab on her knee.

'I now announce you man and wife,' said Joyce, closing the book. 'Now kiss the bride.'

My heart thumped as I turned to my new bride and pursed my lips.

'You look stupid with that hat on,' giggled Mildred.

'Go on, kiss him.' Joyce was getting a bit fed up with the whole thing.

'He's all sweaty,' Mildred observed as I removed the hat. '*Ach y fi!*'

I rubbed my face vigorously with the sleeve of my jumper and puckered up again.

'Not on the lips, you'll spoil my lipstick. My cheek.'

'Old cissy, playing with the girls!' Ronnie Jones appeared at his gate.

I blushed crimson. Before me Mildred had her eyes shut and was waiting resignedly for a kiss.

'Hurry up.' This was Joyce.

I threw the hat on the ground and kicked the wicket stump that formed the pole of the tent. 'I'm not playing any more

– it's daft,' I cried, and walked away without kissing the smooth, cold-creamed cheek that awaited me. 'Anyway, I'm sweating because I haven't been well, so there.'

That was true. I was just getting over a severe bowel infection I had picked up through eating infected ice-cream bought from a street vendor. I had been too ill to go to hospital and so Mam looked after me at home, supervised by Doctor Hefferman, who had brought me into the world. At one stage during my illness I slipped into a coma.

'This is it,' said the doctor. 'If he comes out of this he'll be all right, if he doesn't. . .' he shrugged his shoulders.

I was swathed in cold compresses to bring down my temperature which had reached 105 degrees Fahrenheit, and then they just had to wait and see. After an agonizing time for my family I slowly opened my eyes and the first thing I said, according to my mother, was 'Where's my medals?'

Apparently, to keep me quiet, my father had pinned his war medals on my pyjama jacket.

From that time on I was regarded as the 'delicate' one of the family – always prey to whatever ailment happened to be visiting the neighbourhood. I had already had scarlet fever at seven; chicken-pox was followed by German measles, followed by yellow jaundice. I think it's safe to say that I had a pretty colourful childhood.

Every summer when we were small my father took his holidays with his cousins in Cardiganshire, in a little place called Llechryd. Gran and Grandpa Bloom – we seemed to call anyone over a certain age 'Gran or Grandpa' – lived on a farm there, and were utterly self-sufficient. They had a farmhouse, a bakery, a watermill, pig sties, chickens, cattle and wheat fields. So they grew their own wheat, churned their own butter from their own cows' milk, ground their own grain in the mill, and from the flour made delicious bread.

It was a glorious place for children, and we were always made very welcome. Legs of ham hung from hooks in the kitchen ceiling, and when we came down for breakfast, old Gran Bloom, who spoke only a few words of English, would take one down, cut lovely big slices off it and throw them in a big frying pan along with some fresh eggs. What a wonderful start to the day.

Gran Bloom was Welsh-speaking, and was Dad's cousin. Her husband was of Norwegian descent, and apart from being a farmer he was also a great horticulturist. In the big orchard at the side of the farmhouse he grew huge pears, and at the end of the holiday he always gave us some to take home. He was also the proud owner of an open-topped Sunbeam tourer, in which he and his daughter Sally would drive us to Aberayron on the Cardiganshire coast for a picnic by the sea.

Because I was always recovering from, or about to have a fresh outbreak of some childhood 'crut', I rarely ventured further out into the briny than knee-deep. Mam and the other ladies would tuck their frocks into their bloomers and have a good old paddle, then get back to the car to unpack the hamper for the picnic.

Golden days indeed, and the wrench of leaving was almost too much to bear. We'd say goodbye to the chickens, the pigs, the horses, and the dogs, and I'd promise never again to climb on the bakehouse roof or let the cows out, or try to start the car, as long as I could come back again next year, please Gran. And she'd give us all a big hug and promise us it would be all right.

When we got back home I used to sit on the front gate facing Town Hill, because I knew that was west, and that's where Llechryd lay, towards the setting sun – and I'd close my eyes tightly in an effort to bring back the sights and sounds of the holiday. Then Ronnie Jones would throw a stone at me and I'd be off over to the patch to join the other kids for a game of football or 'mothers and fathers' or whatever was going on.

*

After my disastrous appearance at the school Eisteddfod, it was some time before I could bring myself to attempt anything of a similar nature except within the family circle. In fact it was a couple of years before I was recruited by Carol to perform a double act with her at a social. She was pretty well established on the local amateur concert party circuit by this time, doing funny monologues, and Mam thought it would be a good idea if the pair of us teamed up to do a comedy act. What she had in mind was a piece of material which had been recorded on a 78 rpm record by a Welsh double act called Ted and May Hopkins, who had achieved some success on the music halls in the Twenties. The record was called 'The Welsh Courtship', and as far as I can now remember it entailed me being a straight man to Carol's comic character.

We first performed it at the Central Hall in Swansea and I was in a fair old state before the performance. I couldn't bear to look at all the faces I saw out front when I peeped through the curtains before we went on, so I took my glasses off. To my great surprise I lost a lot of my nervousness when we made our entrance. The fact that I could see no individuals, only a pink sea of unidentifiable faces before me, calmed my nerves. As far as I was concerned I was just doing a 'turn' for the family at home, and when the first laughs came I revelled in them. I had found the secret of success, I thought – until I fell down the steps in the dark as we came off stage.

It's true, though, that from that day on, I was never as terrified about facing an audience again – just as long as I could not see them. The only time I ever wore glasses on stage was when I appeared in *Pickwick* over thirty years later, and that was only because the part required me to wear them.

Back at school I managed to go from form to form without distinguishing myself academically and I was never much good at sport, either – except for one occasion when I succeeded in scoring a goal in a soccer match.

We were playing on the school playing fields which were at the top of Townhill and I was wearing a pair of football boots with studs. These studs had been nailed in by my father,

who, in one of his drives for home economy, had bought a
cobbler's last and announced that he would do all the shoe
repairs in future. (It turned out to be pretty false economy,
because when it rained my soles and uppers parted company
as I walked home from school, prompting the neighbours to
ask, 'What kind of complaint has your Harry come down
with now – him limping so badly?') On this particular day
the nails were coming through into my heels every time I ran
after the ball and I had adopted a watchful crouch back near
the goal-keeper in the faint hope that the games master would
not notice. He did.

'You're not in the slips, Secombe. This is soccer, not
cricket.'

I hopped forward, trying to look keen, and received a blow
in the face with the muddy ball which broke one of the arms of
my spectacles. I was sent in to the changing-room to try to fix
them, but there was no way I could get the arm back on again.
I gave up after ten minutes, put my specs in my coat pocket
and limped back on to the field, peering short-sightedly at
the action before me. Suddenly the ball was at my feet and
I began to dribble as well as I was able, waiting for it to be
taken from me at any second. To my surprise I was able to
waltz through the blurred opposition and from about ten feet
from the goal, painfully booted the ball into the net. I turned,
waiting for acclamation.

'You're an idiot, Secombe,' said Mr Burgess, the games
master. 'We changed sides five minutes ago.'

There were little triumphs, now and again, to counterbalance
my inadequacies. As, for example, when I was picked for the
school choir. Mr Beynon, the music teacher, was very keen on
getting together a big concert at the newly opened Brangwyn
Hall, and he held auditions throughout the school for a gala
performance of 'The Revenge', Tennyson's poem about Sir
Richard Grenville set to music. We were also to learn 'The
Blue Danube' waltz to which special lyrics had been written.

It was the first time I had had any experience of a really big occasion in a proper concert hall with a professional orchestra, and I loved it. There's a wonderful feeling when you're riding on the crest of the music, exulting in the power of communal effort, and giving the conductor your maximum attention.

We had such a tremendous reception from the audience that we sang 'The Blue Danube' three times and Mr Beynon was beside himself with pride, running up and down our serried ranks, patting our heads, beaming hugely. Just to be a small part of such success was like a heady drug, and once I had tasted it I was an addict.

Another lift to my ego was having a short story accepted for the school magazine. The sight of my effort in print almost turned my ambition away from the stage to a life of letters, and I took to leaping around the house, in what I thought was a balletic style, to records on our wind-up gramophone. I started to read poetry, and sat for ages in our back garden contemplating the weeds. My parents began to exchange worried glances until I saw the first 'Andy Hardy' film one Saturday afternoon, and I was Mickey Rooney again and the embryonic poet disappeared for good.

When the time came for me to sit the Central Welsh Board Examination – the equivalent of GCSEs today, I suppose – I was fairly confident about English, French and Art, but not so happy about Geography and Chemistry, and positively miserable about Maths, Geometry and Algebra. The only theorem I had ever been able to come to terms with was that of Pythagorus – all the rest meant nothing to me.

I have to say that I was in pretty good company, because the form I was in had a reputation for unruly behaviour. Some of the lads had stayed on from the previous year and were sitting the exam a second time. They were consequently that much more advanced in the physical sense, especially one lad, whom I shall refer to only as Dai.

Dai used to come to school on a motorbike – he was just old enough to be allowed to ride one – and sometimes wore plus-fours with his blazer. His moustache was heavier than that of Glan Powell, the form master, and his voice had broken when he was twelve. Naturally, all the class worshipped him.

Nothing bothered Dai, and while the rest of us puffed furtively at fags behind the school toilets, he smoked a pipe quite openly in the yard. The masters had no control over him, but he took no physical liberties with them, regarding them all with an amused cynicism. Everything about him was larger than life – when we had pimples, Dai had boils.

His favourite occupation was perpetrating practical jokes on the masters and sometimes he enrolled our aid. But one day he went too far.

Our maths teacher was an old gentleman with a drooping moustache who loved his pint at lunchtime. On his return from the pub he would set us some arithmetical problem, put his feet on the desk and have a little kip. This was a regular routine, and on the day in question, Dai had decided to have some fun.

He went to a joke shop near the back of the Empire called Dirty Black's, where he bought some stink bombs, sneezing powder and a small, neat pile of imitation dog turds. Armed with these purchases, he returned just before afternoon lessons began and distributed them around the classroom. Somewhat fearfully I took a little pinch of sneezing powder and put it in my waistcoat pocket.

When the maths master came in he followed his customary procedure and settled down, as usual, with his feet on the desk and his mortar-board shielding his pate. After waiting for a snore to emerge from behind the mortar-board, Dai went into action. First he put the pile of dog turds on the open book on the master's desk, and then gave the signal for the other lads to drop the stink bombs. In the excitement I forgot to blow my sneezing powder into the air, but there was enough going on without my adding to the confusion.

The master awoke with a start, removed his mortar-board, saw the mess on his open book and collapsed backwards off his chair. We were all seized with hysteria, banging the desks and yelling in a kind of frenzy – all except Dai, who was observing the scene with quiet satisfaction.

In no time at all the classroom was full of masters and prefects who had heard the noise we were making and were convinced that their worst fears about the Lower Fourth were materializing and that a mutiny had taken place. The sight of them had a sobering effect on our hysteria and very quickly order was restored.

In the recriminations that followed, the Head, Mr 'Beak' John, addressed the form in a quiet voice which was infinitely more frightening than if he had yelled at us.

'Hands up all those boys who had sneezing powder.'

I looked around the class, aware of that little pinch of powder in my waistcoat pocket. Other boys looked down fixedly at the tops of their desks. At home I had always been told to tell the truth whatever the consequences, so slowly I raised my hand, my heart banging away.

'Secombe, eh? And your brother's the head prefect?'

I nodded, unable to speak.

'All right, get outside in the corridor.'

Out of all the boys in the form, only about six of us owned up – Dai, of course, being one of the number.

I was called into the headmaster's study first. I stood before his desk as he eyed me sternly.

'Fred's brother. You've let the family down, and you've let the school down. What have you got to say for yourself?'

'Sorry, sir.' I was determined not to cry. 'I didn't actually use the sneezing powder, sir.' I brought a little bit out of my waistcoat pocket on a finger. The head's nostrils twitched.

'I don't want to cane you, boy. You've never been in trouble before.' His nose twitched again.

I began to breathe more easily.

'Your brother would not want to see you caned, would he?'

I shook my head, convinced now that I'd get off without punishment.

'But if I don't cane you now, you'll only do it again. Hold your hand out.'

He gave me six of the best with his short bamboo cane and I managed not to yell out. As I painfully shut the door behind me I had the meagre satisfaction of hearing a gigantic sneeze.

Dai, who was next in line, grinned widely and winked. 'Good lad,' he said.

Dai ran away from school to join the French Foreign Legion not long after, and his parents had to bring him back. I don't know what became of him in later life, but with his charm and ability to manipulate others he had all the hallmarks of a confidence trickster or a politician. Good luck to you, Dai, wherever you are.

The Young Tycoon

I left school with a sense of relief mingled with regret that
university life was not for me. I had always fancied myself
with a scarf in college colours slung carelessly around my
neck and an MG ticking away at the kerb, but with my
profound ignorance of maths and science I would have been
about thirty before I qualified for Higher Certificate. The
four credits I had managed to get in English, Art, French
and German meant that I had passed the Central Welsh Board
Examination, and that would have to suffice.

The time had come to look for a job. The *South Wales
Evening Post* 'Positions Vacant' columns became absorbing
reading, and I began to apply for interviews. The first one
I wrote off for was a vacancy for an insurance clerk in a
rather posh firm in Walter Road, Swansea. To my surprise
I received a letter in reply asking me to attend the office for
an interview. There were quite a few up for the job and from
the look of them they were far better qualified than I was.
However, I did my best 'Young Woodley' impression and
impressed the interviewer enough for him to ask me to come
back. Apparently I was on a short list.

The same week I had a letter from Baldwins Ltd, in Wind
Street inviting me to go along there in response to my
application for the post of junior pay clerk in the Colliery
Department. I turned up in my best suit, purchased, as usual,

To whom it may concern.

I have known <u>Harry Donald Secombe</u>
47 Grenfell Park Road, from babyhood.
He was one of my Choir-boys until
his voice broke, and he has always
attended Sunday School.

He has been brought up in a
good home and has responded well
to his Training.

He is a well mannered, well behaved
lad, of a quiet and thoughtful
disposition, and quite intelligent
and dependable.

He has, I believe, the making of
a good, useful and valuable man.
He has my best wishes.

E Jenkins Davies
Vicar of St Thomas
Swansea.

Sept: 13<u>th</u> 1937

by my mother with a Provident cheque, one of my father's stiff white collars around my neck and my shoes gleaming from his labours the night before. He set great store by shiny shoes, my Dad.

To cut a long story short, my interview was a success and I was advised to start work the following Monday for the less than princely sum of ten shillings a week. My folks were delighted – some more money coming in and, with luck, a future asured in the commercial world for their somewhat wayward son.

When I arrived for work on the Monday morning I found myself in an office at the end of a long corridor with a glass partition separating it from two other offices – Coal Sales, run by Mr Davies, and Transport, headed by Haydn Baptiste. The lad I was replacing, Ken Thomas, had been promoted to the Post Room, and he was there to initiate me in the role of junior pay clerk. He was a fair-haired, slightly aggressive boy who looked me up and down with an air of disapproval.

'Dynevor boy,' he said, looking at my tie. He was a Glanmor boy himself and there wasn't much love lost between the two schools. 'Here's your most important job,' he said, opening a cupboard. Inside on a stained sheet of brown paper were a cracked jug, half a dozen battered cups, a sugar bowl and a kettle. 'You've got to make tea twice a day – eleven o'clock and four o'clock. You charge 'em a penny a cup.'

So much for the elevated status of junior pay clerk. I was a glorified office boy. Still, I decided to make the most of the situation. I was assigned to Bill Layman, who was responsible for Newlands Colliery pay sheets. He was a kind, bespectacled man who suffered my mistakes with a wry grin. My job – apart from tea making – was to copy out all the details of the colliers' pay from the large pay sheets on to individual dockets. I then had to number each one in sequence with a Roneo machine, a task which made a lot of noise and which I enjoyed. Unfortunately the clatter of my machine made the other members of the office wince.

They were a friendly bunch: Haydn Davies, a burly, pipe-smoking ex-officer, was in charge of Bryn Colliery pay matters; Elvet Thomas, a tall, black-haired young man some three years older than me, was his assistant; Emrys Davies, a wise-cracking man in his early twenties ran Aberbaiden and Mr Brew was in charge of the whole department. Nancy Johns, a tall, pretty blonde who operated the comptometer, was the only female member of the team.

As time went by I became the office clown. I was able to do impressions of some of the staff – an accomplishment which once nearly cost me my job.

It was on a Friday afternoon when, with all the senior members of the department absent at the collieries paying out the miners, Elvet, Nancy and I were alone in the office. The game of firing paper clips from a rubber band at a target on the tea-cupboard door had begun to pall and a desultory silence had descended.

From behind the partition in the Transport Department we heard signs of Haydn Baptiste preparing for an early departure. 'You can hold the fort, Harry,' we could hear him tell his assistant, Harry Vickery.

Elvet tapped me on the arm. 'Go on,' he said. 'Do your J P James impression on the phone.'

J P James was the overall boss of Baldwins' Colliery Office and ruled the place with an iron hand. He also happened to be one of my best impersonations.

I picked up the phone and dialled Haydn's number. He was half-way out of the door when my call rang.

'J P here,' I said.

There were urgent whispers from behind the partition as Harry caught Haydn in mid-flight. 'It's the governor,' he said hoarsely.

'Oh crumbs,' said Hayden, who never swore but often felt like it.

'How many empty wagons have we got at Port Talbot Docks?' I said, J P-like.

'Just a minute, sir.' He turned away and said to Harry, 'Get the figures for Port Talbot Docks.' There followed much searching of ledgers and frantic whispering as the two of them tried to come up with a figure. With empty coal wagons all over the place at Port Talbot Docks, they were faced with a daunting task just when they thought the day was over.

Figures were bandied about which in my role as the boss I pretended to reject. Elvet and Nancy were stuffing handkerchiefs in their mouths to stop themselves giving the game away.

In the end I over-played my hand. 'Bring the ledgers up to my office,' I said, secure in the knowledge that J P James had gone home ages before. When we heard Haydn stagger out of his office loaded with ledgers on his way up three flights of stairs to J P's eyrie at the top of the building, the three of us gave way to hysterics.

What we did not know was that J P James had had a meeting and was still in his office when Haydn tottered in, bearing his pile of ledgers.

'There you are, sir,' he panted, dumping the lot on the boss's desk. 'Count them yourself, sir.'

The governor backed away in alarm as Haydn defended his total of empty wagons. Then the penny dropped.

'It's that new boy – Secombe – he does impressions of you.'

J P James turned to his secretary, Leslie Davies, who told me the story afterwards. 'Get Secombe up here at once,' he said.

I was still laughing downstairs when the furious Head of Transport stormed into our office. 'You're going to cop it,' he said. 'J P wants to see you straight away. That'll teach you.'

My heart was thumping when I reached the glass door of the boss's domain. I knocked with trembling fingers.

'Come in.' J P sat behind his desk with a grim look on his face. He didn't waste time with preliminary chat. 'They tell me you do an impression of me.'

I shuffled, red-faced, before him. 'Er, yes.' There was no point in denying it.

'Let's hear it, then.' He sat back in his chair and folded his arms.

I cleared my throat and attempted to do his bidding. Nothing came out.

'Come along – say "How many empty wagons have we got at Port Talbot Docks?"'

My voice, which could usually break through the sound barrier, refused to function in anything but a broken whisper. 'How – er – many – wagons – have – you – er – got – er – in – Port Talbot Docks?' I croaked, near tears.

J P looked at me for a full half minute, while I saw visions of myself explaining to Mam how I had lost my job.

Finally he spoke. 'Nothing like me at all.' He dismissed me with a wave of his hand.

As I crept thankfully away I heard the sound of laughter.

Having to make tea for everybody still irked me, until one day while waiting for the kettle to boil up in Mrs Puplett's kitchen, I had a brainwave. Mrs Puplett was the wife of the commissionaire and was responsible for the catering. She had to provide teas and light lunches for the bosses of the Steel Department as well as for J P James himself, and had a couple of huge teapots always on the go.

'Any chance of buying one of those teapots?' I asked her. 'If I had one like that I could extend my tea round and make it pay off.'

She was a good old soul, and had travelled the world as the wife of Sergeant-Major Alf Puplett who, with waxed moustache and immaculate uniform, kept unwanted visitors at bay at the front door of the Head Office building. For some reason she had taken quite a liking to me.

'Tell you what,' she said. 'I'll get you a new one and you can pay me when you can.'

I was delighted and began to make plans for my venture into tea-making on the grand scale. No more broken cups and chipped saucers for me. I went to the china stall in

Swansea Market and bought a dozen cheap but whole cups and saucers. Next, I had a chat with Mr Goldsworthy, the grocer whose shop was opposite the front of the office, and negotiated a good price for not too broken biscuits. A new tin tray completed my tea set, and I was ready for business.

The size of the teapot meant that I was able to take a lot more customers on, and with the broken biscuits in each saucer as a 'come on', I was able to up the price of a cup of tea to three ha'pence. Before long I had spread my tentacles all over the office building. Eventually I was earning more money from tea-making than from clerking and was becoming known as Joe Lyons Junior.

Looking back on those days from this distance in time my recollections are to say the least kaleidoscopic. I remember being happy with my lot: I had a ready-made audience in most of my work-mates, though some found my boisterous nature a bit hard to take. Odd memories do stand out though, with a quite startling clarity.

One day I shall never forget was when Bill Layman returned to the office after an operation for gall stones. We all gave him a great welcome back because he really was a very popular fellow. He had brought with him in a matchbox lined with cotton wool the stones which had been giving him so much trouble. They looked remarkably like the sweets we used to have in those days called marzipan bon-bons, being brown and crystalline in appearance. Bill was quite proud of his trophies and passed them around for us all to admire.

One person who had not joined the group which had collected to greet our returned invalid was an old gentleman who worked in the Coal Sales. His name was Joe Meagher and he was a special mate of mine. He was in his sixties and was profoundly deaf, the result of a boating accident in the Bristol Channel. If anyone wanted to tell him something, he always had a pad and pencil on his desk so that the message could be written down.

This particular morning he was completely absorbed in his work and was not aware of what was going on in the pay department. I was determined to bring him up to date with all the excitement and, with Bill Layman's somewhat reluctant permission, I borrowed one of his gall stones to show to Joe in the other room. I tapped him on the shoulder and held out my left hand containing the gall stone, then reached for the pad with my right hand to write down what it was.

Joe looked up, saw the shiny object in my hand and popped it into his mouth, thinking it to be a sweet. I stared at him aghast as he thanked me and bent his head back to his writing, crunching away as he did.

Frantically I wrote 'Bill Layman's gall stone' and pushed the pad under his nose. He read it, still chomping, then with a strangled cry headed for the toilet at the end of the corridor.

Bill Layman was not very happy at losing one of his treasures, and poor old Joe went home. A memorable day indeed.

Another vivid memory remains of the day I was taken from the office to my mother's hospital bedside. She had been admitted for an operation for kidney stones after months of terrible back pains. It was shortly after Bill Layman's own operation, and he had been most kind to me when he knew that Mam had been taken to hospital, allaying my fears and playing down the seriousness of the situation. However, when the call came from the hospital requesting me to attend, I was in a terrible state. My brother was in college and my father was off on his rounds of the grocers' shops and could not be contacted.

Apparently the surgeon had opened her up – awful phrase – and discovered that the kidney was useless and had to be removed. She was in such a bad way that they decided to send for the next-of-kin straight away.

The next couple of hours were a nightmare. I sat holding my mother's hand, willing her to live and trying not to cry; a boy sent to do a man's job. I couldn't imagine what life would be like without her. Mam was the strong one of the family –

the dynamo who kept everything ticking over, who treated all three children alike, but made each of us feel special.

For a long while there was no response from the hand I held so tightly. Then I felt a gentle squeeze and she opened her eyes and smiled, and I could have run up Kilvey Hill a dozen times for her. I made a mental vow never to give her any cause to worry about me ever again. But I did, I'm afraid. I joined the Territorial Army.

In April 1939, Hore-Belisha, the War Minister at the time, introduced conscription. When war broke out on 3 September, anyone over the age of 18 and up to 41 years old was, subject to passing the medical examination, liable to be called up to serve eighteen months in the services. The only way to escape the conscription net was by joining the Territorials. This meant reporting once a week to the barracks and spending two weeks away in camp.

There were several men in the Head Office who were eligible for call-up. Johnny Otterson, who was the assistant to Leslie Davies, and Emrys Davies of the Pay Department were two of them. They decided to opt for the Territorials and consequently joined the 132nd Field Regiment Royal Artillery (TA), with the result that they would both be away at the same time for summer camp. And as I helped out Johnny Otterson in the Post Room some of his work would fall on me.

I thought carefully about this, and decided I would follow their example. The only snag being that I was not yet eighteen. However, Johnny told me that nobody asked for a birth certificate and that it was easy to get in.

Another thing which swayed me was the fact that war was definitely going to come sooner or later. My father had been an infantry soldier and I had heard enough stories about his First World War experiences not to want to follow his example. The Royal Artillery, though, seemed a much better proposition. It required clerks and specialists, and to be perfectly honest I fancied myself in breeches and spurs, which was the uniform of an artilleryman at that time.

Mam went very quiet when I told her that I was joining my mates, but she accepted the fact with a sigh. My father was secretly pleased that I was going to be a 'five-mile sniper' as he called it.

The only trouble I envisaged was passing the eye test at my medical. My eyesight, without spectacles, was still extremely poor, but I could see perfectly well with them on. When the time came for me to see the doctor at the Drill Hall, I had already learned the eye chart from memory, thanks to Johnny Otterson. He had copied it out for me beforehand. Thus, when I had stripped off, blushed and allowed my head to be searched for nits, I rattled off all the letters on the chart down to the printer's name.

'Remarkable,' said the MO with a twinkle in his eye. 'All right, son, if you're that keen to join the Terriers, you're in.'

I was given an army number, a second-hand uniform and the rank of Gunner. Hitler in his eyrie at Berchtesgarten must have felt just a slight *frisson* of foreboding. I'm sure Neville Chamberlain did.

'Sex appeal in brackets,' was my family's unanimous decision when they first saw me in my puttees and spurs, looking bandy-legged in the somewhat clown-like breeches, and with a tunic that had taken on a greenish tinge with age. But I fancied myself in the uniform, trying all sorts of military poses in the big mirror in my parents' bedroom. 'Not bad,' I thought to myself, turning smartly. I caught one spur in the other and crashed to the floor.

The regiment went to camp in July and we all began to feel what real soldiering was all about. We were under canvas on Malvern Links in Worcestershire for two weeks, and the sergeants really put us through it. The officers were as raw as we were, with one or two exceptions, and mostly concerned with being saluted. After two weeks a lot of friendships had been cemented and a few enemies made, but it was all smiles when we broke camp. We tossed our Sergeant-Major in the air in a blanket, nearly breaking his neck in the process; not realizing that in a few short weeks we were to be soldiers in earnest and that Sergeant-Majors have long memories.

War had been in the air for some time and it clouded everything we did that summer. But it still came as a shock.

I have particular reason to remember the day I was called up. It was a Friday and I was at Newlands Colliery with Bill Layman that morning preparing to pay out. Briefly, what happened on these occasions was that, along with the Chief Clerk at the Colliery, we would put the money for each miner in a tin with a number on it. The number would correspond with that on a counterfoil called a pay docket. Each docket would show what each miner was entitled to, and was made up by the clerks at Head Office from the pay sheets which were sent down to us from the Colliery. The person responsible for numbering each docket with its tear-off counterfoil was myself. I used a Roneo machine which stamped the numbers twice on each docket, and when I had finished I was supposed to check each ticket with the pay sheets to make sure that all numbers were correct. The pay dockets were then sent back to Newlands by rail so that the tins could be prepared. All that happened at the Colliery then was that the miner would hand in his numbered counterfoil and he'd receive the money from the tin with the corresponding number on it.

However, owing to the heavy amount of business I was doing on my tea round – I had even extended to an office across the road which had nothing to do with Baldwins – I did the tickets in a hurry. It was getting near to the train time and so instead of checking each ticket individually from the pay sheets, I just made sure that the first and last numbers tallied. What I was not aware of was that the Roneo machine, owing no doubt to its enthusiastic handling, had slipped and in consequence some of the numbers were out of order. However it had righted itself some twenty tickets later and the last digits were correct.

The first few miners were soon dealt with as they handed in their slips through the pigeon-hole in our corrugated iron pay office and I happily handed down the tins from the shelves around the walls. Then, slowly, a trickle of men began to bang on the side of the office demanding attention.

'I done five shifts at 7/6d and I've only got half a crown.'

'What's going on in there? My butty's got the wrong money . . .' etc. etc.

The shouting got louder and the banging more insistent and Arthur Kingdom, the Chief Clerk of Newlands, slammed the door shut over the pigeon-hole. He and Bill Layman turned to me.

'Did you check the tickets, Secombe?' It had been 'Harry' all morning.

'Sorry,' I said weakly.

Outside the miners were getting angrier as they counted their money, and the clamour reached frightening proportions as we tried to put things right.

Suddenly there came the cry of someone in authority. 'Come out, Secombe.'

I backed away in a corner. I thought I might be lynched – I'd seen too many Westerns to think otherwise. But it was not a lynch mob, it was the Seventh Cavalry in the shape of Adolf Hitler.

'You've been called up, son.'

'Thank God,' I said.

Playing Soldiers

We lined up among the tents, the uneasy laughter hushed, and listened to Neville Chamberlain on the radio making his reluctant declaration of war. One thing is for sure, I thought, we're not playing at soldiers any more.

It was Sunday, 3 September and we had been detailed to strike the tents which had housed other Territorials from a Nottinghamshire regiment who had been camping at Parkmill on the Gower coast.

Only a few weeks earlier my family had rented a bungalow in a field not far away in Pennard and, where we now stood, a travelling fair had blared out 'South Of The Border' and 'Roll Out The Barrel'. Our task was to pack up all the gear the other lads had left behind and load it on to lorries which would take it back to the Midlands.

There was an air of unreality about everything we did in those first few weeks of the phoney war. There didn't seem to be any kind of order and at the very beginning we were even allowed to stay at home. This was a bit embarrassing for me, because after I had reported to the Drill Hall on the Friday evening I was sent home and told to report the following morning. Consequently on Saturday morning I made a big farewell tour of the patch and St Leger Crescent as I was driven to war. Archie Roberts, a friend of Fred's and mine, possessed a Daimler car of which we were all extremely envious. The only means of private transport available to most of the denizens of Grenfell Park Estate were push–bikes. The sight of a car in our street usually brought out a posse of kids to sit on its running boards to have their photographs taken. So when Archie offered to drive me back to the Drill Hall, I made the most of it.

The car had a sunshine roof, and by standing on the front passenger seat I was able to emerge in true VIP style to wave to the neighbours, who stood at their front gates to see me off. With the aid of a black pocket comb I performed my locally celebrated impression of Adolf Hitler to the accompaniment of good-natured boos from the onlookers. The only person who seemed apprehensive was Archie, who winced as he saw the damage my army boots were doing to his front seat.

Of course, I was sent back home again that afternoon, and although I had to report for duty at Parkmill on the Sunday, I made so many farewell appearances that I became a bit of a joke. Men who had waved goodbye to me from their gates were in the British Expeditionary Force in France while I was still hanging about the district.

For a while we were billeted in a dance hall in Neath, just a few miles outside Swansea, and then we went to Carmarthen for three weeks where we were stationed in Lamas Street Barracks. The food there was dreadful, and at night most of us haunted the local fish and chip shops rather than tackle what our sergeant cook had to offer us. We had to queue up with our mess-tins at lunch-time and the contents of an old Soyer stove were slopped into them. The official title was 'stew', but the concoction contained ingredients which were too awful to contemplate, and there was strong evidence that an old army boot provided the basis for the stock. However, anyone with the temerity to complain had to face the fury of the sergeant cook, who was ready to rush out from his kitchen with a butcher's knife at the slightest sign of criticism. Fortunately for us all he was discharged from the regiment for being mentally unstable, and by the time we had settled in at our next destination – Usk – the standard of cuisine had risen slightly.

The place itself was very forbidding – as well it might be, because it was a recently vacated Borstal Institution, which before that had been an adult prison. Inside the high walls and behind the big green door it was just like a scene from one of the 'Big House' epics which Hollywood turned out so often in the Thirties. The two-tiered rows of cells radiated like the spokes of a wheel from the hub of the central hallway. Wire mesh was stretched across the cell wings separating the top row from the bottom one, and trestle tables and wooden forms were placed in the space between the cells. We were allocated two to a cell and were given straw palliasses upon which to sleep. This was to be our home for the next six months or so, and this was where we were going to be made into proper soldiers, whether we liked it or not.

Up until November, the regiment consisted of two gun batteries – 321, the Swansea Territorials, and 322 battery, the Neath volunteers – and the strength numerically was only about 250 men. We had started the war with eight 4.5 gun howitzers which were taken from us to go to Finland. They were replaced by iron-tyred guns. The transport which drew these guns and carried us to and fro around the area consisted of a varied assortment of pop lorries, brewer's drays and officers' cars. The two Scammells which pulled 322 Battery's guns were bright scarlet in colour and could not be painted dark because they were on hire for a pound a day.

I belonged at this time to the specialist section, as did most of the lads I joined up with. We were all clerks of some kind and regarded as potential NCOs or possibly officer material. We formed the basis for the office staff of both batteries and were being trained in the mysteries of how to direct the fire of the guns, an art I was never fully to master because it involved complicated mathematics.

My particular friend then was Danny Williams, an athletic lad about two years older than me. We used to sit up at nights at the tables between the cells discussing philosophy, the quality of the beer in the pubs, and the possible availability of the barmaids. Another mate was D K Griffiths, a jolly type with a moustache that made him look older than his years. Everybody wanted him as a friend because of his ability to play the piano. When he sat down at a pub piano to do his celebrated Charlie Kunz impressions the drinks were always on the house for D K and his mates in uniform. Sometimes I'd join in after a pint or two and do some of my bits and pieces, which usually resulted in a packet of crisps being hurled my way. I still had a long way to go as a performer.

The winter of '39 was a particularly severe one and the snow piled up everywhere. The heating in the cell blocks was not very effective and soon a lot of the boys were coming down with all sorts of ailments. There were a few cases of scarlet fever, some caught pneumonia, and the first flush of excitement had evaporated in the dreary drilling and training. I remember one incident that gave us all a laugh one weekend, although it backfired in the end.

One of the specialists among us was Gunner Thomas A C G, known to one and all, for some unaccountable reason, as 'Titty-bottle' Thomas. I had known him before the war when he worked in an office on the Swansea docks. He was always a good source for postage stamps at a cut price.

At the end of our row of cells was the padded cell in which those prisoners who were getting a bit too stroppy had been incarcerated until they cooled off. It was too dilapidated for use as living quarters, so it was left locked – that is, until one Saturday afternoon when one of the lads with nothing to do managed to open the lock with a screw driver. Then someone had the bright idea of getting old 'Titty-bottle' to enter the cell and shutting him in there for a lark.

I can't remember what ruse we employed to get him to go in – it must have been a dare of some kind. Anyway, in he went and we slammed the door on him, intending to let him out after a few minutes. He pounded away on the mildewed padding for a while, shouting and yelling at us, and then Danny Williams, who had a natural authority even though he had no rank, said, 'All right, that's enough, let the lad out.' Unfortunately, the lock had sprung and no amount of sweating and straining could shift the cell door – after all, those doors were supposed to stay shut. Poor old Thomas was getting hysterical by this time, and the RSM was summoned. He read the situation at a glance, and turning on the half a dozen or so of us who were gathered around the cell door he said, 'There's no chance of getting a locksmith up from Newport at the weekend. He's got to stay there till Monday, and you clever buggers are going to sit here outside this door and keep him company.'

And that's what we had to do. We managed to open the iron flap in the door through which food was passed in the old days, and kept up a non-stop conversation with poor 'Titty-bottle', taking it in turns to read to him and pass him the odd bottle of beer. Most of us had made arrangements to do other things that weekend, but the RSM made us keep up our vigil until the locksmith arrived from Newport early on Monday morning and released a tearful Thomas. It didn't appear to have done him much harm, because he left us for an officer training course not long after, and finished the war as a Lieutenant-Colonel in the Intelligence Corps. I finished up as a Lance-Bombardier – and I was on the outside.

We stayed in the prison up to the time of Dunkirk, when some of us were detailed to meet the ships coming in to Newport docks from the beaches. Our job was to help the chaps ashore and take them back to Usk to clean them up and provide them with fresh kit.

I'll never forget seeing those soldiers – real soldiers, not like us – bandaged and unshaven, and for the most part grim and unsmiling, their eyes full of what they had just gone through. I felt ashamed and ineffectual as we directed them to the waiting trucks and, for the first time since the war started, I realized what my uniform was all about.

There was one unbearably poignant incident that day. A soldier who had escaped completely unscathed from France, and had just been kitted out with a fresh uniform, crossed the road from the prison to send a telegram home to tell his family that he was safe and well. On the way back, a few minutes later, he was knocked down by a lorry and killed. That took some getting over for all of us.

With the war having taken a more dramatic turn, training was intensified and the regiment was strengthened by reservists and militiamen. After several local moves, we found ourselves deployed along the South Wales coast with no infantry and eight guns. We had to look after about sixty miles of coast and our ammunition consisted of one hundred very old rounds per gun. (I quote from the regimental history, so I'm not making it up.)

One day we were taken down to the seaside near Margam to watch one of the guns being fired. Our officers thought it would be a good idea for us to see just what a howitzer could do. The gun was manhandled down on to the shore and we were all instructed to get well behind it and watch. The gun was loaded with due ceremony and the order was given to fire. There was a flash, the shell landed with a disconcertingly light plop about two hundred yards out to sea, and a wheel fell off the gun carriage. Of course, we all fell about with laughter.

As specialists we were detailed to take turns with our officers at an observation post which had been set up on the dunes at Margam, and one morning it was my turn to take over just before dawn after a heavy air raid on Port Talbot. I was equipped with a revolver which I had never fired and an officer named Major Sims, who always seemed to regard me with a kind of detached amusement. A few weeks before this incident he had passed me out as a driver, on the strict condition that I was never to drive a lorry within three miles of where he happened to be. I had demolished three concrete posts in Usk cattle market during the course of my test. 'I like your style, Secombe,' he said, signing my licence application with a flourish.

We arrived together at the dug-out in the dunes and my head was still buzzing with the events of the night before. It had been a nasty raid on Port Talbot and we were told to be on the look out for parachutists. This was the period when we were expecting an invasion at any time – well, I certainly was.

After we'd been at the observation post for about half an hour, Major Sims decided he had to go back to HQ for some reason, leaving me in complete possession of the fire power. It was still fairly dark when he left and I squinted fearfully into the expanse of sand before me. Off to the right I could just about make out some smoke from the direction of Port Talbot and as my eyes came back from looking at it I thought I saw movement in the near foreground. Sweatily I reached for the binoculars and trained them on what I thought I'd seen. Sure enough there was something there. My glasses steamed up with fear and I had difficulty focusing the heavy army binoculars. It was definitely a man in uniform of some sort, and he had a bicycle with him. We'd been warned about parachutists with bicycles.

I was transfixed with terror as the figure crept nearer, then I forced my trembling fingers to ease the big 45 from its holster. It was getting lighter, but not enough to distinguish what kind of uniform the figure before me was wearing. 'Who goes there?' I yodelled. No reply. I said it again, and pointed the wobbling weapon in the figure's general direction. I knew it was loaded but I was not sure where the safety-catch was. Trembling like a leaf I fumbled around trying to find it. 'Oh God, oh Mam,' I was saying mindlessly over and over. 'Halt or I fire,' I croaked for the last time, and shut my eyes, taking a fearful first pressure on the trigger.

'Hello there,' said a cheerful Welsh voice. 'Playing soldiers here, are you?' A postman stood before the entrance to the dug-out. 'Thought I'd look in on the way to work. I was in the Welch Fusiliers in the last lot, cosmopolitan crowd we were.' He seemed prepared for a long chat. 'Be careful with that thing,' he said, pointing to the revolver in my hand. 'You can kill somebody, mun.' He was quite surprised when I began to cry.

We moved from Usk to a country mansion at a place called Clytha, not far from Abergavenny, where we were put under canvas, a great relief to all after the shocking conditions we had suffered in the prison. It was a time of route marches through the lovely Monmouthshire countryside, and often the wild life would be disturbed by the harsh tones of Adolf Hitler as I led the column doing my by now celebrated impression with the pocket comb. I was pretty firmly established as the regimental idiot, a role I found to be rather useful on one or two occasions.

I was on leave one weekend from Clytha, and while walking down Swansea High Street with my pal from the regiment, 'Dixie' Deans, I was arrested by an over-zealous Redcap for being improperly dressed. To compound the felony I had left my AB64 – my army pay book and identification document at home along with my weekend pass. The result was that I was put under arrest in the Military Police HQ in Swansea High Street railway station until Dixie got back with my means of identification. Dixie said that when he told my mother what had happened she burst out laughing. I was released and told that I would be reported to my regiment and consequently, on my return from leave, I was called up before the Battery Commander, Major Thomas.

I was marched in along with Dixie as a witness and the charges against me were duly read out by the Sergeant-Major. 'Improperly dressed, not in possession of his AB64 and leave pass, and insisting on whistling the German national anthem when in custody.'

Major Thomas's mouth twitched under his large brown moustache. 'Is that the lot?' he said.

'Yessir,' said the Sergeant-Major.

The major looked down at his desk for a moment and then looked up. 'Sergeant-Major, as you well know, Gunner Secombe is not responsible for his actions. Case dismissed.'

Major Thomas featured in another episode, this time one in which my reputation played against me. I had applied for an officers' training course after seeing a notice in regimental orders referring to an urgent need for officers in the Indian Army. I seemed to have all the necessary scholastic qualifications – the Establishment was obviously getting desperate – and so I filled in an application form. A week or two later I was on fatigue duty, unloading coal from a lorry, when I was summoned to the battery office. 'No time to change,' said the messenger. 'Go as you are.'

I duly found myself standing to attention in a pair of filthy overalls, my face smudged and my glasses askew.

Major Thomas sat at his desk with my application form before him. He was obviously under some stress. Across the office, Bombardier Otterson was also suffering from a deep emotional crisis.

'Ah, Secombe,' began my battery commander, his fingers fiddling with his moustache. 'I see you've applied for a commission. . .' He broke off and held his head in his hands for a moment. Then he looked up at me and could no longer contain himself. He began to laugh, silently at first, then he started to cackle. Otterson, my erstwhile comrade from Baldwins, was pounding his desk as an accompaniment to his wild whooping laughter.

I still stood at attention, my dreams of gin slings and punkah wallahs and a starched khaki drill uniform with a gleaming Sam Browne dissipating rapidly. I was hurt – cut to the quick. And then I caught sight of my reflection in the window behind the major's desk. God! Was that me? The merriment was infectious and for several minutes we clung together, the three of us fused with laughter, until eventually I stumbled out of the battery office clutching my aching stomach. And that was as near as I ever got to becoming an officer. Some of my friends did go as officers to the Far East and were taken prisoner almost as soon as they got off the boat. There's a lesson in there somewhere.

My nineteenth birthday found me in Staffordshire at a place called Rugely. The town had one claim to fame – Dr Palmer, a notorious poisoner, had lived there, and it was the favourite joke in the battery that he was still around and working in the cookhouse. It was 8 September 1940, and the day that our fighter aircraft brought down a record number of enemy planes. That night I was on guard duty in a bell-tent at the entrance to the camp alongside an ornamental lake.

Ammunition was so short that there was only one magazine for all four sentries, and as each one came off duty he had to unload it from his own rifle and hand it over to the next man on sentry-go. At this time our 303 rifles had been taken from us for more deserving soldiers and we were issued with ancient Canadian Ross rifles which, unlike the Lee-Enfields we were used to, had no cut-out. The cut-out was a piece of metal which, when depressed, prevented the bullet from being loaded into the breech. To operate this cut-out, you pulled back the bolt, pushed the metal plate over the contents of the magazine and then slid the bolt back home over the empty breech and pulled the trigger. As I said, the Ross rifles did not have this safety precaution.

It was warm that night and some of the sentries were sleeping outside the tent on groundsheets because it was cooler by the lakeside. However, because I found the gnats a nuisance, I had opted to sleep inside the tent. When my turn came to take up my post, I sleepily loaded the magazine that had been tossed to me by the man I was relieving, pulled back the bolt, operated an imaginary cut-out, pointed the rifle towards the wall of the tent and, after pushing home the bolt, pressed the trigger. There was one hell of a bang, and a hole appeared in the tent wall. There was a loud yell, followed by splashing sounds, and then another shout, more high-pitched this time.

What had happened was like a scene from a Laurel and Hardy comedy. The bullet had penetrated the ground near where Gunner Haydn was sleeping. He woke up with a start and instinctively ran into the lake, where he stubbed his bare toes on a wooden crate of Molotov cocktails which had been put in the water to keep them stable. His yells and the rifle shot brought the duty officer running down the path in his pyjama top, revolver at the ready. 'Call out the mobile,' he cried, invoking what was supposed to be a flying column of guns which was to go into action immediately the invasion began. (When they were called out a couple of days later on a false alarm only the gun towed by a pop lorry made it to the rendezvous – all the others broke down.)

Then he saw me at the entrance to the tent, still in a state of shock, with a smoking rifle in my hands. 'Oh shit,' he said. He turned back to the other men, who were now running down the path behind him to find out what the fuss was all about. 'It's all right, it's only Secombe.'

This time I did go on a charge – for wasting ammunition. I got off with a few days confined to barracks which, under the circumstances, was pretty lenient.

By Christmas 1940 the regiment had undergone a period of intensive training in Aldershot and 496 Battery was formed from personnel from my Battery, the 321, our sister Battery, 322, and a fresh intake from London. From being a wholly Welsh regiment at the start of the war, we now became a mixture of cockneys and northerners – and for the first time I heard myself being called 'Taffy'.

In spite of myself I was gradually becoming more proficient as a soldier – not enough to keep Hitler awake at night, but I now knew how to fire a rifle properly, and the workings of the 75mm guns which we had been issued in September were no longer a completely closed book. One thing I wasn't too bad at was the drawing of a panorama, which was a sketch of the countryside viewed from an observation post. I liked drawing little trees and smoke coming out of the chimneys of the farmhouses and cottages which were our imaginary targets. When I began to put in cows and horses my officer, Captain Gordon Davies, would remonstrate with me. 'Come on, Secombe. You're a gunner not a Constable.' There was no answer to that, although it was around this time what I was working on the 'raspberry' or the Bronx cheer which was to become a feature of my variety act a few years thence.

I spent most of my time working in the battery office along with Johnny Otterson, who was the chief clerk, and Ken Jenkins, with whom I was responsible for making out the acquittance rolls, or pay sheets, for the battery pay parade. There seemed to be no escape from adding up figures, although there was no chance of a repeat of my Baldwins fiasco. Ken Jenkins supervised my figures and he was a phenomenal mathematician. He also knew the name, rank and number of every member of the battery. By nature he was a nice, quiet, kind sort of bloke and I'm afraid my boisterous nature must have got on his nerves at times, though he never showed it. On the other hand, Bombardier Otterson was not averse to heaving an ebony ruler in my direction.

Danny Williams was now a bombardier with two sparkling stripes on his arm, and one day he came to me and said, 'How would you fancy a trip to Scotland with me?'

It appeared that he had been detailed to collect a prisoner from Maryhill Barracks, Glasgow. The man – whose name, incidentally, was Jack Dempsey – had not returned from leave and had been arrested as a deserter. He hadn't been with the battery very long and neither of us knew him by sight. 'It's a nice little trip, Harry,' said Dan, and I accepted readily. We drew our rail passes and haversack rations and headed for the station.

The journey up to Glasgow was not very comfortable and we were forced to sit most of the way in the corridor. 'Don't worry,' said Dan. 'On the way back I've got authority to commandeer a reserved compartment because we'll be bringing back a prisoner.'

'That'll be nice, Dan,' I said, stepping on my haversack rations as I stood up to let an officer go past.

Danny's intention was to report to Maryhill Barracks that evening, spend the night in the YMCA, and pick up the prisoner in the morning. However, the moment we stepped through the entrance of the barracks in Sauchiehall Street we were made to double march across the parade ground by an aggressive sergeant-major. In the guard room we were stood to attention while the prisoner was brought in from the cells.

'Gunner Dempsey,' said a laconic sergeant, handing over a short, nervous lad wearing spotless battledress. Danny signed for him and then the three of us were marched back across the parade ground and out into the street.

'Sorry to cause you all this trouble,' said our prisoner.

'Don't mention it,' I said cheerfully.

Danny gave me a hard look. After all, he was in charge.

It transpired that poor old Dempsey had gone home on compassionate leave because his home had been bombed in an air raid and he couldn't get everything sorted out in the forty-eight hours he had been given. We felt sorry for the lad, and when we had settled down in the compartment Danny had duly commandeered, we treated him to a bottle of beer from the station buffet.

By the time we arrived in London we were fast friends, and after breakfast at a Church Army mobile canteen, Danny decided that, as we had plenty of time to spare before getting the train back to Aldershot, we'd take a little walk around the Victoria area. We went to a cartoon cinema, had a few beers in a pub, and then Danny looked at his watch and declared that we'd better get cracking. Before catching the train we were supposed to report to the RTO at Victoria Station, which involved us getting into a lift. By this time Dempsey was carrying my rifle over his shoulder, because my shoulder was getting sore. There was the usual crush of servicemen in the station, laden like us with equipment, and as the lift arrived there was a surge forward and Dempsey was thrust into the lift in front of us. The gates shut and we watched open-mouthed as our charge disappeared upwards without us. Danny and I looked at each other in alarm and then started for the stairs, only to be impeded by a solid phalanx of Canadian servicemen coming down them. By the time we reached the top of the stairs the lift had gone down again and there was no sign of Dempsey. We ran back down, having to push our way through the soldiers, only to find the lift on its way back up, and still no glimpse of our prisoner.

We sat down on a bench and discussed the situation calmly. 'He's gone – he's deserted again. Oh God, oh Mam, what are we going to do? He's got my rifle. It's the glasshouse for me.'

'Shut up,' said Danny. 'We'll have to tell the RTO we've lost our prisoner, that's all we can bloody well do.'

I had wild thoughts of pretending to lose my memory and wandering off into the crowds. I had played a blind beggar in John Masefield's *Good Friday* with the St Thomas Players and had perfected a marvellous out-of-focus look. It would come in handy now. Danny took a firm grip on the back of my battledress jacket and propelled me towards the lift again. As we turned the corner, there on a bench outside the RTO's office was Gunner Dempsey, looking very anxious. 'Where've you been? I've just reported that I've lost my escort.' We grabbed him thankfully and hustled him away.

I'm glad to say that he was dealt with very mercifully by the commanding officer, and after a week's detention he was allowed to go back home on leave to attend to his family.

By the time spring came in 1941 the regiment was posted down to Sussex in an anti-invasion role. It was a pleasant part of the world to be stationed, and our battery's temporary home was Gote Farm near Ditchling, just below the wooded 'V' on the northern slopes of the South Downs. The battery office was set up in the farmhouse itself, with the Battery Commander and some of his officers billeted in the bedrooms on the first floor. Behind the main farmhouse the barn had become the officers' mess. The BC was new to us and obviously on his way to a higher command in the future. His name was Major Townend, his manner brusque but fair. He had a clipped, no-nonsense way of talking which I found fascinating. It was the way officers spoke in films – most of our lot from the TA days had more than a leavening of Welsh in their speech. This man was a pukka sahib and I managed to work up a pretty good impression of him. It was soon to get me into trouble once again.

During this period in Sussex, the officers were going through very intensive training. It was a far cry from the very early days of the war when some of the specialists had to carry their officers through the trickiest methods of bringing down fire on the enemy. There was one lieutenant who was sent on quite an extensive course on hygiene in the field. When he returned he was detailed to give his first lecture to the specialists and signallers. He assembled us and addressed us thus: 'If there's one thing I've learned, it's this. Don't kick the turd about – bury it. Now, who's got a pack of cards?' And that was it. We were very sorry to lose him.

Things had changed, and there were tactical exercises without the presence of the lower orders called TEWT (Tactical Exercises Without Troops), of which Major Townend was particularly fond.

One morning he set off early on one of these TEWTs, leaving me in complete control of the battery office. Only Townend's batman, Protheroe, was left behind. His job was to light the fire in the office grate and tidy up generally while I got on with the laborious job of typing out the battery correspondence with one finger.

Protheroe was not exactly a ball of fire, and given the opportunity was not averse to using his officer's camp bed to kip on when the latter was out. He was a grizzled soldier with an armful of long-service stripes. At eight o'clock on what had started off a lovely sunny day, but which was now beginning to cloud over, Protheroe had still not made an appearance. No amount of persuasion would induce him to come down and take over his duties. I resorted to a desperate measure. Tiptoeing out through the front door I made a great fuss of entering and slamming the door behind me. Then, using my Townend voice, I called up the stairs from the hallway.

'Protheroe,' I yelled. 'Come down here.'

There was a muffled cry from the major's bedroom and a dishevelled batman appeared at the top of the stairs, hastily buttoning his trousers. When he saw it was me and not the Battery Commander he let fly with a few choice phrases picked up in various parts of the empire, including some in Urdu. He then went back into Townend's bedroom and banged the door shut.

There wasn't much I could do about making him come down to carry out his chores – I was only a gunner like him – so I muttered a few oaths of my own and lit the fire myself. Afterwards I went back to my painful typing.

Outside the sky darkened and a light rain began, which gradually became heavier. Then, in the distance, came the sound of a motor bike putt-putting down the path to the farmhouse. It was, of course, the Battery Commander, who had gone off earlier without his mackintosh. He was now on his way back to collect it.

From my typewriter, as if in a dream, I watched open-mouthed as Major Townend stepped damply over the threshold and slammed the front door shut behind him. He shook the rain off his cap, gave me a curt nod and went to the foot of the stairs.

'Protheroe,' he shouted.

'Eff off,' cried his batman, who was lying on his back on the camp bed smoking one of the BC's Perfectos cigarettes, his uniform shed and strewn on the floor.

Major Townend turned to me in complete disbelief. I raised my eyebrows in a travesty of surprise.

Once again he called, this time adding Protheroe's rank. A fresh outburst of abuse came from upstairs, including a few sexual suggestions which I found quite remarkable.

The major took the stairs three at a time and, strangely calm and aware of the outcome, I followed him. As Townend opened the bedroom door I was able to get the full reaction on Protheroe's face as he stood to attention in his long johns, his wedding tackle swinging in the breeze. Smoke rose from the cigarette cupped in one hand, and a whimper came from his open mouth. Then he saw me and said, as Haydn Baptiste had said only a couple of years before, 'I thought it was Secombe, sir. He takes you off.'

Townend fixed me with a steely eye. 'Does he, by God?'

I shrugged my shoulders helplessly.

'I'll deal with you later,' he said to me and turned back to his by now ex-batman. 'Get out at once and report to the Battery Sergeant-Major.' He grabbed his mac from behind the door and marched angrily down the stairs.

I was still typing away late into the evening, wondering fearfully what my fate would be, when I heard a roar of laughter from the officers' mess in the barn behind the farmhouse. Shortly after, the BC came into the office with a glass of brandy in his hand. He put it down on the army blanket covering the trestle table which served as my desk.

'Drink this,' he said. 'I've been with this regiment for some weeks now, and that was the first laugh I've had from my officers. I told them about Protheroe.' He barked a short laugh and left, smiling.

Later he was to become a headmaster famous for his unorthodox methods. I thought he was a great chap, but I never did an impression of him again – I felt it would have been extremely dangerous.

Ditchling was, and is, a pretty little town and its inhabitants didn't seem to mind too much that their pubs and institutions were being taken over by the army. I managed to get involved with the local concert party which was run by an extremely nice girl called Joy, who was a school teacher. She persuaded me to agree to perform in a variety concert at the Town Hall.

I made a list of my impressions – Stainless Stephen, a Sheffield comedian who always announced that he was speaking from the 'B full stop B ditto C ditto Studios, London full stop; then there was Sandy Powell – 'Can you hear me, mother?'; Stanley Holloway reciting 'Albert and the Lion', and Windy, the toothless sidekick of Hopalong Cassidy, the cowboy star. Not exactly show-stopping material, but I was learning to handle an audience. I would usually finish with a falsetto rendering of a Deanna Durbin song which always seemed to go down well. However, I was always careful to blow a few raspberries in the middle of it, just in case anyone got the wrong idea.

Everything was going well on the night of the concert, until someone introduced me to a pint of old and mild followed by a whisky chaser. I thought it was a great innovation, especially as I was being treated, and my confidence increased as I tried it again. Across from the pub the concert was proceeding apace with the local talent scoring heavily with the mixed audience of servicemen and civilians. I was the life and soul of the pub, and when my time came to go back to the concert I strode confidently towards the stage door. Unfortunately the mixture I had been drinking hit me as I got half-way, and by the time I arrived backstage my legs could hardly support me.

Joy eyed me anxiously as I assured her with nods and winks that I was fine and ready to paralyse the audience. Reluctantly she informed the compère that I was all set for my entrance and I stepped sweatily on to the stage.

What happened after that I cannot remember very clearly. I know that I got all the impressions mixed up and my Deanna Durbin song was punctuated with hiccups and burps. The bewildered audience gave me a spattering of applause out of respect for my uniform, and I collapsed in a giggling heap at the side of the stage after my wobbly exit. It was a very sorry performance indeed, and Danny Williams told me the following day that I had let the whole regiment down, as indeed I had. It taught me a lesson I never forgot. Alcohol and performing don't really mix – at least, old and mild with a whisky chaser don't mix. Mind you, brandy on the other hand, taken in moderation. . .

I would have been far more careful about my performance had I realized that Joy's younger brother, a lad a couple of years my junior, was destined for a glittering future in the theatre, films and television. He was a quiet chap who, on one occasion, had carried my kitbag when he came with Joy to meet me at the station on my return from leave. He did it with that panache for which Donald Sinden was to become famous. For it was none other than he, gentle reader. A memory to cherish.

The Real Thing

We stood at our boat stations on deck, fully equipped and wearing Mae West life jackets. It was customary for us to muster one hour before dawn and one hour before dusk just in case Jerry caught sight of our convoy. Johnny Owens from Tumble, for whom I had acted as best man at his wedding the previous year, leaned over the ship's rail and pointed to the line of snow-covered mountains tracing the horizon to the north of us.

'That's the Sierra Nevada, boyo,' he said.

'All things considered, I'd much rather be looking at Kilvey Hill,' I replied, reflecting the mood of all of us on board the *Stratheden.*

The ship was part of the great 'Operation Torch', the code name for the invasion of North Africa, and we were now well past Gibraltar. All around us, corvettes and frigates fussed over the passenger liners which now served as troop ships, signalling every so often in Morse code to each other. So far, we appeared not to have been spotted by the enemy – a fact I found unbelievable, such was the size of the convoy.

We had embarked at Greenock on 15 October 1942, completely unaware of our destination.

We knew, of course, that we were going to war, and for security reasons embarkation leave had been dispensed with. I was lucky enough to have been given ordinary leave on 27

September, and because of my work in the battery office I was able to intimate to my parents that I would not see them again for some time.

I vividly remember Mam and Dad coming to see me off from the old LMS station in Swansea. We chatted gaily on the platform before the train came in. The conversation was about important things like not catching cold and how well the Russians were fighting and how I was to take care of myself and about Carol's new boyfriend and about what we'd do at Christmas. And when the train did come in, my mother held me very close and Dad coughed and blew his nose on his handkerchief several times. As the train drew away from the platform I waved farewell, leaning as far out of the carriage window as I dared, watching them as they stood hand in hand, trying to smile as their son went off to war.

The regiment was no longer a second-line support unit, we were now part of the 78th Division. At the end of July 1942 we had moved up to Dunblane in Perthshire where we were completely re-equipped and reinforced up to strength. We were trained for assault landings, and 'loading and unloading of guns and vehicles were intensively practised on the Clyde', as the Regimental History states laconically. We were also taken out into the hills around Dunblane at night-time in closed trucks and ordered to make our way back to base with the aid of a prismatic compass. I wasn't too bad at this; I already had a very strong sense of survival and I had learned to find my way about pretty well. If anyone had to lead a retreat I was going to be the first one to volunteer.

There was now one gleaming stripe on my arm. I had achieved the highest rank I was ever to attain in the army, that of a lance-bombardier. I had been sent on a course to Edinburgh Castle in August so that I could become a fully-fledged army pay clerk. It was an easy task after the experience I already had and I came out top of the course, a fact which caused great merriment when I got back to the battery office.

'Come on, snap out of it.' Johnny Owens tugged my arm. 'Let's have a sing-song.'

This was always easy to arrange, especially as a lot of our original Welsh complement were still with the regiment. In no time at all the deck rang with the sound of three-part harmony as we sang ourselves through the Mediterranean night. Welsh songs, rugby songs, songs that were unrepeatable in polite society, and lastly, hymns, which have always been my favourite kind of music. Then the inevitable 'Come on now, lads, break it up. You'll wake the bloody Jerry submarines,' from someone in authority, and we'd break off reluctantly and shuffle our way back down to the hammocks that were our sleeping accommodation between decks. Back to the smell of sweat and fear, and our own thoughts.

Ten days out at sea we were informed of our destination, and for some reason the knowledge of where we were going removed some of the foreboding we had felt. In the army it was always the fear of the unknown that was hardest to take; once a task was made clear it was somehow more bearable, however hard it might be. We also heard over the ship's tannoy system of the great victory at El Alamein and that cheered us up no end. Between us – the First and the Eighth armies – we'd soon have Jerry bottled up. We thought like that then.

Our part of the convoy, the second echelon, as we were called, landed a couple of days after the rest of the regiment. We came ashore at Algiers without incident and I was greatly excited by the sights and smells of the place. There was one particular aroma which I always associate with Algiers and that was the gas they used to power the cars and lorries. There was a great shortage of petrol and all the vehicles seemed to carry large gas containers on their roofs. It smelled like rotten apples, but was not exactly unpleasant. However, there were also plenty of pongs of the unpleasant kind about.

The political situation was uncertain for a while and the guns were deployed on the golf course all set to fire on Fort L'Empereur where Darlan, the head of state in French Africa, was rumoured to be in hiding. Nothing came of it, however, and we sat around waiting for our next move. It was not long in coming. It was decided on 15 November that 11th Infantry Brigade, with our regiment in support, was to head for Tunis, five hundred miles away.

My duties, apart from being a command post officer's assistant and pay clerk, now included riding a motor cycle as a relief despatch rider, and I was called upon to ride MC 13, a 500 cc Norton, all the way from just outside Algiers to our ultimate destination in Tunisia. It was a hair-raising and backside-bruising journey that included hairpin bends and long stretches of badly maintained roads. On occasions, because I spoke fairly reasonable French, I was sent on ahead with Lieutenant John Booth as a pillion passenger to arrange billets for the regiment.

We were generally the first British soldiers that the local inhabitants had seen, and in one small town near the Tunisian border we were fêted by the mayor on the town hall steps. Johnny Booth and I stood and toasted 'La France' and 'L'Angleterre' in glasses of some potent anisette which were presented to us on a silver tray, and we were offered the freedom of the town hall. It was decided that we needed somewhere a little less grand in which to billet the troops, and settled finally for a tobacco factory on the outskirts of the town.

The following morning I had a monumental headache and every bump in the road sent shock waves of pain up the back of my neck. But it wasn't long before the sheer exhilaration of being part of an advancing army took over. We were heading, it transpired, for a town called Medjez-el-Bab, where we had been ordered to secure the bridge over the Medjerda River. This little white Arab town was the gateway to the valley that led to Tunis, and we were to see a lot of it before the campaign was over.

When we eventually reached Medjez-el-Bab the excitement had begun to wear off, at least it had as far as I was concerned. We had been subjected to enemy attacks from the air ever since we had crossed the mountain range which marked the Algerian/Tunisian border. By this time the Germans were pouring men and equipment into Tunisia by sea and by road from Tripolitania – but nobody had told me that. Our supplies had to come from the Bône which was seized early on and made safe for shipping, but the port was bombed so heavily and consistently day and night that there was no Arab labour to unload the ammunition and petrol, and so the lads had to do it themselves.

The regiment went into action on the night of 24 November in support of the three infantry battalions which made up the 11th Brigade – the 2nd Lancashire Fusiliers, the First East Surreys and the 5th Northants – who went into the attack the following day. Unfortunately the attack failed after coming under heavy machine and field gunfire, the Fusiliers' CO, Colonel Manly, being killed as they approached the river.

It was in this engagement that our regiment got its first MC. Captain Barker-Benfield, who was forward observation officer, managed to cross the breast-high river with a wireless set strapped to his back and brought fire down on the machine gun posts, enabling the Fusiliers to withdraw.

On the next day, when the Brigade attacked again, Medjez was found to be empty of German troops, and though the vital bridge had been blown, our engineers started building a hundred-foot span bridge – their first in action – and there it remained for the rest of the campaign. There were rumours later on that one of the engineers had 'sold' it to an Arab entrepreneur who began charging vehicles a toll to cross the bridge.

The next move as far as I was concerned was on the 28th, when we left Medjez and headed for Smedia Farm, a large, prosperous farm about five miles to the north. I kept an intermittent diary at this time and as it's the only means I have of recollecting what happened, here are the entries for 28 and 29 November 1942:

'28th: Left Medjez for Smedia Farm. "B" Troop went forward to Tebourba. Dive bombed and 2 killed. BHQ left for Tebourba.

'29th: Arrived early morning. Started to dig slit trenches at once – till daybreak. Command Post set up in cactus grove. "A" Troop in anti-tank role in strip of wood on main road just outside Tebourba in front of Command Post. Rather severe air attacks in early afternoon. One Stuka shot down by Lt anti-aircraft guns.'

Earlier, on the 27th, our sister battery, 322, which was supporting the East Surreys, was attacked at mid-morning by seventeen tanks at close range. Our gunners knocked out fourteen of them, and at the end of the day seven out of 322's eight guns had been put out of action. The one remaining gun had been manned by Sergeant Busty Eustace on his own, 'and the knocked-out ranks formed a ring around the battery, one of them only three yards from the muzzle of the gun that had destroyed it.' (The quote is from the book about the 78th Division, *From Algiers to Austria* by Cyril Ray.)

Sergeant Eustace won the DCM, and my old mate Signaller Dixie Deans got the MM for keeping up communications throughout the battle from an unarmoured truck.

The next few days from 30 November to 3 December were sheer hell for everybody. Dive-bombers and tanks had almost wiped out 496 Battery with a high percentage of officers and men being killed and wounded.

Our Battery, commanded by a very brave Major Giles Brocklebank who was awarded the MC for his part in the battle, was now in the thick of things. I had dug myself a slit trench which not only went straight down several feet, but also went lengthwise. 'One more inch, Secombe,' said the Sergeant-Major, and I'll charge you with desertion.'

I remember going to obey a call of nature during a lull in the battle, taking with me a shovel as we were required to do. As

I was fearfully carrying out my duty in a squatting position, I heard something whizz past my right ear. When I looked behind me I saw that a bullet had punched a neat hole in a prickly pear cactus. My first instinct was to stand up and tell whoever had done it to be more careful, and then the realization crept over me that the person who had fired the shot had every intention of killing me. After I had scrambled back to my slit trench I was never the same carefree lad again.

As the battle progressed our position came under mortar fire from almost every direction, and then came the sound of tank fire. Major Brocklebank decided that he would try to find where the tanks were situated, and as I happened to be out of my slit trench at the time, he summoned me to accompany him. 'Put these in your battledress blouse,' he said, handing me two hand grenades. I had never really got on with hand grenades, and as we set off on our reconnaissance I was more afraid of them than I was of the Germans.

'Keep close behind me,' he said as we crawled on our bellies towards the crest of the hill behind BHQ.

The sweat was pouring down my face as I tried to stop the grenades from banging against each other inside my jacket.

Brocklebank beckoned sharply to me from his position just below the top of the hill. 'Look at that,' he said, pointing towards two large German tanks which were laying up, hull down, in a hollow on the other side of the crest.

I stared in sheer terror at the sight below, the big black crosses on the sides of the tanks leaping out at me. In the near distance a couple of British tanks were on fire and puffs of black smoke floated lazily into the air. It was like a scene from a film, but I was only too aware that there would be no interval with ice-cream and chocolates.

'Check my reading,' whispered the Battery Commander, handing me a prismatic compass which shook like a small blancmange in my hands. As I was reading off the scale, Brocklebank calmly took out his cigarette case and offered me a fag. I shook my head wordlessly. I just wanted to get back to the comparative safety of the Command Post. It was remarkable how degrees of danger shifted in one's mind in battle. Regimental Headquarters could seem like the front line when you first went into action, then when you went forward to the gun position you yearned for the security of RHQ, and the gun positions seemed like paradise when you were at the observation post with the infantry.

'Keep your distance on the way back,' said Brocklebank after he had smoked half his cigarette, which he pinched out and replaced in his case. I overtook him three times, the hand grenades clanking ominously under my blouse. When we finally got back to the command post and I had been relieved of my unwanted cargo, the major came over to where I was standing – outside my slit trench – and said 'Secombe, I think I left my cigarette case up on the ridge. Could you go and look for it for me?'

I don't know to this day whether or not he was joking but I went around the corner of the Arab huts in the cactus grove which formed our command post, stayed there out of sight for about ten minutes, and then reported that I could not find his case.

'Oh, all right,' said Brocklebank, rather too readily accepting the fact.

Another very courageous man was Bombardier Ken Harling, who in Civvy Street worked in the city. He was quite a bit older than the rest of us but when the chips were down, as they were in Tebourba, he showed absolutely no fear at all. He, too, was awarded the MM for his coolness in action, and was wounded by a mortar shell on the last day before we were forced to withdraw. When we got back to Smedia Farm after the battle I wrote a letter to his wife in Epsom. Here's part of it:

'I felt I must write to you to let you have some first-hand information of the whole incident, as Ken was my best friend – rather he was more like a brother than just a friend – and I know he would like me to tell you all I know.

'It happened on the afternoon of December 3rd when we were in action and were undergoing a rather fierce bombardment from the air and from gunfire. Ken, in his capacity as signal NCO, was out repairing a break in the line caused by a shell burst. Prior to this he had been manning a telephone and doing other routine jobs which in action take a lot of nerve to carry out. . .

'Unfortunately, however, a mortar shell landed some few yards away from him before he had time to take proper cover. He dropped forward on his face, saving most of the blast, but too late to stop three pieces of shrapnel which struck him – one in each arm and the other just above the knee. He managed to crawl into a slit trench and there his wounds were dressed by an officer. They were not very serious – just rather deep flesh wounds, but he lost quite a lot of blood from them.

'We got a stretcher for him and he was taken to our nearest dressing-station. Then came the worst part. We had orders to move from our own area, owing to heavy enemy pressure, and fight our way out. But because the dressing-station was some distance in front of our position, we were unable to evacuate all the wounded except those who could actually walk. Thus Ken, who had a leg wound, had to be left in the dressing-station with other casualties to await inevitable capture by the Germans. The doctor, however, stayed with his patients and you can rest assured that Ken was as comfortable as he could possibly be.

'Throughout the whole of the incident, especially when his wounds were being dressed, he displayed really marvellous courage – even to the extent of getting onto the stretcher himself. He smiled at me as he was carried away and said "I'll be all right, boy."

'. . .A spirit like Ken's will always be undaunted, whatever the circumstances.'

In the event Ken was not taken prisoner, but after a series
of bizarre accidents was ultimately evacuated by an American
half-track and in due course was invalided out of the army.

The evening of 3 December was a nightmare. We had been
firing open sights with all the ammunition we had left – smoke
shells and armour-piercing shells which were normally used
against tanks. The Hampshires had fought magnificently, one
of their officers, Major le Patourel, winning the VC, and
their strength had diminished to only ten officers and two
hundred men. Led by their CO, Colonel Lee, they cut their
way through Tebourba, firing their Bren guns from the hip.
Then came the order for all troops to withdraw, and it is a
credit to our Battery that we brought out what guns we had
left. What remained of the East Surreys came out with us.

I found myself clinging to the back of a three-ton truck,
while overhead the tracer bullets seemed to travel in slow motion. The Germans, fortunately, were not too sure about what
was happening, and most of us managed to reach the safety
of Smedia Farm back down the road towards Medjez-el-Bab.
Johnny Owens and I made the escape together, but some of
our lads were taken prisoner after we'd had an argument
about which track to take. They went one way and were
captured, Johnny and I went the other and survived. The
luck of the draw, I suppose.

Our brave bid to take Tunis quickly did not come off,
though we had come to the very brink of success. We failed
only because our force was too small. Nobody could ever say
that we didn't try. There could be no reproach.

Ask anyone who fought in the First Army in Tunisia what
his abiding memory of the campaign was – apart from the

My father, Frederick Ernest Secombe *(above left)* during the
First World War, and *(above right)*, Grandpa Secombe

Grandpa Secombe with my mother

With my elder brother, Fred, in 1924, wearing my father's tie

As a twelve-year-old choirboy

Seated, third from right,
at St Thomas' Boys
Elementary School,
Swansea

My sister, Carol

Age 14, with Carol

With Carol in the Welsh Courtship act

CENTRAL

WELSH  BOARD

SCHOOL CERTIFICATE EXAMINATION

This is to certify that:

I. *Harry Donald Secombe* _____

_____ born *September 8*ᵗ *1921*

attended the following Secondary School:

Swansea, The Dynevor Secondary School from *September* _____ *1933* to *July* _____ *1937*

and _____ from _____ 19 ___ to _____ 19 ___

and pursued a Course of Study in the subjects enumerated on the back of this Certificate.

Llewelyn John　　　　Head Master.
　　　　　　　　　　　　　　　　　　Mistress

and that having been examined in the following Groups of Subjects:

    (i) ENGLISH SUBJECTS,

    (ii) LANGUAGES,

    (iii) SCIENCE AND MATHEMATICS,

    (iv) OTHER SUBJECTS,

II. (s)he passed the School Certificate Examination of the Central Welsh Board in *July* _____ *1937*,
passing with Credit in the following subjects: *English ; French (Written and Oral); German (Written and Oral); and Art* _____

Signed on behalf of the Central Welsh Board,

Chairman.

and that

III. The Board of Education have inspected the School(s) and recognized *it* ~~them~~ as (an) efficient Secondary School(s),
and accept the Examination as reaching the approved standard and as being suitable for the ~~last-named~~ School.

Signed on behalf of the Board of Education,

W. P. Wheldon

*Permanent Secretary to the
Welsh Department.*

My School Certificate, 1937

As Lance-Bombardier Secombe in the army in Italy in 1945

In the army, 1943

Welcome home from St Barnabas Church

Saint Barnabas Parish Church

1939 1945

Swansea

Presented to *Harry D. Seacombe*

It is with a profound sense of Thankfulness and Gratitude that the Church extends to you a cordial Welcome on returning home safely from the perils and hazards of the World War, being deeply conscious of the grave dangers and hardships you had to endure whether serving on Sea, Land, or in the Air.

The Thoughts and Prayers of your Church have always been a constant petition for your protection and well-being, believing that your Loyalty, Fortitude and Sacrifice will enable future generations to live in peace and security.

May the remainder of your life be blessed with every Happiness.

On behalf of the Church,

D. Luther Thomas
Vicar.

Out of uniform at last

Entertaining fellow soldiers in Italy, 1944-5.
Fairy queen – fair enough

Shaving for a living at the Windmill Theatre, October 1946

With Jimmy Edwards at a *Weekly Sporting Review* party and *(left to right)*, a pretty lady, self, Johnny Mulgrew and Leslie Welch, the 'Memory Man' (who would know the name of the pretty lady)

Courting days, with
Myra Atherton, 1946

Myra, before our
engagement

'Resting' in digs

Picture of a desperate second-spot comedian on tour

Matinée idol

Our wedding day, 19 February 1948: *(left to right)* Beryl Atherton (Myra's cousin), Josh Williams (best man, later to marry Carol), Jim Atherton (Myra's father) and sister Carol

With Norman Vaughan *(left to right)*,
Johnny Mulgrew and Myra in London,
1948

Returning from a rough fishing trip
in Brixham harbour, 1949, with
father-in-law, Jim.

With my mother, Gladys

Proud grandparents

Baby minding is a serious business,
Torquay, 1949

Jennifer, asleep at last,
on the front at Rhyl

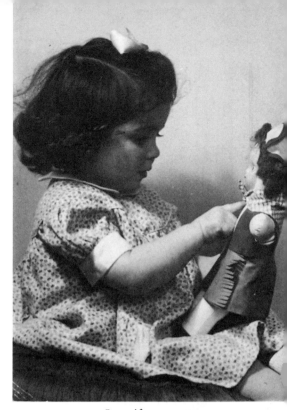

Jennifer with Myra, my mother,
Carol and neighbour

Jennifer, age 2

With Jennifer in 1950

In yellow bowler hat and check jacket for the 'Toot, toot tootsie' number in the Blackpool season of 1951 – a lovely mover

At the opening of St Stephen's Garden Party, Blackpool, 1951 – cue for a song?

Judging a beauty competition with Jack Radcliffe, Blackpool, 1951. I won

With fellow artistes backstage in Blackpool: Vera Lynn, Jack Radcliffe *(at the rear)* and Norman Evans

With Milligan upstairs at Grafton's – the monkey was the real brains behind the show

Goons at Grafton's – we could only afford two scripts

Funny faces on radio

Persuading the Goons to sign their second contract at the Aeolian Hall, 1951 *(front, left to right)*: Dennis Main Wilson, Jimmy Grafton, Spike Milligan and Larry Stevens. Behind, next to me, are Michael Bentine and Peter Sellers. The money was obviously laughable

In descending order: Michael, Spike, Peter and guess who

Germans, of course – and he'll answer 'the mud'. Mud was everywhere, in our hair, in our food, and it plastered our uniforms like liquid cement. Tanks sank up to their turrets in it, and even when the surface of the ground dried out there was always three or four feet of oozy clay underneath.

The rain began in our sector on about 6 December, and it fell for three days and nights. There was no respite from it and no protection either. I had always imagined North Africa to be a hot, sandy place with oases and palm trees, but it soon became clear that the climate was more European than African. Down where the glamorous Eighth Army were fighting it was more like the popular conception of desert warfare, but where we were that December it might just have been Ystalyfera with Arabs.

We spent most of the month around the Medjez area, patrolling and waiting to be re-equipped and for reinforcements. The food we were getting was not too bad. It was called 'composite rations' officially, but we knew it as 'compo rations'. A box containing food for fourteen men for one day, it consisted of forty-two tinned meals, along with boiled sweets, cigarettes and, most importantly, toilet paper. The best combination was the box that held steak and kidney pudding, golden syrup sponge, and Players cigarettes. If you were unlucky you got McConochie's stew and soya links with Capstan full-strength. It also contained a tin of tea, sugar and dried milk all mixed up together. This concoction we would throw into water which we boiled in the tin in which the hard tack biscuits had been packed. I could never get used to the stuff, but most of the lads thrived on it, taking every opportunity to brew up.

The biscuit tins were very useful for collecting water and for boiling our lice-ridden underwear. They were also supposed to act as ovens when turned on their sides and punctured with holes to let out the steam. It certainly didn't work for Johnny Owens and myself that Christmas. We were billeted on a farm and I had managed to persuade the Arab farm manager to sell me a chicken for twenty cigarettes. He took the fags and handed over a live bird. Now, neither Johnny nor I had ever killed anything – not even Germans as far as we knew – but our desire to have a change of diet was stronger than our qualms and we set about slaughtering the poor creature with a machete. I'll draw a veil over the actual killing, except to say that I think it died from laughter at our attempts to despatch it.

Faced with the dead chicken, we began to prepare it for our dinner. First, we realized, it had to be plucked – and our clumsy efforts removed as much surface skin as feathers. Then there was the problem of cooking the damned thing. We started a fire with petrol-soaked wood in a circle of stones, placed the bird inside the biscuit tin, laid the tin on its side, duly peppered with holes as instructed, and sat back to await results. They say that a watched pot never boils – well, I can assure you that a watched chicken never cooks, at least ours didn't. We went off to collect some bottles of beer which had come up with the rations and supplemented them with a couple of mugfuls of our Christmas rum ration. Soon, a rosy glow came over us, which was more than could be said for the chicken. It just lay there, smoking. Eventually as evening approached and no fires were allowed after dark, we dragged the blackened corpse from the biscuit tin and tried to carve it. The stench was awful when we cut into it, and only then did we realize that you were supposed to take out the insides of poultry before cooking it. We had stew Christmas night and some more rum, and when the padre came along and asked me to lead a sing-song in the barn I couldn't even answer him.

There is only one entry for January in my diary for 1943:

'Friday, 1 January: Broke my glasses on way to Green Hill.'

JANUARY, 1943

MON.
4

TUES.
5

WED. *Epiphany* ● New Moon, **12.37** p.m.
6

THURS.
7

FRI.   JANUARY, 1943
1   *New Year's Day*

FRI.
8

Bank Holiday, Scotland

Broke my glasses on way to Green Hill

SAT.
2

SAT.
9

SUN. *2nd Sunday after Christmas*
3

SUN.
10 *1st Sunday after Epiphany*

Behind this brief sentence lies a story.

We were ordered up to the northern sector to support the Buffs of 36th Brigade in an attempt to take Green Hill, a dominating position ten miles short of Mateur. I know this now because I read it later on in the official history of the 78th Division. At the time I was only aware that I had to ride the dreaded MC 13, which was now a Matchless 350 cc, the Norton having been left behind somewhere in Tebourba. The mud was so bad that every few miles I had to undo the butterfly screws on the back mudguard and scoop out the liquid glue that clogged the wheel. Then I lost one of the screws in the stuff, and finally finding it after nearly a half-hour of searching, I kicked the starter so savagely that my glasses flew off and shattered on the petrol tank. I managed to make the rendezvous but my eyesight was so bad without my spectacles that I was useless for any duties other than carrying ammunition boxes and peeling spuds in the cookhouse. The attack failed – and we withdrew to positions near Medjez. Here it was decided that I was going to be a liability until I had a new pair of glasses, and I was duly sent off to the rear to get them.

For some reason I was officially classified as a 'walking wounded' and put on the ambulance train to Souk Ahras, back over the border in Algeria. I was issued with a brown label with my name, rank and number on it and told to report to the General Hospital. The journey back to base was very embarrassing because there were infantrymen with bullet and shrapnel wounds sharing the same compartment. I could not bear to tell them what was wrong with me, so I cultivated an air of mystery about myself, hinting at some obscure disease.

We arrived at Souk Ahras at night-time in the middle of an air raid, and things were pretty chaotic at the hospital. Those of us who could walk, shuffled in a line before a desk where our labels were taken from us. Then we sat around for a while as the bombs fell. When the all-clear went, an orderly summoned me, gave me a pair of pyjamas and told me to undress. I was in no position to question his orders, indeed I welcomed the chance of a kip in a real bed. 'This is the way the British Army looks after its lads,' I thought admiringly as I pulled the blankets over my head. My memory of the next few hours is hazy – I know I was awakened and given something to drink, and remember nothing more until I was shaken awake by a doctor in a white coat.

'How are you now, Brown?' he asked.

'Pardon, sir?' I tried to bring him into sharper focus by narrowing my eyes.

He repeated the question.

'My name is Secombe, sir. Lance-Bombardier 924378.' I knew that much.

The doctor looked at something tied to the foot of the bed. 'Aren't you Fusilier Brown?'

'No, sir.'

'Have you got dysentery, then?' The doctor was getting irritable by this time.

'No sir, I've broken my glasses,' I stammered.

'Get out of that bloody bed, man.' The MO was furious. 'Give him his uniform and send the bugger to the optician,' he said to the orderly with him.

As I dressed I learned that there had been a monumental mistake and that some poor fusilier had been up all night filling sandbags in between rushing to the latrines. Then, to cap it all, he'd been given an eye test, which must have seemed a strange treatment for what ailed him.

I was given pretty short shrift, and was provided with two new pairs of spectacles in no time at all. Secretly I had banked on having to wait a couple of days while they tried to fix me up with the strong lenses I required, but I had to be content with just the one night's bed and board. I don't know what was in the drink they gave me that night but it was nearly a week before I had a bowel movement – and it took a mortar attack to move me.

At the beginning of February we were once more in support of the 11th Infantry Brigade – the 2nd Lancashire Fusiliers, the 1st East Surreys and the 5th Northants – south of Medjez overlooking the Goubellat Plain. Battery Headquarters was set up in a farm and conditions became static for a week or two, with the wind and rain adding to our discomfort. A lot of spare time was spent trying to chip away the mud from our uniforms and equipment, because when the stuff dried it was like concrete. The Arabs made bricks out of it.

Then, according to my diary, on 27 February (which, incidentally, appears to be a day behind the official regimental history – but then I never knew what day it was when we were in action) we were attacked by a much bigger force and nearly over-run. My diary for that day says:

FEBRUARY, 1943

MON.
22

TUES.
23

WED. *St. Matthias*
24

THURS.
25

FRI.
26

SAT. ☾ *Last Quarter,* **6.22 p.m.**
27 *Party started at 4 o'clock in morning. Lasted throughout day with terrific casualties for Jerry. Capt. Reader Newall killed by a mine.*

SUN. *Sexagesima*
28 *Battle continued on Plain but consisted mostly of small pockets lying up in gullies nullahs.*

MARCH, 1943

MON. *St. David's Day*
1 *lunch quieter — met Lt. in A.A. who knows Dewi Williams. Down south — Capt. Browne - Kenyie wore*

TUES. *Fairly quiet.*
2 *Bag counted down South consisted of 2 Mk IVs 1 88 mm gun, 15 lorries, and 3 staff cars !!!*

WED. *Quiet during day. Lots of*
3 *own planes in sky. Bit of misunderstanding between own and French infantry caused quite a flap!*

THURS.
4 *Lovely day — nothing much doing. Lot of banging down far South. Jerry plane down*

FRI.
5 *Fairly quiet. Planes came over — ours plus but nothing in our area*

SAT. ● *New Moon,* **10.34 a.m.**
6

SUN. *Quinquagesima*
7

19

'Party started at 4 o'clock in the morning. Lasted throughout day with terrific casualties for Jerry. Captain Reader and Newall killed by a mine.

'Saturday, 27 February: Battle continued on Plain but consisted of small pockets lying up in gullies and nullahs.

'Sunday, 28 February: Much quieter.

'Monday, 1 March, St David's Day Fairly quiet. Bag counted down south consisted of two Mk IV (tanks), one 88 mm gun, fifteen lorries and three staff cars.

'Tuesday, 2 March: Quiet during day. Lots of own planes in the sky. Bit of misunderstanding between own and French infantry caused quite a flap!

'Wednesday, 3 March: Lovely day – nothing much doing. Lot of banging down south. Jerry plane down.

'Thursday, 4 March: Fairly quiet. Planes came over – ours and his, but nothing in our area.'

Those few sentences conceal a hell of a battle with the 10th Panzer Division, the one that was the spearhead of the Germann Army in the smashing of France. Along with them were parachute troops and the Potsdam Grenadiers; altogether about forty-five thousand hardened fighting men. If only I'd known what we were up against, I would have set off for Algiers on MC 13, mud or no mud.

At the end of March, the regiment moved down into the Le Kef area to prepare for the big offensive which was to drive Von Arnim's army out of Africa. The weather was getting warmer and there were longer periods of sunshine between the rainstorms, so it was obvious to those in command – though not to me – that it was time to strike back.

Reinforcements were arriving all the time and on one particular occasion we were instructed to dig gun-pits for a detachment of 7.2 gun howitzers which had just come into the area. They were to be deployed on a plateau for the purpose of destroying some enemy gun positions which were sited in rock caves deep in the hillside.

We dug the gun-pits, as ordered, in the daytime and the guns moved in under the cover of darkness. I happened to be sitting in an eight-hundredweight wireless truck in a gully below a steep cliff which led up to the plateau where the guns were intended to come into action.

Meanwhile, up above us the big guns with their rubber tyres and huge barrels had been manhandled into position. It was the custom when artillery of this calibre was used, that the first round was fired by just one gun, using a rope attached to the firing mechanism. The gun was duly fired, but, owing to the fact that we had been given the wrong specifications, the gun-pit was too shallow to accommodate the recoil of the barrel. Consequently it bounced out of its pit and careered backwards over the cliff under which our little wireless truck was positioned.

The noise was quite terrifying and my first reaction was that if the enemy had now taken to firing entire guns at us and not just shells, it was about time we packed in the whole business. Nobody seemed to know exactly what had happened and because it was night-time, there was not much point in running about looking for trouble.

Suddenly the canvas flap of the truck was swept aside and a dim face appeared in the light of our paraffin lamp.

'Anybody seen a gun?' inquired the intruder.

'What colour?' we replied.

It was a certain Bombardier Milligan who was to play quite as prominent part in my life in the near future, but who was then, like myself, only playing 'walk-on' parts in battles. At the time I had no idea who he was, and it was only much later on in Italy, when we were discussing the North African campaign, that I realized it was he who had lost the gun.

On 7 April the division launched an attack which was designed to clear the hills to the north of Medjez; Djebel Ang and Tangoucha along with the Berber villages of Toukabeur Chaouach and the Heidous. When these were taken Medjez would be free from the possibility of counter-attack and the final battle for Tunis could begin. To give a flavour of what went on from our battery's point of view, here are some more extracts from my diary:

'Wednesday, 7 April: Fired at 0350 hours, heaviest barrage seen in Tunisia – 15,000 rounds. Moved forward after 2nd objective taken.

'Thursday, 8 April: Fired Y targets and U targets ['Yorker' targets required the three batteries to fire, i.e. the whole regiment of artillery, and 'Uncle' targets called for all the division's artillery] nearly all day. Osbourn killed at observation post. Very windy and slight rain. Eight Stukas shot down.

'Friday, 9 April: Discovered gun positions to be in minefield. Recce of new locations prior to move, which later cancelled. Captain Browne gets MC.

'Saturday, 10 April: Move took place after all into hills behind Pt 667 [north of Chaouach village]. Arrived after dark and set up command post.

'Sunday, 11 April: No firing done. Two Stukas shot down. Battle going well so far.

'Tuesday, 13 April: Preparations all day for big barrage supporting attack by 11th and 36th brigades. Biggest load of shit going off at 2300 hours ever!

'Wednesday, 14 April: Took all objectives by tea-time with exception of Tangoucha. Not held in much strength. Fired Y and U targets.

'Thursday, 15 April: Jerry counter-attacked on Bou Diss. Driven off. Start day beating off counter-attacks. Still hold all ground. Barrage fired at night.

'Friday, 16 April: Captain Browne went into action with feet [infantry]. Injured. Guthrie and Chamberlain wounded. Attack unsuccessful. Situation remains unchanged.'

Although Tangoucha was still held by the enemy, Medjez was now free from attack and our ten-day battle had been a success. The division had taken 1,080 prisoners and the First Army Commander, General Anderson, wrote in his despatch: 'I consider that 78th Division deserves the highest praise for as tough and prolonged a bit of fighting as has ever been undertaken by the British soldier.'

The one hill which had been a thorn in the side of the British advance from the very beginning of the campaign was Longstop Hill, which dominated the Medjez to Tunis road. Until it was taken, the guns positioned on it could prevent any assault on Tunis. The Guards Brigade and the American combat team attached to our command had tried unsuccessfully to take it at Christmas. Now, on Thursday, 23 April, on the eve of Good Friday, it was the task of 36th Brigade – the Buffs, the Royal West Kents and the Argylls, along with the East Surreys and the tanks of the North Irish Horse – to take Longstop once and for all.

I have a vivid recollection of line after line of infantrymen moving up the slopes before us, silhouetted against the evening sky. The red poppies were out and a profusion of spring flowers carpeted the hills around, as these brave men walked silently upwards into their attack positions. We gunners could only stand in silent awe and admiration as we watched them go by our guns.

'Friday, 23 April: Infantry encountering fierce opposition on Longstop and Tangoucha. Fired barrage.

'Saturday, 24 April: Big final attack expected on Longstop and Tangoucha. Heidous evacuated by enemy.

'Sunday, 25 April: Fired lot of ammunition. Tangoucha taken. Most of Longstop in our hands.'

By the 26th all of Longstop had been taken and in the fighting leading up to its capture, Major Anderson of the 8th Argyll and Sutherland Highlanders won the VC.

On 29 April we were issued with khaki drill for the first time and we all shed our lousy battledress with whoops of delight. It had been getting warmer every day and the wool uniforms were becoming unbearable in the heat. White knees were exposed for the first time as we donned our new shorts, and we all had red 'V's where the sun had tanned our necks.

The battle for Tunisia was now virtually over for the division, although our regiment's twenty-five pounders were still in demand as we advanced along the Tunis road. On 3 May we met up for the first time with the Eighth Army. We were somewhat embarrassed by the newness of our uniforms and the whiteness of our knees, but in the face of their undoubted glamour and bronzed complexions we felt we had done at least as good a job as they had. When one of them shouted 'Get your knees brown' at me, my raspberry came into good use.

'Friday, 7 May: Moved in afternoon. Roads in bad condition and blocked with traffic. Tunis fallen!!

'Saturday, 8 May: Moved forward into area two miles from Tunis. Went through streets of Tunis and Carthage. Terrific response from people.'

That was a tremendous day, and none of us could stop smiling as our dust-covered trucks and guns bearing the yellow battleaxe insignia of the 78th Division crawled at a snail's pace through the packed streets of Tunis. We were cheered and pelted with flowers, and here and there German soldiers stood and watched us in bewilderment. The final advance had been so fast that we took several days to round up all the prisoners and take them to hastily prepared prison stockades.

There was a glorious moment on the beach near Carthage. The band of the Hermann Goering Jaeger Division had been captured, complete with instruments, and they sat on the sands in a roped-off enclosure, guarded by Redcaps. There they played selections from Strauss and 'Roll Out the Barrel' and 'Mademoiselle from Armentiers', while we all stood around in our drawers, cellular, short, clapping their efforts. We threw cigarettes in a couple of hats that the Redcaps had set down in the sand, and none of us could really believe it was happening.

It was a heady time for us and when we had settled down under canvas outside Carthage, we were allowed some time to ourselves. On the Monday after Tunis fell, Lieutenant Joe Cattermole, our Command Post Officer, and myself were driving around the back streets when we came across a huge green door. Joe, who had an inquisitive nature, naturally wanted to know what was behind it, though my own instinct was to leave well alone. It turned out that on the other side of the door were dozens of Jewish people who had been rounded up by the Germans and then left to their own devices as the battle for Tunis developed.

We were the first British soldiers they had seen, and they were pathetically grateful to us for saving them, although all we had done was open the door. In no time at all they dragged out tables and chairs into the courtyard of the place in which they had been incarcerated and produced bottles of anisette and sweet wine which they had hidden from the Germans. We were able to do some of them a favour by borrowing a three-ton truck from the battery vehicle park and moving them back into their homes again.

Lieutenant John Booth, who had ridden behind me on MC 13 to fix billets for the regiment when we first went into action, decided we should have a concert in the little George Metaxas Theatre in Tunis.

We got together those who could do a bit of a turn and I did my impressions, along with a parody to the tune of 'Waltzing Matilda' called 'Lost at Tebourba'. After the withdrawal from that unholy place, any piece of equipment missing from a kit inspection was deemed to have been lost at Tebourba. I can only remember the first verse, which went:

'Lost at Tebourba, lost at Tebourba,
Lost all my kit at Tebourba I did,
And they moaned and they sighed
As they went up to the quarter bloke,
Lost all my kit at Tebourba I did.'

After three weeks' rest we moved to a place called Guelma for a month's training. The area was infested with mosquitoes and on 6 June I finished up in hospital with a temperature of 102°F. Fortunately it wasn't malaria but sand-fly fever, and I was discharged from hospital on the 13th. Ten days later, after we had moved east to Hammamet, at the southern end of the Cap Bon peninsula, I had a narrow escape.

We were positioned in an olive grove which had previously been used as some kind of depot by the Italians. All about the place lay red oval plastic objects, looking for all the world like Easter eggs.

On the 23rd it was my turn to be in charge of the guard and consequently Bombardier Reed, the specialist with whom I shared a pup tent, had the job of erecting it. I had started the job by clearing away some of the 'Easter eggs' and was then called away to mount the guard. A few minutes later there was one hell of an explosion, and when I ran towards the cloud of black smoke I found Bombardier Reed with part of his leg blown away. He had kicked an 'Easter egg' to one side and it had exploded. None of us had realized that these pretty-looking toys were actually Italian hand grenades, and only a few minutes before, I had been casually throwing them to one side. Someone 'up there' must have been keeping an eye on me.

The big moment of our stay in Hammamet was the visit to the unit of General Montgomery. He came to welcome us as part of the Eighth Army, the First Army now being behind us.

He arrived in style, the great man, wearing his famous beret and carrying a fly whisk, and sitting in the back of an open staff car. We were all standing to attention in a three-sided square when his car came to a halt in the middle of us.

He stood up and called, 'Bweak wanks and gather wound.'

Willy-nilly I was propelled forward by the press of the ranks behind me, and I found myself immediately beneath him, hard up against one of the rear wheels.

He looked around at us all and then said, 'Take your hats off, I want to see what you chaps look like.'

Now, I wasn't looking too good at this particular time. For one thing I had just had sand-fly fever, and I had also developed a fine crop of shiny boils; my glasses had been repaired with black tape – although I still had a spare pair in my kitbag – and under my beret, my hair had grown long. So it was with much trepidation that I complied with this illustrious general's command. My sand-coated hair fell over my face, and I was conscious of not looking my best as I lifted up my head.

Monty took his time reviewing his new acquisitions, nodding approvingly as his gaze swept around the assembly. And then he looked down and caught sight of me. He gave a kind of start of disbelief, then went on with his pep talk about 'hitting the Hun for six' and what a good job we'd done. And every so often his eyes drilled down in my direction.

I felt impelled to say something – 'I've been ill, sir' or 'I'll get my hair cut tomorrow, sir'. Instead, when there was a tiny lull in his speech, I called, 'We're with you, sir.'

He looked down at me once more for quite a few seconds, shook his head slightly and said, 'Ye-es,' without much conviction. Then he spoke a few more words and drove away, waving his fly whisk. I must have reminded him of Wellington's words after a march past of his troops before the Battle of Waterloo: 'I don't know what effect these men will have upon the enemy, but, by God, they terrify me.'

Italy – Shells and Showbiz

We knew that the advent of Montgomery meant that another invasion was imminent, and on 10 July, Sicily was the target.

Shortly afterwards we embarked at Sousse in tank landing-craft and two days later we came ashore at Syracuse. Our route took us north, through olive groves and vineyards, over very rough roads towards our rendezvous with the Canadians at a place called Catenanuova. In Tunisia we had had liquid mud to contend with; here we had dust, white and choking, which turned us all prematurely grey and got into everything we ate and everything we wore. It even filtered through the handkerchiefs we tied around our faces when we were on the move.

After we had taken Catenanuova, the division's next task was to remove the Germans from Centuripe, a fortress town on a jagged mountain ridge. It was a bit like the Gibb's Dentifrice Castle which used to be pictured on the toothpaste adverts, and it was held by a very tough bunch of lads – the Hermann Goering Division and the 3rd Parachute Regiment. According to captured documents, Centuripe was the pivot of the German defence strategy, and the resulting battle was as hard as anything we had encountered in Tunisia.

The attack began at first light on 31 July, twenty-four hours ahead of schedule, and continued until 3 August when the Royal Irish Fusiliers of the 38th Brigade broke through the town. It was a remarkable feat of arms, and though the gunners had to manhandle their guns over jagged lava beds, the victory belonged to the infantry.

My diary entries are very brief for this period – I must have been too busy carrying ammunition or trying to dig my way underground to find time for making notes.

'Wednesday, 4 August: Went through Centuripe. Awful place.

'Thursday, 5 August: Catania falls!

'Friday, 6 August: Adrano taken. Regiment moves up towards Bronte.

'Saturday, 7 August: Heard multiple mortar. Very shaken as usual.'

The sound of this multi-barrelled mortar – the nebel-werfer – was absolutely terrifying, and had me looking through my German – English dictionary for 'I'm on your side'. Later on it proved to be pretty inaccurate, but I never got used to the sound of the thing, and I don't think anyone else did either.

Bronte proved a hard nut to crack because it was on the lowest slopes of Etna's lava fields and there was only one single-way road into the town. We had to break down stone walls to get the guns into position, and in some cases fired from the road itself. However, on the afternoon of 8 August – the 7th Sunday after Trinity, as my diary tells me – the infantry of our 11th Brigade took the town. Incidentally, I found out from Joe Cattermole that Nelson had been made Duke of Bronte, and as far as I was concerned he was more than welcome to the place.

Randazzo was the next objective, and Jerry made his last stand in the area because the roads and the country were so difficult that advancing was a slow business. We were now moving around the western side of the massive Mount Etna towards the north, and ultimately Messina.

By 13 August Randazzo was taken and we met up with the Americans for the first time. Our division's engineers and the American infantry entered the town together, but there were no Germans left. When we went through there a couple of days later, not one building in the place was left standing, and the town had a population of ten thousand. The devastation was tremendous, worse than anything we had seen in Africa.

On Monday, 16 August we came out of action and my faithful diary records that on Wednesday, 18 August, I left to join the Divisional Concert Party.

We were a fairly mixed bunch of amateur performers gathered from units within the Division. There was a tall, melancholy chap called Garth who did female impersonations with two saucepan lids for a bust; a baritone, whose name escapes me; another lad called Robertson who did a comic vicar turn; a funny little comedian from a Field Ambulance Unit called Shorty Howard, who was very good, and – more importantly for me – Len Lightowler from 322 Battery of my regiment, who was the pianist for the show. A smiling, thick-set Yorkshireman, he was to become my accompanist and personal manager later on in my career. The party was commanded by Lieutenant Bracken of 56 Reconnaissance, who did monologues.

Our stage was a three-ton truck which had been adapted for the purpose, and for spotlights we had to use the headlights of another truck which carried all our personal gear. On the sides of the lorry ran the legend 'The Sicily Billies – Lava Come Back To Me'.

For our opening ensemble number Garth had written special words to Gershwin's 'Rhapsody In Blue', and – God forgive us – it went something like this:

'We come to you from out of the blue-oo,
With something to entertain-ain you-oo,
Give you a song to help to cheer you along
When you feel rather blue-oo.'

And it went downhill from then on. However, the audiences had been so starved of entertainment for the past few weeks that they laughed and applauded our efforts as if we had been a West End revue company.

It was my first experience of doing an act night after night and performing little sketches, and I began to feel like a real professional. We lived like gypsies, driving around the divisional area to give performances wherever the troops happened to be. Sometimes the audience would contain local peasants who sat mystified throughout, and would only laugh when Lieutenant Bracken came on to do his serious monologue.

We had a great time swanning around the Sicilian countryside, drinking the dark local wine which we collected in jerricans and which was apt to take the enamel off your teeth. There were luscious grapes the size of plums hanging in the vineyards, and we picked them greedily until we found that some of the best bunches had been booby-trapped by the retreating Germans. We chatted up the local girls, but there was no chance of romance with any of them – there was always a brooding relation lurking in the background to make sure there was no hanky-panky.

The party broke up on 16 September, and I returned to the regiment prior to our move to Italy. The Italians had already surrendered and when we landed on 20 September at Reggio di Calabra after a short trip from Messina, we all thought we'd have a walk-over. We travelled in convoy across the foot of Italy through glorious scenery until we got to Bari, where we were billeted for a while on the outskirts of the city.

One afternoon Johnny Owens and I were discussing the meal we'd most like to have when we had the chance, and we decided that roast chicken and chips would be favourite. The nearest we had come to it was the disastrous Christmas dinner in North Africa.

We had leave to go into Bari that day, and after sauntering through the streets, marvelling at the cheapness of the watches on display, we found a posh restaurant and marched inside. We must have looked a villainous pair, tin-helmeted and dusty, with our rifles slung over our shoulders. The tables were laid with white napkins and gleaming cutlery, and a bow-tied waiter approached us nervously. Neither of us spoke any Italian, but Johnny took it upon himself to explain what we wanted. He clucked like a hen and waved his arms in the air. The waiter backed away from him fearfully.

'Now do an impression of chips,' I said helpfully.

Between us we managed to make the waiter understand that we were not dangerous lunatics, but just two hungry squaddies in search of a good meal. He told us to come back in a couple of hours, and though we thought that we'd return to find the place bolted and barred, the dish we had longed for was waiting for us.

It was a sight to cherish – a whole roasted chicken on a silver dish, surrounded by a pile of chipped potatoes just as we'd ordered. We sat down and polished it off, helping it down with glasses of beer. We paid in British Occupation money, which caused the waiter's face to drop considerably, but when we threw in all the cigarettes we had on us, he managed a wan smile. I have to say that I've never tasted anything as delicious as that chicken – months of compo rations had dulled my taste buds and they had had a sudden glorious reawakening. Johnny and I returned to our olive grove, burping and patting our bellies in sheer contentment.

This feeling of goodwill stayed with me as we eventually headed north towards the coastal town of Termoli. I was riding MC 13 as usual, and as we went through some of the little towns on the way we were greeted like conquering heroes by the local inhabitants. After all, they were out of the war now. As we entered one town some miles out of Bari, I think it was called Cerignola, I had to sit on my bike and make sure that the convoy took the right road. People were throwing fruit and flowers to the soldiers in the trucks, and not wishing to miss out, I held out a hand to a dark-eyed beauty across the road from where I sat. She smiled and threw a pomegranate at me with such force that it knocked my goggles off and sent me flying off the bike. She then disappeared into the tittering crowd. It must have been an omen of some kind, because shortly afterwards we were strafed from the air.

I found myself cowering in a gully with a couple of lads from REME. ''Ere,' said one of them. 'Wasn't you in that concert party?'

I nodded, keeping my face close to the ground.

'Sing us a song, then,' he said, as the planes wheeled overhead.

'Bugger off,' I said.

When we reached Termoli it was soon obvious that Jerry was going to make a stand and that our comparatively easy run up the coast road was over. The rain came early and hampered movement south of the Biturno River where the bridge leading into Termoli had been blown up. Some of the 11th Brigade crossed the river into the town in small craft, but most of us, including our battery, were still on the south side. Commandos had landed by sea to the north, but what we did not know was that the 16th Panzer Division were racing towards Termoli with orders to retake the town.

The battle raged for three days and in the fighting Major Anderson of the Argylls, who had won the VC at Longstop Hill, was killed at the brickworks to the west of the town. One of our officers, Captain Jim Gilburtson, got the MC here. He had gone ahead as forward observation officer and had found himself fighting along with the infantry.

By nightfall on 6 October the battle was over, and on the 9th I was sent back to Rear HQ to go to Tunis with a small party to collect the baggage the Division had left behind in Tunis. I welcomed my new orders with a joyful heart. All the fighting had affected my nerves, and it was an act of compassion on the part of Major Dennis Carey, our Battery Commander, to include me in the baggage detachment. It took us a week to get back to Tunis, because we had to hitch-hike our way from Taranto on an infantry landing-craft going to Syracuse. From there we boarded a French boat bound for Malta, arriving on the 23rd. We were not allowed to go ashore, so we stood on the deck of our somewhat battered boat, waiting for our next lift.

All around us in Valletta harbour there were sleek naval vessels. The officer in charge of us, a morose man, suddenly bucked up when he saw an Aldis lamp on board the battleship HMS *Rodney* signalling in our direction.

'Just a minute, chaps,' he said, stopping a noisy argument which had arisen about who could spit the furthest over the rail. 'It's a message about us.' He was a signals officer, so naturally he could read the message which was being sent in Morse code. 'Apparently we're to be picked up and taken on board this evening for the trip to Bizerta.' His back straightened and his face brightened. 'It's a rare honour for the Royal Navy to offer us a lift, especially in such a grand ship as the *Rodney*.' He looked at his scruffy command lolling about the deck. 'Get yourselves spruced up, chaps. We represent the 78th Division.'

We all went down below and cleaned ourselves up as much as we could and returned on deck to be met by our officer, resplendent in his best battledress jacket from which one pip had been removed on either epaulette. He had obviously been recently demoted from captain to lieutenant.

We stood around for a couple of hours, and then a naval officer came aboard our boat carrying some documents. Our officer advanced, smiling, and saluted smartly. 'Are you the party for Bizerta?' asked the naval bloke.

'That's right, and we're all very grateful for the honour you're doing us.'

'It's not much of an honour, mate,' replied the RN officer. 'Those LSTs roll something shocking when they're empty.'

'But what about our going on board the *Rodney*?' Our lieutenant was querulous now.

'*Rodney*? What do you mean?'

We explained that we had seen the Aldis lamp on the *Rodney* sending the message to our ship.

The navy man laughed. 'Oh, I see. That was the *Rodney* doing a favour for the tank landing-craft that'll be taking you on to Bizerta. It was passing on the message by Aldis because your bloke's out of sight around the harbour.'

Our lieutenant seemed to crumple, and shortly afterwards he went below to get drunk. As for us, we resumed our spitting competition over the rail until they came to transfer us to the LST.

Our sojourn in Tunis took quite a few weeks as we tried to trace the whereabouts of the contents of some of the kit-bags. The store had been broken into and there were quite a few Arabs walking around wearing Sam Browne belts and sporting officers' shoes. We all felt deeply embarrassed at the comparatively small amount of kit we had to take back with us to Italy, but there was nothing we could do about it.

We eventually returned to the division in late December, and I found our battery in Vinchiaturo, where the snow lay deep over everything. My first job was to get stuck into helping to clear the blocked roads, and after the balmy air of Tunis I found the bitter cold hard to bear.

On 6 January we were off up the Adriatic coast and on the 8th we arrived at Casola. My diary for that day reads:

'Saturday, 8 January: Reported sick to MO in Casola. Twenty miles in open jeep in the snow. Arrived with temperature of 101. No ruddy wonder.'

It transpired that I had developed an inflammation of the gall bladder and kidneys, and after being transferred to the New Zealand Division Casualty Clearing Station at Vasto, I was eventually evacuated in an ambulance train to the 76th General Hospital in Trani.

Termoli was the last battle in which I was to take any part, and I was not to rejoin my regiment again. It was a fine unit, and I was proud to have been one of its members. 132 Field Regiment was home to me for four years, and I could not have grown up with a better bunch of lads.

We left a lot of our comrades lying under the ground in Tunisia and Sicily, and the regiment was to go on gathering glory in the slow slog up through Italy, finally finishing up in Austria. Those of us who are still left have a regimental reunion as often as we can, and we greet each other like brothers.

I spent five weeks in 76th General Hospital and lost about two stones in weight. At the end of my stay I was admitted to 11th Convalescent Depot just up the road from the hospital in Trani. It was a large Italian Army barracks and had a cinema which also doubled as a theatre. After I had parked my kit on the bunk bed allotted to me, I set out to find if there was a concert party associated with the theatre. To my delight there was a notice outside the cinema asking for volunteers for a variety concert that night. I gave my name to the sergeant in charge, Brian Sherman, and was given a spot on the show.

Fortunately my act went well and I became enrolled on the semi-permanent staff as a member of the concert party. It was a much more professional set-up than the divisional concert party had been. We had a band which was led by Brian Sherman, who also did the vocals, and there were some good entertainers among the group. One of them was a young lad who had been an actor before being called up. His name was Tommy Thompson, and as well as doing excerpts from Shakespeare, he did a very funny take-off of the Inkspots singing 'Whispering Grass'. He had been through a bad time as an infantryman and drank more than he should, but he was a great companion. Another member of the cast was Harold Nightingale who compèred the show and told some good stories. Later he was to become famous as the umpire who fell asleep during a televised tennis match at Wimbledon. There was a Belgian lad, Alan Van Houtem, who played the clarinet and was the scourge of all the ladies in the camp, and a fellow Welshman, Ivor Williams, who had a very fine baritone voice.

Ivor was an amazing character who was forever thinking up schemes to make money. One of his favourite methods was to buy a cheap, flashy watch in the town and then raffle it in the camp. There were lots of Yugoslav soldiers at the depot convalescing from wounds, and they loved to gamble. They were also fiery-tempered, and when one of them won a watch that stopped shortly after he had strapped it on his wrist, he chased poor Ivor all over the camp with a nasty-looking knife. However, Ivor's Welsh charm won the Yugoslav over, although it did cost him another watch.

The concert party became quite well known in the area and we began to perform for other units. My diary states:

'Friday, 10 March 1944: We did show at Barlatta Garrison Theatre. Not very big audience but very appreciative.

'Saturday, 11 March: Bigger audience tonight. Show went down terrific [sic]. Left for Bari at night for "Services Cocktail". Slept in Caruso's room.'

The last sentence referred to the dressing-room once used by Caruso in the huge Petruzelli Opera House in Bari, where I had been invited to perform in an all-services concert. According to my entry for the following day, the two performances went down well and the RAF Command Band wanted me as a compère. However, that must have fallen through, because on the following Monday, my diary entry reads:

'Arrived back at dinner-time from Bari wet through and a little fed up. Still – experience, old cock, experience.'

I settled down into a nice steady routine with the concert party. Every Sunday we did a show at the Eighth Army Rest Camp just outside Bari, where the troops came out of the line for a few days' rest. The experience of playing to different audiences was invaluable and I became convinced that when the war was over I was definitely going on the stage.

One morning Ivor and I saw our names in the Forces newspaper, *The Union Jack*. We were asked to report to Bari for a special 'Services Cocktail' show with Carroll Levis, the famous talent spotter.

'Saturday, 6 May: Left for Bari at 5 o'clock. Got lift on train with Sikhs and arrived just in time for rehearsal of broadcast.

'Sunday, 7 May: Broadcast with Carroll Levis in "Services Cocktail". Fame at last. Ha-ha.'

Carroll Levis appeared to have been impressed with my work and asked me to look him up when the war was over. He must have said that to lots of budding comics, but when I did get in touch with him after the war he put me in one of his 'Discovery' programmes as a 'star from the services'. It was to be my very first BBC broadcast.

Nothing spectacular happened for a few months apart from the fact that I caught malaria and had to go back to the 76th General Hospital for treatment. I had met an American GI in Bari called Joe Allen who was running the USO shows down there, and he gave me the odd date or two working American Air Force bases. It was a salutary experience because nobody seemed to listen to what I was saying. To be honest, I don't think they understood what the hell I was talking about in my Welsh-accented speech, which got faster and more incoherent in pace with my nervousness. However, Joe seemed satisfied and was quite content to pay me a few hundred lire for my pains.

All was going well until one day I returned from one of my jaunts to find the depot buzzing with rumours of a big clean-out. The comanding officer had been posted elsewhere and all superfluous personnel were to be sent back up the line. I was given a medical check-up and though I was not a hundred percent fit I was told to report to the Royal Artillery Training Depot at Eboli, which was across the other side of Italy from Trani, near Salerno. I had made many friends in the camp and quite a few friends in Trani itself. Alan Van Houtem and I had long been chatting up two eminently respectable and extremely well-chaperoned young sisters, Bianca and Teresa. Their father was a doctor and their brother a lieutenant in the Italian Army, and they had a cook who made wonderful pasta dishes. She was the one we were going to miss.

I arrived wet and miserable at Eboli some time in November – my diary holds no more entries. The place was a vast tented camp on the side of a hill and at first sight seemed very unpromising. Then I found that the depot boasted an extremely well-equipped theatre and that it had a permanent concert party of almost professional standard. I was allotted a place in a bell-tent under the supervision of a Bombardier Ticehurst, who had seen me perform back at the Eighth Army Rest Camp. He made some enquiries for me and arranged for me to meet Lieutenants Langston and Laurie Turner, the officers in charge of entertainment for the depot.

They didn't hold auditions, they put on a sort of 'talent night' concert every week, and I was put down as an entrant. I was determined to do my best that night and I gave them all I'd got. Fortunately I was well received and I was offered a place in the regular show. Christmas was not far off – a big revue was being planned, and I was going to be given plenty to do.

For the time being I was to stay in the tent to which I had been first detailed, and later I was to move to a bigger tent in which all the regulars were billeted. I couldn't wait to move, because the tent in which I was sleeping also contained four amateur magicians, three of whom specialized in card tricks. The other was an illusionist called Max who spent all his time constructing a wooden lamp-post which kept collapsing on him. As far as the other three were concerned, I was the only one they could practise on.

I can see the tent now. The rain drumming on the canvas and a thin trickle of water gradually becoming a stream as it flows down the slope between the beds. A paraffin lamp swinging from its mooring place on the centre pole; in its dim light I am being exhorted to 'Take a card' by three eager lunatics, while in the background Max groans as his lamp-post falls down on him for the umpteenth time.

When the NAAFI closed I would wander about in the rain rather than return to the tent and be told, 'Shuffle the pack well; now cut them, and the next card you turn up should be the ten of clubs. Ah – now, just a minute. Something's gone wrong 'ere.' I was saved from pneumonia only by the departure from the concert party tent of a vocalist who had sung out of tune once too often.

The occupants of the 'show' tent were a motley crew, and I was surprised how untidy it was. The other tents in the camp were inspected every morning, but because the Camp Commandant, Major Derek Attwood, had a soft spot for 'theatricals', our tent was left alone.

It was here, in this tent, that an event occurred that was to have a profound effect on my future career. The audiences to whom we played demanded new material as often as possible, and it was essential that we changed our acts before the lads got fed up with them. By the time I had been there a few weeks, in spite of getting a good reaction from playing the

Fairy Queen in the pantomime, I was beginning to scrape the bottom of the not terribly deep barrel of my impersonations. The competition within the regular show was fierce, and if I didn't come up with something soon there was a real danger that I would have to go back up the line again – a prospect I did not relish at all.

The morning before my next scheduled performance, I was still desperately trying to think of something different to do in the act. I was shaving in a mirror attached to the tent pole, watched by a couple of the lads. One of them, Bombardier Sammy Lambert, was in charge of the tent's discipline, such as it was. He was a professional musician and before the war had been a saxophone player with Sid Dean's Band in Brighton.

'Come on, Secombe, hurry up,' he said, 'I want to use that mirror.'

I was slowly lathering my face at the time, still lost in thought about getting together some new material, and when Sammy gave me the 'hurry-up' I began to shave at a maniacal speed, covering myself in lather as I did so. Bill Hall, a magnificent violinist, but as eccentric as they come and a notoriously bad audience, was lying on the bed next to Sammy. He burst into laughter at my antics, and I suddenly realized that I had the beginnings of a new act.

When I had eventually dried myself off I went up into the hills behind the camp with a pad and pencil and worked out the basis of an act which was to launch me into the variety theatre and enable me to bring up a family.

It was quite simple, but nobody else seemed to have thought of the idea. All I did was to demonstrate the way different people shaved. First was a small boy playing about with his father's shaving gear, then came a soldier doing his ablutions in a bucket of ice-cold water with a blunt blade – all the lads appreciated that one – and I finished with an impression of a person who became embarrassed at being observed while shaving, which required me to drink the soapy water from the mug I'd been using. That was all there was to it, and I closed with my version of Jeanette MacDonald and Nelson

Eddy singing 'Sweethearts' as a duet – which included a fruity raspberry.

I began to use the raspberry as a device, blowing one every time I told a joke, and saying 'I was first!' It was really a desperate attempt to give myself the bird before the audience did, and in most cases it worked.

With this material behind me – can you believe this? – I became the principal comedian in the RATD show, and I was safe from being transferred back into action.

It was a very good place in which to learn the serious business of comedy. The theatre itself was run by Les Dodds who had been stage-manager at Wolverhampton's Grand Theatre, and he made us all behave like professional actors. A very clever Geordie named Harold Major wrote West End-standard revue sketches, and the music was written by Tony Thompson, a wild-eyed pianist who was a great enthusiast. Other members of the company were Haile and Beatty, two inseparable lads who were hysterically funny as a couple of NAAFI girls; little 'Chug' Steele, who did a comedy parson routine; Eric Hayes, a fiddle player with a wicked sense of humour who, because of his gold tooth, was known as the 'flash in the pan'; and Jack Bridgeman from Somerset, who played the clarinet, tap danced and also did comedy.

Jack, Eric and Bill Hall would come back pie-eyed from a session in the sergeants' mess and, lying on their backs, would produce sensational music until the guard on picket duty would bang on the side of the tent around dawn to ask for a bit of peace and quiet.

The shows were produced by John Langston, who also played the straight characters when required. Laurie Taylor was a solo pianist who left RATD during the time I was there. We also had a singer from Sheffield whose name was Harold McGee. His speaking voice was quite high, not unlike George Formby's, but when he sang he had the depth and power of an operatic bass. It produced quite a startling effect when he came on to announce in his high-pitched soprano that he was going to sing 'Old Man River', but the titters would stop as soon as he let fly à la Paul Robeson.

To all intents and purposes we were a completely professional company, and when the ENSA parties came to perform in our theatre they were always surprised by the smart dressing-rooms and the lighting boards which Les Dodds had installed. We, in turn, would sit out front and smugly criticize the real professionals, not knowing how much we still had to learn. There is the world of difference between the best amateur and even a mediocre professional comedian, and to cross the gap is an arduous and painful business. But I suppose, considering the circumstances, we could be allowed our little vanities.

I played the Tom Walls part in the Ben Travers farce, *Tons Of Money*, working in a lot of funny business with a false beard, something to which a professional actor would never have resorted, but I must say it used to bring the house down every night.

When VE Day came on 8 May 1945, there was no longer a need for a Royal Artillery Training Depot because we were not going to be firing the big guns any more – not in Europe, anyway. It was decided that because the show was so good, we ought to take it on tour as a kind of travelling fun-fair which, as well as helping to keep all the servicemen happy while they waited to be demobbed, could also be a source of income for the Royal Artillery Fund.

It was a great idea, and we were soon travelling around Italy wherever there were large concentrations of troops, setting up a marquee as our theatre. The fun-fair part of the unit consisted of various games of chance operated by sergeants or warrant officers. One of these was a large wheel of fortune upon which a big metal arrow was fixed. The wheel was divided into segments, like the spokes on a cart-wheel, which were numbered from one to twenty. The punters would place their money on a flat wooden board, similarly numbered, and when the arrow stopped at a particular digit – for example, ten – the winner would receive ten times the amount of lire he had placed on the board, plus his original stake.

There was a sergeant friend of mine who used to take his turn at managing this stall, and whenever I was short of money I would go along to it and try to catch his eye. He would then wink at me and I'd place my lire on twelve or fourteen, and by some strange coincidence my number would always come up. I didn't know how he did it – and I didn't want to know – but I was careful not to try it too often.

At one time a few of us were at a loose end for a few days in Salerno, and having exhausted all the sights and delights of that battered city, we hired a rowing boat and rowed all the way up the coast to the beautiful resort of Amalfi. We liked it so much, that after rowing the boat back to Salerno, Jack Bridgeman, Bill Hall, Eric Hayes and Sammy Lambert packed their instruments and we managed to persuade one of the fun-fair truck drivers to take us all back there.

For two days we lived like lords. The Cappuccini Hotel just outside Amalfi had been taken over as a rest camp for officers, and just a hundred yards or so away, the Santa Catarina had been designated as a warrant officers- and sergeants-only hotel.

Both places were starved of entertainment, and we performed impromptu cabarets there, with Tony Thompson in his element on the Bechstein which the officers' hotel boasted. We were fêted and fed, and it was here in Amalfi that I began trying out a song or two. Previously I had sung only as a joke, doing the Nelson Eddy and Jeanette MacDonald duet, but loosened by a few glasses of vino rosso I belted out a ballad or two, adding my raspberry every time I became embarrassed. It was not until after I started broadcasting that I began to think about adding a song to my routine of impressions.

At the end of the summer of 1945 recruiting began for a new Entertainment Unit to be called the Central Pool of Artists, and as the RATD show was about to break up, Bill Hall and I applied to join. We were both accepted and in due course reported to a building in Vomero, near Naples, which had been taken over as the CPA Headquarters. Here, under the command of Lieutenant-Colonel Phillip Slessor, all the best available talent among the servicemen in Italy was to be gathered in. From this pool of artists, shows were to be put together, rehearsed and sent out on the road all over Italy and the central Mediterranean.

The living quarters were not great, but we all had individual beds, not double bunks, and I sat gratefully on mine as I looked around the room. Bill Hall had dumped his kit all over the floor, as was his wont. He opened his violin case, took out a stale sandwich from some previous officers' mess party and chewed it solemnly. A sad-looking soldier from a recce regiment busied himself with the unloading of his double bass, and a bombardier removed a guitar from its battered case then strummed a few chords. Bill Hall, brushing crumbs off his violin, put it under his chin, his lank hair, which fell either side of his face, making him look for all the world like Paganini. As he started to play along with the guitar, the sad soldier joined in on his double bass. The effect was truly magical, and the rest of us in the room – all new to each other – applauded in sheer delight as Bill Hall, Johnny Mulgrew and Spike Milligan began a musical partnership which was to last for a long time.

Johnny Mulgrew was a dead ringer for Buster Keaton and his sad, deadpan face belied his sly humour. Like Bill Hall, he had been a professional musician, and had once played with the famous Ambrose orchestra. Spike, Johnny and I became friends straight away and I was delighted when it was decided that we were all going to be in a brand new production called *Over the Page*. I was to be the comic, working through the show in sketches as well as doing my own act, and the three lads were to be called the Bill Hall Trio with the star spot – just before the finale.

I didn't know what to make of Spike at first, but when I discovered that it was he who had come looking for the 7.2

gun howitzer back in North Africa, we soon found that we had a lot in common. Then, as now, he was bursting with ideas for way-out comedy sketches, and we shared a dislike for comics who just told jokes. I was also aware that he had experienced a bad time in action and had just been discharged from a psychiatric hospital near Sorrento. There but for the grace of God I too might have gone.

Soon the unit began to fill up as fresh talent came in from all over Italy. Ken Platt (who became well-known for his catch-phrase 'I'll not take my coat off – I'm not stopping') joined us, along with various singers and straight actors who were only too eager to lay down their weapons and start getting back into shape for Civvy Street.

Those performers who were still 'on probation' were tried out at the officers' club which was on the premises. I remember one North Country comic who joined us, sitting on the bed he'd been allotted, feeling the springs and saying gleefully, 'Ain't it grand to be a bloody turn?'

That night he did his audition at the club under the critical gaze of the officers and their lady friends. He opened his act by vamping a few chords on the piano and then, lifting his backside off the piano stool, he broke wind with a pane-rattling ferocity. 'Ain't I a dirty bastard?' he said, grinning at the shocked audience. I'm afraid we never saw the rest of his act, but I'm glad to say he was kept on at CPA in the cookhouse because we all secretly admired his nerve.

One afternoon during rehearsals for *Over the Page* I was detailed to do my act at a hospital concert. The fellow on before me was new to the unit, and when I saw him perform I regretted the fact that I had to follow him. He was a thin young lad who told crazy gags and finished with a very accomplished tap dance, and it was clear that he was no amateur.

After I had finished my turn he came up and congratulated me. 'Are you a pro, then?' he asked.

I was flattered beyond measure, but shook my head. 'I hope to be,' I said. 'Do you think I've got a chance?'

'Of course,' said Norman Vaughan, and became my friend for life.

The run-up to the opening night of *Over the Page* became frantic with fittings for costumes and rehearsals for sketches and dance routines. They had me leaping around in a ballet scene with three other blokes and four Italian girls, who were about as flat-footed as I was. We were put through our paces by an ex-ballet dancer, Jean Veidt, who used to shed tears at our incompetence.

All this hard work made us very keen to get away for a drink in the evenings and Norman, Spike, Johnny Mulgrew and I used to belt down the stairs from our living quarters as soon as we had changed out of our rehearsal kit. One evening I was a bit late, having decided to dress up my uniform with a fancy scarf under the collar of my battledress blouse, and in my hurry to catch up with the other three I hurtled down the steps straight into Lieutenant-Colonel Slessor, our Commanding Officer. When he'd recovered his breath, he took one look at me and yelled, 'Take that bloody scarf off!'

A few years later, when he was the BBC compère for the radio show *Variety Bandbox*, he announced me as 'my old war-time comrade'. The only words he had ever addressed to me had concerned my scarf. But that's show business, folks!

Spike rather fancied himself as a vocalist and was given a song to sing in, of all things, a gypsy camp-fire scene. He wore a spotted red bandana on his head, perilously close to his eyebrows, and a loose-fitting blouse. His trousers were of hessian material dyed black, and on his feet he wore army plimsolls. A more unlikely gypsy you couldn't imagine as he sang, with feeling, 'Down in the forest, playing his old guitar, lives an old "dreams" man', accompanied by his own guitar. He gets a bit upset whenever I remind him of this episode.

The over-all direction of the show was in the hands of Major Hector Ross, an actor who had frequently played in West End productions and who fortunately thought I was very funny. He had chosen an Italian film star, Luisa Poselli, as the centrepiece of the show, and it was decided that we would open at the Argentina Theatre in Rome.

Special scenery was built in the form of a huge open book, and the idea was that an acrobat dressed as a clown should come on to turn a page at a time, revealing the name of the next act or sketch. Unfortunately, on the opening night the acrobat fractured his ankle and the idea was abandoned.

The orchestra was completely professional and consisted of army and civilian musicians, some of them Jewish refugees.

Altogether it was a well-mounted production, and the opening night was a big success, marred only by the news that Hector Ross was in danger of being court-martialled for exceeding his budget! The hit of the show was undoubtedly the Bill Hall Trio, but I managed to impress the theatre critic for *The Union Jack* newspaper, a Canadian Captain in the British Army by the name of Andy Grey. He came to see me after the show and promised to help me get started after I'd been demobbed.

When we had finished at the Argentina we went to the Bellini Theatre in Naples where Captain William Chappell, the choreographer and revue producer, dropped in to see the show and afterwards told me that the next time he'd see me would be in the West End. Ten years later, when I was topping the bill at the London Palladium, I was told by the stage door-keeper, George Cooper, that a Billy Chappell wanted to speak to me.

'Send him in,' I said, and as Billy walked into the dressing-room I asked him, 'Where have you been till now?'

The tour took in Florence, Milan, Bologna and other big cities, and Spike and I chased girls, discussed philosophy, but most of all wondered what would become of us when were demobbed. That time was getting nearer for me. Owing to the fact that I had been in the army as a Territorial since April 1939, I had quite a bit of service under my belt, and it was length of service and age which determined what number demobilization group a soldier was given. Although I was still only twenty-five years of age, I was designated Group 28.

When you knew what number you were, the agonizing wait began for the news that your group was due to be called.

Over the Page closed eventually and I found myself hanging about in Naples again. Ivor Williams had turned up at CPA and was making himself useful as a stage-manager. I was glad to see him, because I didn't know anyone else there. Norman was out on tour in another show and I applied for permission to join him. Meanwhile, Ivor and I frequented the local bars and cafés. One night I sat at a table and recorded my impressions of my surroundings. I still have the piece of paper, and because it was a first-hand account of a long-vanished moment in time, here it is in its entirety. It's called 'Italian Café'.

'Band of quarrelling musicians. Three waitresses – one fat, one tall and thin, one deformed but pretty. Little girl with

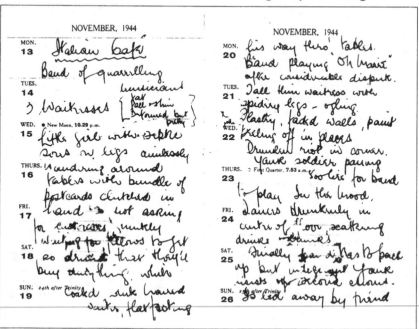

septic sores on legs, aimlessly wandering around tables with bundle of postcards clutched in hand – not asking for customers, mutely waiting for fellows to get so drunk what they'd buy anything. White-coated, white-haired waiter flat-footing his way thro' tables. Band playing 'Oy Maria' after considerable dispute. Tall, thin waitress with spidery legs – ogling. Flashy faded walls, paint peeling off in places. Drunken riot in corner. Yank soldier paying 500 lire for band to play 'In The Mood'. Dances drunkenly in centre of floor, scattering drinks and drunks. Finally band has to pack up but indignant Yank insists on second chorus. Is led away by friend.'

My application to join Norman's show came through and I hitch–hiked my way from Naples all the way up to Mestre – just outside Venice. The night I arrived I was informed that it was the final performance – the show was coming off. I insisted on doing my act, on principle, and the following day we set off back for Naples. Norman and I happened to be on a truck that conveniently broke down in Rome, and we spent a quite hysterical few days in a hotel near the Central Station called the Albergo Universo. It was a rather drunken spree, until one afternoon we went to a cinema and saw *The Lost Weekend*. The film made tee-totallers of both of us for at least two days.

When we did eventually get back to base at Vomero I found that my group number was now due for demobilization and after saying my farewells and exchanging addresses with Norman and Ivor I set off for the demob centre, Lammie Camp. It was a tented base camp on the side of Mount Vesuvius which was almost ankle-deep in lava dust from a recent eruption. I spent a couple of anxious days here waiting for my name to appear on the lists posted outside the camp office. There was no one I knew there and I missed the company of my old friends. Spike had decided to get demobbed in Italy and remained with CPA as a civilian. The Bill Hall Trio was in great demand, and he thought he'd stay with it for a while.

It was a strange time for me. I had been in the army for seven years and had been dying to get out of it. And yet, faced now with the prospect of leaving and making my own way in the world, I felt very insecure. Home, of course, was beckoning and I was really looking forward to seeing the family again. I had been home for four weeks in August 1945 and had had a great time, but I could not see myself settling down in Swansea after I'd seen so much of the world and had a taste of the theatre. I had plenty to think about on the long train and boat journey back to Aldershot.

Out of the Frying Pan into the Foyer

I had first come to Aldershot in December 1940 as Gunner Secombe, H D 924378, and now, in April 1946, I was leaving it as Mr Harry Secombe, in a pin-striped demob suit, new squeaky shoes, a pork-pie hat and a light blue overcoat. In a pocket nestled a Post Office savings bank book containing £82 gratuity and a one-way travel warrant back to Swansea.

The family gave me a tremendous welcome when I got home, making admiring remarks about my tan and on how long and bleached my hair had become. In spite of Spike's description of me at about this time in one of his books as a fat, sweaty idiot, I was in fact fairly slim, weighing under twelve stone. My mother, like all mothers, was sure that I hadn't been eating properly and began to make huge meals for me in the first few days I was home.

Home was now at 48 Hazel Road in Uplands, Swansea. The folks had been bombed in Grenfell Park Road whither we had moved, just before the war, from the house in St Leger Crescent – a short trip of about one hundred yards for the removal van. The Uplands was quite a posh area, very close to where Dylan Thomas lived. But I have to admit that I never even saw him. Mind you, I don't think he ever saw me, either.

My homecoming was a joyous reunion with Carol and Fred and all my relatives, but my attempts to tell them about the fighting I had seen were countered by their tales of the bombings that Swansea and its surrounding district had suffered. I couldn't get a word in edgeways – but it was great to be home.

A couple of days after I'd been demobbed I met some of the lads from the regiment in a pub in town and we arranged to go to a dance the following night. I had no regular girl-friend – the only girl I had taken out was called Elsie Rew, but she had eventually deserted me for a taller suitor before I went overseas.

And so Danny Williams, Josh Jones, Vic Kelly, myself and a few other mates from 132 Field Regiment met at the Mumbles Pier Dance Hall, a few miles out of town on the electric railway. It was packed that night, and after a few beers I plucked up enough courage to ask a pretty, dark-eyed girl for a dance. I took off my glasses out of sheer vanity and sauntered over to where she stood chatting with a couple of her friends. I was going through my 'Canadian phase' at the time, the result of playing a lumberjack in a sketch, and I also happened to be wearing the heavy red-and-black checked shirt I had removed from the property basket before I left *Over the Page*.

'Can I have this dance, please?' I pretended to chew gum as I spoke.

'Pardon?' said the girl.

I repeated my request, toning down the fake accent a bit, and swept my four-foot eleven-inch partner on to the dance floor. Forty-four years later we're still dancing – not quite so nimbly perhaps, but Myra can still do a pretty good 'fish tail'.

She had been about to leave for her home in Pennard where she lived with her parents in a holiday bungalow, their house in Manselton having been destroyed in the blitz, but one of her friends persuaded her to stay at her place in Swansea for the night. I saw Myra to the Mumbles train, escorted by a phalanx of her pals, and made arrangements to meet her the following night outside the Plaza Cinema at six o'clock.

The next morning I had quite a hangover, and for the life of me I couldn't remember what my date for the evening looked like. I decided that I would arrive early at the Plaza, get behind one of the pillars outside the cinema and keep a furtive watch. If I didn't fancy what I saw I'd stay where I was and forget the whole thing. It was at a quarter past six when, tired of waiting, I stepped out from behind my pillar to go home, just as Myra daintily made an appearance from behind hers. And in this atmosphere of mutual mistrust, our courtship began.

It was a glorious summer that year, and Myra and I spent a lot of time together. We used to go down to the many beautiful beaches on the Gower coast and laze on the sand, or go for long walks along the gorse-clad cliffs. We fed lamb sandwiches to sheep in Pwlldu, and I sprained my arm trying to make pebbles skip on the sea at Pobbles Bay. In the evening we'd go to the pictures and once a week we'd pay a visit to the Swansea Empire. Every time I saw a show there I'd be filled

---

RICHARD THOMAS & BALDWINS LIMITED

Memorandum from
COLLIERIES SECTION :—
41, WIND STREET,
SWANSEA.
	To **Mr. Seccombe,**
	      Hazel Road,
	      Uplands,
	        SWANSEA.

Dept.	*Your Ref.* *Our Ref.* FEJ/WT. Date 29th July 1946.

Dear Sir,

     I wish to contact your son Harry, who was formerly employed at this office, and I should be obliged if you would forward me his present address. I may say that I have some information to his advantage which I wish to convey to him.

                        Yours faithfully,
       FOR RICHARD THOMAS & BALDWINS LIMITED.

                         (COLLIERIES SECTION)

with the desire to get up on the stage myself and show them what I could do.

It was time that I did just that, and after having politely refused an offer of my old job back at Baldwins – they were a very forgiving firm – I wrote to Andy Grey as I had promised. He was the Canadian Captain who had offered to help me after seeing my act in *Over the Page* in Rome.

I went up to London to meet him and he suggested that I applied to the Windmill Theatre for an audition. This was the theatre which featured nudes and comedians in a revue which ran for six shows a day, six days a week – a total of thirty-six performances a week. It was a gruelling schedule, especially for the comedians who had to battle to get the attention of an audience which had only come in to see the nudes. Men in dirty raincoats would fight to get a seat in the front row of the tiny theatre, while on stage some unfortunate comic would be trying to get laughs. However, it was a marvellous show-case for any performer due to its situation in the West End, just off Shaftesbury Avenue, and it really was a matter of 'if you can get a laugh here – you'll get a laugh anywhere'.

To my delight, mixed with trepidation, I received a letter from the Windmill management offering me an audition.

I went up to London on the train the day before the audition and stayed the night in Ilford with my cousin Margaret – Uncle Harry's daughter from Llangyfelach – who was sharing a house with a fellow teacher, Joan Fox. They gave me a good meal that night and sent me on my way, wishing me all the luck in the world and waving crossed fingers as I got on the bus for the West End early the next morning.

The audition was not until 9.30 am, and at 8 o'clock I was wandering around Piccadilly in a muck sweat of fear and apprehension. All around were hoardings featuring star names advertising the latest shows, and I felt very inadequate. In the battered attaché case I carried, my shaving mug rattled in sympathy with my knees as I surveyed the huge board outside the Windmill which listed the names of all the famous comedians who had appeared there, alongside the year they had made their debuts. Little did I think that one day my name would be up there as the star of 1946.

When I eventually plucked up enough courage to enter the stage door in Archer Street, the backstage area was busy with fellow auditioners preparing for their acts. I asked the stage-manager, a portly chap called Johnny Gale, if I could possibly have a small table. He gave me a grin. 'All right, mate, take that gold one over there.' He pointed to a rather delicate-looking piece of furniture in a corner of the prop room. I thanked him and proceeded to prepare it for my act. First of all I laid some newspaper on it, and then, having filled my mug with water from a basin in the toilet, I began to get lathered up.

Johnny Gale saw me and tapped me on the shoulder. 'You should have done that before you came here, lad,' he said gruffly.

I turned to him, my face full of Yardley's shaving soap. 'It's my act,' I said.

He clapped a hand to his forehead. 'Gawd Almighty,' he said, moving quickly away.

I had already given my sheet of music to a sympathetic Ronnie Bridges, who was one of the two regular accompanists at the theatre, and told him roughly what I wanted. He made a couple of helpful suggestions, and I felt a little less nervous as I stood in the wings, constantly lathering away as I waited my turn.

One of the acts on in front of me was a short, stocky lad who was also ex-army. We wished each other luck and I watched as he went on to do his audition. He told one joke, fell down, and before he could rise to his feet, a voice from the blackness of the auditorium said, 'Thank you, that will be all.' It was Vivian Van Damm, the famous impresario who ran the Windmill, who was sitting out front along with his producer, Ann Mitelle. Norman Wisdom left the stage door shortly afterwards to make a fortune.

The act immediately before me was a Chinese illusionist whose elaborate make-up and carefully organized props suggested that he must have been up all night getting ready. He went on, shuffled forward in Chinese style, and bowed.

'Thank you,' said the voice of Van Damm, and the stunned illusionist was dismissed before he'd even done a trick.

Before I could take in his demise, I heard my name called. Ronnie Bridges swung into a chorus of 'Wild About Harry' and I was on stage, pierced by the spotlight and wondering what time the next train to Swansea left Paddington. I launched myself into the well-tried routine, scattering lather all over the stage, expecting that at any minute the voice out front would call, 'Thank you – next.' But it didn't come, and I even fancied that I heard faint laughter from the stalls as the act proceeded. When I had finished on the last note of 'Sweethearts', I stood, soap-stained and fearful, waiting for the verdict.

'Come and see me afterwards,' said the voice, and as I gathered up my table and shaving gear I was not sure whether I had got a job or whether I was going to be given a damned good telling-off for wasting the great man's time.

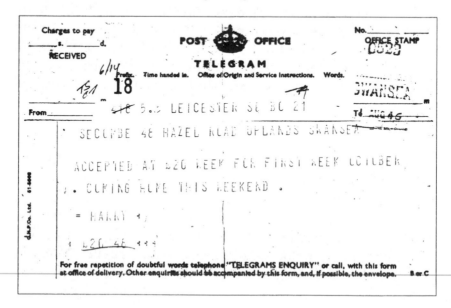

As it transpired, however, I had passed the audition and I was summoned to Ann Mitelle's office to work out the details of my engagement. Ann was a nice, jolly person who told me she and Van Damm liked my act, and asked how much money I was expecting.

I had no idea what to ask. In my mind I could hear the words of Norman Vaughan in one of our many conversations about the business. 'Always ask as high a figure as you can think of and you can always come down.'

A suitably high figure came into my head. I'd been getting three shillings and sixpence a day in the army, and using that as a starting price I said, 'Twenty pounds a week.'

'Done,' said Ann, and I signed a contract there and then for *Revuedeville 187* to begin on 17 October, an auspicious day because it was also my sister Carol's birthday.

I left the theatre with a chorus of angels ringing in my ears, and the first thing I did was to send two telegrams home, one to Mam and one to Myra to tell them the good news. 'Have been accepted at Windmill at twenty pounds a week' was the substance of the first one, and I pushed the form under the grille to the girl behind the counter expecting at least an eyebrow raised in admiration. She counted the words expressionlessly and asked me for four shillings. The chorus of angels dimmed and I was back down to earth again.

My gratuity from the army was looking pretty sick by the time I got back from London, so I signed on at the Swansea Labour Exchange as an actor. I used to be the life and soul of the dole queue, and I think the staff heaved a sigh of relief when I left to take up my job at the Windmill.

Myra and I had an 'understanding' by this time and we had both been looked over by our respective parents. My folks thought she was right for me and she passed the 'Uncle Harry test' with flying colours. She sat next to him at tea-time at our house and was on her best behaviour. Uncle Harry was not. When peaches and cream were served, he said to Myra, 'Do you like those?'

'Yes, thank you,' she said.

'I'm glad,' said my wicked Uncle Harry, 'because I've just dropped my glass eye in your dish.'

Myra didn't turn a hair. 'If I see something staring back at me,' she said, 'I'll let you know.'

My first encounter with Myra's relatives was when I was taken to meet her Uncle Walter and Aunty Elsie in Manselton. I behaved myself, for once, because Myra was very anxious that I should make a good impression. Apparently everything went well and I was over the first domestic hurdle.

However, her grandmother was not very pleased when she found out that Myra's new boyfriend was on the stage. 'Don't bring any actors home here,' was her reaction to the news. So I had to pass the 'Gran test' before I was accepted, but fortunately no glass eyes were involved. I got on well with Myra's parents, Jim and Flo Atherton, and once the initial examinations were over we all enjoyed each others' company.

Before I began work at the Windmill, Andy Grey – who wrote the show business column in the *Weekly Sporting Review* under the name of Ken Gordon – arranged for me to be the cabaret at a party thrown by the publication. I was very nervous before going on, but once I was in the spotlight I felt at home, and the reaction was very warm. This was my first paid engagement, and I was enormously relieved when it was all over. If I could get laughs from people who had paid to see me – and civilians at that – then perhaps I might do well in my new profession. Isador Green, the *Sporting Review*'s editor and founder, had also been in Italy on *The Union Jack*, and promised to give me plenty of free publicity in his paper. He was true to his word, and he and Andy Grey gave me great encouragement in those early days when I was very unsure of myself.

I had fixed up digs in Kilburn for the run of the Windmill Show, at 4 Brondesbury Villas, to be exact. It was a guest house on three floors run by a Mrs Isaacs, a lady who suffered from asthma and, ultimately, me. I began life there as a privileged lodger with a nice room on the first floor, but as my career fluctuated I was moved further up the house, until at one period – after being out of work for several weeks – I found myself sleeping in a converted broom cupboard with my feet quite close to the wash basin. Mrs Isaacs was a nice old lady, and was always concerned that I had enough to eat at breakfast, because that was the only meal of the day to which I was entitled. She had a large marmalade cat which was always sitting in the dining-room when I came down just before breakfast was about to be cleared away. Usually by this time the other lodgers had gone off to work and I was left to finish what remained on the table. This sometimes involved me in a fight with the cat for the last kipper. The damned thing never liked me and would take every opportunity to give me a side swipe with its claws. I hated the animal.

That first week at the Windmill I was so determined to make an impression on my first appearance that I gave my 'all', forgetting that there were five more shows to do that day.

Jimmy Edwards was the resident comedian at the time and he gave me some good advice: 'Pace yourself, mate – there are ninety–nine steps up to the dressing-room and you've got to climb them at least seven times a day.'

He didn't seem to have any nerves at all. Perhaps after what he'd been through as a pilot at Arnhem, the Windmill seemed like a picnic. He had won the DFC for landing his Dakota plane after being hit by anti-aircraft fire, refusing to bale out and leave his crew behind. I admired him tremendously, especially when I watched his act from the wings. He used to sit on a beer crate in his dressing-gown pretending to read bits of a newspaper to the audience. When they started to clamber over the front row to get to the best seats he used to insult them, and they loved him for it.

The leading dancer, Keith Lester, certainly didn't love me for leaving the stage full of water and soap suds, and he complained bitterly to Johnny Gale. It must have been very difficult to follow my act with a dance routine, because apart from anything else, the floor of the tiny stage was made of glass. We reached a compromise eventually and I did a couple of gags in front of the curtain while the stage-hands mopped up the mess I'd made.

Someone else who had reservations about my performance was Vivian Van Damm, who was known to one and all as V D. He was coming down the stairs from the dressing-rooms one day during my first week, and he met me as I was half-way up after coming off stage from my second performance of the day.

'Secombe,' he said. 'That noise you make with your mouth . . .' He attempted a raspberry and failed miserably.

'You mean this?' I blew one of my best efforts for the boss.

'Yes, that,' he said. I waited proudly for acclamation. 'Cut it out,' said V D, 'I don't like it.' And he continued on his way down the steps.

I was devastated – half my act was gone! For the next couple of days I struggled valiantly to remove the raspberry stain from my performance, but it didn't seem the same, and the audience sensed my unease. Then one day, as I was coming down from the dressing-room on my way to the stage, still worried about the gap in my act, I met VD who, on this ocasion, was on the way up.

'I've been thinking about that noise you make,' he said, without attempting to do it himself.

'This – er – sound?' I blew a half-hearted Bronx cheer.

'That's it,' said VD. 'Put it back in.'

I went on stage for my next performance and filled the theatre with a welter of raspberries.

During my time at the 'Mill' I was besieged with visitors wanting to see me backstage – friends from the army, relatives, and quite a lot of curate colleagues of my brother, who was now the Reverend Fred. It was the custom to take anyone who came to see a performer to the canteen for a cup of tea, and it was only after the first week that I realized that I was not the real reason for the backstage visits. The ladies of the chorus would sit around the canteen in their stage costumes with, at the most, a scanty dressing-gown tossed carelessly over their shoulders. All the time I was at the Windmill I don't think any of my visitors ever looked directly at me in the canteen, and I've never seen so many spilled cups of tea, either.

One visitor who came backstage was genuinely only interested in me and my performance. His name was Cecil Madden and he happened to be a BBC television producer. He was always on the look-out for fresh talent for the fledgling medium, and the Windmill had a reputation for putting on new comedians. Thanks to him I was invited to do a spot on a variety show called *Rooftop Rendezvous* which led to quite a few subsequent TV appearances.

Something else happened during my stint at the Windmill that I knew nothing about until the day of Jimmy Edwards's funeral, when I met up again with script-writers Frank Muir and Denis Norden. Frank, who had known Jimmy in the RAF, had recommended him as a potential comedian for a new series that a BBC radio producer was about to launch. Consequently the producer sent a colleague along to the Windmill to have a look at Jimmy's act.

He came back from seeing the show and reported to the producer that he didn't think Edwards was any good. 'Waste of time,' he said. 'He comes on and does a bloody awful piece of business with a shaving brush and blows raspberries all the time. He won't get anywhere.' So Jim didn't get the job.

Towards the end of the six-week run of the show I began to get rather weary and my face was starting to feel the effect of being shaved seven times a day – though only once with a blade in the razor. I remember waiting for a bus back to Kilburn one Saturday night when a light drizzle began. By the time the bus arrived some ten minutes later, soap bubbles were forming in my hair and the West Indian conductor took a step back from me as I mounted the platform. 'Ju-ju!' he cried, crossing himself. I was too tired even to raise a raspberry.

There was one place in Great Windmill Street to which everybody in the show's company seemed to gravitate – Allen's Club, it was called, and it was run by Daddy Allen and his wife. We all called him 'Daddy', but nobody ever told me why. It was a small drinking-club with a little restaurant attached, and a lot of us went there because Daddy Allen ran a slate. This meant that we could eat on 'tick', paying our bills when we got our wages. The club was in a very convenient position, just across the way from the Windmill stage door, and it was easy to slip a coat on and nip over for a drink or a meal between performances. When Myra came to town to see me, the poor girl saw nothing at all of the bright lights of the West End – just the inside of Daddy Allen's Club.

It was a rendezvous for a whole posse of up-and-coming comedians. Frank Muir would meet up with Jimmy Edwards there; Alfred Marks was a frequent visitor, and so was Bill Kerr, the Australian comic who has since turned into such a fine straight actor. When Norman Vaughan was demobbed he used to meet me there, and I remained a member for many years. Someone else who frequented the club was Michael Bentine.

I first saw Mike at the dress rehearsal for the show that followed the one in which I had made my debut at the Windmill. He and a pianist named Tony Sherwood performed a crazy double act called Sherwood and Forrest – Mike being 'Forrest'. Their performance consisted of a wild musical act all done in 'cod' Russian, with Tony on piano and Mike playing drums. My sides ached from laughing at their antics, and I went backstage and introduced myself to them. Mike had already seen my shaving routine and congratulated me on my fresh approach to comedy. The two of us got on like wildfire and we were to spend many hysterical hours in Lyon's Corner House which, in those days, was open all night. We'd stay there till dawn talking about the things we'd like to do in the theatre.

He was a slim, curly-haired lad then, full of restless energy and throwing out ideas for comedy situations like sparks from a Catherine wheel. During the war he had been in the RAF and had finished up in Intelligence, a fact which impressed me no end. I was still mentally a lance-bombardier and I felt sometimes a little inferior to all these ex-officers I was mixing with. One of them was Reg O'List, who had been a major with CPA in Italy, and whom I had often had to salute. Now he was a singer and guitarist at the Windmill, where he'd worked before being called up. He was delighted that I was now a fully-fledged performer and even gave me one of his suits. I accepted it with enthusiasm – my demob suit was getting to look a little threadbare, and the money I was earning after I had finished my engagement at the 'Mill' was practically non-existent.

I managed to get a broadcast on the Carroll Levis show as a 'star from the services', thanks to the good offices of Levis himself, who kept his promise to me back in Bari. When the *Radio Times* appeared for that week I couldn't wait to open it and see my name in print. I turned the pages with trembling hands. There it was . . . 'Harry Fecombe, a successful discovery,' it said. This was the first of many occasions on which my name was misspelt. I was to be called everything from Seagrave to Snelgrove, and later, when my agent decided I should have some kind of descriptive title on the programmes, I became 'the golden-voiced Goon', which usually finished up as 'the golden-voiced Coon'.

For the Carroll Levis programme I received ten guineas which didn't last all that long, and apart from the odd cabaret date I managed to wangle through the influence of Andy Grey, there was not much work for me in the final weeks of 1946.

It was a time when the business was becoming swamped with returning ex-servicemen who had had a taste of performing in army or RAF concert parties and were now, like myself, eager to try their luck in show business. People like Benny Hill, Tommy Cooper, Frankie Howerd, Max Bygraves, Norman Wisdom, Dick Emery, Eric Sykes, Peter Sellers, Arthur English – all different from each other in style, and all clamouring for a chance to show what they could do.

I remember once sitting in the BBC canteen in the basement of the Aeolian Hall Studios in Bond Street. A lot of comics would go down there for a cheap, subsidized meal on the pretext of meeting some non-existent producer. A chap came and sat opposite me and, over a cup of tea, Max Bygraves announced that he was thinking of packing it in. 'I could go back to carpentering,' he told me. 'I've still got my tools.'

'You're lucky,' I said. 'I can't do anything – I haven't got a proper trade.'

Learning the Trade

Christmas 1946 was spent at home. Back at my digs in Brondesbury Villas, Kilburn, I was now in the converted broom cupboard, and poor Mrs Isaacs was having to wait for the rent. The euphoria of playing the Windmill Theatre and being a 'rising comedy star' had worn off and it was difficult meeting old army friends in the dole queue. They all thought that I had hit the big time. Myra, of course, was glad to see my face again, as were Mam and Dad, but I was desperate to get more work.

Then I had a bit of luck. I was offered a tour of Germany with a Combined Services Entertainment Show featuring Peter Waring, a popular radio comedian, and Adelaide Hall, the coloured singer. Sam Kydd, Pamela Matthews, Pamela Cundell, Harry Robins, the xylophone player, a dance troupe and myself were among the supporting cast.

We went out to Germany in January, sailing from Hull in bitterly cold weather. When we got to Hamburg there was thick snow everywhere and one night at the Garrison Theatre, the water actually froze in my shaving mug before I went on. Everywhere there was devastation and people were dropping dead in the streets from hunger and exposure.

The star of the show, Peter Waring, was a strange character who claimed to have been a Lieutenant-Commander in the Royal Navy, but eventually turned out to have served as a fireman in the London Fire Brigade. He was an excellent raconteur who was always immaculately dressed in white tie and tails. The man responsible for keeping his suits pressed and seeing that his shirts were blindingly white was a lad called Bill Montague who was always darkly suspicious of his boss's claim to have been in the Royal Navy, but could never prove it. He and I, along with Sam Kydd, used to make the most of what was a rather arduous trip. Sam had been a prisoner of war and had a lot of reasons to be glad to see the Germans suffer, but the deprivation that we saw all around us as we travelled through the shattered cities of the Ruhr and into Berlin, affected him as much as it did the rest of us.

Poor old Peter Waring had a sad end not too long after we got back from Germany. He hanged himself in a cell where he was being held on a fraud charge. I always felt sorry for him because he was obviously playing a part all the time he was off stage, and could never afford to relax in case he gave himself away. And yet we were all prepared to accept him for what he really was – a remarkably good comedian who was possibly the best story-teller (apart from Terry-Thomas) that I have ever come across.

The money I received for the tour allowed me to buy an engagement ring for Myra. She had seen one for forty pounds in a jeweller's window in Swansea, and that was the one I presented her with shortly after I got back from Germany.

In May I had another television engagement on a variety show and the next month I passed an audition for 'Variety Bandbox'. This was the really big radio comedy show of the time, with people like Frankie Howerd and Derek Roy alternating as resident comedians. The producer was Joy Russell-Smith who was very good at spotting new talent, and had given many of us new boys a chance to shine. Bill Kerr, who used to begin his very laconic act with the statement, 'I've only got four minutes', was another young act she had been the first to encourage.

I can't remember exactly what I did for my first 'Bandbox', but I know that part of it was a rather wicked take-off of someone doing animal impressions. I finished with the 'Sweet-hearts' duet accompanied on the piano by Ronnie Bridges, the musician who had been so helpful at my Windmill audition. The act was received quite well and, as I have already related, I had a nice introduction from the resident announcer, Phillip Slessor.

Norman Vaughan was now back in Civvy Street and intro-duced me to his agent, who kindly offered me a date at the Grand Theatre, Bolton, where Norman was already booked. It was to be my first music hall – I had played quite a lot of night-clubs in the sleazier parts of Soho and dark, somewhat dangerous venues like the Blue Lagoon and the Panama Club, where the clientèle was as shady as the wallpaper. This, then, was my chance to break into the more profitable and slightly more respectable area of the variety theatre.

Norman fixed digs for us in the town and we met there on the Sunday night. I was staying down in Swansea with my folks by then, having abandoned my pied à terre in Kilburn, where even the broom cupboard had become too expensive for my slender resources.

'We'll have to get along to the band call early,' said Norman over breakfast. 'The first acts to get their band parts down on the stage have their rehearsal with the orchestra before anybody else, regardless of how far down the bill they are. It's first come, first served.'

I was learning all the time, suddenly realizing how little I knew about the proper theatre.

'What do you work in?' asked the stage-manager after we'd put our music in position, Norman's brightly covered orchestrations making my solo piano part look very poor indeed.

'A white shirt and black trousers,' I replied.

Norman grinned. 'No, he means what kind of curtain do you want to work in front of when you do your act? The street cloth, the one with shops and houses painted on it or the ordinary black tabs?'

'What do you think?' I asked.

'Perhaps the blacks,' Norman decided. 'You'd look funny shaving in a street.'

I sat in the stalls while Norman did his rehearsal with the orchestra, marvelling at the way he got exactly what he wanted, giving instructions to the drummer that were completely new to me. 'I'll have the temple blocks there, Charlie,' and 'Give me a "boom-boom" at the end of the lion-tamer gag.'

When my turn came I was petrified. 'Where's the rest of your music, son?' asked the bewildered conductor, waving my single sheet of piano music in the air.

Norman again came to my rescue. 'Give him a few bars of "I'm Just Wild About Harry" to get him on – you can busk that, lads, and then it's just piano for the "Sweethearts" duet, and finish with "Wild About Harry" as a chaser.'

The band leader shrugged his shoulders and raised his stick. 'All right, let's give it a go.' It was a good orchestra and they 'busked' what was to become my signature tune with no difficulty at all. I explained to the pianist what I did with the 'Sweethearts' duet, and my first-ever band call was over in less than four minutes, which pleased the lads in the pit. Norman's meticulous rehearsal had taken a good fifteen minutes and they were already looking at their watches to see how long they had to go before opening time.

The theatre was absolutely packed that night. It was Wakes Week in Bolton and the whole town was on holiday. I stood in the wings lathering for the act and heard roars of laughter coming from the audience as two men dressed in comedy kilts did funny walks and performed miracles on a tightrope. They came off to thunderous applause, and then the lights went down and Norman introduced me on the off-stage mike as 'The star from "Variety Bandbox"', which is what I had asked him to say.

I came on carrying the table with my shaving mug, brush and razor on it, and a towel slung over my shoulder.

'Hello, folks!' I said, my lips cleaving to my gums in a death's-head grin. 'I've only just arrived in the theatre. The train was late and I haven't had a chance to shave yet. So as I'm doing it, I'll give you some idea of how other people shave . . .' And I went into my usual routine of the small boy shaving with his father's razor.

The audience sat grimly in their seats. 'This lad hasn't had the decency to shave before coming on to entertain us' seemed to be their attitude, and I went through my performance without getting so much as a titter. In my nervousness I actually swallowed some of the soapy water in the mug instead of spitting it out, and my throat was on fire as I struggled to reach the soprano register for the Jeanette MacDonald part of 'Sweethearts'. I finished on a cracked note, bowed, picked up my table and props and walked off stage accompanied only by the sound of my own footsteps.

Norman helped me off with the table. 'Don't worry,' he said. 'They're always tough here on a Monday first house.' I took some comfort from that, but an icy chill seized my heart when I went for a much-needed drink in the interval, heavily disguised, with my overcoat collar turned up. All around me, as I sipped my rum and pep, I could hear the word 'shaving' being bandied about, sometimes in bewilderment, at other times with sheer lynch-mob fervour. When the bell sounded for the interval I ordered another drink and a large man who had his back to me heard the sound of my voice and turned to face me.

'It was you,' he said accusingly. 'You're that shaving feller.'

I nodded, trying to smile and failing.

'You should be ashamed of yourself. You're Welsh, aren't yer? You ought to be down a mine somewhere doing some real work.'

I was stung by this. 'Who do you think you're talking to?' I said. It was not the cleverest remark I've ever made, but it was all that came to mind.

'I know who you are,' he said. 'But do you know who I am?'

I had to admit that I didn't.

'I own this theatre,' he said. And he followed up this shattering news with: 'You can get t'train in t'morning. You'll not shave in my bloody time.'

And that was it – I was paid off, the thing that every comedian dreads.

I had one tiny triumph though. Norman had arranged for a stage-hand to come on in his act. After he had told the audience, 'My father was a lion-tamer. Every day for years he used to put his head in the lion's mouth. Ladies and gentlemen – my father,' he gestured to the wings and on would come the stage-hand wearing a lion-tamer's uniform which buttoned right up over the top of his bonce, making him appear headless.

That night I persuaded Norman to let me do the 'headless lion-tamer', and as I came on from the side of the stage I undid a couple of buttons on the uniform and gave that audience as juicy a raspberry as I've ever blown.

The next day I got on the first train out of town, leaving behind a sympathetic Norman and a week's rent which the landlady insisted that I paid. All the way back to Swansea I reflected on my future, and actually considered going back to Baldwins.

When I arrived home the first thing I did was to send a telegram to Mike Bentine which read, 'Audience with me all the way. Managed to shake them off at the station.'

That was sheer bravado because I was deeply worried about what would happen the following week when I was due to play the Empire, Oldham, which Norman's agent had also booked for me. It was obvious that the news of what had happened at Bolton would have spread around the business like a fire in a paint factory, and there was no way that I could keep it a secret.

I decided that attack was the best method of defence and so I placed an advertisement in *The Stage*, the weekly theatrical newspaper.

It began 'Vide Press' and listed imaginary notices I had received: '"... and Larry Felcombe"' – *Blackpool Argus*. "Harvey Snelgrove also featured" – *Bradford Examiner*. "Larry Stenchcombe should not have been on the bill" – *Bolton Bugle*. With only one adverse criticism how can this lad fail?'

A lot of the older pros appreciated the fact that I wasn't going to be too daunted by my failure. Two of them were topping the bill the following week at the Empire, Oldham – Reub Silver and Marian Day, piano duettists who were very popular radio performers. They gave me lots of encouragement that day, helping me through my band call, and they were in the wings to give me moral support as I went on in the second spot – the position on the bill after the dancing girls had done their first routine.

In the prompt corner the stage-manager was all set to give me a 'blackout' and get me off the stage if I was as bad an act as he had been led to believe. But he did not have to pull any switches that night. From the moment I went on, the audience was ready to laugh and my confidence grew with every second. I came off with a good solid round of applause which was echoed in the wings by Reub and Marian, and the fear that had half-strangled me receded in the warm glow of their appreciation.

To this day I cannot fully understand why I could be so disastrously received in Bolton and yet the following week, only a few miles away in Oldham, I was a moderate success. 'That's show business,' as they say, and I don't suppose any of us in the profession can ever predict what's going to happen when we go out to face the public. If we did, everybody would be a star and there would be no supporting acts.

After Oldham I went back to London and began to look for more work with the BBC. It was essential in those days to appear as often as possible on something like 'Variety Bandbox' to keep your name before the public. And if you had a catchphrase it was a good handle for them to remember you by.

The ideal way to conduct a career was to make a name on radio and having done so, go out on the Halls to exploit it. The fact that the BBC didn't pay much money was vastly compensated for by the salaries the variety theatres were prepared to hand out to the radio stars. The infant medium, television, was not considered to be much help in making a name because so few people could view it.

The most important item in my new itinerary for success was to find a good scriptwriter. Michael Bentine was very generous with ideas for some of the 'Variety Bandbox' broadcasts I was getting on a semi-regular basis, but he was busy making a career for himself. The problem was solved one lunchtime when Michael took me to a pub he knew in Victoria. It was known as Grafton's and was in Strutton Ground, a turning off Victoria Street. A tall smiling man behind the bar greeted Mike like an old friend, and when I was introduced he laughed. 'Ah – you're the lad from "Variety Bandbox".'

I was flattered that he knew my name and it turned out that he wrote scripts for Derek Roy, one of the resident comedians on the programme, who happened to be his second cousin. We didn't know this at first. It was only after Mike and I had spent about ten minutes criticizing Roy that Jimmy Grafton told us that he wrote his material. He didn't seem to mind the criticism and our visit extended well beyond lunchtime and into the early evening. We discussed every aspect of comedy from the Marx Brothers to the current crop of radio comics. It was a most propitious day for me, because this was the place where 'The Goon Show' was to be born, and in due course Jimmy Grafton was to become my agent and manager. However, at that time, all I knew was that our host had been a Major in the Beds and Herts, had played a vital part in the relief of Arnhem – and was prepared to write scripts for me.

The Bill Hall Trio were now back from working for Combined Services Entertainment and I was able to introduce Mike Bentine to the man I had been raving about – Spike

Milligan. I can't remember exactly where we all met up, but I think it must have been at Grafton's, because that was where I now spent a lot of my time. Jimmy and his wife, Dorothy, were very generous with free meals for starving comics and were even prepared to loan us a couple of quid from the till every so often.

I had now moved into a flat in Linden Gardens, Bayswater, with Norman Vaughan and another bloke called Roy, who was a trumpeter in a band. The place was only supposed to accommodate two people, but we used to take turns to sleep on the floor. Reg O'List and his wife, Jennifer – who were both at the Windmill – also had an apartment in the building, and eventually Spike and Johnny Mulgrew moved into another flat.

We had a lot of fun at Linden Gardens, even though none of us had much money. We were not too well liked by the people who ran the place – we were always slamming the door and making a noise. Once we attempted to make spaghetti in the bath on a gas ring. It turned out to be not only a culinary disaster, but took a lot of enamel off the tub.

There was also the time when I borrowed Spike's Crombie overcoat – we were the same size then, apart from height – because my demob one had become too shabby to wear. I walked about in it for a month, until one day when I was absolutely strapped for cash I sold it to a second-hand clothing dealer for thirty shillings. To my everlasting shame I told him that someone had pinched it in a restaurant, and it was only a few years ago that I could bring myself to tell Spike the truth. He laughed.

There was one venue in the West End of London which always provided a wonderful 'shop window' – and a meal for young ex-services performers. It was called The Nuffield Centre and catered exclusively for servicemen in London. It was run by a lady called Mary Cook who provided coffee and sandwiches in lieu of a fee and was always a great help to aspiring comics. She seemed to know every agent and BBC producer in London and tipped them off when she thought a performer showed promise.

The Green Room there was a great meeting place for those of us she liked – and we were legion. The names of the acts who were appearing at The Nuffield were published every week in *The Stage* and in *The Performer*, the trade papers for the variety profession, and enterprising agents would rub shoulders with the raw talent on view. Many a big name comic began his career at The Nuffield and Mary Cook, God bless her, was like a fairy godmother to us all in those early days after the war.

Things began to buck up towards the end of 1947 when I was offered the part of the Dame in the pantomime *Dick Whittington*, which was to open at the East Ham Palace and then do a tour of the other venues that were called 'The Syndicate Theatres' – The Empress, Brixton; The Palace, Walthamstow; and The Palace, Chelsea. It was a good contract and meant that I could start saving up to get married. The only snag was that I had never before played any part in a pantomine, except for the Fairy Queen in the RATD show, and I knew nothing about how to play the Dame, probably the most traditional role of all. To make matters worse, I had only ever seen one pantomime in my life. It was at the Grand Theatre, Swansea, when I was about ten – and I didn't see much of it, because I was sitting behind a pillar.

I went along to my first read-through of the script in the bar of the East Ham Palace, filled with foreboding. I was introduced to the rest of the cast and sat with the others on chairs placed in a semi-circle. The principal boy was Delyse Hendy, a friendly lady whose husband was the director, Charles King. The principal girl was a tiny lady called Dot who played the piano accordion, and the leading comedian was a very funny man by the name of Hal Blue who was also a very accomplished tap dancer. In addition, there was a straight actor who was playing Demon Rat, and a quite elderly gentleman in a long back overcoat who was on his hands and knees on the floor. Thinking he had lost something I got down alongside him and offered to help him find the missing item. 'Piss off, I'm Puss,' he said, not unkindly.

As the read-through progressed I became aware that there was not much substance in the part I had to play. Every so often I'd come across notes like 'Dame does business with knitting' or 'This is where Idle Jack and Dame do "I'm not here" gag'. I was completely mystified by this but was afraid to ask what it all meant. However I managed to nod intelligently when Charles King said, 'You know what goes on there,' whenever these bits came up. It also came as a blow when I was told that I had to provide my own Dame costumes and props. I was at my wit's end when I got back to Linden Gardens.

Jennifer O'List came to my rescue. 'I'll help you,' she said. And God bless her, she managed to come up with a couple of comedy dresses which she made herself from material she borrowed from the Windmill wardrobe, even providing me with the props for the 'knitting' gag.

The show opened on Boxing Day, and Myra and I spent Christmas Day with Mam and Dad who were staying with Fred and his wife in Machen, outside Newport. We walked miles with our cases that night, unable to get a taxi, and we were about half a mile from the station before we got a lift.

The opening night from my point of view was a disaster. My wig fell off in one scene, causing the kids to cry out in disappointment, 'It's a man – it's a man!' although it must have been pretty obvious from the start that I was no lady. I thought it would be rather funny if I appeared in one scene with a false moustache and a cigar à la Groucho Marx, but the audience was not happy about their beloved traditions being tampered with. Hal Blue, the comedian playing Idle Jack, helped me through the bits of business which I had found so mystifying at rehearsal, but the applause I received in the final walk-down at the end of the performance was lukewarm.

I was sitting in my dressing-room taking off my make-up while Myra tried to reassure me that I was not all that bad when the door opened and the man who was financially responsible for putting on the pantomime stood in the doorway. Apparently he was not a very well man and my performance had not helped his condition. He shook a finger at me for a full minute, trembling with rage as he sought to utter the words to express his feelings. I stood up, out of respect, ready for the tirade which never came – he was the first man I had ever come across who was actually speechless with rage. Charles King, the director, led him away by the arm, still wordless. I wondered what it was about me that could arouse such strong passion in some people – the owner of the Grand Theatre, Bolton, and now this chap. I had a feeling that there would be many more like them before I finished in show business.

It was obviously too late to get a replacement for me in the pantomime, and gradually I began to enjoy myself. Things were constantly going wrong with the production and I have always thrived on disaster.

The 'knitting gag' turned out to be quite a simple piece of business. When I made my first entrance, usually in a blaze of indifference, I carried on stage with me a shopping basket which contained two giant knitting needles from which hung a half-finished woollen scarf. I told the audience that I was going to hang my basket on a nail on the side of the stage and that if anybody went to touch it they were to shout, 'Put that down!' (Really sophisticated stuff, as I'm sure you have gathered.)

Unfortunately, I could not always find the nail in the proscenium arch owing to my short-sightedness, and after fumbling for it, I would more often than not leave the basket on the floor, where everybody coming on from that side would trip over it, particularly my friend, the cat. He used to complain bitterly about it, but one matinée he caused quite a bit of excitement himself.

It was the Highgate Hill sequence where Dick Whittington did a soliloquy with Tom, the cat, who was supposed to appear on the cue 'But I still have Tom, my faithful friend'. Delyse delivered the line, but no Tom appeared. She repeated the cue, adding a few extra lines under her breath which did not augur well for the cat after the show. Meanwhile, Tom, who was rather deaf, had forgotten to turn up the loudspeaker in his dressing-room and at the very moment when his big scene was about to unfold was sitting down with his cat's head off, drinking a glass of stout.

The assistant stage-manager raced up the stairs and banged on his door to tell him he had missed his cue. Tom was so confused that he rushed down the stairs and on to the stage without his cat's head. The sight of a bald cat standing upright sent the audience into shock and Dick into hysterics.

Incidentally, this happened at Walthamstow, a place which features in one of the funniest ad libs I've ever heard. Charles Henry, a producer I had the good fortune of working with later on at the Palladium, was once asked how he thought 'Goodnight Vienna' would go down in Walthamstow. His reply was: 'About as well as "Goodnight Walthamstow" would go down in Vienna.'

Towards the end of the tour things began to deteriorate and props would go wrong quite regularly. In one scene the Demon Rat had to sink the ship upon which we were sailing to Malabar. He did this by pointing dramatically at the left side of the ship's bridge where a couple of powder flashes were concealed, and declaiming, 'I'll sink this ship. Come, fire!' Then the flashes would go off. Turning, he would then point at the right side of the bridge and say, 'Come, thunder!' And two more flashes would rend the air.

Unfortunately, one afternoon at the Chelsea Palace, after a hearty lunch, the Demon Rat became slightly confused and got his moves the wrong way round. Instead of pointing first to the left, he pointed to the right, and received a fairly hefty charge of powder flash up the back of his tights. If he'd stayed where he was and indicated the right side again, he'd have been all right. However, unnerved by his singed backside, he turned and pointed left, and got the second charge full in the rear. He clutched his backside and cried, 'Bollocks!' Then he limped painfully off stage. The kids loved it.

There was a speciality act about half-way through the pantomime which was quite bizarre. It opened with a man in a striped blazer and carrying a tennis racquet walking on stage backwards into a dining-room set. A large table laid for a dozen guests, with a candelabra in the middle, was situated centre stage. The man did a few tricks with the tennis racquet, and then on came a dwarf dressed as Hitler in a tin hat. He marched up and down for a while, and was followed on stage by a lady in a short, fringed jacket and tights carrying a saxophone, upon which she began to play 'Smoke Gets In Your Eyes'. In the background the man in the striped blazer was preparing himself to lift the table into the air. He always appeared to have difficulty, and on some nights the tiny Hitler and the lady saxophonist would go to his assistance. The climax of the act was when he balanced the table on his chin by one of its legs. The candelabra would then light up and all three would take their applause. Sometimes the light would refuse to go on, and together they'd put the table back on stage and the man in the striped blazer would work underneath it with a screwdriver. Meanwhile, the lady saxophonist would play another few choruses of 'Smoke Gets In Your Eyes' until her partner announced that he was ready to try again. It was the most surreal performance I have ever seen, and made Pinter's *The Birthday Party* seem like *Postman Pat*. I never failed to watch it.

After the pantomime had finished I got a couple of dates in northern variety theatres. I was very anxious to put something in the bank, because I had fixed the biggest date of my life – my marriage to Myra. 19 February 1948 was to see the union of Harry Donald Secombe and Myra Joan Atherton, spinster, but there wasn't much in the kitty.

Then I was offered a contract for a touring revue to do 'act as known' and 'appear as required in sketches' at a salary of forty pounds a week. This was the lifeline I had been praying for and meant that I'd be in regular employment for at least six months after we'd come back from our honeymoon.

The day of the wedding was sunny but chilly. Myra's wedding dress was made by her Aunty Elsie from six yards of material, which was all that was allowed in those days of rationing. It had a heart-shaped neckline and she wore her grandmother's pearls. My suit came off the peg. We were married in St Barnabas Church, Sketty, Swansea, and my brother Fred performed the ceremony. When it came to the part of the service which goes 'with this ring I thee wed', I was about to put the ring on the wrong finger. 'The third one, you idiot!' whispered the Reverend Fred. My sister, Carol, was one of Myra's two bridesmaids, and Carol's fiancé, Josh Williams, whom she married the following April, was my best man. The other bridesmaid was Myra's cousin, Beryl Atherton.

Ronnie Bridges came down from London for the occasion, and while we were waiting for the bride to make her entrance he played 'I'm Just Wild About Harry' in the style of a Bach fugue.

After the church service all the principals went off to Chapman's, the photographic studio, for the mandatory wedding pictures, and there was a reception for seventy-five people at the Glanmor Country Club. There's posh for you.

Myra's Dad, who really was unaccustomed to public speaking, made an excellent short speech and a good time was had by all. We caught the five o'clock train from High Street Station for Bristol, our night-stop on the way to Penzance for our week's honeymoon. Ronnie Bridges travelled in our compartment as far as Cardiff, and when he left the train he was so covered in confetti he looked like a bridegroom who had mislaid his bride.

We had a slap-up meal in the hotel and retired early. That night it snowed, but I must confess we didn't notice.

We had chosen Penzance because it was as far as we could go without actually going abroad. Travel overseas was restricted and I don't think we could have afforded a continental trip anyway. At least there were palm trees on the front, even though they were being blown all over the place in the wet, windy weather when we first arrived. We seemed always to be last down to breakfast in the hotel – a fact which occasioned a few smiles. We walked for miles in the surrounding countryside, getting to know each other and generally having a great time. Need I say more? I decided then that if marriage is a lottery, I held a winning ticket.

When the honeymoon was over we went to London to stay in digs in Kensal Rise for the rehearsal period of the new show I was joining. I was told to report to a church hall in Clapham for my first day with the new company, and had difficulty finding the place. When I did find it, I thought I had made a mistake. Lots of young men wearing ladies' clothes were cavorting around to music which came from a battered piano. I went back outside, found a call box and phoned the agent who had booked me for the job.

'You've given me the wrong address,' I said, laughing at his mistake. 'There's a whole bunch of fellers dressed like women dancing around in there.'

'That's right,' said the agent. 'The show's called *Forces Showboat* and it's a drag show.'

'Oh dear,' I said. 'Look, I hope I'm not expected to dress up like that, I've just got married.'

It was the agent's turn to laugh. 'Don't worry, I saw you play Dame at the Chelsea Palace, remember? You're just doing your act and appearing as yourself in a couple of quick blackout sketches.' And he put the phone down.

I swallowed hard and went back into the church hall to rehearse. After all, I needed the money.

Topping the bill was a double act called Bartlett and Ross, female impersonators who were seasoned professionals with immaculate timing that was a joy to watch. Colin Ross, who never looked right in men's clothes, took a fancy to Myra and used to go shopping with her. His partner, Terry Bartlett, had a good singing voice.

It was the singing in my act which bothered me at first, especially the Jeanette MacDonald impersonation, so I began to blow a veritable hurricane of raspberries in case anybody got the wrong idea about me. The rest of the company thought this was extremely funny, especially one young lad called Danny Carroll, whom Myra took under her wing because she felt that he was a cut above the rest of the chorus boys. He was – and Danny La Rue always makes a big fuss over Myra whenever we meet.

I was still doing radio broadcasts on the odd Sunday and was involved in trial recordings for two separate BBC comedy series. One of them, called 'Get Going', got nowhere, but another, produced by an avant garde veteran of comedy, Pat Dixon, was taken up. It was called 'Listen, My Children' and featured Robert Beatty, Carol Carr, Patricia Hayes, Benny Hill, Bennie Lee, Jon Pertwee, and the Vic Lewis Orchestra. The writers were Paul Dehn, Frank Muir and Denis Norden. It was way ahead of its time, as was Pat Dixon, a tall professorial type with thick spectacles who operated from a room in the rabbit warren that was Aeolian Hall in Bond Street. The walls of his office were lined with hundreds of files and books about comedy. He was a great enthusiast and gathered around him a stable of young comedians who shared that enthusiasm. He would go into paroxysms of laughter reading pieces from the Canadian humorist Stephen Leacock's book *Literary Lapses* and he knew the dialogue of all the Marx Brothers' films.

The pilot, or trial recording, for 'Listen, My Children' led to a series of eight programmes and the first one was broadcast on the BBC Home Service on 1 June 1948.

Between broadcasts and *Forces Showboat* appearances I spent a lot of time at Grafton's with Mike and all the other comics who used to congregate in the saloon bar until the early hours of the morning, intoxicated not only with what we'd been drinking, but also with each other's company. Dick Emery would be there and the bar would ring with the uninhibited laughter of Bill Kerr and Spike as they exchanged filthy army jokes.

Incidentally, the second time I went along to see Jimmy Grafton at the pub I was on my own and went into the saloon bar for a drink and a chat. When I ordered my half pint of mild – business was bad at the time – he smiled, handed over the beer and moved away without saying a word.

I was rather hurt by his behaviour because Jimmy and I had enjoyed such a great evening the previous week, so I took my drink and sat alone in a corner of the bar. Then he came up to me, made a big fuss of me and asked me what I was going to have to drink. Puzzled, I indicated my half pint of mild and reminded him that he had only just served me.

'That wasn't me,' he laughed. 'That was Peter, my twin brother.' And he called over the person I could have sworn was Jimmy.

They really were identical twins and were extremely difficult to tell apart. Years later I remember Peter turning up at a party for Jimmy in Melbourne wearing the same patterned cravat and practically identical sports jacket and trousers as his twin – and they hadn't seen each other for about three months.

Myra and I went on touring around the halls with *Forces Showboat*, staying in some strange lodgings along the way. There was one landlady in Plymouth who would come into our bedroom with the breakfast tray and then stay talking until eleven o'clock, telling us all about her ailments and how badly they'd been bombed in the war, and we couldn't get a word in edgeways. I used to fall asleep in the middle of the conversation and wake up to find her still yapping on and my bladder bursting.

Theatrical landladies were a strange breed. They always had tickets for the first house on the Monday and if they didn't like your act, you'd suffer for the rest of the week. One old dear would just thump my meal on the table in front of me, sniff loudly and walk out of the room mumbling, 'Call yourself a comic.' But if the landlady took a fancy to you it was roses all the way for the week.

Once when I was sharing digs with Norman Vaughan we had a letter from Les Henry, a comedian who had been in one of the Central Pool of Artists shows in Italy, and later became 'Cedric' in the comedy harmonica act, the Three Monarchs. He had heard that these particular digs were good and asked us to fix him up there the following week.

We wrote back saying that we had booked him a room, but offered him a bit of friendly advice about the landlady. We told him that she was very deaf, but out of pride refused to wear a deaf aid, so it would be a good idea if he spoke loudly when addressing her. There was, of course, nothing wrong with her hearing at all.

What he didn't know was that we had told her the same thing about him, and by the Thursday of the week he was staying with her, he had lost his voice completely. It was only when he started writing down instructions to her on a writing pad that they both realized the joke we had played on them.

There was one very nice landlady in Halifax who, while perched on the loo one morning, became aware that she was being watched through a knot-hole in the door. She recognized the eye as belonging to one of her week's lodgers – a randy old stage–manager with an unsavoury reputation. That particular time she was unable to do anything about the Peeping Tom. However, the following morning she went into the toilet well prepared. She waited until the eye made its appearances and jabbed at it with a knitting needle she had taken in with her. There was a horrible yell and she heard the stage-manager – for it was he – stumble up the stairs. He turned up that evening for his dinner with his eye heavily bandaged, but never a word was spoken about the incident.

To get back to the *Forces Showboat* tour, there was one awful week Myra and I suffered when the show was playing Harrow in North London. The landlady of the digs which had been recommended had to turn us down at the last minute, and we finished up on the Sunday night at an evil-smelling house in a back street. The character who ran the place was straight out of a Dickens novel, hatchet-faced and dressed in black. She informed us that she was doing us a favour by letting us have her best room. After she had shown us into the room, Myra said in a whisper – because it was that kind of atmosphere – 'If this is the best room, what must the others look like?'

A naked bulb hung from the ceiling, and the flimsy wardrobe had a door that wouldn't stay shut. There was bare linoleum on the floor, and the bed was a single one. Myra refused to unpack any of our clothes and we were so cold we had to put our dressing-gowns on to go to bed. During the night some drunk began banging on the door asking to be let in, and it was some time before he went away.

At breakfast the next morning our hostess informed us over a cup of tea in which grease floated, that her real job was laying out the corpses in the local mortuary, and she regaled us with some jolly tales of the vicissitudes of her profession.

When Myra and I left for the band call we took one of the suitcases containing my stage suit and props, leaving behind the cabin trunk which held my street clothes and Myra's dresses and shoes.

Fortunately, that afternoon I met a friend of ours from the Windmill days – Barry Brigg, an RAF pilot who had married Daddy Allen's daughter. When we told him of our experiences of the previous night, he said, 'For God's sake don't go back there, come home and stay with us – June will be delighted to see you.'

We gladly accepted the offer and the following morning Myra went back to the digs to pay what we owed and retrieve our trunk.

She found the door to our room locked and a huge padlock and chain had been fastened outside. The landlady refused to let her in to get the luggage until the week's rent had been paid. Myra came back to the Briggs' house with the news, and I had to go down from the theatre, where I had been rehearsing, to claim the trunk. When I gave the woman the money she unchained the door and I took the trunk away.

There was a strong sense of evil in that house, and in order not to be caught out again I applied to the Actors' Church Union for their list of recommended accommodation for actors. We found it extremely useful and it became our 'bible' when we were on tour. Appropriate, really.

All the time I had been working in *Forces Showboat* and doing the odd radio or television broadcast, I never considered singing seriously. If I sang at all, it was always in a burlesque way, because I was so concerned with being a comedian that I had no real desire to add a straight song to the act. I was afraid of using my voice in a serious way in case I got laughs in the wrong places. Anyway, it was a big, untrained voice, liable to go out of tune when under pressure – although in the bath I sang like a dream. However, the more often I broadcast on 'Variety Bandbox', the harder it became to find enough material to fill in the time, and it was always good to have a finish to your act. Some comics closed with a monologue or a tap dance like Norman Vaughan – but tap dancing on radio was obviously out. Arthur English had a unique way of finishing his performance when he did a stint on 'Variety Bandbox'. He would get louder and louder and faster and faster and then shout 'Open the cage!' as a way of getting applause. Reg Dixon, a resident on 'Variety Bandbox', would sing 'Confidentially' to open his act, and end with a ballad of some kind, but the only comedian who sang in a full-throated way was Issy Bonn. Some of the older pros had good voices – people like Tommy Handley, Stanley

Holloway and Arthur Askey all used their vocal ability to bolster their performances.

Jimmy Grafton was all for me doing the same. 'Try a song to finish with on your next "Bandbox",' he suggested. 'You've got one coming up in October.'

I decided to have a go at it and picked a song which seemed to suit my voice. It was called 'When You're In Love', and was a Spanish song, originally entitled 'La Paloma', to which English words had been added.

Myra and I were staying in digs in Brixton at this time. She was expecting our first child, something that didn't stop her doing cartwheels in the street on the way home from the theatre the evening after her pregnancy was confirmed. But now she was suffering from morning sickness and wasn't feeling too well. The week before the broadcast in which I was to sing my first straight ballad, we had very little money left and we'd used up all the meat coupons on our ration books. We lived on potatoes for several days – fried, boiled, and in their jackets. Sketching had always been a favourite pastime of mine, and I became preoccupied with drawing heads and flowers and God knows what else with a soft-leaded pencil all over the marble mantelpiece in our room in the digs. The landlady, Mrs Rattray, was used to the eccentricities of her theatrical guests and didn't mind at all, but I have no doubt that she wiped the lot off as soon as we had gone.

On the day of the 'Variety Bandbox' broadcast, I went along to the band call with a full orchestration of 'When You're In Love' provided for me by the publishers. The conductor, Billy Ternant, who knew me by now from previous shows, was very patient with my fumbling attempts to come to terms with the music. It sounded very different from the simple piano part and I had trouble sorting out exactly where to come in. In the end he got the pianist in the orchestra to give me a bell note when it was time for me to start.

Jimmy Grafton was very keen that I didn't muck about with the song. 'No going cross-eyed in the middle or anything like that,' he admonished in the dressing-room before I went

on. I didn't. When I came to the end of the comedy routine
Jim had written, I announced the song, and sang it straight, all
the way through. However, at the end, after I had got the top
note, I fell flat on my back. It was my way of compromising.
It was a start, though, and it gave me enough confidence to
begin to think of adding a straight song every time I did a
radio show.

It wasn't always successful, however. After one programme
Stanley Black, the conductor, said to me. 'Do you know that
you sang "Granada" all the way through a quarter of a tone
sharp?'

I looked at him and said, 'Do you think it's easy?'

He threw his baton at me.

Christmas 1948 was a traumatic time for Myra and me. *Forces
Showboat* was playing Bristol the week before Christmas
and everybody was looking forward to going home for the
festivities. However, on the Friday when we were supposed
to be paid, the man responsible for financing the show had no
money, and the company was stranded. It was like something
out of a Hollywood musical, with tears being shed all around,
everybody looking very desperate, and me with a pregnant
wife. Fortunately I knew a man in Bristol who had taken a
liking to Myra and myself and I managed, with his help, to get
enough money to pay the train fare home for the company.
Bill Pavey was his name, and I am eternally grateful to him.

We spent Christmas at home with Myra's parents and had
a great time. Even though we had experienced the worst thing
that can happen to a performer, apart from being taken off the
bill – and I'd already been through that – I felt that things were
getting brighter. I had a radio series with Pat Dixon to come
in the New Year, and on New Year's Day I had a television
show to do – another *Rooftop Rendezvous*.

The radio series I was contracted to do was 'Third Division', and Pat had gathered around him a team which would
take some beating. Robert Beatty headed the cast, and other

members of 'Listen, My Children' were also included – Bennie Lee, Pat Hayes, Benny Hill and myself. The newcomers were Bruce Belfrage, Michael Bentine and Peter Sellers. This was the first time that Mike, Peter and I had worked together and was a forerunner for 'The Goon Show'. The comedy was thought to be too way-out for Light Programme listeners and went out on the Third Programme – the equivalent of today's Radio 3.

Naturally, Mike and I took Peter along to Grafton's. He was so obviously one of us and his repertoire of impressions was formidable. Like the rest of us, he had been in the services and shared our lunatic sense of humour. Spike and Peter took to each other immediately and soon the four of us were meeting regularly.

Rooftop Rendezvous on New Year's Day 1949 was a live television programme – as they all were in those days – and was broadcast from the Alexandra Palace Studios. I was required to wear full evening dress for my act, and that was the cause of some concern because I didn't possess it. Fortunately a fellow lodger at Mrs Rattray's knew somebody who worked at the theatrical costumiers, Fox's. 'He'll fix you up with a really good outfit,' he said. 'Just tell him I sent you.'

Of course, when I went along to Fox's the lodger's friend was not there, and the selection of evening wear was very poor – all the good stuff had already gone out. 'Christmas and the New Year is a busy time for us,' explained the assistant who served me. 'Have a look through this lot.'

I eventually chose a tail jacket which was too long and a pair of trousers which were too short and which turned out to have a greenish tinge under the studio lights. Seeing my disappointment, the assistant let me have the dress shirt and waistcoat for nothing. 'But don't forget to bring the lot back on time,' he said, pocketing the thirty shillings I gave him. I was only getting ten guineas for the show.

As a change from the shaving act I had worked out a routine of how different people ate sandwiches – the hungry man, the laughing nibbler, the man who was allergic to mustard, and a

couple of others I've forgotten now. I had asked for very thin
sandwiches so that I wouldn't have too much in my mouth at
any one time, otherwise I would not be able to speak.

'You shall have them – don't worry, old chap,' said the floor
manager cheerfully. (That always makes me suspicious – give
me a floor manager who worries, I always say.)

There was no time for a proper dress run-through, and
when the red light came on in the studio, signalling the start
of the show, I still hadn't seen the sandwiches I was to use in
the act. I was also having trouble keeping my starched shirt
front in position. It was not a proper shirt; the collar, the
bow tie and the starched front part with the three black studs,
were all one piece, fastened at the bottom by a tab which fitted
over a button in the top of my trousers. I have a long torso,
and the fake shirt front was too short. It was all right when
I bent forward, but when I straightened up, the tab attached
to my pants was under great strain and put my manhood in
jeopardy.

They had placed me in a corner of the set, seated at a
table, and the idea was that a waiter came on, put a plate
of sandwiches before me and left me to it. The band struck
up my signature tune – 'I'm Just Wild About Harry' – and
the waiter duly appeared bearing a plate of six of the biggest
doorstep sandwiches I'd ever seen. When they were placed
before me it was obvious that they had been left under the
lights somewhere and, big as they were, they were curling at
the edges.

There was nothing I could do but go into the routine –
this was live television. I announced the first sandwich eater
– the very hungry one – and began stuffing the dry bread
into my mouth. It was a horrible experience, and as I progressed I was spitting bread everywhere. The effort of trying
to bend forward to keep the pressure off my groin was getting unbearable, and when I eventually came to the 'laughing
nibbler' bit I was forced to straighten up. The tab on my shirt
front snapped and the whole lot unrolled upwards like a blind,
revealing an expanse of bare, sweating flesh. The band went

hysterical and the camera swung away from me. I thought I had blown my chance of becoming a TV star for good, but the producer came around to my dressing-room afterwards and congratulated me. 'Sheer genius, that bit with the shirt front,' he said. 'I thought the act was going downhill at one point, and then you produced that glorious piece of business. Beautifully timed. Congratulations.'

I went home on the bus from Alexandra Palace that night determined to try that same 'piece of business' in my act, and then in the cold light of a Brixton morning I realized that there was no way I could ever repeat that completely unrehearsed moment.

On some occasions, however, it is possible. Fourteen years later, during the trial scene in the musical *Pickwick*, I accidentally broke off the wooden bar which formed the front part of the dock I was standing in. I looked so surprised that the audience laughed uproariously. It was such a good reaction and, coming at a dramatic part of the play, relieved the tension at just the right moment, so I thought I'd try to do it again on purpose the following night. I arranged for the bar to be loosely attached to its moorings and when the time came I broke it off deliberately in the same way I had done it accidentally the night before. It worked again, for some reason, and it stayed in for the rest of the run. People would come up to me and say, 'I was in the audience the night when you broke off the wooden bar on the dock.' And I'd nod and smile, but I never let on.

New Responsibilities

I had quite a lot of radio shows in the first couple of months of 1949 – 'Third Division' was going out, and on 26 January I did a trial recording for the 'Cyril Fletcher Show'. Cyril had a regular summer season at the Pavilion Theatre, Torquay, and was looking for a comedian. To my delight I got the job, probably on the strength of the broadcast, and the summer looked nice and secure. There were to be a couple of weeks in Hastings at the White Rock Pavilion, a further two at the Knightstone Pavilion, Weston-super-Mare, and a short run at the Theatre Royal, Bath, after the Torquay season. In addition, there were to be some television appearances in Cyril's own show. All this meant that Myra and I could look forward to the arrival of our first child knowing that I would be getting a steady weekly wage.

As I have already mentioned, radio did not pay much. My fee was ten guineas at the time, so I had to fill in with as many theatrical dates as I could. My act was getting more polished – I suppose you could say that I was being fired in the crucible of the music halls. It was the proud boast of the stage door-keeper of every theatre up north that 'If yer can please 'em 'ere you'll please 'em anywhere.'

Once, as I left the stage door of the Theatre Royal, Barnsley, a cloth-capped gentleman grasped my arm firmly and informed me, 'You nearly 'ad me laughing when you were on, lad.' And he meant it as a compliment.

Discipline was always strict in the better-class venues – the Moss Empires and Stoll Theatres – but it was also rigidly applied in the smaller establishments. If you went over your allotted time by too many minutes you were in trouble with head office. The stage-manager put down on his report sheet the time you went on stage and the time you came off, and stage-managers were unbribable. There was no excuse for coming late to work either – every artist had to be in his dressing-room by the time the half-hour was called by the stage-manager. There was also a rule that no fish and chips were to be brought into the theatre.

I was not aware of this, and one Friday night when I was playing a northern Palace, I went out to the chip shop down the road and brought back a couple of bob's worth of cod and fried potatoes. The stage door-keeper was on the phone when I got back, and obviously didn't notice me enter. I was in the middle of my meal in the dressing-room when I heard the thundering cry come up the stairs, 'Who's eating bloody chips in 'ere?'

The accordionist in the next room to mine rushed in and started wafting the air with a towel. 'I thought it was you,' she said. She pointed to the window. 'There's a ledge you can stand on out there.'

Without thinking I climbed out of the window and stood on a rather narrow ledge, with the remains of my supper in one hand. When I looked down I nearly fainted. Because of my lowly position on the bill, I was on the third floor. The star had the stage-level dressing-room and the lesser acts ascended the building in order of size of billing. I was lucky not to be on the roof. I've never had a head for heights, and I spent a very uncomfortable few minutes clinging to the brickwork around the window until the accordionist announced the all-clear. I never did it again.

*

The week that Myra was expecting our baby to arrive I was playing Feldman's Theatre, Blackpool, and she was at home in Swansea with her parents. I had been down at the weekend but had to leave on the Sunday to be in Blackpool for band call on Monday morning.

There were two comics on the bill. I was one of them, and the other was a young ex-serviceman who had been in the RAF *Gang Show*. Tony Hancock was a slim, nervous lad in those days – as was I – and we had a lot in common. We had met at Daddy Allen's Club and he was a frequent visitor to Jimmy Grafton's pub in Westminster. His act was completely different from mine, but like Peter and Mike he spurned the 'string of gags' approach to comedy, and among other things he did an impression of a British Movietone Newsreel.

As I came off stage after my first performance that Monday night, 11 April 1949, the stage-manager said there was a phone call for me. I rushed up the stairs to the manager's office, my face full of shaving soap, to receive the news that Myra had given birth to a six-and-a-half-pound baby girl. I was over the moon with delight and asked Tony to join me in a drink and a meal after the second house.

By the time we had both cleaned up, all the pubs were shut and the only place open was a fish and chip bar down a side street. Over our steaming fried haddock and sixpennyworth of chips we toasted my new daughter's health in a couple of glasses of Tizer. Then we walked down to the promenade, leaned over the rails, and discussed our futures. We were young and ambitious and the night seemed strangely full of promise as we looked down into the dark water, seeing only stars there. I shall always remember Tony as he was then, before the drink got the better of him. He was uncertain of himself and talked a lot about the art of comedy, especially about Sid Field, upon whom he was beginning to model himself. He was not content just to accept the laughs he got for a piece of 'business', he wanted to know why the audience found him funny. I was always only too ready to take the reward without questioning it too closely. Tony never was, and eventually embarked on a quest for perfection that led him to get rid of all the stalwarts who worked with him on his radio and TV shows.

As I was to write much later in a foreword to a book about Tony written by his widow, Freddie Ross, together with David Nathan: 'The demands of his profession shaped him, ground him down and eventually killed him, but he served it well. If anyone paid dearly for his laughs, it was the lad himself. May he lie sweetly at rest.'

I couldn't wait to get back to Swansea at the weekend to see the new baby. She had a mop of black hair like her mother, and big, dark brown eyes like her mother, but by God she had my lungs. Seeing her I realized that I now had increased responsibilities, and as yet Myra and I had no home of our own. It was time I started to get enough money together to buy one.

I travelled to Cardiff on 13 May to record 'Welsh Rarebit', a long-running variety show which had a high listening figure, and I was keen to make an impression. The producer was Mai Jones, a lady of tremendous energy and talent who also conducted the orchestra. Her husband, Dai, was the programme's engineer.

Mai went through the script I had brought along, looking for innuendoes, putting her pencil through the odd line. 'Mustn't have anything naughty on "Welsh Rarebit", love,' she said. What she had crossed out was a reference to a 'district nurse'. I could not see what harm there was in it but as it was my first 'Rarebit' I kept my mouth shut. At least she allowed me one raspberry.

We then ran over the music and Mai made some helpful suggestions about how I should handle the song. It was 'Falling In Love With Love', which had been made famous by Alan Jones, the Hollywood musical star whom I admired very much. My reputation had gone before me, and as I went into the number she wagged her baton at me. 'No making funny faces in the middle, now.' I promised to try to sing it properly – and I did. The result was that I became a regular item on 'Welsh Rarebit' for the next few years, and it helped to build my career. The theme song, 'We'll Keep A Welcome', for which Mai wrote the music, has been a feature of my stage act as long as I can remember, and if I don't sing it I get complaints.

The shows were recorded in Corey Hall in Cardiff, a place with excellent acoustics and ideal for the purpose of broadcasting. However, it had one unfortunate drawback – there were no toilets backstage. Quite a number of the cast members were getting on a bit, especially the actors who were involved in the regular 'Tommy Trouble' feature, and after a few pints they would begin to feel very uncomfortable. There must have been a few bladders ruptured in the cause of radio, until a bucket was provided for surreptitious relief in the corner of the dressing-room.

It was a great show to do and I made many friends, including Frank James, the compère, Alun Williams, the announcer, comedians Wyn Calvin and Stan Stennet, Albert and Les Ward, a comedy musical act, and Ossie Morris. Ossie was a naturally funny man to whom fame came late in life. For years he had worked in the steelworks at Port Talbot and performed locally as an amateur, until Mai Jones discovered him. He had a good singing voice and his gimmick of 'I must 'ave 'ush' became a popular catch-phrase of the day. Another regular who became a star in middle age via 'Welsh Rarebit' was Gladys Morgan, a dear lady with a high-pitched cackle.

The programme also gave me an opportunity to work alongside some of the top singers and comedians of the day. Donald Peers was very popular at that time and I used to watch in awe as he stood among his fans, signing autographs with a flourish, his overcoat draped over his shoulders in the manner of a Continental film star. I wondered if ever I'd get to that stage, and even practised the overcoat bit, but it always fell off.

Although Mai discovered a lot of future stars, there was one who slipped through the net. A young singer once auditioned for her and was told to 'go home, love' – and Shirley Bassey went back, temporarily, to Tiger Bay.

The television series of Cyril Fletcher's show went very well and I was given plenty of work in the sketches, although I had no singing to do. I had a couple of good notices in the press and I was looking forward to the rehearsals for the summer show, which was called *Magpie Masquerade*.

It was a sumptuously dressed seaside revue, and the men wore full evening dress for the opening and the finale. Betty Astell, Cyril's wife, wore crinolines and wonderful beaded and sequinned gowns which she made herself, and the ladies of the company dressed in the height of fashion.

I had never been in a show of this kind before, and I felt a bit like a fish out of water. However, I was determined to make the most of it.

Myra had answered an advertisement for a cottage to rent in Brixham, a fishing village not too far from Torquay which could be reached quite quickly by a converted motor torpedo boat which plied between the two harbours.

We had no car as yet, and Myra came down from Swansea on the train with her mother, all our luggage, a pram, and three-month-old Jennifer. We had liked Reg O'List's wife's name so much that we decided to call our first-born after her.

The scene was now set for what should have been a glorious summer season, but it didn't quite turn out that way. For a start, Cyril was a laid-back comedian whose humour was gentle, as witness his 'odd odes' which made him famous on radio. My approach to comedy was still rather rough and ready, and I had not yet learned the art of subtlety – especially when performing in the sketches. I was apt to ad lib when the fancy took me, and after a Guinness or two, my raspberries got fruitier.

For the show's finale, all the male members of the company had to stand in line and unfurl opera cloaks, revealing their crimson linings, as Betty came down the staircase to take her bow. On one occasion I thought it would be a great idea to write 'Eat at Joe's' on the inside of my cloak. The laugh I got when the message was revealed completely spoiled poor Betty's entrance, and I was quite rightly given a severe telling-off.

There was another scene, set in Bath, in which the whole company was dressed in elegant Georgian costumes. Betty sang a song and we finished with a number called 'Oh Listen To The Band', the last lines of which went, 'To the shouts of here we come, and the banging of the drum, Oh listen to the music in the park.' However, I got into the habit of singing slightly different words to the real ones. One night, the rest of the cast – on the instructions of Nugent Marshall, who had been at the Windmill when I was there and had a wicked sense of humour – stopped singing before they came to the afore-mentioned lines. The result was that the audience heard, 'To the shouts of here we come, put your finger up your bum, and listen to the music in the park,' sung as a solo by yours truly. Actually, I thought I sang it rather well, but Cyril and Betty did not appreciate my efforts.

To be honest, Cyril didn't know how to handle me, and, looking back, I would have felt the same if some zany young idiot had started messing about in one of my summer shows. His only complaint to my agent was that I was rather 'ro-bust', an understatement if ever there was one. Cyril and I have discussed the show since and had a good laugh about it, but it wasn't too good an experience for either of us at the time. I was a misfit in the elegant atmosphere of the concert party. There were still traces of the NAAFI performer in me, and my overdeveloped sense of the ridiculous kept getting me into trouble.

Back at the cottage in Brixham, Myra was having difficulty with Jennifer, who seemed to be crying incessantly for no apparent reason. It was lonely for Myra being stuck on her own when I was out every night doing the show, but she never complained, God bless her.

I thought it was time that I bought a car – it might cheer everybody up. Gordon Holdom, the baritone in *Magpie Masquerade*, had a car which he said I could have for forty pounds. I snapped up his offer. It was an old Humber – a very old Humber – but it had the look of having been a great car at one time. Perhaps it had belonged to someone of substance – at any rate it now belonged to someone of very little substance, because the forty quid nearly cleaned me out.

The first difficulty I encountered was the fact that although I had driven all sorts of vehicles in the the war, including a Bren carrier, I had forgotten to renew the licence I had been given by Major Sims back in Usk in 1939. Consequently I had to take the driving test again. This was a blow, because I now had a car but was unable to drive it. I could see the damned thing parked down at the quayside, slowly disintegrating before my very eyes.

I decided to apply right away for a test, and obtained a provisional licence. As a refresher I fixed up a crash course of driving lessons – very appropriately termed, as it turned out. When my driving instructor arrived I found, to my surprise, that he had only one arm. I showed him what I could do and he pronounced that I would have no difficulty whatsoever in passing the test. We then adjourned to the pub.

The following week I took my driving test, thanks to the influence of my one-armed friend. He and I went out for a quick drive before the examination, which was arranged for two o'clock that afternoon. Afterwards we adjourned to the pub again and I had a couple of bottles of Guinness.

It was a very hot afternoon, and I parked the car outside the place where I was supposed to meet the examiner, about half an hour before the appointment. I put my head back against the seat and dozed. The next thing I knew was that a hand was shaking me awake. The examiner was anxious to get going, and after checking my name and particulars on his clipboard, he told me to proceed. He watched patiently as I tried to start the car. The Humber was a slow starter and I was beginning to despair of the ignition ever firing, but finally it clattered into life. I smiled at him in relief, put the car smartly into reverse and moved backwards into a parked bicycle. As I got out to see if the bike was damaged – fortunately it was not – I saw the examiner writing something down on his clipboard.

Torquay is a town of many hills, and I chatted away desperately as I tried to coax the old banger to negotiate some of them – and all the time the examiner was writing away on his clipboard. The climax came when, attempting a flashy three-point turn, I drove inexorably into the back of a stationary bus. The examiner got out, grim-faced, and, giving me a yellow slip, announced that I had failed on everything.

'You didn't try me on the Highway Code,' I said plaintively. 'I'm good on that.'

But he had gone, leaving me to deal with an irate bus driver. I drove back to my driving instructor's office on my own, which afterwards I realized was quite illegal because every learner has to have a licensed driver alongside him.

The instructor was quite surprised that I'd failed the test. 'Pity he didn't try you on the Highway Code,' he said in an attempt to mollify me. 'You're good on that. Never mind, better luck next time.' And we adjourned to the pub.

I did pass the second time, a few weeks later, but the old car was on its last legs and I used the one-armed gent's vehicle for the test. When I came to drive the Humber regularly I found that if I went over twenty miles an hour the perspex windows of the two rear doors slowly wound down, with the result that anyone who rode in it eventually finished up with a head cold. Myra's parents would sit in the back seat wrapped up like Scotts of the Antarctic.

When we finished the season in Bath I tried hard to sell the car. At one point I was about to secure the deal at a garage, but made the fatal mistake of taking my foot off the accelerator with which I was keeping the mortally wounded engine alive. It died immediately I did so and nothing could revive it. The garage owner, who was about to pay me twenty pounds for it, subsequently charged me five pounds for having it towed away.

The rest of the year was pretty quiet with only a few broadcasts, mostly 'Variety Bandbox' shows, and a sprinkling of theatre dates. My only television appearance was on 23 December when I played the Judge in *Toad Of Toad Hall*, which went out live from Alexandra Palace. The cast was excellent, with Cameron Hall as Toad, Kenneth More as Badger, Jill Balcon the Narrator, Andrew Osborne as Ratty, Jack Newmark as Mole, and Desmond Walter Ellis as the Usher. Sam Kydd, with whom I had toured Germany in the show with Peter Waring, was one of the water rats, and Oscar Quitack, who was to play Mr Winkle to my Pickwick much later on, was the back-end of the horse.

I welcomed the opportunity to work with actors and found them all very generous. My part as the Judge in the courtroom scene required me to sing a song as well as deliver quite a lot of dialogue. There was one piece of business which always reduced Kenny More to giggles. In the sleeve of my judge's robe I concealed a huge red-spotted handkerchief, which I used to produce at intervals and pretend to blow my nose. It was a perfect excuse to blow a raspberry, and I grasped the opportunity with both lips.

When the programme was repeated on 2 January, 1950, we had to perform it live all over again, because in those days it was not possible to make a recording for later use. A lot has been said about the transmission of live television shows, with opposing views about their virtue. Those in favour say that the adrenalin of performing live gives an artist that extra edge, but I must admit that I prefer the controlled atmosphere of a recorded show, without the air of desperate gaiety which comes with the knowledge that if you make a mistake, millions of people are going to see it.

❖

I had now become a resident comedian on 'Welsh Rarebit', and from 26 January 1950 I appeared every week. There was no pantomime engagement for me during the Christmas period of 1949/50, which was no real surprise after my disastrous debut in *Dick Whittington*, and I was content to do the radio programmes and consolidate my career. The variety theatre bookings were coming in steadily, and my salary had increased to fifty pounds a week.

One week found me playing the Metropolitan, Edgware Road, one of the Syndicate Halls, and the only theatre in the group that I had not played during the tour of *Dick Whittington*.

It was a very good 'shop window' theatre to play, because it was easily accessible for all the London agents and bookers, and it had one feature that I don't think any other theatre possessed. The bar in the stalls had a huge plate glass window through which the customers could watch the acts while having a drink. This was where the men who did all the bookings could stand with large whiskies and decide the fate of the sweating performers on the other side of the glass.

The top of the bill the first week I played there was Jack Train, the impressionist, who was a regular on 'ITMA', the great wartime comedy show which starred Tommy Handley. For some reason, perhaps because there were a lot of young people in the audience, I did really well on the opening night. I was beginning to achieve a radio popularity and when I came on the audience applauded. That was what we all aimed at. It was a sure sign of recognition, and brought with it the realization that you no longer had to struggle to coax the first laughs from those all-important people out front – the paying public. And it meant that some of them had even come in especially to see you.

I did so well that week that the management moved my position further down the bill. It was the first time that I had vacated that spot that every young comic dreaded – second act on. We used to make desperate gags about our position when we came on to face the audience: 'I wouldn't give this spot to a dry cleaner,' was a favourite line.

One night that week I learned that Lew Grade of the Grade Agency had been in to see me, and had liked my act. He had left a telephone number for me to ring the following day.

When I told Norman Vaughan back at Linden Gardens, where I still shared the flat whenever I was in London, he said, 'Great, mate. He's a really big agent - he can get you the Palladium.'

I got very excited and rang the Grade Agency's number first thing the following morning and made an appointment to see Lew and his brother Leslie the same afternoon.

I was ushered into their posh premises in Regent Street, introduced to Leslie (who was later to become a dear friend) and offered a seat in Lew's office. He was on the phone.

'Well, I've got the boy in the office with me now, Val,' he said, waving his cigar at me in greeting.

Val? That has to be Val Parnell, I thought, the head of Moss Empires and the man who puts on the Palladium shows. I began to twitch with excitement and apprehension as Lew made a few complimentary remarks about me to Val before going on to discuss other business. When he had put the phone down, Lew shook my hand across the desk and asked me who was representing me. As it happened I was between agents. I had not been satisfied with the way things were going and had left the Will Hammer office, a fairly small-time agency.

I told Lew that I had no agent at the moment and he sat back in his chair and recited all the benefits which would accrue to me if I'd sign up with his outfit. I would be put on a sliding-scale salary, increasing on a yearly basis, and in a few weeks' time, God willing, I could be playing the Palladium.

It was a great temptation and I almost signed there and then as Lew wanted me to. But something held me back. Jimmy Grafton and I had been talking the previous week about how my career should go and we had decided that the 'parabola' was the best way – a gentle rise and a slow fall, rather than the 'rocket' – going straight up and, energy spent, falling quickly. Besides, I did not think that I was ready for the Palladium, which, though it was the Mecca for every aspiring performer, was also the focus for the national press, and failure there could be fatal.

I asked Lew if I could think about the deal, and promised to come back with my answer in a couple of days. He was surprised that I had not snapped up his offer, but was gracious enough to agree to see me again.

Sleep did not come easily that night. I was doing quite nicely as I was, slowly acquiring a name on radio and gradually learning my craft on the stage. But, on the other hand, if I made a big impact at the Palladium I could almost be a star overnight. . .

The following morning I went down to see Jimmy Grafton, whose opinion I valued, and he took me out on to the golf course with him for my first-ever game. On the way around, in between retrieving balls from various inaccessible parts of the rough, we decided that in the long run and all things considered it would be better for my future career if I turned down Lew's offer.

'You'd be far better off with a smaller agent who only has a few acts. Then he could concentrate on shaping your future, nurture you, and then when you're ready – and not before - you can play the Palladium,' said Jim, sinking a long putt on the seventeenth hole.

I agreed, and went back to see Lew Grade.

When Lew heard my decision he was rather upset and shook his cigar at me. 'All right, lad,' he said. 'But one day you'll come crawling back to me.'

'I don't think so, Mr Grade,' I replied, and left his office.

Six years later, when I was starring at the London Palladium in *Rocking The Town* Lew came into my dressing-room. 'I didn't come crawling back did I, Lew?' I said. And he laughed and offered me a cigar.

*

The fact that I was now singing every week on 'Welsh Rarebit' made me a target for the song pluggers. These were the men who worked for the music publishers and it was their job to persuade artists to sing the songs published by their companies. I would frequently be visited in my dressing-room by anxious middle-aged men who would stand about a foot away from me and sing into my face their latest melody. 'My grey-haired mother' they would croon unaccompanied, or else a song about 'an old lamplighter' or 'an old cobbler' or whatever profession was considered to be romantic at the time. They were earnest gentlemen who, on closer acquaintance, proved to have a great sense of humour.

If a singer agreed to perform one of their tunes on a broadcast, they would provide a free orchestration which saved the artist paying a quite hefty sum of money, and they invariably put the singer's photograph on the front of the piano copy with the words 'as featured by so-and-so on such-and-such radio show'. There were also rumours of plug money being paid as an extra blandishment, but I was not big enough to be offered that.

I became very friendly with one of the song pluggers – a man called Leslie Simpson, who would also spare the time to run over songs he thought might be suitable for my voice, even if his company did not publish them. He taught me how to interpret a ballad rather than just belt it out, which I sometimes did out of sheer embarrassment. I was slowly becoming aware that my voice could be used to more advantage, but it was still slightly unfocused, and under pressure I was in danger of singing sharp.

However, I was now using a couple of straight songs in my stage act. 'Falling In Love With Love' was one, and 'We'll Keep A Welcome' (the theme song of 'Welsh Rarebit') was the other. My band parts soon became rather tattered as my work in the variety theatres increased. They were also getting pretty illegible because of the pencilled notes all over them. Members of the brass section in one pit orchestra would leave little notes for their counterparts in the next town on my touring schedule. 'Good for a pint, here' perhaps, when there was a long pause in the music, or 'How's Lily?' from one double bass player to another. It got so that I could hardly make out the musical notes from the pencilled notes.

The problem was solved when I was booked to appear at the Finsbury Park Empire, which in terms of our profession was the next best thing to playing the Palladium. All the big American acts were to be seen there and it was a much sought-after date.

When I put my tatty music down on the stage prior to the band call it looked very much out of place among the red and blue leather books which held the orchestral parts of the other artists, and I felt very uncomfortable when my turn came to rehearse.

'What's this lot, then?' Syd Caplan, the resident musical director, handled my little pile of scribbled notes as if they harboured some dread disease.

'I'm very sorry, Mr Caplan. I've been meaning to get some new ones done.'

He sniffed and shook his head disapprovingly. A lot of people seemed to be doing that to me, I thought miserably.

'All right, leave it to me. I'll do you a new set of books by the end of the week. These are really disgusting.'

I agreed readily, little realizing that by the time I had paid for the band books there wouldn't be much left out of my week's salary. Apparently Syd Caplan always used the same ploy when an artist turned up with music in a tatty condition. The bill came as a blow, but I have to confess that those red leather books with gold embossed letters on the front that spelt my name and the name of the instrument section of the parts it contained are still in good condition today, so in the long run it was a very wise investment.

Myra was with me for the week, along with little Jennifer, who was now twelve months old. We had booked into a small bed and breakfast hotel in Russell Square which was on the Actors' Church Union list of lodgings. It was not a very happy week for Myra, because she was left alone practically all day with the baby, and, in addition, the hotel had been freshly painted.

I have never been able to stand the smell of fresh paint and my throat became affected by it. To make matters worse, on the night that a big agent came in to see my act, I had forgotten to bring a clean shirt for the second show, with the result that I had to go on stage in the shirt in which I had performed the first house. I was nervous too, and it showed. At the end of the performance, Ted Gollop, who was the assistant to Cissie Williams, the lady responsible for booking all the acts for Moss Empires, came backstage and took me to task for the state of my shirt. Miss Williams had the final say about whether an act was fit to play the circuit and had an extremely powerful influence on the variety scene as a whole. Ted Gollop was always at her side when she came to a theatre, and was forever running through the pass door to the stage to convey her likes and dislikes to the artists concerned. There was a story going the rounds that when her pet dog died she made Ted wear a black armband.

It was quite some time before I played a Moss Empires theatre again. I heard that she had declared my act to be dirty. Whether it was because of the shirt I wore that second house, or whether the lady took a dislike to the raspberries I blew, I never found out. But to call my shaving act 'dirty' was a bit thick – after all, I always boasted that it was the cleanest act in the business.

There were some astonishingly eccentric performers doing the rounds at the same time as myself. Take Henry Vadden, for instance, who had a most unusual finish to his act. He would stand in the centre of the stage and strap on a helmet upon the top of which was a large spike. He would give a signal for the drummer in the pit to begin a dramatic roll on the tymps and the lights would go down, leaving him in a white spotlight. He would then give a cry, and from the flies above the stage, a large cartwheel would fall and he would catch it on the spike. Then he'd give the wheel a twirl and the curtains would close as it spun on the helmet.

I watched him from the wings one Monday night at the first–house performance. As the cartwheel thudded down on to his helmet I heard him utter a strangled cry as his neck disappeared into his shoulders. This was the first show of the week, remember, and he had to go through the whole business another eleven times.

There was another act that always intrigued me, and indeed I used it as the basis of an episode in my novel about the variety theatre, *Twice Brightly*. It was a lion act, and though it was billed on the theatre posters as 'a forest-bred animal', it was more likely 'Epping Forest-bred', and was practically toothless.

For the breath-taking climax to his performance, the lion's trainer would announce that the beast would now eat a hunk of raw meat which he would place on his lady assistant's chest. She lay down, the dripping joint was placed on her bosom, and the lion would commence to slobber over it as the tabs came down. What the audience at first house did not see was the battle between the trainer and the lion as he removed the meat from its jaws to be re-used in the second performance of the evening.

Then there were foot jugglers, ladies and gentlemen who lay on their backs on specially designed padded wooden supports, and balanced barrels and large, painted spheres on their feet, sometimes tossing them to a similarly positioned partner on the other side of the stage. There were incredibly daring clowns who did comedy routines on slack wires high off the ground with no safety net, pretending to be drunk and seeming about to crash to the floor at any moment. But they never did. I saw a knife-thrower who, blindfolded, would throw his shining deadly weapons all around the body of his sequin-clad assistant while she was strapped by her arms and legs to a revolving wooden wheel – and not a drop of blood to be seen at the finish. I remember a one-armed dog trainer who used to put a little black and white terrier through a most complicated routine of tricks without one word of command. As Spike Milligan remarked after he'd seen this particular turn, 'He must have had a bloody big dog in the act at one time.'

Touring the halls could be a monotonous business. The daily routine after the Monday, when all the preparatory work such as band call and setting out your dressing-room was done, was always of the same pattern.

I would arrive at the theatre at about eleven o'clock, following a leisurely nine o'clock breakfast at the digs. If the act had gone well on the Monday night I would enter the stage door with a light step, eager to revisit the scene of my success, ready with a smile for the stage door-keeper as I collected my mail, and then up the stairs to my dressing-room to read the letters at leisure. Then, back down to the stage level for a chat with the stage-manager, who usually brought me down to earth with some kind of criticism of my performance – either I'd run over time or I'd made too much mess with the shaving soap and ruined the front tabs.

Chastened, I would wait for the entry of some of the other acts and discuss what was on at the local cinema or exchange the latest showbiz gossip. 'I see Bygraves is going to play the Palladium' or 'I hear Frankie Howerd died a death at Bradford' or 'Who was the comic who was taken off the bill at Bolton?' And I'd say 'It was me,' and conversation would slacken for a while.

Then it was off to the pub for a couple of pints and a meat pie and back to the digs for a kip before first house.

On the other hand, if the act had not gone well on the previous night, I would stay in bed until lunch-time, worrying, and asking myself why I had chosen the theatre as a profession. Then, after walking through the stage door on leaden feet and surreptitiously checking the trains out of town in case I was going to be paid off, I would set out to face the audience like a Christian in Roman times entering an arena full of lions. And if I was lucky, I'd get an audience that liked what I was doing and I'd walk home to the digs that night about a foot off the ground, and the glass of stout with supper would taste like champagne and the landlady was an angel and I was going to top the bill at the London Palladium.

Then along would come Thursday night, and I'd spend the day in bed again.

It was always a relief to get away from the theatre and join in the revels at Grafton's on a Sunday night. Spike, Peter, Mike and I were fast developing a team spirit and enjoyed bouncing ideas off each other. All the time Jimmy Grafton watched approvingly, sometimes curbing our excesses with a constructive suggestion, which won him the nickname KOGVOS ('King Of Goons And Voice Of Sanity').

Peter was the only one of our quartet who had a theatrical background. His grandmother on his mother's side was a descendant of Daniel Mendoza, the Portuguese Jew who was the heavyweight champion boxer of England around the beginning of the 1800s – a time when they fought with bare fists. She was left a widow with several young children, and rather than passively bemoan her fate, started a touring revue. Her real name was Welcome, but she called herself Ma Ray and became a big attraction on the halls. Her daughter Peg, who had married a Protestant from Yorkshire, Bill Sellers, followed in her mother's footsteps, specializing in 'tableaux' with her pianist husband as her accompanist.

Oddly enough, Peter was born on 8 September 1925, exactly four years to the day after me. In his youth he became fascinated by the skill of the drummer in a band which played at the Victoria Pavilion in Ilfracombe. The theatre was managed by his uncle, and Peter used to help out with the chores. The drummer caught him playing his drums one day and, instead of giving him a good telling-off, he gave him instruction, and soon Peter was playing with some of the established dance bands. When he was eighteen he joined the RAF and was eventually posted to the Ralph Reader *Gang Show*, finishing up in India. He was often in trouble with his superiors for impersonating them – a habit we had in common. Also, like me, he had performed at the Windmill, where he had earned £25 a week – five quid more than I had got – and his name finished up along with mine on the famous board outside the theatre.

To get his first BBC Radio job, Peter rang a producer called Roy Speer, and by impersonating the voices of Kenneth Horne and Richard Murdoch, he recommended himself for an audition. For his cheek he was granted one. From then on his reputation grew apace and, as I have already recounted, we met on several radio programmes. He was a perfectionist who even at that early stage in his career was showing signs of greatness. But he was never completely happy, always feeling that he could have given a better performance.

Of the four of us, he was the most nerveless. I don't think that I ever saw him show any kind of nervousness about performing before an audience. He was always completely in command of himself and was never afraid to experiment with gags on stage. I can best illustrate this by leaping forward in time a couple of years to when Peter, Spike and myself were all performing together in a show at the Coventry Hippodrome. It was November, and the cold seemed to have seeped into the souls of the audiences who, at times, appeared to be completely baffled by what was going on up on stage.

One night Peter walked on carrying a chair and addressed the audience thus: 'I've been out shopping today, and I came across a little EP record of Christmas Carols performed by the Wally Stott Orchestra. I was so enchanted by it, I decided I'd like to share it with you.'

He then gave a nod to the electrician side-stage, who had been primed in advance to have the record ready to play over the house sound system.

The music started. Peter sat down on the chair, crossed his legs and hummed along with the music.

The audience looked at one other in complete confusion as this went on, but at the end of the music gave Peter a desultory spattering of applause.

'I knew you'd like it,' he cried, leaping from his chair. 'So let's hear the other side, shall we?'

And he sat down again as the rest of the record was played. When the music finished he got up, bowed to the audience, and brushing away an imaginary tear, walked off stage with the chair.

And I had to follow that lot with 'Bless This House'.

Spike was born on 16 April 1918 in the Military Hospital in Ahmednaga, the son of an Irish sergeant-major in the British Army. His Christian names are Terence Alan but as Michael Caine might say, 'not many people know that'. His boyhood was spent in the army barracks of India, but his father became the victim of a cut in the armed forces and at the age of forty left for England with no prospects of work.

The family settled in a terraced house in Catford, and in time Spike found himself working in a tobacco factory for thirteen shillings a week. He bought a trumpet on the instalment plan and joined a dance band in Brockley. In between gigs he did a variety of jobs after he'd got the sack from the tobacco firm for pilfering fags. He worked in a laundry and at Woolwich Arsenal as an unskilled labourer.

In June 1940 he was called up into the 56th Heavy Regiment RA at Bexhill-on-Sea. I can testify to the fact that he was a good soldier and, surprisingly enough, a very smart one, but he could never accept unnecessary regimentation and was constantly at war with the establishment. Come to think of it, he still is.

At Monte Cassino Spike was caught up in the blast of a mortar shell and was wounded and severely shell-shocked. This put an effective end to his involvement in any more fighting, and as I've already mentioned, he spent quite a long time at a psychiatric hospital near Sorrento.

After his spell with the Bill Hall Trio he got fed up with touring, and Jimmy Grafton offered him work as a script-writer. He began writing for Derek Roy – a job he hated –

and for an up-and-coming comedian, Alfred Marks. In time he was to live in a room above Grafton's which could only be reached by a ladder, so we all christened him 'The Prisoner Of Zenda'.

If I was asked to sum up Spike at this point in his career, I'd say he was a half-educated genius with an over-developed sense of the ridiculous and a healthy disrespect for the status quo. Looking back on those days, I find it hard to believe some of the wild things we got up to.

Once, when Spike and I were staying at the Mapleton Hotel in Piccadilly, he bet me that I would not run around the block in my vest and underpants. He underestimated me, I'm afraid, and fortified by several brandies, I set off. It was early evening as I ran out of the room, down the stairs and out through the main door into the street. Fortunately it was pouring with rain, and I made my way around the block with only a few ladies of easy virtue to cheer my efforts and offer me various rewards for my athletic prowess, at reasonable prices. Nobody else took a blind bit of notice, and I padded back into the hotel past the commissionaire who nodded at me in a friendly way. 'Been for a run, Harry?' he said.

When I got back upstairs, very wet and extremely short of breath, Spike had locked the door. It took twenty minutes of pleading before he opened it again.

There was a time when everyone seemed to be wearing duffel coats. Spike had one and so did I, and they were rarely off our backs. I developed a way of buttoning mine right up over my head, so that I looked like Norman Vaughan's 'lion-tamer's father' in the gag I did in his act at Bolton. It became a party trick which I'd do at the drop of a hat, until one afternoon it came unstuck.

Spike, Johnny Mulgrew, Peter and myself were having a meal in a rather posh café in Golders Green, and after we'd eaten, the other lads said, 'Go on, Harry, do your duffel coat bit.'

In a trice I buttoned my coat over my head in my now familiar way and proceeded to make Goonish noises from within. I kept this up for several minutes. Then, gradually, I became aware that the place seemed to have gone very quiet. I opened one of the toggles and peeped out. The others had gone, the bill was on a saucer before me, unpaid, and the café owner was standing at the table, glaring at me. I struggled out of my coat, red-faced with embarrassment. Not a word was said as I fumbled through my pockets looking for money to pay the bill. I had just enough, without a tip, and the whole transaction took place in an eerie silence as the rest of the customers looked on. As I reached the door I turned and blew a raspberry, but it was a Pyrrhic victory at best.

Another time, after a liquid lunch at Bertorelli's Restaurant in Shepherd's Bush, Spike noticed that there was an undertaker's parlour a couple of doors away. He promptly lay down outside on the pavement in the duffel coat, with his eyes closed and his arms crossed over his chest, as the rest of us hammered on the door calling 'Shop!'

Mike Bentine was the only one of us with a 'pedigree'. He was born to a Peruvian physicist father and an English mother, and we always claimed that he was the only Peruvian born on the Watford by-pass. He had been educated at Eton and the Lycée in Paris, spoke several languages fluently, and claimed a degree in nuclear physics. During the war he had trained as a pilot, but a vaccination which went wrong affected his eyesight and instead he became an Intelligence Officer with a Polish Squadron.

He seemed to be capable of anything – he was an accomplished swordsman, a fine shot with a pistol, an expert with the long bow, a very good artist and an excellent cook. We could never fault his prowess in these areas, although we frequently tried, and if sometimes we became suspicious of this wealth of talent we had to accept the fact that he was indeed an extremely versatile young man.

His contribution to our evenings of comedy experimentation at Jimmy's pub was immense, and his enthusiasm was boundless. Yet there was the beginning of a rift developing between Spike and himself about who had thought up some particular piece of funny business, or how a theme should be developed. It wasn't a yawning chasm, because they both respected each other, but there were differences between them. There was a whiff of the establishment about Bentine which I found fascinating, but Spike was, perhaps, less attracted by it.

Something else to bear in mind was the fact that Mike was the first of the four of us to make an impression in the West End. He scored a big success in *Starlight Roof* at the Hippodrome, with an act in which he used the back of a chair as a prop. It was a brilliant performance in which he used this most unlikely piece of carpentry as a comb, a flag, a plough and God knows what else. Peter and I were now making some headway in the halls, but Spike had not yet worked out a solo act for himself.

Mike was always good company, so when one Sunday, early on in our acquaintance, he invited me to spend the day with him at the house of a recently acquired girl-friend, I accepted readily.

She lived with her family in the outer suburbs of London, and as neither of us had a car, we took the train. It was a lovely summer afternoon, and the house was quite grand. The company consisted of the girl's mother and father and an aunt, who were all dazzled by the brilliance of Mike's conversation.

Throughout a beautifully cooked meal he regaled us with stories of his days in repertory with Robert Atkins, and when it came to playing a spot of croquet on the lawn he beat everybody, performing wonders with his mallet. At tea, which was sumptuous and extremely filling – especially after our huge lunch – he enthralled us with tales of his adventures in the Air Force. By the end of our visit everyone, including myself, was captivated by Mike's wit and eloquence.

Farewells were said, and then the three ladies decided to walk us to the station, leaving the father behind. Mike enlivened the short walk with descriptions of ballets he had seen, and as we walked on to the gravel leading to the station platform, he decided to show us Nijinsky's famous leap as performed in *The Spectre Of The Rose*.

He took a little run and leapt into the air. Unfortunately, the amount of food Mike had consumed throughout the day – the roast beef and apple tart at lunch and the pastries and the boiled ham at tea – proved too much, and as he took off he gave vent to a blast from his nether regions. It was gargantuan, and had it been properly harnessed it would have propelled him over the roof of the railway station. It seemed to me that the shock of it actually delayed his return to earth, exactly like Nijinsky's celebrated leap.

I immediately collapsed in hysterics against the wall of the station, and the three ladies, who were standing watching arm in arm, abruptly turned around and began to walk off without a backward glance. Mike followed them for a few steps, making little raspberry sounds with his mouth in a vain attempt to convince them that he had made the sound from that end. But their retreating backs offered no forgiveness. He turned to where I lay, kicking my heels in the gravel in helpless, uncontrollable laughter, and, seeing the funny side of the incident himself, he joined in the hysteria.

Another ex-serviceman who used to join in the cut-and-thrust of the impromptu comedy sessions was Larry Stephens, who eventually collaborated on 'The Goon Show' scripts with Spike. He had been an officer with Brigadier Orde Wingate in Burma and had seen a lot of action.

This was the cast which was slowly but inexorably heading towards the creation of a comedy show which we hoped the BBC might accept as a series. However, before this happened I had to do more slogging around the provinces and the London surburban theatres.

It was not exactly an uneventful time for me; I was fired on by an air pistol wielded by some lunatic in the gallery at the Grand Theatre, Clapham; a penny struck me forcibly on the forehead when I was playing the Hippodrome, Wigan; and once I had to do my act wearing a dinner jacket and brown tweed trousers. I had forgotten that it was half-day closing and when I went to collect my soap-stained dress pants from the cleaners that afternoon, I had found the place shut. 'I'm trying to set a new trend,' I said lamely to the audience, but I don't think they were ready to accept the joke.

Myra had decided that touring every week with the baby was not really good for either of them, and so until I got an engagement that enabled me to stay in the same place for a reasonable length of time, she opted to stay at home with her parents in West Cross, Swansea, and I would join her there at weekends.

As the year 1950 rolled into autumn, a request came for me to do pantomime in Hull. It was far enough away from my less-than-successful appearance in *Dick Whittington* and I was offered the part of Simple Simon – a much easier role to play than Dame. The subject was *Jack and The Beanstalk* and the venue was the New Theatre, which showed straight plays for the rest of the year. I accepted the offer with alacrity and Myra was delighted at the prospect of the three of us being together for a good spell.

The digs we had booked into must have slipped through the net of the Actors' Church Union because they were not very good. When we lit a fire in our room the smoke always blew back down the chimney and nearly suffocated us. We decided to move to a very nice little hotel called the White House, which we could not really afford, but we were worried about Jennifer's health. It was a great idea as it turned out, and we were very well looked after. Myra's parents came up from Swansea to spend Christmas with us, and they were able to give Myra a break from looking after the baby.

The pantomime was much easier than *Dick Whittington* and I had no trouble learning the part of Simple Simon. The Dame was played properly and traditionally by Alan Modley, the brother of the more famous Yorkshire comedian, Albert Modley. Gordon Norville, who was a rather camp Demon

King, also produced the pantomime. The Principal Boy was Valerie Ashton, who was later to marry Sid James, and the Princess was a lady called Primrose Gordon. The Giant was a large gentleman who made 'Fee-fi-fo-fum' seem like an invitation. It was a nice, happy show and I can only remember one instance when something went wrong with the production.

In the prologue to the show, Gordon – dressed all in green, with sequins stuck to his eyelids – had to make a speech, lit by a green spotlight, about what he was going to do to Simple Simon and his mother when he caught them. At the conclusion of the diatribe he disappeared through a trapdoor in the stage and then up went the lights and on came the full company to sing the opening chorus.

One night something went wrong with the trapdoor and Gordon only disappeared up to his shoulders. The lights went up and revealed him swearing away at the stage-manager while the boys and girls of the chorus danced around him. Suddenly the trap moved again, and he struck his chin on the stage as he finally dropped out of sight. His cursing could be heard throughout the theatre.

While we were in Hull, Len Lightowler, who had been in the 'Sicily Billies' concert party, came with his wife, Maude, to see the show, and Myra and I went over to Leeds to stay with them on a couple of weekends.

I went back to the hotel one night to find Jennifer drunk. She had somehow got into a room where a private cocktail party was being held and had gone around drinking out of the sherry glasses on the tables. I must say that she slept well that night, and for the first time in weeks, so did we.

Those Crazy People

On 3 February 1951 I travelled down to London on the night train to make a trial recording of 'The Junior Crazy Gang', produced at the BBC by Pat Dixon. At last the perseverance of Spike, Jimmy and the rest of us had paid off and we had a chance to make a break-through in comedy. For three years the recordings we had made at Grafton's had been turned down by the BBC as being 'too way-out'; but now the powers that be had relented.

We were not too happy about the full title, which was 'The Junior Crazy Gang – starring those crazy people, the Goons'. The Crazy Gang, as everyone at the time knew, was a collection of very funny veteran acts – Flanagan and Allen, Nervo and Knox, Naughton and Gold, and on occasions, Monsewer Eddie Grey. They were noted for their shows at the Victoria Palace and for them, nothing was sacred. We admired them but we didn't think that we should be called the 'Junior' anything – we felt we had our own identity, and didn't want to share anyone else's.

I cannot now remember what that first show was all about, except that it was fast and furious and disjointed, containing musical items by the Stargazers, Ray Ellington and Max Geldray. After the show we weren't sure whether we would get a series or not.

Meanwhile, on the theatrical side of my career, I was

taken up by George and Alfred Black, the sons of the great impresario George Black, who had controlled the gigantic Moss General Theatre Corporation during the 1930s and the war period. They had their father's flair for putting on shows, and as ex-servicemen themselves, they had a soft spot for entertainers from the forces. They signed me up for some variety dates and their big season at the Opera House, Blackpool. This was the Palladium of the summer season theatres, and the shows they mounted there were equal to any big West End production. I was thrilled because it meant that Myra and Jennifer could have a good long holiday by the seaside with all expenses paid, so to speak. The show was to be called *Happy Go Lucky* and would run from early summer until the Blackpool lights were switched on. The stars of the show were Vera Lynn, George and Bert Bernard, the American mime artists, and Jack Radcliffe, a Scottish comedian who specialized in 'old men' parts. There was also the spectacular Jimmy Currie's Waterfalls – a scene which involved thousands of gallons of water. How the stage was not flooded every night I'll never know.

In between variety dates and the opening of the summer show, I did quite a lot of broadcasts, including 'Variety Bandbox', 'Welsh Rarebit' and 'Music Hall'. Then came the news that Spike, Peter, Mike and I had been waiting for. The BBC had granted us six shows, the first one to be recorded on Sunday, 27 May, to be transmitted the following day at 6.45 pm on the Home Service.

On the strength of this news I decided it was time to buy another car, preferably one which had rear windows that stayed in position when I drove it. I happened to be home in Swansea that week and Myra and I made a tour of the various garages offering second-hand cars for sale. She was keen on an Austin Princess which would have knocked me back £900, but, with uncharacteristic caution, I settled for an Austin Ten for about £300. At last I was mobile – no more waiting for trains on draughty stations – I could head for home as soon as my week's work was finished. The car was in good condition and was sturdy enough to accept the large cabin trunk which carried all my clothes.

It was in this magnificent vehicle that I set out for the first recording of the new BBC comedy series, which was to be at the Aeolian Hall, Bond Street. I was no stranger to the place, having previously broadcast many programmes from the studio. For the rest of the series I had to drive down to London from Blackpool on the Saturday night to arrive in time for the Sunday morning rehearsal, which prompted the rest of the cast to refer to me as 'he who drives through the night'.

When I arrived I was greeted by our producer, Dennis Main Wilson, who was to collect a fine crop of stomach ulcers as time went by as the result of trying to handle the four of us. Pat Dixon, having set up the pilot programme, was content to let Dennis take over the actual series. I think we began the first read-through of the script at about 10.30 am. This was an exciting moment for us and we were all in a state of near hysteria, laughing at lines in the script whether or not they were funny. It was the first time I had seen any of the show written down because I had been travelling around the country so much, but it didn't take us long to get a rhythm going. We had become used to each other's timing during the sessions at Jimmy's pub, and the first signs of the almost extra-sensory perception we were later to develop began to show.

The 'warm-up' for the show consisted of a string of mad routines. I came on and began to sing 'Falling In Love With Love' accompanied by Ray Ellington's pianist, Dick Katz, and as soon as I had sung a few bars Peter came on, removed my braces and walked off the stage with them. As I continued with the song, Spike made an entrance and, for no reason, took an exaggerated bow. I then sang the final top notes, stepped forward, and pulled his trousers down.

Then there was a bit of a jam session with the Ellington Quartet and Peter on drums and Spike on trumpet. When the red light flashed, on came Andrew Timothy, the regular BBC announcer, to tell the audience that the recording was about to begin. Tim, as everybody called him, had been a chaplain in the 'Para' brigade, wore a monocle and looked absolutely fed up with the whole business.

I remember little about the show itself, but in a book by Alfred Draper called *The Story Of The Goons* (Everest Books, 1976) he recalls that we did a sketch about BRM, the racing car made in Britain, which was a target for many jokes.

Bentine, as a Grand Prix entrepreneur, says to Sellers, 'Here's five thousand pounds. I want you to go to Italy and bring back the finest motoring brains that money can buy.'

Peter races away on a sound effect, and Mike remarks, 'Three weeks later he arrived back with a glass jar. In it were the finest motoring brains that money could buy.'

In the show we also did a parody of a very popular radio serial, 'Dick Barton Special Agent', which finished like this:

PETER (as Barton): Look, they've thrown something through the door!

HARRY (as Jock): What'll we do?

PETER: Quick men – put your fingers in your ears.

Then came a very loud explosion.

Listen again tomorrow to 'Dick Barton's Special Funeral'.

The show finished with Mike declaiming the following words to the accompaniment of 'Land Of Hope And Glory':

Today the motherland can still raise her proud face to the skies and say . . .

HARRY: HEEEELLPP!!

It was not vintage stuff, and a lot of what we did mystified more than entertained the audience in the studio. I also sang a song on the show – I've forgotten which ballad it was, but I do know that by having to dash from one microphone where I was performing a sketch with the other three to another nearer the orchestra, I became a bit breathless and consequently didn't sing too well.

Afterwards, Michael Standing, the Head of Variety, told Dennis Main Wilson that I should do no more singing on the programme because I was out of tune. When Jimmy Grafton conveyed the news to me a few days later, I began to wonder whether I should continue to sing or pack it in altogether.

I now had a new agent, Frank Barnard, a canny old Geordie from Newcastle who had at one time managed the affairs of Jack Hylton, the famous dance-band leader. He was Derek Roy's agent, and after Jimmy's talk with me before I turned down Lew Grade's offer, it seemed a good idea to put my career in his hands. He had a small agency, he was shrewd, and above all he was respected in the business for his integrity. We had no contract, we just shook hands on the deal, and I stayed with him until he died about fifteen years ago. Jimmy became his partner, and between the two of them they piloted me through the dangerous waters of the profession.

During the year I had played Dudley Hippodrome, a beautiful theatre in the Midlands owned by Bob and Maurice Kennedy. Bob became a particular friend of mine, and he too was eventually to work for me, and at the age of eighty-two, still does, thank God.

When the time came to go to Blackpool for the first rehearsals, Myra packed the car with her typical thoroughness. Before our marriage she had worked in the rag trade, and when she folds a garment, brother, it stays folded. The interior of the car was loaded right up to window level, and on the top of all the luggage, Jennifer was placed in a carry cot. It's a tribute to Myra's expertise that throughout the long trip from Swansea to Blackpool, not one piece of luggage became dislodged. However, the cabin trunk – which I had personally strapped to the open boot – fell off three times.

We had chosen our accommodation carefully, because it was going to be a long season and we wanted the three of us to be as comfortable as possible. When we arrived in Blackpool, Myra pronounced herself very satisfied with the rooms and Jennifer seemed to be more contented than she had been at other places where we had stayed.

It was always a nightmare for a mother and child to travel around the country on tour in those days. Some goods were still in short supply, bread was rationed, and so were sweets. There were no huge supermarkets where you could buy everything all under the one roof – you had to shop around for what you required. It was essential to have a place for washing and drying the nappies as there were no disposable ones then, and prams in the hallway were discouraged in some digs. Myra always seemed to manage without a fuss, and had the happy knack of making friends with even the most taciturn landladies. Except, that is, for the one in Harrow.

Before I let Myra unpack the car I took her on a tour of Blackpool, to show her the Tower and the famous Promenade. It was getting dark and the lights were on. There was a bustle and excitement about the town – an 'all the fun of the fair' atmosphere. Everywhere there were posters for the big shows and famous faces grinned down from the hoardings. Arthur Askey, Norman Evans and Vera Lynn were just a few of the big names who were appearing at the many theatres Blackpool had to offer. There was the smell of candyfloss and beer, and people strolled arm in arm along the seafront, savouring the salty evening air. It was brash and noisy and we both loved it.

'Mind you,' said Myra, on the way back to the digs, 'Swansea Sands takes a bit of beating.'

She always sticks up for her home town. When I took her abroad to Italy and she had her first glimpse of the Bay of Naples she remarked, 'Very nice, but Swansea Bay is just as pretty. Smaller perhaps, but just as pretty.'

Backstage at the Opera House the following morning I met
the people with whom I was going to work for the next few
months. Vera Lynn was in her dressing-room with her hair
in curlers, and was warm, friendly and completely down
to earth. She made me very welcome and introduced me
to Harry Lewis, her husband. The next person I met was
Jack Radcliffe, a smartly dressed Scot, who was to teach me
a lot about repose on stage. If I moved at the wrong time in
a sketch with him, he would actually hit me. It's a great way
to learn.

George and Bert Bernard had been a big hit at the London
Palladium. Their act consisted of miming to records by Bing
Crosby and the Andrews Sisters, among others, and they
were also very good dancers. Bert was married to Zoë Gail,
an English revue artist, and was great fun. It was the first time
I had encountered any American show business performers
and I was fascinated by their stories about Hollywood and
the sexual proclivities of some of the stars. From their tales,
it was obvious that sex was in its infancy in Britain.

They were both friendly and outgoing, but George, I
discovered later, could get a bit temperamental and Bert had
to calm him down. However, on this, our first meeting, they
gave me a warm welcome.

On the enormous stage the hands were busy setting up the
scenery for the run of the show, getting all the sets into position in the flies with cries of 'Up on your short bit, Charlie' or
'Down on your long – all right, tie off', as the stage-manager
and the producer supervised their efforts. This side of the
theatre has always mystified me, probably because I never
wear my glasses on stage and consequently can't see what's
going on. But the very smell of backstage never fails to thrill
me. It's a combination of dust, sweat, glue, size, paint and
rosin, the hint of perfume from a passing chorus girl, and for
me, a tinge of fear – especially in a theatre that's new to me.

Alec Shanks, the producer, greeted me and introduced me
to the stage-manager, Dan, a tall man with a military moustache who, like all the best of his kind, was unflappable and

extremely competent. When I had met everybody it was obvious that I was going to have a good time, and that's how it worked out.

I was actually given a song and dance number to do, and my Uncle George's tap dancing lessons came in handy for a soft-shoe shuffle, with the ladies of the chorus backing me up. The song was 'Toot-toot-tootsie' in a Jolson medley, and a photograph taken of me at the time shows a still reasonably slim Secombe in the costume of a yellow bowler hat and a check suit.

Working with Jack Radcliffe in sketches could be painful, as I've mentioned, but he was a great character actor as well as a comedian and he had a good singing voice. His permanent 'feed' was Helen Norman, an accomplished actress who was never thrown by Jack's frequent departures from the script. What I learned more than anything from both of them was not to indulge in private jokes on stage.

'There's nothing more annoying to an audience, son, than to see somebody laughing on stage and not being allowed in on the joke,' he said to me once.

I could hardly hear what he said for the ringing in my ears. He had given me a hefty clout on the side of my head for giggling in the sketch we had just performed. Of course he was right, but it was a bruising way to learn.

He also helped me to develop a better dress sense. I had always bought clothes off the peg, and although Myra always saw that I was neat and tidy, my wardrobe was not extensive or varied – a sports coat I had bought in Bath in the *Magpie* days and a suit from the thirty shilling tailors in Swansea was about it. Jack had a tailor friend in Glasgow who came down and measured me for my very first hand-made suit. It was a great success, and when I wore it to the 'Goon Show' recording I was greeted with cries of 'Secombe's a pouf' from my colleagues. What I really needed, though, was something to protect my ears from Jack's heavy-handed assaults on stage.

Someone else who taught me a lot was Norman Evans – the famous 'over the garden wall' comedian who was the star of

the show in our sister theatre, the Winter Gardens. He was
an extremely generous man and looked after the members of
his company as if they were his own family. He would sometimes hire a coach and take everybody in the cast, including
the stage-hands and the orchestra, on a trip into the lovely
countryside which surrounds Blackpool. A sit-down meal
would be arranged at an hotel, and everyone was his guest.
Then he'd pick somebody at random and ask them to make
a speech, because he believed that everybody should be able
to express themselves in public.

I was lucky enough to be invited along on several of these
occasions, and Myra and Jennifer came too. For me Norman
offered a glimpse of how a star should behave – with respect
for those who worked with him, and maintaining a visible
presence in the theatre, not shut away in his dressing-room in
splendid isolation, but accessible to all. It worked for Norman
because he always had a trouble-free company and no one
ever took advantage of his good nature.

I found out later on in my career that the danger of a long-
running show is that 'cliques' may begin to form within the
cast – and bad feeling can sour the whole season. Most of the
trouble arises from insecurity. Someone might feel that he or
she is being upstaged in a certain scene, or a song sung by
a supporting member of the cast is being ruined by a scene
change in the middle of it. If their complaints are ignored
they become resentful, and the company may then divide
itself up into factions for and against. On the other hand,
if they feel they can approach the person who is leading the
cast and express their feelings openly, something can be done
to smooth out the differences before they start to affect the
show. Because there's no doubt that an unhappy company
communicates its unhappiness to the audience. The people
out front may not know what the reason is, but inevitably
they begin to feel uneasy. End of lecture!

Whenever we could Myra and I used to drive into the
Trough of Bowland, a beautiful part of the country which
is not too far from Blackpool. Jennifer loved these outings

where we took a picnic basket and got away from the noise of the resort. My parents came up for a couple of weeks with us and so did Myra's Mum and Dad. The Austin Ten used to get a bit crowded with all of us crammed inside, so I used that as an excuse to buy a larger car.

I had become friendly with a car dealer near the theatre, and one day he showed me a second-hand vehicle which had just come on the market. It was a big black American Packard with a canvas top which folded back, turning it into an open tourer – the sort of car which I used to drool over in the Hollywood movies. It had a 'straight eight' engine with a satisfying rumble, and you could have held a dance in the back. Myra had reservations about the colour, but the salesman said he would be delighted to have it resprayed any colour we liked. We chose light grey, and when I took delivery of it a week later I was like a little schoolboy. My dreams were slowly coming true.

All through the summer I had to drive down to London for the 'Goon Show' recordings which were now billed as 'Crazy People'. The option of another six more shows was taken up on 18 June 1951 and later an option for five more was signed.

I used to leave Blackpool at the crack of dawn on the Sunday morning, and I revelled in the pleasure of driving a powerful car on almost deserted roads. My first port of call when I got to London was Grafton's, where Jimmy and Dorothy would provide coffee and bacon and eggs. I would then have a kip on their sofa in their private sitting-room upstairs until the time came for me to leave for the first read-through of the script at the BBC studio.

This was always the best part of the day for me, because I had no idea of what I had to do in the show until I got to the studio. My contribution to the writing of the script was fairly negligible, especially now that I was up in Blackpool, and I was just happy to be in the show. When we met up, we spent the first half-an-hour swapping gags and generally behaving like kids in school at playtime. Then Dennis Main Wilson would try to get some semblance of discipline into the proceedings, which was not easy. Bentine might be standing on his head demonstrating some new yoga position, Peter would perhaps be practising on Ray Ellington's bongo drums, and Spike would either be playing his trumpet or bashing out jazz chords on the piano. As for me, I'd be blowing raspberries or belting out a couple of strangled top 'C's.

Once the read-through of the script was over we'd go off to the nearest pub for a few lunch-time drinks and a snack, and then we'd return to the studio for a run-through with music and effects at four o'clock. Then there was time for a look at the Sunday papers in the stalls, or a nap, or both.

The script took on a new dimension with the addition of the musical links and the sound effects. There was always a 'spot-effects' man behind a screen with a miniature door with a knocker on it, half coconut shells for horses' hooves, a swannee whistle, a rattle as used by football fans, and anything else that Spike or Mike had decreed. In the sound booth an array of turntables were set up with all kinds of records of weird and wonderful noises, all ready to go. This was in the days before tape came into use and the sound engineers had to work with discs – 78s which had been marked up ready for the needle to fall into the exact groove required. Spike would perhaps want the sound of Big Ben mixed with a chicken cackling, so the engineer would need two turntables going at the same time. Sometimes four or five machines would all be going together with the poor fellow going berserk to keep up with all the effects – like a juggler spinning plates on the top of bamboo poles and running from one to the other to keep the momentum going so that none of them fell off.

The 'warm-up' was sometimes funnier than the show, because the gags were mostly visual and the studio audience did not have to strain to hear what was being said. That was the main criticism of those early 'Crazy People' shows – the dialogue was delivered at a tremendous rate and in so many different accents that it was frequently hard to understand. It was a common saying among the members of the cast that we had to listen to the repeats ourselves to find out what the show was all about.

After the performance there would be a post-mortem, and that was when the difference of opinion between Spike and Mike would sometimes surface. There were never big rows, it was usually the interpretation of a character, or coming in too soon, or someone else's lines that was the cause of contention.

As soon as the show was over we'd go back to Grafton's or perhaps Peter would ask us up to his place in Finchley. I never stayed too late because I had to drive back to Blackpool. Myra had someone with her every weekend to help with Jennifer, but I always felt guilty about leaving her. Still, it was important to get the exposure on radio even if the money was not very much.

Every Sunday my dressing-room at the Opera House was used by the star of the concert which went on every week during the season. I would always leave an array of drinks out on the dressing-table with a note telling the temporary occupant to help himself, with the result that I had quite a collection of thank-you notes from celebrities. This was a practice I kept up whenever I played a theatre in which my room was used in a similar way. In 1953, at the same Opera House, I had one note which I still cherish: 'Thanks for the drink, Harry. Love, Frank.' Sinatra had drunk out of one of my glasses! The funniest note was from Russ Conway, who wrote, 'I don't drink, but thanks for the offer. I let the tap run for half-an-hour.'

A well-furnished dressing-room can make a week in variety go much more quickly, and for a run of several months it is essential that your comfort is assured. In the Opera House, I had a very nice room with a chintz-covered armchair and settee and matching patterned curtains at the windows. Vera had made her room very comfortable indeed, and I often nipped in to have a cup of tea with her and Harry. She was a lovely lady to work with and is still the same today. The audiences worshipped her, and she held them in the palm of her hand as soon as she walked out on stage. She closed the show – nobody could possibly follow her.

I used to watch George and Bert Bernard's act as often as I could from the wings – with the permission of Dan, the stage-manager, of course. They relied on an off-stage assistant to put the records on at the right time, in the right order and at the right speed, and to his credit he never missed a cue. Mind you, I think George would have throttled him if he had.

George himself used to give the management a few heart attacks. Every weekend he flew to Paris where he had a flat, and sometimes the plane would be delayed. The whole cast would hold its collective breath until we heard the news that he had arrived at the stage door. He must have had a special clause written into his contract to allow him to do it, but it gave poor old Bert some stomach-churning moments.

The shaving act was still the main part of my performance and I was beginning to get fed up with it, but nothing could beat it for that second spot, and so it stayed. My singing was slowly improving, and the large orchestra was a joy to work with. My previous doubts about my voice had evaporated and I had regained some of my confidence after what Michael Standing had said.

In September, a few weeks before the show finished, I heard that I had been picked for the Royal Command Performance. This was something that I had dreamed about but never expected would happen to me. Vera Lynn and Jack Radcliffe and his partner, Helen, were also to be in the show, and so was Norman Evans from the Winter Gardens. The performance was to be on 29 November 1951 at London's Victoria Palace Theatre in the presence of King George VI and Queen Elizabeth. I could think of nothing else for weeks, and when the time came for the end of the summer season, my regret at leaving Blackpool was lightened by the excitement of the impending Royal Command.

The only time I had ever seen the King was when he drove quickly through Carthage after the end of the North African campaign, and then I didn't recognize him. On 29 November I'd be able to take a good look at him, and he would be watching me. This was the frightening part. Every old pro I spoke to said the same thing: 'The audience always look up to the Royal Box to see if They are laughing, and if so, they'll laugh too. If They're not, they won't.'

I drove the Packard home to Swansea, eager to show it off, and the journey at first was infinitely more comfortable than it had been in the Austin Ten. Then it began to rain, and we discovered we had a leak in the canvas roof. We arrived at Myra's parents' house somewhat damp, but happy to be home.

I stood side-stage at the Victoria Palace on the afternoon of Monday, 29 November, my mouth agape at the line-up of stars. It was dress-rehearsal time, and the stage and stalls were packed with celebrities. Gracie Fields was there – I had once worked the spotlight for her act in Rome when I was with the Central Pool of Artists. Then there was Florence Desmond; Frances Day; Adelaide Hall from the CSE show in Germany; Charlie Kunz, the man every NAAFI pianist aspired to imitate; Johnny Hutch and the Seven Volants – his brother was the clown who had broken his ankle on the first night of *Over the Page* at the Argentina Theatre in Rome. The Crazy Gang – after whom the four 'Goons' had been so reluctantly named – were easing the tension of the moment with some earthy jokes. Gordon Richards, the famous jockey, was in the stalls along with Joe Davis, the snooker player. Kenneth Horne and Richard Murdoch from the radio show 'Much Binding In The Marsh' were chatting together; Cicely Courtneidge was there, too. 'Professor' Jimmy Edwards, my mate from the Windmill, waved his trombone in greeting.

Arthur English nodded in my direction. Vera Lynn smiled at me, and a heavy hand clipped my earhole. 'Hello, son,' said Jack Radcliffe.

The Royal Box was bedecked with flowers, but we had received the sad news that the King was too ill to attend the performance. However, Her Majesty Queen Elizabeth would be coming, and the show was to go ahead. It was a tremendous bill, and included celebrities from the world of sport as well as show business. Apart from the ones already mentioned, also taking part were Stanley Matthews, every soccer fan's hero; MacDonald Bailey, the West Indian runner; Sydney Wooderson, the famous athlete; and the Cambridge Boat Crew.

I had already done my rehearsal in the morning, and as usual I was the second spot comic. The evening arrived – my first Royal Command Performance. The opening scene was from the Blackpool Opera House show and I was glad of the familiarity of the props as I waited for the fanfare which announced the entrance of the royal party. I stood to attention as a soldier should when the national anthem was played, and then went into a frenzy of lathering in preparation for my act.

Standing in the wings with my little table with the shaving gear on, I was reminded forcibly of my Windmill audition, and of that day years ago when I made the lads laugh in the tent at Eboli. Then I remembered that Frankie Howerd had suffered badly in this same spot on the bill the previous year. My knees began to shake as I heard the opening bars of 'I'm Just Wild About Harry'. I said to myself, 'Myra's out front' – and I grabbed my table and walked into the spotlight.

'Hello, folks,' I said.

STRAWBERRIES
&
CHEAM

The Autobiography

of

HARRY SECOMBE

Vol 2
1951–1996

To Myra
who has always been there for me.

Why *Strawberries and Cheam* for a title, I hear you ask. Well, I called the first volume of my autobiography *Arias and Raspberries* because it encapsulated my career as a performer, and for this one I wanted something to sum up my private life. For over thirty years my family and I lived in Cheam. The strawberries? We grew them in the garden. I hope that answers your question.

Now read on . . .

Acknowledgements   xi
Preface   1
The Goons   5
Radio Days   18
Treading the Boards   25
Hits and Mishaps in Film and TV   46
Life on a Main Road   80
Pickwick and Other Musicals   108
A Wanderlust   141
Entertaining the Services   167
On the Highway   181
Pickwick Again   200
Grand Finale   211

Acknowledgements

Just as there is no such thing as a one man show, no book is the work of the author alone. I owe a great debt to my elder daughter, Jennifer, who has had to sort out my scribbled notes from various exercise books and put them in some semblance of order, to my younger daughter, Katy, who did a lot of research on the films and theatre productions I have been involved in, and to David, my younger son, for helping to transcribe some of my manuscript.

My thanks go to my editor, Louise Dixon, who has had the unenviable task of ploughing through the morass of paper and making sense of it all.

Thanks also to Ronnie Cass for his help with the *Highway* chapter, to the Theatre Museum, Covent Garden and to the British Film Institute.

Preface

It seemed as if the elements had conspired to bid Peter Sellers a final, dramatic farewell. Thunder rolled around the black sky, lightning flickered overhead and rain lashed down as we drove into the crematorium.

In spite of the weather there were crowds of people outside the chapel.

'Look at them,' said Michael Bentine, who had been unusually serious on the journey up from the house. He and his wife, Clementina, had decided to come to the funeral with Myra and me.

'We'd better make a dash for it.' I eyed the torrential rain as I spoke.

Mike was the first out, followed by Clementina and Myra, and I was a poor fourth, hampered by my girth from leaping with any sort of agility from the front passenger seat of the Rolls.

Inside the chapel, a small group had already assembled in the vestry. Tony Snowdon greeted Myra with a warm kiss and David Lodge and Graham Stark came across to join us. We were all smiling nervously, making bright conversation, still too shocked by Peter's death to know what to say to each other. Spike Milligan had not yet turned up and there was speculation as to whether Peter's second wife, Britt Ekland, would make an appearance. Theo Cowan, an old friend and Peter's publicist, introduced the weeping widow, Lynne Sellers, and Denis Selinger, who had been our old mate's agent for many years, smiled and nodded in our direction. He looked lost without his pipe.

Father John Hester, to whom Peter had turned so many times for guidance in the past and who was an ardent *Goon Show* fan, announced that it was time for the service to begin.

We filed into the chapel and took our seats. My eyes turned to the coffin, unable to take in the fact that it contained the body of an old friend. Henry Crun and Bloodknock and Gritpype Thynne and Clouseau were in there. And poor old Bluebottle had been 'deaded' for the last time.

Only a few days earlier we had planned to meet for dinner – just the three of us – Spike, Peter and myself.

'It's about time we had a meal together before either one of us finds himself walking behind a coffin saying "We should have had a meal together".' That's what Peter had said to Spike on the phone from Gstaad.

So Spike had called me to fix a date and we made it for the previous Tuesday, but Peter had collapsed that afternoon, a couple of hours before we were due to meet. He never really regained consciousness after that.

And now here we were. There was a stir in the chapel and Spike came in. Behind him was Britt Ekland.

The four Goons were together for the last time. Three greying, respectable gents come to say farewell to our dear friend. Where were the four frenetic lads of the 50s, the anti-establishment rebels of yesterday?

I shifted uneasily in my seat as John Hester spoke lightly

and well about Peter as a man and as an artist. In the pew across the aisle Spike was looking down into his folded hands. Alongside me Mike was nodding gravely in agreement at what was being said.

Then, his short address over, Father Hester announced that it was Peter's wish that a certain piece of music should be played at his funeral. In accordance with that wish, a recording would now be played.

We all sat back, dutifully solemn, waiting for the music to begin. I didn't know much about Peter's taste in serious music. I expected Sibelius, perhaps, or maybe an extract from Dvořák's New World Symphony.

There was a crackle on the loudspeakers and through the chapel came the sound of Glenn Miller's 'In the Mood', an old dance band foxtrot which was completely out of keeping with the occasion.

I looked along at Spike and he grinned back. On my left, Mike Bentine was stifling a giggle. Suddenly it was all as it should be. There were smiles all round again and I gave Myra's hand a reassuring squeeze. I let the music wash over me.

The Goons

We are old men now, we who were the angry young men of comedy – Spike, Mike and me, grizzled veterans cloaked in respectability; Commanders of the Order of the British Empire to a man; absorbed by the establishment; our teeth drawn and our illustrious partner Peter dead and buried, only to be resurrected in a flurry of tabloid controversy at least once a year.

Goon but not forgotten.

It is amazing to me how the *Goon Show* still lives on. Only last year the Goon Show Preservation Society held a three-day seminar at a Bournemouth hotel and fans came from all over the place – including America and Canada. The recordings that the BBC put out every year appear on the bestseller list every Christmas and, surprisingly, the royalties have increased over the last couple of years.

The show, then billed as *Those Crazy People*, was first broadcast on 28 May 1951. At that time the profession was full of stand-up comics who came on, told a string of jokes and finished either with a song or a dance. We were different. The Grafton Arms in Strutton Ground, Westminster, was our unofficial headquarters where the four of us would meet up and get high on drink and each other's company. We were all in the same boat then – young ex-servicemen determined to overthrow the established comedy of the day and create something which would appeal to the kind of people with whom we had served. We all thought that there was more to comedy than telling jokes about mothers-in-law and a funny thing happening to us on the way to the theatre. James Thomas of the *News Chronicle* said of the first series, 'Goon humour is obviously crazy and clever. It will either be loved or detested.'

Our backgrounds were very different. Spike was born in India, the son of an Irish RSM in the Indian Army.

When I first met him he was Lance-Sergeant Milligan, Terence A, and one of the crew of a large 7.2 gun howitzer which had been installed in a gun-pit insecurely dug in the hard rock of a Tunisian plateau. His howitzer was being fired by a lanyard – a rope attached to the firing lever which was used when the gun crew was not quite sure of what might happen. As the sergeant pulled the lanyard, the crew turned their backs to the gun as it fired, and when they turned round, the gun had disappeared.

At the time I was in an artillery regiment deployed nearby, and I was sitting in a small wireless truck at the foot of a sizeable cliff. Suddenly there was an enormous noise as some monstrous object fell from the sky quite close to us. There was considerable confusion, and in the middle of it all the flap of the truck was pulled open and a young helmeted Milligan asked, 'Anybody seen a gun?'

When I was demobbed in 1946, I started at the Windmill Theatre, where I had the good fortune to meet Michael Bentine. He was half of an act called Sherwood and Forest, and played the drums while Tony Sherwood played piano. I first saw him when he and his partner did the dress rehearsal for the show that followed the one I was in. From the beginning we found that we had the same sense of the ridiculous. We used to sit in the Lyons Corner House in Coventry Street and spend most of the night over a cup of coffee and beans on toast, sometimes pretending we were Russian . . . until we picked on a Hungarian waiter who spoke Russian.

Although Mike's mother was English, his father was a distinguished Peruvian physicist and he refers to himself as the 'only Peruvian born on the Watford bypass'. Of the four of us, he was the most cerebral, having gone to Eton and the Lycée in Paris. At the beginning, he was also the only married man among us.

Peter Sellers was the only one of us who had a 'show business' background. His mother came from the Mendoza family, a well-known name in the theatre, and his father was a pit orchestra pianist. Peter was more professionally experienced than we were because he had played the drums in a band before the war. I was introduced to Peter at a radio broadcast I was doing for the Third Programme. The producer was Pat Dixon, a man with an ear for unusual comedy who was always on the look out for new talent. It was said that Peter had recently got himself a broadcast by the simple expedient of ringing Pat Dixon and, using the voice of another radio producer, recommending this new comic Peter Sellers to him. Minutes later, Sellers turned up at Dixon's office and was booked on the spot.

I was very impressed with Peter, by his friendliness and by the uncanny way he had of becoming the person he was impersonating. I was always amazed at the way he could shrink himself down for Bluebottle and then, seconds later, puff himself out for Bloodnock. Yet when he was called upon to do his own natural voice, he was always worried. 'I can't, lads,' he'd say. 'I don't know what I sound like.'

So it was that this motley quartet got together and started stirring the ingredients that went into the making of the

Goon Show. As I mentioned earlier, our unofficial headquarters was the Grafton Arms, run by the very gallant Major Jimmy Grafton, who, besides being a Westminster city councillor and a publican, was also a scriptwriter for Derek Roy, a regular comedian on the popular Sunday evening radio show *Variety Bandbox*. In due course, Jimmy became my agent. Our name for him was KOGVOS – 'Keeper of Goons and Voice of Sanity'.

Larry Stephens, an ex-commando who had served in Burma, worked with Spike on the early scripts and was another character who was tuned in to our wavelength.

For several years, Spike and Peter lived in a block of flats in Shepherd's Hill, north London, while I was living in Cheam, well south of the Thames. It was not unnatural then that being in such close proximity to each other sometimes led to the occasional spat between Spike and Peter. I would always know about it because I would get a phone call from the producer asking me to get along to rehearsals early on the Sunday morning to act as a kind of pacifier when the other two arrived. As far as I can remember, any differences they had would soon dissipate when the first read-through began.

As the second series wore on, Mike Bentine began to show signs that he was not too happy with the way things were going. When we all sat around discussing the show, he and Spike used to throw off ideas for scripts like sparks from a Catherine Wheel and it became inevitable that when some of these ideas actually appeared in the script, both would claim authorship. This led to some friction, and Dennis Main Wilson, the producer of the first three series, did not seem to be able to control us. After all, we were all about the same age and, like most ex-servicemen, we were not too willing to accept authority. We had had enough of that.

I was not privy to the other reasons why Mike decided to leave the *Goon Show*. My Variety commitments took me all over the country, and the only time I met the others was on the Sunday of the recording, so I was not aware of any power struggles that might have been going on.

Looking back on those days, I realize that I must have been surprisingly naïve. In any event, I was sorry to see Michael go. He went on to do great things on his own and was the first of us to make a name for himself.

On a typical *Goon Show* recording day, I would arrive at the Camden Theatre at around 2.30, musing on which car Peter had rolled up in. He was always changing his cars. As I entered the stage door I'd sing a burst of 'Return to Sorrento' in reply to which Sellers, lying in a prone position and playing the bongos, would cry 'It's Singo, the approaching tenor, folks,' and Milligan would announce my arrival with a NAAFI pianist's rendition of 'We'll Keep a Welcome' and a shout of 'Ah! The well-known danger to shipping has arrived. Ned of Wales is here!'

I'd reply with a raspberry and then the jokes would begin – mostly gags of a scatological nature.

Then it was time for our producer to try to exert some control over us (you could tell the producer by the worry lines on his forehead), and get us to have a look at the script. This was the time we all loved best. Peter and I would fall around giggling as we read the script for the first time. Spike would watch anxiously for our reactions to his efforts before joining in the general laughter.

Spike used to drive the studio managers mad with his insistence on getting the sound effects he wanted. In the beginning, when the programme was recorded on disc, it was extremely difficult to achieve the right sound effect. There were, I think, four turntables on the go simultaneously, with different sounds being played on each – chickens clucking, Big Ben striking, donkeys braying, massive explosions, ship's sirens – all happening at once.

It was only when tape came into use that Spike felt really

happy with the effects – although I do remember one particular time when he wanted to record the sound of someone being hit with a sockful of custard. He tried all sorts of ways to get the desired squelch, but to no avail. Eventually, he went into the Camden Theatre canteen and asked the very helpful Scottish lady behind the counter to make him an egg custard. 'Certainly, Spike,' she said, knowing that he sometimes ordered fancy meals on account of his weak stomach. 'Come back in twenty minutes.'

When he returned, the canteen lady proudly presented him with an earthenware bowl of egg custard, beautifully prepared with a sprinkling of nutmeg on the top.

'Here you are, Spike,' she said warmly. Spike thanked her and immediately began to take off the grey woollen army socks he often wore. She watched in utter amazement as he proceeded to spoon the contents of the bowl into both socks. She gave a little whimper and ran into the kitchen.

Back in the studio, Spike had already placed a sheet of three-ply wood near to a microphone. Swinging one of his socks around his head, he hurled it against the wood. The result wasn't quite what he wanted, so he did the same with the other sock. Alas, that too failed to produce the elusive SPLAT he was looking for. Realizing that he only had two feet and that nobody else would volunteer to try again, he stomped off crying 'Shit!' because, if truth be known, that was what he *really* wanted the sock to contain.

The run-through over, we would be joined by Wallace Greenslade, who, having finished his news reading duties for the day, acted as our announcer and linkman. Then the musicians would arrive, preceded by conductor Wally Stott, who always looked too frail to pick up his baton.

When the third series began in November 1952, The Ray Ellington Quartet and Max Geldray came into the show. By this time, the incomparable Peter Eton had taken over as producer. Peter would take no nonsense from any of us. I remember him having an argument with Peter Sellers about something or other, during which Sellers threatened to leave the show.

'All right,' said Eton. 'Bugger off then!' and Sellers, having started to leave the room, came back and sat down again.

He and Spike worked well together. Eton's work as a radio drama producer meant that he was prepared to experiment with sound effects – which was manna from heaven for Spike.

The two musical items from Ray Ellington and Max Geldray proved very popular. Ray was a huge success, not only because of his music but also because of his personality. It wasn't long before Spike was writing him into the script with exchanges like, 'Are you the colour sergeant?', to which the black Ellington would reply, 'Are you kidding?'. During the warm-up for the show Peter Sellers, no mean drummer himself, would join Ray on the bongos.

Max is a great jazz harmonica player. Dutch by birth, he now lives in Los Angeles, where he is a counsellor at the Betty Ford Clinic. It says a lot for his musicianship that his playing on the *Goon Show* tapes is still fresh today. Spike often put Max in the scripts with a Dutch expression or two. He was always referred to as 'Ploogie'. God knows why.

Anyway, back at the Camden Theatre, with the arrival of Ray and Max, we were ready for a run-through with effects and orchestra.

About this time, the pub next door to the theatre was always a welcome sight, and we would nip in for a couple before the recording proper. It was always full of friends of ours and Goon addicts, all of them would-be Bluebottles and Eccles and Neddies. Then it was back to the theatre, remembering to take a bottle of brandy and a pint of milk with us for the musical interludes – which might explain why the last part of the show was always so frenetic.

The warm-up for the show was sometimes funnier than

the show itself. It would begin with a 'jam session', with Peter playing the drums, Spike on trumpet and Wally Stott's session musicians – some of the best in the country.

Then Peter would announce that I was going to sing 'Falling in Love With Love', and while I was getting ready to sing, Spike would unclip the back of my braces without me knowing it.

I would then step forward, having already released the front buttons of my braces, and launch into the song. Along would come Spike, flexing his muscles. He would then put his hands up my jacket and pull my braces out. As he raised them aloft with a cry of triumph, I would get behind him and pull down his trousers.

One night, in an excess of zeal, I pulled down his underpants as well, eliciting a gasp from the audience followed by a round of applause which Milligan, a well built lad, gravely acknowledged before pulling his pants up.

After that lot of nonsense the *real* nonsense would begin as Wally Greenslade would ask for silence, wait for the green light and, with 'This is the BBC Home Service. Tiddly pong', we were off.

The only time the three of us appeared on stage together was at the Hippodrome in Coventry. It was the policy of the theatre to put on what they called a Birthday Show in the run-up to Christmas, and we were booked as the headliners.

I was to do my usual performance – a mixture of gags and straight songs; Spike was at that time still working on his act; and Peter, who was completely without nerves, was experimenting with all kinds of comic ideas because he hated doing the same act night after night. The only piece of material which we did together was a skit on Morris dancers (called the East Acton Stick Dancers) which Eric Sykes had written for one of my television shows. For this we wore farmers' smocks and shapeless hats and had bells round our ankles and waists. For some reason best known to himself, Peter appeared as a hunchback, à la Charles Laughton in the film *The Hunchback of Notre Dame*. We also carried sticks with bells attached, with which we bashed each other in time to the music of the 'Blue Bell Polka'.

One night Spike had a particularly bad reception from a bewildered audience and, after delivering the immortal line, 'I hope you all get bombed again,' he walked off to his dressing-room and locked the door. He could be heard from the corridor outside as he jumped up and down on his trumpet. After the interval, when the time came for him to join us on-stage for the East Acton Stick Dancers routine, he refused to leave his dressing-room.

Picture the scene as two grotesquely dressed idiots banged on his door, pleading with him to come out, our bells ringing merrily away while Sam Newsome, the theatre owner, the stage manager and the front of house manager wrung their hands in unison.

Meanwhile, in the auditorium, the restless citizens of Coventry started a slow hand clap.

Eventually, about fifteen minutes after the curtain should have gone up, a dishevelled and unrepentant Milligan responded to our pleading and emerged from his lair. We went on to do our act before a grim-faced audience.

After the performance, Spike was adamant that he was not going to continue with the show, but by the following day he relented and decided to stay on. The only snag was the fact that his trumpet, which was an essential part of his act, was flattened beyond repair and he had to borrow one from the pit orchestra. There were no recriminations from Peter or myself because we knew that Spike was going through a bad time with his manic depression, though I was beginning to think I might catch it off him.

One night, Peter went on stage armed with a chair and announced to the audience that he had been shopping that afternoon and had come across an EP recording of Wally Stott's orchestra playing a selection of Christmas songs. 'Having heard it,' he said, 'I was so delighted that I thought I'd like to share it with you.' He then gestured to the electrician in the sound box, whom he had previously briefed, and the theatre speakers resounded to a spirited rendering of 'God Rest You Merry Gentlemen'.

Peter then sat down centre stage on the chair that he had brought on, and rocked and swayed to the music, a beatific smile on his face.

The first side of the record completed, Peter stood up clapping, and the long-suffering folk out front joined in half-heartedly. 'I knew you'd like it!' he said, beaming at them. 'Let's have the other side.' And he sat down again as the Christmas music continued. When the EP was finished, he just picked up his chair and walked off with a cheery wave. I then had to follow this piece of stage magic with a slightly hysterical rendering of 'Bless This House'. This house was not very pleased.

Chaotic though it was, I thoroughly enjoyed the weeks in Coventry in the company of my anarchic friends – though I think the theatre management was glad to see the back of us.

The last *Goon Show* proper – 'The Last Smoking Seagoon' – went out in January 1960. But, twelve years later, in 1972, we were summoned back to record a special show as part of the BBC Silver Jubilee celebrations. The *Last Goon Show of All* was transmitted on 5 October 1972.

When we got together for the recording, which was done at our favourite studio, the Camden Theatre, we had not seen each other for a long while. I remember feeling quite nervous about the show and I wondered whether the old chemistry between us would still be there.

When I arrived at the theatre, I was greeted by John Browell, the producer of the last couple of series back in late

1959 and 1960.

'They're in the back room,' he said, referring to the small studio at the side of the theatre where we used to do our rehearsals for the show. Peter and Spike were indeed already in there, and after the excitement of meeting up again and the exchanging of reminiscences, we got down to reading the script. Initially, both Spike and Peter had difficulty in finding the voices of some of the characters. At first Peter could not get the right pitch for his Bluebottle, and Spike had a spot of bother with his famous Eccles. I was all right because Neddy Seagoon was my normal voice, pitched a few decibels louder.

There was one sad note. Wally Greenslade, who had taken over the part of the announcer from Andrew Timothy from the start of the fifth series in September 1954 right up to the end, had since died, but it was great to have Andrew Timothy back for this special show. Ray Ellington was there too, and Max Geldray had flown in specially from the States.

By the time we had read the script through, the old timing began to come back and we were all more relaxed. Peter was now a really big star and I had wondered whether he would be the same old Pete of ten years ago. I need not have worried and soon the years fell away as we tried our characters on for size.

There could not have been a greater contrast between this *Last Goon Show of All* and the early ones. In the audience that night were Prince Philip, Princess Margaret, Lord Snowdon and Princess Anne. Unfortunately, our greatest royal admirer, Prince Charles, was unable to attend, but had sent a very funny telegram regretting his absence.

I first met Prince Charles at a luncheon at Lancaster House prior to his Investiture and it was then that I found out that he was an avid *Goon Show* follower. We discussed important matters of state, such as what was the Welsh word for 'chips' and I asked his equerry, Squadron Leader David Checketts, if HRH would like to meet Spike and Peter. He said he was sure that he would be delighted to do so.

Eventually a date was fixed and Prince Charles and Checketts drove down from Cambridge together to have lunch with the three of us at Peter Sellers's house in Elstead, Surrey, where he lived in some style. It was a most memorable meal during which the young Prince revealed an astonishing knowledge of past Goon Shows and an uncanny ability to imitate most of the characters. I remember saying at the time that if anything happened to the Royal family he could join us, a case of 'Heir today and Goon tomorrow'. He laughed and said, 'It's very draughty in the Tower these days, Ned.'

Myra, my eldest daughter Jennifer and I were lucky enough to be invited to the Investiture Ball at Caernarvon Castle and on the drive up there we were listening to the ceremony being broadcast on the radio. The newly invested Prince of Wales was making his speech in Welsh and I happened to hear the word 'Goon' mentioned. I said to Myra 'I didn't know that there was a Welsh word "Goon", I wonder what it means?' Then when he repeated his speech in English I realized what he was saying. He said that 'Wales had produced many a poet, tragedian and a most memorable Goon.' I nearly drove the car off the road.

'I wonder what the historians of the future will make of that?' I said proudly.

'Never mind about them,' said Myra. 'Keep your eyes on the road.' Phlegmatic some Welsh people are indeed.

When we arrived at the Castle we found ourselves in the midst of hundreds of Welsh singers and I sang myself hoarse with my mates Geraint Evans and Stuart Burrows. It was a night to remember but I'm afraid that I imbibed a little too much Welsh ale and I honestly cannot do so. Myra said I enjoyed myself and I'll take her word for it. It was a good job I didn't have to drive home until the next morning.

The next day I sent a cable to HRH in Malta saying

'Thanks for the free plug. Milligan and Sellers are clamouring for Welsh citizenship.' He took the time to write a very funny letter in reply which I shall be proud to pass on to my children.

Back in 1951 we had been four young comics determined to change the face of comedy one way or another – iconoclasts and rebels, chopping away at the feet of the establishment of which we were now a part. It is a typical characteristic of the British hierarchy that it absorbs its rebels and makes them respectable. Makarios in Cyprus and Jomo Kenyatta both came to power after leading revolutions. Milligan might yet be Prime Minister.

The *Last Goon Show of All* went down extremely well with the studio audience, and the appearance of favourite characters such as Bluebottle and Eccles was greeted with rapturous applause. But, to be honest, it was by no means a vintage show, and the presence of Royalty out front lent a kind of reverence to what should have been an irreverent occasion.

However, it was great to be back in harness again working with two wayward geniuses. It was a pity that Mike Bentine had not been invited back for this last show. As a founder member of the Goons, he should have been with us at the finish.

Radio Days

I was involved in a lot of radio programmes in the early fifties of which *Welsh Rarebit* was one. This was produced by Mac Jones and came from Corey Hall in Cardiff. The closing song of the programme was 'We'll Keep a Welcome' which eventually became part of my stage repertoire.

There were two radio series in those days which also helped my career. They were produced by Pat Dixon who pioneered the *Goon Show* and were very advanced comedy shows for their time. One was called *Listen My Children* and the other was *Third Division*, both containing material by Muir and Norden.

I joined the cast of *Educating Archie* in 1953. The radio series featured the ventriloquist Peter Brough and his dummy Archie Andrews, and I took over the role of Archie's tutor from Tony Hancock. It was an amazingly popular show at the time – especially considering that the central character was a wooden doll!

Edgar Bergen had broken new ground in America when he did a radio programme with his famous dummies Charlie McCarthy and Mortimer Snerd. (Incidentally, the voice of

Mortimer Snerd became much imitated in radio programmes as the quintessential 'idiot', and was adopted by Spike in a slightly different form for his Eccles character in the *Goon Show*.) However, a strong cast had been built up around Archie. Max Bygraves and Julie Andrews were in the first series, which was written by Eric Sykes and Sid Colin. Tony Hancock had joined the team for the second series as Archie's tutor, and started to make a big name for himself. Beryl Reid, Hattie Jacques and myself were the newcomers to the team, and I stayed until the end of the fourth series in April 1954. I was also doing the *Goon Show* during most of this time, rehearsing and recording both programmes on the same Sunday. In between times I managed to squeeze in an hour's singing lesson.

Eric, Max and I became great mates – we had all been in the services and had the same sense of humour, which was not always shared by Peter Brough.

I remember one particular Sunday when the three of us came back late from our lunch break. We had been held up in a restaurant around the corner from the Paris Cinema in Lower Regent Street where we recorded the show. Brough was furious with us and gave us a good ticking off, which we resented because the delay was not our fault. We sulked a bit and then decided that we would somehow get our own back on the following Sunday.

I don't remember exactly whose idea it was to play a trick on Brough by doing something to Archie when his master wasn't looking, but I think it was Eric's.

Peter's usual routine was to walk on stage first from behind the curtains which hid the cast from the audience, leaving Archie sitting on a stool to await being picked up and presented to his fans out front. This meant that we had the dummy to ourselves for a minute or two while Peter started the warm-up. Max had brought a red rubber glove from home, and we quickly stuffed it into Archie's little trousers, opening the buttons on his flies and leaving one finger sticking out. We had just finished doing this when Peter came back behind the curtains to snatch up the now tumescent little Archie, not noticing that he had been tampered with.

We waited for the reaction from the audience.

'Hello, Archie,' said Peter, his lips moving behind his cigar as he settled the dummy on his knee.

There was a moment of shocked silence as the audience took in Archie's condition. This was followed by some stifled laughter and a shriek from Peter when he discovered what had been done to his dummy. He raced back to the safety of the curtains, red-faced with embarrassment. It was obvious to him who the culprits were, but to give him his credit he took the joke very well.

Peter might not have had a great sense of humour, but he did have a good sense of injustice. During the series I had been given a song to sing in each programme, which meant that I had to leave the microphone into which I spoke my dialogue and rush over to another one near the orchestra for the song. Quite often this left me out of breath at the beginning of the song with the consequence that I occasionally strayed off the note. This was the cause of some complaints from listeners with finer-tuned musical sensibilities than I possessed and led to the Head of BBC Radio Variety, Michael Standing, banning me from singing solos in future shows.

To his eternal credit, Peter stood up for me and through his musical associate, Wally Ridley, who was then the recording manager of HMV, I was introduced to the man who ultimately saved my singing career – Manlio di Veroli, an Italian singing teacher.

Manlio took my voice apart like an expert mechanic strips down an engine. He lived in a flat at the back of Marble Arch and had a remarkable history. He had trained at the Academy of St Cecilia in Rome at the same time as Gigli. As a very young boy he had met Verdi, and he had been chorus master for

Puccini. He employed the famous bel-canto technique, using the diaphragm as a bellows, giving the singer greater control over his voice, carrying the sound up through the chest and into the head cavities and preventing too much strain on the vocal chords.

To reach Manlio's flat, I had to climb a very steep staircase, at the top of which was a door that led into his studio, where a grand piano filled the room. There were dozens of photographs on top of the piano, all signed by famous singers – Chaliapin, for whom Manlio had been accompanist at many concerts, expressed his eternal gratitude for Manlio's help; Gigli declared his affection; Valente, a fine operatic tenor who had recorded *Turandot* under the baton of my new maestro, thanked him profusely for his assistance.

In another room, Manlio's devoted wife, Selma, would be preparing spaghetti sauce for the evening meal, and it was difficult to stop salivating at the very aroma of her cooking.

My first task, after I had recovered my breath from the climb up to his studio, was to run through a few scales, and the rest of the lesson would be concerned with interpreting a phrase or two of 'Caro mio ben', an aria by Gluck which requires a tremendous amount of breath control. I would be dying to let rip with a bit of 'Vesti la giubba', or one of Mario Lanza's belters, but Manlio very firmly and sensibly confined me to singing only those things that would improve my technique.

It took years of sacrifice on my part – driving down from northern towns after the second house on a Saturday night to be in Marble Arch for a lesson with the maestro on the Sunday morning, prior to a *Goon Show* rehearsal, and then driving back early on the Monday morning for another band call in another town.

Manlio insisted that I took opera seriously and had a fervent desire to see me on stage at Covent Garden. 'Give up these Goons,' he would say. 'You can earn hundreds and pounds with the voice.'

I refrained from telling him that I was already earning 'hundreds and pounds' in Variety, but part of me wanted to believe him.

'Please don't go cross-eyed in the middle of the aria, Harry,' he'd say, half-jokingly. 'Puccini was up all night writing it.'

I remember him ringing me up after a record of mine was played on *Housewives' Choice* one morning. 'You sang better today, Harry,' he said.

The result of my first course of lessons was that my voice improved tremendously – so much so that when *Educating Archie* won the *Daily Mail* Top Variety Series Award at the Scala Theatre in February 1953, I was allowed to sing 'Vesti la giubba' on the programme. I had Peter Brough to thank for that and, to my surprise, *I* also received the thanks of Michael Standing, who complimented me on my performance. I felt good that night.

One Sunday at the *Goon Show* rehearsals at the Camden Theatre, I received a frantic telephone call from Dennis Main Wilson, who was calling from the Paris Cinema Studio. 'Can you come down here and take over *Hancock's Half Hour*? It's the beginning of the second series and he hasn't turned up.' Tony had apparently walked out following a disagreement with the management of a show he was appearing in at the Adelphi and couldn't be found anywhere. Dennis, who was the producer of the Hancock show, had already spoken to my agent and to the producer of the *Goon Show*, both of whom had agreed to alter the rehearsal schedules to accommodate my doing the two shows.

I knew Tony Hancock well, but I also knew that his timing and delivery were different from mine, and before I read the Ray Galton and Alan Simpson script I was afraid that it might not work as well with me in a role that had been tailor made for Tony. As it turned out, the script was so beautifully written and the supporting cast of Sid James, Bill Kerr and Kenneth Williams was so strong in performance that anyone could have done it.

I did two more shows – this time with scripts written for me – and I was enjoying myself in the part, although it was still announced as '*Hancock's Half Hour* featuring Harry Secombe'.

On the Monday following the broadcast of the third programme, Tony unexpectedly appeared at the stage door of a theatre I was playing in Shrewsbury. He came into my dressing-room and apologized for his absence. I didn't think it was right to ask him where he'd been and he didn't offer any explanation. After he had thanked me for holding the fort he drove off in his green Jaguar.

The following Sunday, Galton and Simpson wrote a special opening piece in which I handed over to Tony – and away he went.

It was a real pleasure to perform those three scripts and when, after the second one, Dennis Main Wilson hinted that perhaps I could take over the series, I admit I was tempted. But Tony was an old friend and I had enough on my plate with the *Goon Show*, so that was that.

Anyone who does a job of work and at the end of the day has nothing tangible to show for it, apart from his salary, has every reason to feel insecure. This is perhaps particularly true of show business – you can't frame applause, you can't place cheers on your mantelpiece and you can't plant a chuckle in a pot and expect it to raise laughs. All the average comic is left with at the end of his career are some yellowing newspaper cuttings, perhaps an LP or two and a couple of lines in *The Stage* obituary column. But, if he is one of the few greats, he leaves behind a legacy of laughter when he has gone, especially, it seems, if there was an element of tragedy in his life.

Tony Hancock was one of those rare ones who are bedevilled by success. He was never completely happy in the

Variety theatre; the strain of repeating the same performance night after night and trying to invest it with apparent spontaneity was more than he could bear. His timing and delivery were never better than when he was doing something fresh – creating and not recreating. That was why he took to television so well, it took him from the treadmill of the music hall and gave him new situations in which to work his magic.

Of the rampaging, drunken, self-destroying Hancock depicted in so many stories, I knew very little. I had drunk with him and been drunk with him in the days when we were both young and inexperienced comics fresh from the services, but it was all good-natured tippling then. The truth we were searching for wasn't far away – it was there in the bottom of the glass.

The time I remember Tony with most affection was when we were playing on the same bill at Feldman's Theatre, Blackpool in April 1949. I was doing my shaving act, in which I simply demonstrated the different ways people shave, and Tony was doing his Gaumont British News impressions and some hesitant patter. On the opening night – Monday 11 April – I was rushed to the manager's office to receive a telephone call telling me that Myra had just given birth to our baby daughter, Jennifer. I waited until Tony came off and told him the news. 'We'll celebrate, lad!' he cried.

With twelve shillings between us and it being too late to get to the pub, we ended up in a fish and chip shop with rock salmon and Tizer. Later, we wandered down to the sea front and argued about what we would do with the world now we had fought to save it, leaning over the iron bars of the promenade, looking into the dark sea and seeing only brightness.

I will always think of Tony Hancock as he was then – pristine and shining with ambition at the threshold of his career. The demands of his profession shaped him, ground him down and eventually killed him, but he served it well.

If anyone paid dearly for his laughs, it was the lad himself.

Treading the Boards

'I'm going fishing, love,' I said to Myra.

'Be careful on those rocks, now.'

'Don't worry,' I replied. 'I'm wearing my guaranteed non-slip American sports shoes.'

This exchange – somewhat fateful as it turned out – took place at the Ariel Sands Hotel in Bermuda at Easter in 1956. Myra and I had just come back from New York where I had been appearing on the *Ed Sullivan Show*. It had been a hectic time, so we were spending a few quiet days in Bermuda on the way back to London and my first starring role at the Palladium in *Rocking the Town*.

'Relax and enjoy yourselves,' was the advice of my agent, Jimmy Grafton.

I had read somewhere that fishing was a great way to relax, and according to the Ariel Sands' brochure there was great sport to be had off the rocks in front of the hotel.

And so it was with great expectations that I sallied forth from our bungalow, festooned with fishing equipment and head held high – which turned out to be a mistake, because I tripped over a large piece of coral. The sight of a corpulent tourist sprawled on the sand was too much for a group of local children who began jumping around with glee. After I had managed to sort myself out, they decided to follow me and see what further entertainment was in store.

I was reminded of the time on the beach at Cap d'Antibes when I was mistaken for ex-King Farouk, who happened to be staying in the area. Some French kids elected to walk behind me, pointing and giggling, until I turned around and gave them a fruity raspberry. This unregal action convinced them that I was not the man they thought I was and they reluctantly dispersed.

Unfortunately the same tactic only seemed to increase the mirth of the Bermudian children, so I decided to find a place on the rocks which was as far away as possible from my new 'fan club'. They still followed my scrambled progress for a while, until a swimmer in difficulty off to my left, presented a better opportunity for merriment and they drifted away.

I was now able to concentrate on my fishing. The sea was calm and I made my first cast in high anticipation. Unfortunately, the hook snagged on an underwater rock about ten feet out and no amount of tugging would free it. I realized I would have to swim out to retrieve it.

There was a nice flat rock just in front of me from which I could launch myself into the sea. However, the moment I put my foot on it I lost my balance and fell. In order to break my fall I stretched out my left arm, with the result that the bone snapped. It went off like a pistol shot and when I eventually got to my feet in my guaranteed 'non-slip' American rubber shoes, my arm hung uselessly at my side. I could move my fingers but that was all.

'I open at the Palladium in three weeks' time,' I thought, as I trudged painfully back to the hotel, leaving the equipment behind. On the way I met some of the lads who had enjoyed my earlier antics. 'You missed the best bit,' I said through gritted teeth.

The return flight to London was a turbulent one, and every

jolt went through my freshly plastered arm like a knife. The doctor who treated me in the hospital in Hamilton said that I really should have an aeroplane splint with my arm sticking out at a right angle to my body, but I persuaded him that I could not possibly perform on stage like that. So, against his better judgement, he plastered the arm with my elbow bent, and bound it in a cocoon of crêpe bandages across my chest. At least my hand was free.

'Juggling is definitely out, but you can still sing,' said Myra, comfortingly.

Rehearsals for the Palladium began in earnest when I got back. An excellent cast had been gathered together, some members of which I had already had the pleasure of working with previously.

Beryl Reid was an old mate from *Educating Archie* and I was delighted to learn that we would be working together in sketches. Beryl has a tremendous sense of humour and a wicked wit and is one of the few Variety stars to make it big as a character actress. Whenever we worked together at the Palladium, she took great pains to make sure that the clothes she wore were exactly right for the part. She always said that the secret of finding the right clothes was to begin with the shoes. Once she felt that her feet were comfortably settled, the rest was easy. The lovely singer Alma Cogan was also in the show and Winifred Attwell – along with her two pianos – completed the female line-up.

Eric Rogers was the conductor of the orchestra. He and I went back a long way. He was a Swansea boy, and his brother Alan had been in the Swansea Territorial Regiment in which I had served. Eric and I often walked to school together down Morris Lane – a very steep hill which led down from the Grenfell Park Road estate, where we both lived, to the road which crossed the East Dock bridge and was the main thoroughfare into Swansea town.

Eric could play nearly every instrument in the orchestra and in addition to being a fine conductor, he was an extremely talented arranger and composer, providing the music for most of the *Carry On* films and many other, more serious, epics. He was later to arrange Lionel Bart's music for the film of *Oliver!* in which I would play Mr Bumble, the Beadle.

It was very reassuring to find that I had a friend in the orchestra pit, because I usually found myself somewhat inhibited in the presence of musicians, mainly owing to my lack of formal musical training and a tendency to stray from the note when under pressure.

The main supporting acts on the Palladium bill were The Cinq Peres, a very funny French singing act, Gene Detroy's performing chimpanzees and an amazing young juggler called Rudy Horn.

The first time any of us saw Rudy's act was at the dress rehearsal. I was sitting in the stalls with Charles Henry, who was responsible for the comedy production of the show, a man with a legendary dry sense of humour. It was he who, when asked how well *Goodnight Vienna* would do in Walthamstow, replied 'About as well as *Goodnight Walthamstow* would do in Vienna.'

On to the stage on a unicycle rode Rudy Horn, dressed in short pants and knee-length white socks, accompanied, on foot, by a sequin-clad lady (who, it transpired, was his mother). It was her task to throw various articles to Rudy which he would then balance on his head, nose or chin, while he simultaneously circled the stage on one wheel.

The climax of his act was truly staggering. One by one he tossed up from his foot on to his head, six saucers and cups. When they were all balanced in position, he flicked up a spoon which landed in the top saucer. Then, as if that was not enough, his mother placed a lump of sugar on his toe and up it flew to land in the top cup.

The audience of performers watching from the stalls burst

into spontaneous applause and loud cheers. But not Charlie. He sat alongside me, shaking his head.

'What's up, Charles?' I was amazed at his lack of enthusiasm.

'He's not as good as he used to be.'

'What do you mean?' I asked.

He sucked his teeth reflectively before replying. 'He used to use demerara.'

During the try-out at the Birmingham Hippodrome I was experiencing such discomfort with my plastered arm that I made a morning appointment with Sir Osmond Clarke, a noted bone specialist, at the London Clinic.

When he cut the cocoon of bandages away he discovered that the lime in the plaster had burned into the flesh on my side. 'You poor man,' he said. 'We'll have to do something about this.' He then made a phone call to a colleague who came down to see the damage that the plaster had done.

'Try some Mycil ointment on that,' was his colleague's advice.

After he had left I said to 'Nobby' Clarke, ' I think I've met him somewhere before.'

'That's Archibald McIndoe, the man who helped all those airmen who were so badly burned in the war.' He started cutting away the plaster as he spoke.

'Of course, I did a show for his "guinea pigs" at East Grinstead Hospital,' I managed to say just before I passed out.

After my arm had been re-set and pads of soothing Mycil ointment placed between the plaster and my ribs, I caught a train back to Birmingham and was at the theatre in time for the first performance.

The producer of the show was the legendary Robert Nesbitt and to be honest I was slightly in awe of him. He was always immaculately dressed in a dark suit and always wore a tie and a shirt with snowy white cuffs.

When rehearsals began on the stage proper – we would go through our paces in different bars around the theatre – he always had a work space towards the back of the stalls, which consisted of a wooden trestle table laid over two rows of seats. On it he would have a couple of telephones, a bottle of champagne in an ice bucket and all the paraphernalia of music scores and lighting plots, etc., together with a mike through which he would issue instructions to the stage-manager, the redoubtable, unshakeable Jack Matthews.

Robert was most meticulous about his lighting and would spend what to some would seem an inordinate amount of time getting the effect he wanted. There is a story that once, during a break in rehearsals, a stage-hand went to pick up a pot of paint that was sitting centre stage. 'Don't touch that,' said Jack Matthews. 'Mr Nesbitt's just spent two hours lighting it.'

Sometimes, in his search for perfection, Robert would become irritable and raise his voice. That usually got results. 'But I don't *understand*, dear boy,' he would call out in exasperation, and some poor stage-hand would fear for his life.

There was one occasion in the early hours of the morning during a last dress rehearsal, when everything seemed to be going wrong. His telephone rang loudly and because Ros, his secretary, was elsewhere at the time, he answered the call himself.

'Yes, what is it?' he said, bringing the proceedings on stage to a halt.

It was Maude, the wife of Len Lightowler, who was my manager at that time. 'What time will Harry be home for his supper?' said Maude in her strong Yorkshire accent. 'We've got steak and kidney pie for him and Myra wants to know when to put it in the oven.'

Robert stood silently for a moment with the phone to his ear. 'I don't know,' he said with something like a whimper. 'I honestly don't know.' And sat down.

Once I got to know him better, I realized that he had a good sense of humour and was an excellent dinner companion. He has left us now and, after he died, it was said with affection by one of his friends that Robert's first job upstairs would be to re-light the Pearly Gates.

Rocking the Town opened on 17 May 1956 and, to everyone's relief, it was a triumph. I thought the best way to deal with the broken arm was to draw attention to it at the beginning of the show and then carry on as normal.

I made my first entrance in a lift which came down from the flies disguised as a dressing-room door bearing a bright golden star. It came down quite fast and then just a couple of feet from the ground it slowed down to land me gently on to the stage. I opened the door and stepped out to a gratifyingly warm reception from the audience.

'It's always been my ambition to play the Palladium with a huge supporting cast – and here it is,' I announced, tapping my plastered arm. 'It doesn't bother me any more – and I hope it won't bother you.' And off we went . . .

They were a wonderful audience that night and the whole evening's entertainment was received with great enthusiasm. I finished the show with the aria 'E luccvan le stelle' from *Tosca*, wearing what I used to call my 'singing suit' – a white silk shirt and a pair of black trousers. I sang it as well as I had ever done – for Myra's benefit as well as my reputation.

During the applause that followed, Myra turned to her friend Maude with tears in her eyes. 'Look at him up there,' she said, 'and I have to wash his crutty underpants.'

Nineteen-fifty-six was a big year for me, as it also featured the most memorable Royal Command Performance in which I've been invited to perform: the one that never was. It was the fifth of November – Guy Fawkes Night, the traditional time for fireworks in England, but unfortunately the biggest bangs were going off elsewhere – in Hungary, where the

Russian tanks were brutally quelling the revolution, and in
Egypt where the British and the French were attempting to
overthrow Nasser and take control of the Suez Canal. Not an
altogether propitious time to set a jolly dish of variety
ingredients before a Queen.

Val Parnell had assembled a tremendous array of talent to
perform at the London Palladium that year. Liberace and his
brother George were among the American headliners, along
with Jerry Colonna, who appeared in many Bob Hope films.
Antonio, the famous Spanish flamenco dancer, was also on
the bill, along with home-grown performers such as Max
Bygraves, Bud Flanagan, Beryl Reid, Jimmy Wheeler and
myself among many others. As I was the incumbent of the
number one dressing-room for the summer season, I was only
too delighted to act as host to some of the visiting performers.

The number one dressing-room consisted of two adjoining
rooms, both of which opened into the corridor. Liberace and
his brother had been allotted the make-up room, which was
divided by a door from the reception room which Max
Bygraves and I shared. I had stacked enough booze in our
room to satisfy the most demanding drinkers in the business
– of which Jimmy Wheeler was the greatest – but it was all
being kept in a locked cupboard until after the show.

Those of us who had already done our band rehearsal
gathered in the stalls to watch the other acts going through
their paces with the orchestra. Some used the resident
conductor while the American artists had brought over their
own.

It is always a great thrill for me to watch some of the
legendary names in the profession doing a band call, to hear
the banter between the act on stage and the musicians in the
pit. On these special occasions we are all in the same boat –
the famous performers and the most humble 'wines and
spirits' acts share the same nervousness about the
approaching show, knowing that the star of the evening is

going to be the Queen, who will never *ever* be upstaged. With this knowledge in mind, there is a humility in even the most temperamental members of our business.

I happened to be sitting next to Jimmy Wheeler when Antonio the flamenco dancer came on stage. The Spaniard was wearing a very tight-fitting pair of trousers and a bolero-style jacket, and as he drummed his heels and twisted and turned to the rhythm of his musicians, Jimmy leaned over to me. 'One can of beans and he'd ruin that bloody suit,' he said.

We were about halfway through the dress rehearsal when I was called into the bar at the rear of the stalls. Val Parnell had sent for Bud Flanagan and a few other members of the cast, including myself, because he had something very important to ask us. We gathered around him as he told us that he had just received a call from Buckingham Palace saying that Her Majesty had been advised not to attend the performance because the seriousness of the international situation made it inadvisable.

When Val had given us the news, he wanted our opinion about whether or not the show should go on without the Queen in attendance. It was unanimously agreed that a Royal Command Performance without the Queen being present was definitely out of the question.

Val then went on stage and declared to a hushed and hastily assembled cast that the show was cancelled. There was a stunned reaction from everyone present. Some of the acts were in tears – Liberace in particular, was inconsolable, and he and George shut themselves in their room.

Meanwhile, next door, I decided the time was right to open up the drinks cupboard and drown everybody's sorrows. Beryl Reid and Alma Cogan came in, along with Jerry Colonna, Jimmy Wheeler, Max Bygraves and Eric Sykes – who had dropped in to watch the rehearsal. In no time at all the room was packed with people, while poor Liberace languished next door.

'Come on out,' we pleaded, banging on the door. Eventually he came out to join us and I have the bizarre recollection of Max, Eric and myself standing around him and joining in with Jimmy Wheeler as the comedian went into his routine: 'If you have to get a boil, get a big 'un, and we can all sit round and watch it throb . . .'

This certainly cheered up Liberace, but I don't think he understood a word of it. The rest of the evening was a bit kaleidoscopic but I do know that I arrived home at 129 Cheam Road to a grateful Myra and the kids just in time to let off the fireworks in the garden. In the process I managed to burn a big hole in my white polo-neck sweater, but it got a laugh from the children, so the evening wasn't entirely wasted.

While we are on the subject of Royal Command Performances, 1958 was another one I will never forget. It was at the London Coliseum and the artists included The Beverley Sisters, Frankie Vaughan, Bruce Forsyth, Pat Boone, Eartha Kitt, to name but a few.

The soprano Adele Leigh and I were to sing the famous 'Misere' duet from *Il Trovatore*. Mantovani and his orchestra were to accompany us, and with my customary caution I had asked for the pianist in the pit to give me a bell note so that I'd be able to enter in tune. Adele, of course, had no such difficulty with pitch, having sung the opera many times. Had Adele been the one to begin the duet there would have been no problem, but the sight of Mantovani wincing during rehearsals at my effort to find the note, was enough for me to fix it with the pit pianist.

When it came to the actual performance I stood confidently as the orchestra played the introduction. 'Bom-diddy bom, tiddy bom tiddy bom' they went, while I waited for my note. It never came. I waited for an 'A' but the pianist had gone for a pee. Subsequently I came in half-a-tone sharp, but luckily Adele came to my rescue and got me back on track.

I was forcibly reminded of the time when I sang 'Granada'

on a *Goon Show* recording. When I had finished, Stanley Black, the conductor, hissed at me 'Do you realize that you sang that tune a quarter of a tone sharp all the way through?'

I turned to him and replied, 'Do you think that's easy?'

He threw his baton at me.

But the real reason that the 1958 Royal Command Performance was so unforgettable was because it was one of those rare occasions when an unknown performer became the hit of the show.

I was doing a spot of compèring that night and I was in the wings to watch the act that preceded the one I was to announce. What I saw was a young bespectacled lad who took the bejewelled, dinner-jacketed audience by the throat and had them yelling for more. He danced, he sang, he played the trumpet and he told a few jokes – and they wouldn't let him go.

He came off stage to where I was waiting, his eyes wide in disbelief at what was happening to him. I had to push him back three times to take a bow before the audience would let him leave the stage, and Roy Castle became a star that night. I little knew then how much he would enrich my life, or how interwoven our families would become.

And many years after, when he was battling his cancer and appeared on stage for his last few performances in *Pickwick*, and I used to bring him down to the front of the stage at the end of the show for a special bow, there was that same look of disbelief in his eyes as the audience rose to its feet in an outpouring of love.

I feel privileged that I was there at the very beginning and at the triumphant though tragic end of his brilliant career.

Another memorable Royal Command was the one in November 1963. At the time I was appearing at the Saville Theatre in *Pickwick* and impresario Bernard Delfont wanted a couple of songs from the show for the Royal performance which was held at the Prince of Wales Theatre. It was a big cast which included Marlene Dietrich and the young lads who had recently become the nation's darlings, The Beatles.

I was standing on stage during a break in rehearsals when Marlene's dresser, who it turned out later was her daughter, came to me and said that Miss Dietrich would like to meet The Beatles. As I had met the boys on a couple of occasions, I brought them across to her. They didn't seem to be all that impressed to be meeting her, though she turned the full battery of her charm on them. Looking back, I had no idea that I had brought two great world legends together for one brief moment. The show business equivalent of Stanley meeting Livingstone, marred only by the fact that I didn't know all the boys' names.

That was the night when The Beatles told the glittering audience to 'rattle their jewellery'.

In the finale I had to come forward and call for three cheers for Her Majesty. Just before I did so, I took off my bald wig and put it on backwards, with the grey fringe of hair now in front, saying: 'Look folks, The Beatles in fifty years' time!' It went down quite well for an ad lib and must have made some kind of lasting impression because years later at a charity dinner, Princess Margaret reminded me of it.

'Why did you do it?' she asked.

I could not think of a reply.

My second Palladium revue was *Large as Life*, which opened on 23 May 1958.

Val Parnell was still Managing Director of the Palladium and Bernard Delfont was also on the management side. Once again, Robert Nesbitt was the producer and George Carden was the choreographer. The cast consisted of a lot of my old mates – Terry-Thomas, Eric Sykes, Hattie Jacques and Harry Worth.

This time there was a theme, of sorts, to the show. The first half was all about the world of the theatre going from a Harlequinade to the days of Music Hall. This gave Robert Nesbitt the opportunity to bring on some music hall veterans to close the first act. Hetty King, G H Elliot and Dick Henderson – Dickie's father – all came on to do their party pieces and proved that they could still bring the audiences to their feet.

The second half was concerned with the world of revue and Eric, Hattie, Harry Worth and I did a burlesque of *The Three Musketeers*. But the loudest laughs came for Johnny Puleo and His Harmonica Rascals. Johnny was a Punchinello-type dwarf who had taken over Borrah Minevitch's Harmonica Rascals, an act that had often featured in American film musicals. Johnny was a great little man and I never failed to watch him from the wings – there was a lot to learn from the way he handled his comedy.

There was also a lot to learn from Hetty, Dick and G H Elliot. On the first night, as the curtains came down on the finale, all the cast left the stage as the orchestra played the National Anthem – except for the three old-timers, who stood to attention as the 'Queen' was played. I saw this and felt ashamed and on the second night I joined them. The third night saw the whole company on parade until the orchestra had finished.

Eric had written some very funny sketches for the show including the Marching routine he had worked out for my first ITV comedy show. Another idea of his was the Top Graders, a burlesque of an American pop group in which we were joined by Max Russell, who often worked as a straight man in shows with me.

Harry Worth had gone down so well in the Variety season at the Palladium in the weeks preceding our show that Bernard Delfont kept him on. It was the first time that Harry had ever worked in sketches and he was most apprehensive at rehearsals. When I started to give him a big build-up before his act, he appeared from the wings, quite upset. Shading his eyes from the front spotlight with his hand, he called out to Robert Nesbitt who was in his usual place in the stalls watching the rehearsal. 'Please Mr Nesbitt,' said Harry, 'I can't possibly follow that. I like to come on quietly and cull the laughs.'

So all I said to introduce him was 'Ladies and Gentlemen – Harry Worth' and he took it from there with great effect.

Terry-Thomas was making a film at the same time as appearing at the Palladium and travelled in a private ambulance from the studios to the theatre. He had been placed in the second half of the show to give him a bit of extra time. After his solo act he joined Eric, Hattie, Harry and me in the *Three Musketeers* burlesque. Terry was not unknown to have a drink or two during the day and some nights we had to hold him up during the fencing scene that closed the sketch. He was a great giggler and he used to set off the rest of us, which sometimes puzzled the second house audiences who didn't know what we were laughing at.

Very unprofessional behaviour, I'm afraid, but we enjoyed ourselves. After the show, Terry, Eric, Harry and others would gather in my dressing-room and Terry would keep us in hysterics with his 'shaggy dog' stories. He had the gift of making the run up as funny as the end of the gag itself.

Every Saturday, between the second and third perform-ances, I used to send up a bottle of champagne to G H Elliot's dressing-room for the three veterans to share. They always appreciated it and I was thanked most politely and formally by the three of them individually. G H would save the cork for applying his 'black face' make-up, a ritual he kept secret, and I don't think he was ever approached about the subject by any member of the cast. We all had a great deal of respect for the old-timers because they had all been top of the bill in their day. At times, I felt it was very sad that they had to spend their declining years still working thirteen shows a week, when they should have been enjoying the fruits of their labour in contented retirement. I don't know whether they were reluctant to give up appearing on stage or whether they were forced to do so for financial reasons.

Now that I am in my seventies and find myself doing exactly the same thing as they did, I think I know how they felt. Although I am fortunate enough to be still playing the lead in *Pickwick*, there is a reluctance in me to leave the spotlight and retire to the safety of the wings, leaving the stage for younger, more able actors to take over. Sometimes on a matinée day when I'm doing *Pickwick*, the thought of not having to go out and face another audience ever again is decidedly appealing and I sink lower into the armchair in my dressing-room savouring the thought. Then the orchestra starts up and the voice over the tannoy calls 'Overtures and beginners' and, like an old war-horse scenting the battlefield, I am up on my feet with a last look in the mirror and off down the stairs to the stage, adrenalin pumping away, and there's nowhere else that I want to be.

Yes, I think I know now how they felt.

I have always found pantomime the most difficult type of show to work in. When you are sitting in your dressing-room before curtain up, the loudspeaker on the wall relays the roar of the children's chatter and you wonder whether your voice will last the performance.

It's a battle, folks.

When you do make your entrance, the reek of wet knickers and oranges assaults the nostrils.

But a Palladium pantomime is a different thing. The scenery and costumes are always magnificent and most of the music is original.

In December 1959, I opened in the best panto I ever appeared in. *Humpty Dumpty* was the last panto Val Parnell presented before embarking on his television career. Robert

Nesbitt was in the producer's chair once again, and the lyrics and music were specially written for the show by David Croft and Cyril Ornadel.

It was a change from the traditional pantomime because there was no principal boy – well, there was, but he really *was* a boy. Gary Miller played Tommy Tucker and Stephanie Voss was Mistress Mary. There was no Dame and the story was set firmly in the land of nursery rhyme. Four days before we opened, Sally Smith, who was to play Mistress Mary, had appendicitis and Stephanie Voss stepped in to fill the breach. It was a great tribute to Stephanie that she was word perfect on opening night. Alfred Marks and Paddy O'Neill were the King and Queen of Hearts and Roy Castle was Simple Simon.

I had not really seen much of Roy since the night he took the Royal Command Performance audience by storm the previous year. He had been given his own TV show, which had received an unfair drubbing by some critics, and when we started the rehearsals he was feeling pretty low. However, as the days went by his confidence began to return and when we finally opened his routine as a clown, in which he did not say a word, was one of the funniest things in the show. He soon put his TV troubles behind him and from then on his professional career zoomed into orbit.

It was a very spectacular production and the critics were lavish in their praise for Robert Nesbitt. I remember one particular piece of stage magic which I watched from the stalls at the dress rehearsal. At the end of the first act there was a pageant of the four seasons which ended in a fantastic snow fall and Santa Claus in a real sledge made an entry aloft which came alive with twinkling lights as the orchestra played 'I'm Dreaming of a White Christmas'. The effect on those of us who saw it was electrifying. I don't believe I have ever been moved so much in the theatre. Why, I don't really know, but the combination of 'White Christmas' and the appearance of Santa in his sleigh epitomized the magic of Christmas.

Even the broadsheet critics, who have not always seen eye to eye with me, were effusive in their praise. Philip Hope-Wallace in the *Guardian* said: 'This is the pantomime for me. Not for years have I seen the title role so perfectly cast . . .' 'The Palladium's "*Humpty Dumpty*" triumphantly blends pageantry and fun in a way that Christmas spectaculars in the West End rarely achieve,' wrote Richard Findlater in the *Observer*, going on to say, 'The show also includes a brief venture into Grockery by its Simple Simon, Roy Castle, who in ten minutes of brilliantly gentle wordless fooling puts to shame all those joyless buffoons who misuse the great name of Clown in circus and theatre.' Hear, hear!

It was a very successful show backstage too. Alfred Marks and Paddy O'Neill were always ready to 'break me up' on stage, although this time any ad libbing that went on was shared with the audience. Sticking to the script had always been hard for me and the temptation is always there to come out with an extra bit of business, but I never do it with an actor who is easily thrown. That's my story anyway.

After our season at the Palladium, the following year we took the show to the Palace, Manchester, and it was there that I was involved in the greatest transformation scene ever witnessed.

Every weekend I travelled down to London by sleeper on Saturday night and flew back on the Monday morning plane. One unforgettable Monday, the plane was delayed – not enough to worry about at first, and Tommy Cooper, who was playing the Opera House, Manchester, was a most amiable companion at the bar. The delay continued until it was obviously going to be too late for me to get to the theatre in time for curtain-up. I rang the Palace and told them to put my understudy on. For some strange reason my stand-in was a diminutive lady of slight build who doubled as Mother

Goose, and could easily have fitted into the left leg of my costume. Anyway – on she went.

Meanwhile, back at Heathrow, Tommy Cooper was in the middle of performing his celebrated 'Eskimo taking a leak' impression using a handful of ice cubes as props, when our flight was suddenly called. I was met by a distraught manager at the airport and driven like the clappers to the theatre.

I arrived halfway through the first half, dressed in thirty seconds flat and got to the wings at the very moment that Betty Jumell, my understudy, was about to make her re-appearance on stage after being turned from a chicken into a human being – in the panto, that is. I thanked her hurriedly and ran on stage.

The gasp of astonishment from the kids which greeted my appearance was tremendous. The transformation was so great that there was a deathly hush for at least five minutes. And for pantomime that's a supreme achievement.

It wasn't so good for Tommy Cooper at the Opera House, though – his props had melted.

The next time I appeared at the Palladium, in 1961, Leslie McDonnell had taken over from Val Parnell as managing director. The show was called *Let Yourself Go* and I was re-united with my old mate Roy Castle in a cast that also included Marion Ryan, Audrey Jeans, Ronnie Corbett, The King Brothers and Eddie Calvert, the trumpet player who was then at the height of his career.

The sketches turned out to be less funny in practice than they looked on paper and we were taken to task for it by the critics. 'Mr Nesbitt's production has all the zip to which we have become accustomed over the years but *Let Yourself Go* is all zips and one begs to ask "Where are the trousers?" ' wrote Robert Muller in the *Daily Mail*. 'Harry Secombe ... wondrously has breath enough to exercise his tenor voice at the end, but except for a good moment as the fat woman of the seaside postcards he is lost in tedious and banal sketches.' That was what Michael Wall wrote in the *Guardian*, but he had good things to say about Roy. 'Roy Castle is more fortunate in having two long spots on his own and once again shows he is a relaxed, talented and refreshingly unaffected entertainer.' Roy was now well on his way to the top, but I was not so sure about which way I was going.

There is one particular incident that makes this show memorable for me.

The dress rehearsal had been something of a disaster in which everything that could have gone wrong, did just that. There's a saying in the profession that if the dress rehearsal goes smoothly, the opening night will be a failure, so I fervently hoped that the same would apply to our show.

Miraculously, the opening performance ran without any hitches apart from a lack of laughter here and there and, after the finale, I turned to Eddie Calvert, who was standing next to me, and gave him a hug. 'We've done it Eddie,' I cried, squeezing him hard in my relief.

'You've done my ribs in,' he gasped, clutching his chest.

Unfortunately, in my excitement that is exactly what I had done. He had to be taken straight off to hospital where he was strapped up.

It was a tribute to Eddie as an old trouper that he still carried on with the show on the following day, although he tackled the top notes on 'Oh my Papa' with a great deal of caution.

In spite of the bad reviews, the show ran its allotted span and the business was very good right up to the time we closed. The sketches improved as the show progressed and Audrey Jeans, with whom I had worked in pantomime, proved to be a great help with the laughs. Ronnie Corbett was, as always, worth his weight in gold and it was not long before his own career took off.

*

The last revue that I was due to appear in at the 'Fab Pal' as Beryl Reid used to call it, was *London Laughs* which opened on 6 May 1966.

I had come back from America the previous November and was feeling pretty low after *Pickwick* had closed on Broadway. Then, after Christmas, Jimmy Grafton told me that Bernard Delfont wanted me to go back to the Palladium for the Summer Show. This bucked me up no end and I was looking forward to going to work again.

This time I had the support of Jimmy Tarbuck who had made a hit on *Sunday Night at the London Palladium*, Thora Hird and Freddie Frinton from TV's *Meet the Wife* series, the lovely Anita Harris, and another dear friend who had accompanied me on many overseas tours for the services, and Russ Conway who was billed as a special guest. Someone who was appearing for the first time at the theatre and worked with me in the sketches was Nicky Henson, the son of the great Leslie Henson, who has since turned out to be a very fine actor.

This time the show was almost universally panned. Barry Norman wrote, 'I could have almost wept, but I was too busy yawning.' Herbie Kretzmer wrote, 'It's all very glum and old-fashioned.' The *Punch* critic moaned, '*London Laughs* is a disgrace to the entertainment world.' Well, it wasn't quite *that* bad.

It was the year that the World Cup was hosted in England and business began to drop off quite alarmingly as most people were watching the football on the television.

One day Leslie McDonnell came into my room with a request. He wanted to take out the donkey and cart in which Thora and Freddie made their entrance in the first half finale. I didn't think it was a good idea to cut that particular bit, because it always got a good round of applause when the donkey came on. He accepted my decision gracefully and left.

A week later, when the business was still not picking up,

Leslie came in again, threw his hands up in despair and lamented 'That effing donkey is earning more money than I am.'

Being on stage with Jimmy Tarbuck was quite hazardous. I found him to be a really lovely guy and quite unselfish as a performer. But he would never keep still in the sketches, he was constantly on the move – so much so that one night I grabbed the back of his jacket to make him stand in position. When he went to move away, my grip on his jacket was so strong that I tore part of it off. To his credit he laughed, and the audience all thought it was part of the act. To me he is one of the funniest comics around and I like the way he has mellowed with age.

Hits and Mishaps in Film and TV

After *London Laughs* I began to take more care with the material I had to work with. Too many times I had been presented with a *fait accompli* where the script was part and parcel of the deal, and I had accepted the fact. In reality, by this time television had made great inroads in theatre attendances and the big spectaculars were losing favour.

I had been involved in television very early on – in 1946, in fact, when I appeared in *Roof Top Rendezvous* after Cecil Madden had spotted me at the Windmill Theatre.

I did quite a bit of television work after that, mostly solo spots in Variety programmes, but also in a musical version of *Toad of Toad Hall* in which I played the Judge for two consecutive years. Then, when I appeared in summer season with Cyril Fletcher, I played in sketches in a television series with him.

For the life of me I cannot remember all the television programmes in which I was involved, but one stands out as a sort of watershed in my career on the box. It was a show from Radio Olympia in 1955 – broadcast live, as almost every programme was in those days. I was involved in all sorts of antics: marching with a Guards band, pretending to play a trombone with a busby down over my eyes – even riding a horse at one point in the proceedings. The whole show was performed in the vast arena at Olympia with the orchestra, conducted by Eric Robinson, situated on the far side of the hall.

The finale was my performance of 'Nessun Dorma', and because of the strict rules laid down by Ricordi's, the publishers of Puccini's music, the aria had to be sung in the costume of the opera. This posed several problems. I had to wear a Chinese tunic and a round pillbox hat and the time given for me to change was limited to the time it took for the George Mitchell Singers to sing the introductory bars to the aria. In addition, the pay-off to the sketch which immediately preceded the aria required me to be stranded half-way up a rope. During rehearsals I just about made it and the producer declared himself satisfied. I was a bit apprehensive, but being a dutiful sort of chap, I declared that I could manage the change in the allotted time.

Things did not work quite as planned for the actual recording. First of all, in the black-out which brought my sketch to an end, I was not lowered gently to the ground as rehearsed, but had to drop six feet to the floor of the arena, in darkness. Then, as I was frantically dressing into the Fu Manchu style outfit, I was told that six bars had been taken out of the introduction to save time. The result was that I stood in the arena, transfixed in the spotlight, half-buttoned into my costume, gasping for breath from the effort of falling from the rope.

As I began singing the opening bars I felt my chest heaving in panic, and when I came to the low notes my throat completely seized up. Eric Robinson – on the other side of the arena – was not fully aware of my plight and carried on with the music.

I had two options at this point – walk off in disgrace or explain my situation to the audience, the course of action I decided to take.

'Stop, Eric,' I cried, my voice rising a couple of octaves. 'I'm out of breath.'

Eric turned around in alarm and the whole orchestra came to a halt. Rosin filled the air over the string sections as their bows skidded across their instruments, a series of indelicate sounds came from the trombonists as they deflated their cheeks. The audience, meanwhile, went quiet with only a nervous titter here and there.

It was now up to me to explain what had happened – it was make or break time.

'I'm sorry,' I said, stepping forward. 'I've only had a few seconds to get ready and I lost my breath dropping from that flipping rope. Just give me a chance to get my breath back and I'll have another go.'

For a moment there was silence and I thought, 'That's it, Secombe, you've done it now.' Then there was a ripple of applause and some good-natured laughter and the moment passed.

'OK, Eric,' I called. 'I'm ready.'

The orchestra started from the beginning of the aria – without the Mitchell singers this time, and I launched myself into the aria. By some miracle I sang it as well as I had ever done and received a tremendous round of applause at the end.

After the show Ronnie Waldman, who was then Head of Television, came to see me. I thought he was going to tell me never to darken his screens again. But, instead, he stuck out his hand and said 'That was a real breakthrough, Harry. Now you are on your way.'

As a result of the Olympia show I was given a series by the BBC called *Secombe Here*, which was written by Jimmy Grafton and Eric Sykes. There was one particular programme which caused a bit of a stir even before it went out. In those days – the early 1950s – the BBC used to put on

'Interludes' in the periods between transmissions. One Interlude was a short film of a potter at his wheel, another was of a leisurely trip down the Thames in the Maidenhead area, and in order to publicize my show we filmed a couple of parodies of these Interludes, recorded in exactly the same venues, to go out as trailers.

In the potter's wheel film, everything was as per the genuine one, until the clay on the wheel began to wobble all over the place and the camera panned up from the ads to reveal an idiotically grinning Secombe.

For the Thames one, we pin-pointed the very bend of the river near Medmenham, from which the original film started and, as in the genuine film, our camera drifted down the river, in a scene of riparian tranquillity, until suddenly I popped up out of the water with a notice saying 'Don't forget to watch *Secombe Here* tonight'. Of course, this meant that I had to go, fully dressed, over the side of the boat carrying the camera crew, submerge and appear with the notice held above my head.

The current was pretty strong that day and the clothes I was wearing dragged me down after the boat went past. Everybody on board was laughing and congratulating each other on getting the shot at the first attempt, while I was getting more waterlogged by the minute. It was only when one of the boat's crew realized that I really was in difficulty that I was pulled out of the water. By that time I was beginning to think that there must be an easier way to make a living.

Another gimmick we used to publicize the show was for me to be seen for a fleeting moment on other people's programmes. During the opening sequence of the popular panel show *What's My Line?*, as the camera moved along the faces of the panel, I was revealed with my usual stupid smile. I also turned up on other shows as a member of the studio audience. It was all great fun and everyone concerned entered into the spirit of the occasion, and apparently these ground-breaking ideas seemed to work because we had a huge viewing audience when the programmes went out.

The show itself had a surprise ending too. Eric Sykes had the brilliant idea of having a big fencing finale at the closing credits. Some of the audience had been provided with prop swords and as we came to the end of the programme, Eric, Spike Milligan and I fought our way off stage, past the cameras and up through the audience into the street outside the Shepherds Bush Empire where the show was being televised – live, of course. We got into a waiting open-topped car and waved our swords as the credits rolled over our retreating figures.

It was the custom in those days for the evening news to be read over a static shot of Big Ben with the hands at 10 o'clock. When the news finished there was a live studio shot of Peter Haig reading the weather forecast and wishing everybody 'Good night'.

Bill Lyon-Shaw, the producer of *Secombe Here*, arranged for Eric, Spike and me to burst into Peter Haig's little studio, still brandishing our swords. Peter then moved across to the Big Ben mock-up, removed one of the hands and joined in the fight. After we had been ejected from his studio, Peter calmly combed back his hair, apologized and bade the viewers his customary farewell.

This was the first time that the BBC had agreed to let its hair down on television, and the public reaction to all the shenanigans was most favourable.

The *Secombe Here* shows also saw me singing quite a bit of opera, although whenever a guest opera star joined me in a duet, special permission had to be obtained from whatever opera company the artist was under contract to. My reputation for fooling around was well known and I had to promise faithfully that I would behave.

It was decided that I would do the love duet from *Madam*

Butterfly with the lovely soprano Adele Leigh. This was the first time we had worked together, and she was naturally somewhat nervous at our first rehearsal with Eric Robinson and the orchestra, but she seemed satisfied that I would be able to cope with the music. Once again, the copyrigh for the duet was held by Ricordi, and it had to be performed in the appropriate costume. As Lieutenant Pinkerton, this meant that I had to be dressed in the white tropical uniform of an American naval officer, and Adele was to wear the traditional garb of a geisha girl, complete with black wig, wooden shoes and floor-length kimono.

At the final run-through for the cameras, neither of us was in complete costume, we just went through the duet on the set. It was a pretty setting, based on the Willow Pattern plates, with a little ornamental bridge over which I was to make my entrance. Overhanging the bridge was a fake willow tree and there were two steps at the other end of it down which I was to join Adele for the main part of the duet. Everything seemed to go well, even though I was a bit embarrassed at having to clutch Adele to my chest at the climax, but she didn't seem to mind.

My uniform was ready in time for the show, which again was a live broadcast, and it was not quite as dashing as I had hoped. I was about seventeen stone in those days and the jacket revealed more of my paunch than I would have liked. The epaulets had been sewn on to the shoulders, but didn't look too safe to me. The trousers were not too bad, but I would never have been able to sit down in them. The hat, although realistic, came down low over my ears when I put it on my head. 'Keep your head back a bit,' said the floor manager, responding to a call in his ear-piece from the control gallery. 'You'll throw a shadow over your face if you don't.'

I nodded nervously and the cap came down again. 'See what I mean?' he hissed, as we stood waiting for the introduction to start the duet.

My cue came up and I started across the bridge. Unfortunately a twig from the over-hanging willow tree caught under my right epaulet, causing it to become detached from my shoulder, and it hung down like the red tabs on a general's lapel. My hat slipped forward in the process and I stood on the end of the bridge almost blinded as I sang, in Italian, 'Let me kiss your dear hand.'

Adele, who had never seen me in my costume, didn't know whether to laugh or cry when she caught sight of the man she, as Butterfly, would commit suicide over. Instead, she gave a stifled snort as I advanced down the steps toward her.

I was now at her side, looking straight up her nose. The added height of her wooden shoes and the geisha wig meant that she towered over me. The peak of my cap was jutting into her chest, so I did the only thing in the circumstances – hurled it to the ground. It should be remembered, that while all this was going on we were singing a passionate love duet.

Adele bent her knees under her kimono to accommodate my lack of stature, which was fine until just before the end of the song she developed cramp and, as I sang the final bars, where I was supposed to clutch her to my chest, she suddenly straightened up and I found my nose pressed firmly in her bosom.

It is a great tribute to Adele as a performer and as a person that we managed to finish our duet without her losing any of her dignity.

Mine, of course, was in tatters.

For some years I did an hour-long Saturday evening show for BBC Television entitled *Secombe and Friends*. It consisted of sketches written by Jimmy Grafton along with Peter Vincent and David Nobbs, and was directed by Terry Hughes.

One of my most enchanting guests was a young New Zealand soprano who had only recently arrived to sing at Covent Garden. At rehearsals I had difficulty in pronouncing her name properly. After a few attempts at it, she laughed and said, 'Just call me Tin Knickers.'

That was my first introduction to Kiri te Kanawa. She was a delight to work with and was very patient with me as I wrestled with the tenor part of a duet from Bizet's *Carmen*. We were all very impressed by this lovely lady from the Antipodes and it was obvious that she was going to be a big star in the operatic firmament.

Another great lady with whom I had the pleasure of performing was Eartha Kitt. The first time we met was at the flat she was renting in London, where we were due to go through the script and discuss the routine of a duet we were going to perform together on the show.

I was driving up from Swansea for the meeting and on the way I was caught up in a horrendous traffic jam. The result was that I was over an hour late arriving, something I always dread because I am very particular about punctuality.

I had heard tales of Eartha's fiery temper, and it was with fear and trembling that I knocked on the front door of her mews flat. When the door was opened, the scowl on her face as she greeted me seemed to confirm my worst suspicions. I began to stammer my apologies which she listened to in stony silence. Then, suddenly, she threw her head back and laughed. 'It's all right, man, come in and have a coffee.' She had just been putting on an act – and from then on it was laughter all the way.

The duet we performed was 'Sweethearts' from the operetta *Rose Marie*, which was made famous by Jeanette McDonald and Nelson Eddy. I had queried the choice of music with Jimmy Grafton. 'She'll never get those top notes,' I said. 'Her voice is too low.'

'You'll be surprised,' said Jimmy. And I was. In addition to the well-known 'purring' sound she produced in songs like 'I'm Just An Old Fashioned Girl', she also possessed a lovely, clear top register, which completely bowled me over.

In the actual sketch she lay centre-stage on a *chaise-longue* in a sequinned gown with a feather in a bandeau around her head à la Red Indian squaw. When the music began I sang the opening line off stage.

'When I'm calling you-oo-oo-oo-oo-oo-ooh,' I yodelled as I stood in the wings dressed in a travesty of a Royal Canadian mounted policeman's uniform, with breeches which spread out from my hips and finished about six inches above my ankles, and a hat several sizes too big.

'And I answer too-oo-oo-oo-oo-oo-oo,' carolled Eartha in her sweet soprano.

Then I made my entrance. Eartha had not seen me in costume at the rehearsal, and she nearly choked with laughter at my comical appearance. The scene was a riot in the studio and was such a success that we repeated it later that year for a Royal Command Performance.

Eartha really was a pleasure to work with and we became great chums. The last time I met her, she flung her arms around my neck and there were genuine tears in her eyes.

One of my most memorable early television appearances was when I was involved in the first ever live link between London and New Zealand. I was in New Zealand doing a series of concerts, and the BBC thought it would be a great idea for me to appear live from Auckland on a *Cilla Black Show*.

Owing to the time difference between the two countries, I had to get up very early, and much was made of this for the broadcast. A bed was placed on the top of a hill outside Auckland, and I had to pretend to wake up, chat with Cilla and then sing a song which had been pre-recorded.

At that time there was only one colour television camera in the whole of New Zealand and everyone was keeping their fingers crossed that the enterprise would work. A van containing the sound equipment was driven up on to the hill so that I could hear my music through the speakers that were strategically placed around the area. There was also going to be a time lag between Cilla's questions to me and my answers, and vice versa, so the idea was for each to wait for the other to stop talking before answering, otherwise there would be an overlap.

Everything was set up beautifully and the picture was looking good on the monitor when, with only seconds to go, the sound system refused to work. The director wrenched out the ear-piece he was using to communicate with London and bunged it in my ear. The result was that I had to chat with Cilla and sing my song with only the comparatively faint sound from the ear-piece to guide me. Cilla and I overlapped so badly that it was decided that I ought to get into the song as soon as possible. Because the wire attached to the thing in my ear was not very long, my movements as I sang were severely restricted and I must have looked a proper twit standing on top of a hill in New Zealand wearing a night gown and night cap singing the theme song from *The Onedin Line* at least a bar out of synch.

However, everyone seemed to love the fact that they were watching me being an idiot on live television all the way from the southern hemisphere, and we got a cable later that morning from the BBC engineers saying that we had made history.

To be Welsh and in show business is to belong to a rather exclusive club. We all know each other – indeed we seek each other out – and when we get together we become even more Welsh than ever. Our veneer of sophistication is only finger-nail deep in most cases and we flaunt our working-class backgrounds like battle flags.

Stanley Baker and I were great mates and another good friend was Donald Houston, with whom I first worked in a radio play called *This Vale of Tears* by Cliff Gordon. Geraint

Evans and I performed together several times and the harpist Ossian Ellis was a frequent member of the *Goon Show* orchestra.

It just so happened that one year the five of us were recording a Christmas television show from the ABC studios at Elstree and, in between takes, we got chatting about Richard Burton and his affair with Elizabeth Taylor. What incensed us was the cavalier way that Richard was treating his wife, Sybil, a Welsh girl we all knew. It was the time when the affair was at its height, and Stanley knew that Richard and Elizabeth were filming at the MGM studios in nearby Borehamwood.

The recording took quite some time and in the intervals we availed ourselves of the generous hospitality of the ABC management. As the hours went by, we got more and more 'tanked up' and our determination to tell Richard exactly what we thought of him for what he was doing to Sybil grew to such an extent that Stanley made a phone call to the MGM studios. He discovered that Richard and Elizabeth would be in the pub next door and that the media were not around.

It was decided that we would drive there as soon as our recording was finished and have it out with our recalcitrant fellow Welshman. Recording over, we piled out to the car park. I had a Thunderbird in those days which only took two passengers, but somehow five of us managed to fit in.

Together we stood uncertainly outside the pub and then we burst in. There was no one in the bar except, at the end of the room, Richard Burton and Elizabeth Taylor, who was drinking a pint of beer.

'This is it,' said Stanley, who was the bravest of us, and began to move forward.

Richard watched him coming and suddenly burst into song with the opening lines, in Welsh, of 'Counting the Goats'.

We all stopped in our tracks and joined in with him. Two hours later, after we had sung ourselves hoarse and Burton had silenced Elizabeth's attempt to join in with 'Sing your own bloody songs,' the party broke up amid back slappings and mutual expressions of good will.

Outside again, I turned to Stanley and said, 'We never did mention Sybil, boyo.'

'We didn't, did we? Bloody shame,' said Stanley. And that was that.

When I got home I said to Myra, 'You're much better looking than Elizabeth Taylor.'

She sniffed. 'Now I know you're drunk,' she said.

The author and director Noel Langley approached me in 1954 and asked me to play Barizel, the leader of the students, in a film called *Svengali*. It was a much larger production than any of the previous ones in which I had appeared, and was to star Hildegard Neff and Robert Newton as Trilby and Svengali. It also featured a number of the Rank Charm School graduates – Terence Morgan, Derek Bond and Hubert Gregg, for example. Paul Rogers and Noel Purcell were also in the cast, and Alfie Bass and I were supplying the comedy element. .

Noel Langley was an aficionado of the *Goon Show* and had laughed so much at our antics when lying in a hospital bed recovering from an eye operation, that the tears had run down his cheeks and greatly assisted his recovery. He thought that a bit of lunacy from me would help to give the plot a much needed lift.

The story concerned an artist's model, Trilby – supposedly Irish, but Ms Neff's German accent somewhat strained the credulity of the audience – who meets up with three students, Billy, Taffy and the Laird, in Paris. She also makes the acquaintance of the sinister Svengali. Billy and Trilby fall in love and Svengali becomes wildly jealous. Billy's parents also hate the match and try to make Trilby leave Paris. Svengali takes delight in taunting Billy over this. Billy attacks Svengali and is subsequently trampled by bolting horses and badly injured (making Terence Morgan's portrayal of Billy even more intriguing by having to cope with a limp). Exciting stuff, eh?

Meanwhile, Trilby falls under Svengali's hypnotic powers, becoming a great singer under his influence and forgetting her former life. When Billy attempts to visit her at a concert in Covent Garden, Svengali has him thrown out. Svengali then declares his love for his protégée and tells her that if she dies, so will he. At the opening of the concert he becomes ill and his powers over Trilby fail – and she can no longer sing (Hildegard Neff couldn't anyway, her voice was dubbed). The audience give her the bird, she lapses into a coma (sensible girl) and we assume that Svengali's prophecy will come true. However, limping little Billy brings her back to life and the spell is broken. End of story.

Somewhere in all of this Trilby poses nude in the studio run by Carrel, played by Alfie Bass, and I ran amok as the leader of the art students, mugging disgracefully in the process.

The first days of filming at Shepperton Studios were fine. Robert Newton, a notorious drinker, had promised Noel Langley and George Minter, the producer, that he would go on the wagon until the film was finished. I found him a charming man and he told me lots of stories about the films he had appeared in – *Treasure Island, The Citadel*, etc. – he was great to work with and it was a wonderful experience for me to see screen acting by a master of the genre at first hand.

But I came to work one morning to find that pandemonium had broken out. Newton had arrived at the studios smashed out of his mind and proceeded to drop his trousers in front of the make-up ladies. He then chased the lighting cameraman around the studio with a knife swearing 'I'll teach you to paint your effing pictures in lights.'

He was removed from the set and dropped from the picture. The next we heard was that he had flown off to California. I don't think he ever returned to England after that. It was a pity because he had such a towering talent when he was sober.

Newton's replacement was Donald Wolfit, who gave an entirely different slant on the character of Svengali. I'm afraid that in one scene with him, Alfie Bass and I had the giggles so badly that Noel Langley banned us from the set until we had pulled ourselves together. However in *The Film Bulletin* Wolfit is described as giving 'a performance of uninhibited bravura with moments even, of grandeur'. Ms Neff's Trilby was called 'handsome but spiritless'. In other words, as someone unkindly said, 'A naff Neff performance'.

Mercifully I was not singled out for criticism, apart from being described in the 12 January 1955 edition of *Variety* as part of 'a safe supporting cast'.

One who was well down on the list of supporting players was a young actor fresh from RADA. He had won the Gold Medal for his acting that year and had been given one line in the film as part of his award. All he had to say in a scene with me and Alfie Bass was 'Have you heard that Van Gogh has cut off his ear at Arles?' Not much of a début on the silver screen, but it got Jeremy Brett off on a soaring career. All it got from our two characters after the director said 'Cut' were two resounding raspberries.

It was through my friendship with Stanley Baker that I met the American producer Cy Enfield at a party at Stanley and his wife Ellen's house in Wimbledon. Cy was one of the unfortunate members of the film industry who had been hounded out of Hollywood by the McCarthy witch-hunt.

Fortunately for me, at this time – in 1959 – he was preparing a new production to be filmed at Pinewood Studios. It was to be called *Jet Stream*, but the name was later changed to *Jet Storm* for some obscure reason. Cy thought that I would be just right for the part of Binky Meadows, a vaudeville star who was one of the passengers on a plane heading for New York from London Airport.

In the story, one of the passengers, scientist Ernest Tilley (played by Richard Attenborough), accuses another passenger, James Brock (George Rose), of being the hit-and-run driver who had killed his child. The captain, played by Stanley Baker, questions Tilley and finds that he has planted a bomb on the plane. The other passengers led by an industrialist called Mulliner (Patrick Allen) are stopped by the captain from finding out where the bomb is and so they plot to murder Brock in the hope of appeasing Tilley. Not good old Binky, though. I never left my seat for one minute. Brock, however, brings about his own death in a moment of panic – Hooray! Eventually a small boy is persuaded to appeal to Tilley, who defuses the bomb and the plane touches down safely.

Nearly all my scenes were shot sitting next to dear Dame Sybil Thorndike, another passenger, who was an excellent companion to have and subsequently became a good friend. She was a remarkable lady who never fluffed a line or complained about anything. I learned a lot from her.

The only thing that worried me about the film when we were shooting was that the clouds which appeared outside the windows of the plane never moved. 'Don't worry,' said Dame Syb. 'They'll think of something.' But they didn't – and if you ever see the film on television – about three o'clock in the morning as a rule – you'll see what I mean.

The reviews of *Jet Storm* were not too bad. *Variety* said 'A workmanlike suspense drama with some excellent acting cameos by an all-star cast. Stand out comedy relief is

Four original idiots.

Recording session with Marcel Stellman.

Peter making himself heard. (*Press Association*)

With a bewildered HRH at Peter's house in Elstead.

Busking for my TV show. We collected three quid. (*Daily Mirror*)

Last Goon Show of All – three Goons and a royal flush. (*BBC*)

Me, Spike and Eric as The Three Charlies – a strong-man act.

This Is Your Life in 1958. Peter and Spike duelling, with my parents in the background. (*BBC*)

Me as Pickwick in 1963. The hat hides a bald wig. (*Daily Mirror*)

Secombe on Broadway, folks! (*Daily Mail*)

Making-up for *The Four Musketeers* in my dressing room at Drury Lane. David is holding Katy who isn't too impressed.

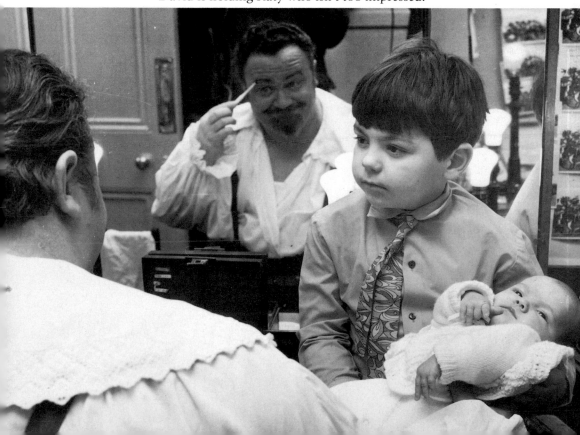

On set for *Song Of Norway*, with my idol Edward G Robinson and Liz Larner.

Myself as Schippel in *The Plumber's Progress*. Roger Kemp watching me go a funny colour as I hit a high note. (*Tom Hustler*)

With Hattie Jacques, Jimmy Edwards and Eric Sykes in the bushes in a scene from *Rhubarb*. The dialogue was easy as 'rhubarb' was all anybody said.

At a Royal Command Performance with Eartha Kitt. Cliff Richard looks
a little apprehensive to my left.

With HRH at an Army benevolent fund concert. Jennifer is enjoying
herself. (*Press Association*)

The lovely Adele Leigh and me on the set of *Davy*. (*Ealing Films*)

Oliver asking for 'more' from Peggy Mount and me. He'll be lucky.

The Queen looking radiant. I think it was something Myra said.
(*Joe Matthews*)

Outside Buckingham Palace in 1963. Andrew and Jennifer check if the
CBE is gold. Unfortunately, it is not.

With Harold Macmillan. He said 'Say something to make me laugh.'
I said 'The Liberal Party.' He laughed. (*Associated Newspapers*)

Tommy Cooper, me and Cardew
Robinson at a cricket match. I was
the heavy roller.

My manager Bob Kennedy in a
helicopter. He was glad to get out.
(*Paul F Cooper*)

My mum and dad at my first *This Is Your Life* in 1958 with Eamonn Andrews. (*BBC*)

My favourite picture of me and the missis, doing a Fred and Ginger impression.

Me and Jim. Jim is the intelligent-looking one.

Jennifer, Myra and Andrew teaching me to read.

Early Victorian-type family portrait with a recalcitrant Andrew.
(*Sunday Mirror*)

Katy's first day at school and my second.

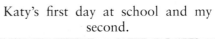

With my dear mate Roy Castle, as Laurel and Hardy. (*Radio Times*)

Johnny Franz and me at a Philips recording session.

Variety Club Luncheon to celebrate my twenty-fifth anniversary in show business. With Arthur Askey, Hilda Baker, Spike, Eric, David Kaye and Jimmy Tarbuck. (*Press Association*)

Signing session for my first novel, *Twice Brightly*. The lady next to me bought two, one for each eye.

With Ronnie Cass on *Highway*.

Dame Thora and me together on a *Highway* from Morecambe. We had called a truce in our Sunday programme war.

Pickwick, Chichester 1993. This time I don't need a bald wig.
(*John Timbers*)

Katy on my shoulders at Margate.
(*Daily Mirror*)

provided by Harry Secombe and Sybil Thorndyke, a most unlikely combination which nevertheless combines like bacon and eggs.'

I'm rather proud of that.

Davy was to be my big chance to score a success in films, something I had longed to do ever since I started in the business. My previous attempts at becoming a film star were pretty poor to put it mildly.

Penny Points to Paradise, made in Brighton with Alfred Marks and Bill Kerr, was great fun to do but hardly advaned any of our careers. *Down Among the Z Men*, an E J Fancy production, featured all the Goons plus Carole Carr and Andrew Timothy, the TV Toppers and a number of small-part players. That too was something of a disaster, emerging every so often through the years on late night or early morning television, forever consigned to that Sargasso Sea of the cinema. *Forces Sweetheart* with Michael Bentine, Freddy Finton, Hy Hazell and myself also failed to impress either the public or the critics. If you happen to come across the title in any of the books which list movies on television, you won't find any stars alongside it. Exclamation marks, certainly.

And so, when Michael Balcon decided to star me in one of his films made in co-operation with MGM at Elstree Studios I was over the moon with excitement.

William Rose, the American writer who was responsible for *Genevieve* and the prestigious *Guess Who's Coming to Dinner?* was signed up to write the script, Basil Dearden was to produce and Michael Relph was to direct. Normally they worked the other way around, with Basil directing and Michael producing. Geoffrey Unsworth was the camera man with a host of credits to his name.

Bill Rose came up to Coventry, where I was playing at the New Theatre, to chat with me about the script. He was an extremely nice man and we got on very well together. The idea he had for the story was one which appealed to me. It was about a young comic called Davy, the mainstay of a family act working in Variety who, because of his tenor voice, had been granted an audition with a famous conductor at Covent Garden. The audition was held on stage at the Opera House but things went wrong when his young nephew, who had come along with Davy, knocked over some scenery backstage just as he was finishing his aria. Without waiting to hear what the conductor had to say about him, Davy grabbed the lad and ran out of the theatre.

However, the great conductor was so impressed by Davy's voice that he tracked him down at the Music Hall where he was performing at and offered him a career in opera.

In the end, Davy, faced with the dilemma of furthering his singing career at the expense of the family act, decides to stay with the act – at the same time turning down the prospect of a romance with a soprano (played by Adele Leigh) he had met in the canteen at Covent Garden.

That, roughly, was the story, but there was an added complication. Bill decided that the action should take place during the actual time the film took to run. In other words, the ninety minutes or so on the screen would be the timescale of the action, thus preserving the continuity of time. This meant that there were to be no flashbacks – all the history of Davy's family act and the undercurrents of past conflict had to be revealed in the dialogue.

Another added dimension was the fact that it was to be shot in Technirama, a new wide-screen process.

The cast list included Ron Randell, Susan Shaw, Bill Owen, Peter Frampton, George Relph, Alexander Knox, Gladys Henson and Joan Sims.

The first week of shooting meant that I had to be on set early every morning, working until late in the evening and so arrangements were made for me to stay at the Edgewarebury Country Club near the studios.

It was my first real experience of what it meant to be a star working in a major studio. Every possible comfort was provided for me – a canvas chair with my name emblazoned on the back, a dressing-room, filled with fruit and flowers, which had only recently been vacated by Van Johnson was mine for the run of the film, and any time I worked up a sweat there was a make-up girl to pat my face with a soft leather cloth soaked in eau-de-cologne. During breaks on the set, tea and sandwiches were brought to me by my stand-in, who also took the brunt of the standing around for the lighting cameraman.

Penny Points to Paradise was nothing to all this, I thought to myself.

When I got home to Cheam on the Friday night of that first week, I sat in my armchair by the fire in the front room. It was a pretty wild night outside which made me appreciate even more the warmth inside, and as I looked into the dying embers in the grate my mind went over the events of the past five days. 'I'm a star,' I thought. 'A proper film star at last. Pampered on the set, provided with every possible comfort off it – this is the life for me.' I crossed my legs and leant my head back against the chair, smiling with self-satisfaction.

My reverie was interrupted by Myra coming in from the kitchen. She had a very heavy cold, her hair was windswept and she had a bucket in her hand. She looked at me for a moment, taking in my relaxed attitude.

'Come on, Gregory Peck,' she said, 'get some bloody coal on the fire!'

Ah well.

The audition scene in *Davy* really worried me because it was going to be filmed on location on stage at the Covent Garden Opera House. I had already recorded 'Nessun Dorma', the audition piece, with the full orchestra and everyone assured me that I had done a good job on it. However, I knew that I would be coming under the scrutiny of real opera singers who would have every reason to regard me as an upstart with no operatic pedigree. So it was with much trepidation that I waited in the stalls while the preliminary shots were taken of the stage, which was packed with the actual members of the current production, *Die Meistersingers*, being cleared for my audition piece. I saw Joan Sutherland and Hans Hoffer, a fine Wagnerian tenor, being ushered into the wings, and my heart thumped.

After what seemed an eternity, I heard my name being called by the assistant director and I weaved my way through the stalls to where I was to make my entrance. The opera chorus had now taken to sitting up in the circle to watch the proceedings and had not, as I had hoped, gone off to their dressing-rooms or the canteen, or anywhere where I could be seen and heard.

Alexander Knox, as the conductor, motioned me to the front of the stage, where I announced what I was going to sing. The actual recording had begun with just piano and then with typical artistic licence the full sound of the orchestra crept in after a few bars.

I was petrified, which was what I was supposed to be in the film, but I was determined to break the ice somehow. So I retreated upstage, and as the piano track started I came forward, opened my mouth and sang 'I've got a lovely bunch of coconuts'. Fortunately, everybody laughed, and the dreadful moment was over.

It's something I have always done, I suppose, to pre-empt criticism – like blowing a raspberry after telling a joke. Sometimes it works and sometimes it doesn't, but on that occasion it certainly did.

By contrast with the Covent Garden scenes, those of the Music Hall theatre were shot on location at Collins Music Hall, where the dampness in the dressing-rooms was so evident, that the walls ran with water. It seemed a waste to me to use a new colour technique on such drabness, though it came in to good effect in a slap-stick routine in which lots of different coloured paint was sloshed about in the family act. Charlie Cairoli, the great clown who was such a feature at Blackpool's Tower Circus, came down at my request to stage the scene and a good job he did of it, too.

Davy premièred at the Empire, Leicester Square on the same night that Peter Sellers's film *Nothing But the Truth*, opened at the Odeon. Spike Milligan declared that he was going to set up a magic lantern in the middle of the square and have his own première, but I don't think anything came of it.

The critics didn't take kindly to *Davy*. Donald Zec in the *Daily Mirror* said of me 'He sings like Caruso – Sugar Ray Robinson Caruso.'

I think part of the reason why *Davy* failed to impress was the fact that it was billed as a 'zany' type movie, over-emphasizing the comedy content, whereas it was mostly a dramatic story. Anyway it was not the stepping stone to stardom that I had hoped it would be.

It was many years before I made another film.

When Jimmy Grafton told me that Richard Lester wanted me to play the role of the Shelter Man in his feature film of *The Bed-Sitting Room*, I was intrigued, to say the least. I had seen the original play by Spike Milligan and John Antrobus and had enjoyed it, but I didn't see how it could be made into a film because the plot was so bizarre.

It was about a group of survivors living a precarious existence three years after a nuclear war had devastated the world. Among them are Captain Bules Martin and Lord Fortnum who is terrified of turning into a bed-sitting room. The survivors are joined by Penelope, her lover, Alan, Father and Mother who have been living on the Circle Line tube. Prior to the holocaust, the Shelter Man had been the Head of a regional seat of government, and the whole society is watched over by two policemen, played by Dudley Moore and Peter Cook, suspended in a balloon.

Eventually, Mother changes into a cupboard, Penny marries Bules Martin and Father is selected as Prime Minister, but is changed into a parakeet and subsequently eaten. Penelope ends her eighteen-month pregnancy by giving birth to a monster and Fortnum becomes the bed-sitting room. The country is eventually saved and Ethel Shroake rules over it as monarch. How's that for a plot!

When Richard Lester's offer came through I was starring in *The Four Musketeers* at Drury Lane and welcomed the opportunity to try something different – the constant repetition of a long run was getting to me.

The cast list for *The Bed-Sitting Room* made remarkable reading – Ralph Richardson, Michael Hordern, Arthur Lowe, Rita Tushingham, Spike Milligan, Mona Washbourne, Marty Feldman, Jimmy Edwards, as well as Peter Cook and Dudley Moore. Who could resist joining a cast of that magnitude? Unfortunately, the nature of the scenes in which I appeared meant that I only met up with two of those illustrious names.

My scenes in the studio were confined to the inside of a corrugated iron underground shelter littered with debris. Mona Washbourne as Mother was called upon to throw crockery at me when, in my role as the Shelter Man, I requested her to remind me of the wife I had lost. Mona threw the pots with such enthusiasm that the poor lady broke her ankle on the china-strewn floor of the shelter. However, like the trouper she was, she carried on with her ankle in plaster.

The rest of my participation in the film was shot on a rubbish dump somewhere off the North Circular, in the company of Michael Hordern, a most pleasant man to be with at any time. We were positioned at perilous positions among the garbage so that as he poured me a cup of tea the liquid appeared to be leaving the spout at an unusual angle – demonstrating the effect of the nuclear holocaust on the force of gravity. I must say that I quite enjoyed my couple of days on the rubbish tip with Richard Lester and Michael Hordern, though I certainly appreciated my comfortable, warm dressing-room at Drury Lane when I returned to it in the evening.

The critics did not much like the film when it was released, complaining about the lack of story line. However, there was one cinema in Sydney which ran *The Bed-Sitting Room* for several months. I happened to be playing at a theatre in the city at the time and the cinema manager invited me to make an appearance on stage between showings of the film. When I did so I was surprised at the reception I received. Later though, after thanking me for coming, the manager said 'It beats me, mate. I can't understand what the fuss is all about.'

One afternoon as I was settling down for a nap on the front patio of our house in Majorca, I heard someone walking up the steps. To my surprise it was Eric Sykes. He had come to ask me if I would like to play a golf-mad vicar in a short film he had written, and rather than send the script by post, he decided to outline the plot to me in person.

The plot concerned a police inspector and a vicar who were very competitive golfers, and the film followed them around the course as they both employed every trick in the book to win the match. In the end the vicar overdoes it by invoking the Almighty to help him once too often and is struck by a bolt of lightning. The vicar is reduced to the remains of two smoking shoes in the sand of a bunker.

The script was very easy to learn because it consisted of just one word – 'Rhubarb'.

It was great fun to make and Eric had dreamed up some unusual methods of cheating at golf. At one point I appear to be walking across the surface of a small lake, pulling my trolley along behind me. This effect was achieved by laying planks just below the surface of the lake along which I had to stride without looking down. I confess that I got very wet before I finally achieved the result that Eric desired.

I understand that *Rhubarb* is still a favourite at various golf clubs for screening on the odd social occasions.

It was while I was performing at the London Palladium in 1966 that Lewis Gilbert invited me to read for the part of Mr Bumble, the Beadle in the musical film version of *Oliver!* I was subsequently signed up – the first member of the cast to be contracted for the film, even before Ron Moody who had been such a wonderful Fagin in the stage production. Not a lot of people know that.

For some reason, Lewis Gilbert was replaced as director of the film by Sir Carol Reed before filming began, but luckily my contract was secure.

It was apparent from the very first day on the set at Shepperton Studios that we were working on a winner. The money being spent on the project was tangible. To wander round the outdoor sets was to be taken back in time. No wonder John Box was nominated for an Oscar for best set design, his recreation of early Victorian London was authentic down to the tiniest detail. There were even real loaves of bread in the baker's shop windows.

Carol Reed was a film actor's dream director. He never raised his voice in anger and before shooting every morning he would sit down with the cast members involved in the forthcoming scene and go over the action. He would remind us of the scene which preceded the one we were about to enact – the previous scene may have been filmed over a week before – so that we all had the right motivation and emotions in mind.

His only notes to me concerned my eyebrows. He warned me to stop moving them up and down to emphasize each point. 'On that big screen,' he explained, 'it will look as if your eyebrows are jumping six feet at a time!'

The first scenes to be filmed were the ones set in the workhouse where Mark Lester, as Oliver, is prodded by the other boys into asking for more gruel. The famous request for more was followed by a frantic chase around the dining tables in which Peggy Mount and I took part. When Oliver is eventually caught, Bumble, my character, had to seize the wriggling Oliver by his ear and march him off between the tables to be chastised by the Governors, all the while singing 'Oliver, Oliver, never before has a boy wanted more . . . etc.'

This was my very first appearance on set and, knowing my own strength, I was very wary that I might hurt the fragile Mark. At the first rehearsal I pulled his ear rather gingerly.

'No, no, Harry,' said Carol. 'You must really seize hold of his ear as roughly as you can.'

'He's such a delicate little lad,' I replied. (Incidentally, he is now about six foot three.)

'Never mind that,' said this previously compassionate director. 'Do it harder next time.'

We waited until the cameras and lights were ready for another take, and off we went again. When we got to the same piece of action, I really put everything I had into grabbing Mark's ear. To my horror it came away in my hand. The props man had fitted a false plastic ear on the boy. I had been set up rather beautifully, but I had to sit down for a while before I was ready for another take.

Peggy Mount, who was playing Mrs Bumble, was a joy to work with. She was the exact opposite of the dragon-like roles she often portrayed on stage and screen. I first met her at the Anvil Studios in Denham where the music for *Oliver!* was recorded, and I was a little in awe of her because of her screen reputation. However, she turned out to be a sweet, gentle soul who was apprehensive about having to sing with me.

The orchestra was under the direction of John Green, a famous Hollywood conductor with perfect pitch, an accomplishment which he was determined to demonstrate at every opportunity. He could pick out a bum note almost before it was played, and would bawl out the offending musician in front of the whole orchestra.

As we stood together watching the run-through of our music, Peggy and I looked at each other in alarm. Even though I had thoroughly rehearsed the number with the rehearsal pianist I was still likely to go off key with the full orchestra, until I had become accustomed to the orchestrations. In addition, the instruments being played were the ones in use at the time of the young Queen Victoria – crum horns, serpents and the like – and not very easy to follow.

It was going to be a bit of an ordeal for me, but for poor Peggy, who was not a singer, it was going to be a nightmare. I made a couple of tentative jokes in an attempt to get a laugh out of the musicians in the orchestra – some of whom I had worked with before. They got a bit of a titter, but not from John Green – who didn't know me from Adam – and was anxious to get on with the recording.

It was my turn to sing first and after a couple of mistakes I managed to get through the rehearsal without too much trouble. Peggy, though, was completely at sea and had great difficulty in picking up her opening note. John Green didn't do much to settle her down and in his exasperation became somewhat sarcastic, which resulted in Peggy shedding a few tears.

Eventually we both got it right and the sound recordist pronounced his satisfaction, but it was an unsettling couple of hours for everybody except Green.

When we were filming the 'Boy for sale' scene, I had to trudge through the fake snow hand-in-hand with Mark Lester, miming to the words of the song. Now, to get the effect of a heavy snowfall, a large fan blew pieces of jabolite, a sort of polystyrene, into our faces as we walked through the outside set. It looked great on the screen, but it was awkward for me to pretend to sing because the 'snow' was stinging my face. After a few takes I started to get the hang of it and Carol Reed told me to open my mouth wide for the long note at the end of the song. This had to be held for about fifteen seconds, and I was doing fine until a particularly large chunk of jabolite went straight down my throat, nearly choking me. Everybody had a good laugh – and so did I once I had managed to cough up the offending object. Once again I had the feeling that I had been set up.

Oliver! was great fun to do and I learned a great deal from being directed by Carol Reed.

My next appearance on film was as Bjornsterne Bjornson in *Song of Norway* and came as the result of the husband and wife, producer/director team of Andrew and Virginia Stone having seen my performance in *Oliver!* They decided that I was just the man they wanted to play the part of the famous Norwegian playwright, Bjornson. They contacted my agent and he set up a meeting in my St James's Place office for them to run over the music for me. They brought with them the film's songwriters, Robert Wright and George Forrest, to play their tunes on my piano.

It was reminiscent of an old Hollywood 'B' feature. Bob and George sat side by side on a small stool playing the music together on my small upright piano, while Andrew Stone, a grizzled veteran of God knows how many films – including W C Fields's final one – shouted out the plot.

'See now, this is when the kid comes into the piano store run by Eddie Robinson an' wants to buy a pianner for Grieg, see.'

'You mean Edward G Robinson?' I had to interrupt. I had seen every gangster film Edward G had ever made and, like many other budding comedians, I used to do an impression of him. If *he* was in the film, *I* had to be in it too.

Andrew Stone was a bit miffed at having his 'spiel' interrupted. 'Yeah, he's in it,' he said and went on with his summary of the plot.

I didn't need to hear any more. I was hooked, but allowed a decent time to elapse – during which Andrew described the complicated lifestory of Grieg (to be played by Toralv Maurstad, of whom I had *not* heard) – before my hand shot up and I agreed to take on the part.

Filming began for me in Lillehammer, Norway after I had enjoyed a break in the sun of Barbados with Myra and our youngest child, Katy.

The difference in climate was extreme. I left the 80 degrees of the West Indies for the minus 30 degrees of the frozen north. It was so cold on location that the hairs in my nostrils froze and ice would form in the corners of my eyes. Moving my lips to speak the dialogue was a distinct effort, resulting in one disastrous episode when I was required to drive an old-fashioned sleigh. Seated beside me was Elizabeth Larner, who was playing Bjornson's wife, and in the two seats behind us, Mr and Mrs Grieg – Toralv Marstad and Florence Henderson.

My single previous experience of driving horses had been in Llangyfelach, holding the reins of my uncle's old mare as we rode round the country lanes delivering blocks of fuel. There was nothing to it – the horse knew all the stops anyway and the only time she broke into a trot was when she could smell the home stables.

Lillehammer was quite a different kettle of fish to Llangyfelach. I found myself in charge of two fjord horses who had never worked as a pair before, and faced with the formidable task of following a complicated track which included a sharp right hand bend at the bottom of a steep hill. All this was undertaken in a temperature well below freezing and with a covering of nine inches of snow on the ground.

To make matters worse, the instruction I was given regarding the commands for the horses required me to make a 'kissing' sound for them to start and a blowing out of the lips to slow them down. I nodded sagely as Andrew Stone took me through the command signals for the horses. I didn't dare open my mouth because I wanted to save my lips for the take.

'Action!'

I managed to produce the starting command and off we went on our merry way. All went well for a while, and even Toralv – who had formerly expressed some misgivings about my ability to handle the sleigh – sang a carefree snatch of some Scandinavian melody.

As we approached the hill which preceded the sharp right hand bend, I attempted to blow out my lips in the slow-down signal. To my horror, I couldn't move my lips. At that moment it flashed through my mind that I had been warned that these old sleighs had no brakes.

I began tugging on the reins in a vain attempt at taking control, but the horses took no notice. Animals always seem to sense when an idiot is in charge of them. We went hurtling down the hill, rocking from side to side, and as we came to the bend, I managed to pull hard enough on the reins to swing the sleigh around. As I did so the runners on the right hand side hit a large boulder hidden in the snow. I let go of the reins and dived off my seat, taking poor Elizabeth Larner with me. Toralv and Florence jumped at the same time and, luckily, we all landed safely in a heap in the snow.

The horses went on in the direction of the stables in Lillehammer, galloping in step for the first time. On their way they ran into three parked cars, ruining the sleigh but fortunately doing no harm to themselves or any passers-by.

Andrew Stone had a few sarcastic things to say to me, and referred to me as 'Ben Hur' for the rest of my time on location. They had to re-shoot the sequence using a stuntman called Yakima Canutt, whose name I had seen many times on the credit list of Hollywood films. I was given a set of dummy reins while Yakima had to lie flat on some planks beneath our seats to steer the horses.

Filming was held up on several occasions, and to complicate matters a rift opened up between Virginia and Andrew. She had taken a fancy to a member of the crew and this caused so much trouble that a couple of executives flew over from Hollywood to try to restore some kind of harmony on location. A compromise was eventually reached and the couple promised to stay together until the filming was finished.

There is a funny, but poignant, footnote to the Stones' eventual split. When the filming was completed and everything was being wound up in Norway, the unit publicist, Eddy Kalish, received a telegram from Virginia asking him to send her the driving mirror from her hired Volvo, because it was in that mirror that her eyes had met those of her new man for the first time. I presume he was sitting in the back.

In the process of removing the mirror from the car, it broke in Eddy's hands. Undaunted, he bought another mirror from a Volvo dealer and sent that one off instead. 'If you've seen one mirror, you've seen 'em all,' was his motto.

I've never much liked looking at 'rushes'. The sight of myself on the big screen – and this film was being made for a *very* wide screen – always puts me off. However, one evening in Oslo I was persuaded to go along with some of the cast and crew to see the rushes at a cinema near our hotel. Unfortunately, they were to be shown without a soundtrack, so we watched our efforts in silence. Until, that is, one particular scene which involved the recital of some of Grieg's work in a concert hall.

The storyline was that some of the composer's friends had hired the hall in an attempt to secure financial backing for his work. Toralv, as Grieg, sat playing the piano while the characters portrayed by myself, Edward G Robinson, Florence Henderson and Elizabeth Larner sat in the almost empty auditorium. From time to time we looked around us and at each other, mutely expressing our disappointment at the sparcity of the audience.

The scene was quite a long one, with the odd re-takes being shown as well, and it suddenly occurred to me to liven up the proceedings by blowing a raspberry. Just after I had done so, the scene on screen showed Edward G Robinson looking at Florence Henderson with his eyebrows raised quizzically. This was followed by Elizabeth Larner giving me a questioning glance.

I could control myself no longer, and piped up from my cinema seat 'I didn't do it.'

Everybody at the rushes screening fell about laughing as our *Song of Norway* characters appeared to be turning around looking for the culprit who had farted. I was banned from attending the rushes thereafter.

I so resembled the character that I was portraying in the film, that children in the street used to run after me crying 'Bjornson!' when I was in costume. When we filmed on location in Bjornson's house, Andrew Stone allowed a genuine portrait of the playwright to remain in shot on a wall behind me in one of the scenes.

It was while we were filming in Bjornson's house that I received a message that an urgent phone call had come through from London. The telephones in the main house had been disconnected so that filming would not be disturbed, and the only working phone on location was in a lodge at the entrance to the property which was situated at the end of the long drive. As I made my way to the telephone it was snowing heavily and I must have resembled Captain Oates of the Antarctic as my mind raced wildly in frantic speculation about the nature of the call. Could one of the children be ill?

Could Myra have had a car crash? Every possible scenario went through my brain and by the time I reached the lodge I had turned into a snow-covered gibbering wreck.

I picked up the phone with trembling fingers. 'Hello?' I said tentatively. 'It's a Mr Milligan for you,' said the operator.

'Neddy! Will you record the voice of an elephant for me?'

'Yes,' I said. Milligan hung up.

On the long, cold trudge through the snow back to the house I thought of other things I might have said to him.

It was a rewarding experience to work with Eddie Robinson. He never seemed to be acting; every move, every piece of dialogue flowed naturally. I was surprised to discover that he was quite deaf. In one scene, we were sitting around a table in a piano shop along with Florence Henderson and a German actress who delivered her lines rather softly.

During the rehearsals Eddie found her very difficult to hear, and this made him late with his own lines. In the break before the actual take, he turned to me and whispered, 'When it's my turn to speak just tap me on the leg under the table.' This I did, but there was always a very tiny pause before he came in with his lines. Yet, when I watched the final result of the scene on screen it appeared that he was carefully considering what he had to say – and stealing the scene from everybody into the bargain.

Sitting beside him on the set was always a rewarding experience. He used to like telling us about his days with Warner Brothers when he and Humphrey Bogart took turns being the villain. Despite his tremendous success at playing gangster parts, he confessed that he hated firing handguns. Whenever he had to shoot at somebody, the make-up artist had to tape his upper eyelids back, because his instinctive reaction was to close his eyes every time the gun went off.

Eddie Robinson also revealed that Humphrey Bogart's

habit of snarling came from the fact that he suffered from heartburn. His condition caused him to take antacid tablets which left a chalky deposit on his teeth. Bogart attempted to remove this by moving his upper lip up and down over his teeth in his familiar 'snarl'.

Off screen Eddie was the exact opposite of the tough guy roles for which he was famed. He was a great collector of fine art, and when he had time off from filming he and his wife spent most of their time wandering around Oslo looking for new paintings. He was a gentle man and it was worth suffering the cold Norwegian winter to have had the privilege of working alongside him.

The film was not a great commercial success – indeed in one of the movie guides it is described as 'a bomb'. But nevertheless, I enjoyed the experience.

However, there is a sad footnote to *Song of Norway*. When the film came out, there were premières in Miami and New York and I was invited to the second.

It was a wash out in more senses than one because a torrential downpour hit New York that night and by the time I arrived at the cinema, after a horrendous journey through heavy traffic, Andrew and Virginia Stone, who shared the limousine with me were no longer speaking to each other. They were escorted up the sodden red carpet to the canopy in front of the cinema by a flunkey carrying a large umbrella. I followed behind umbrella-less, only to be accosted half-way by a drunk who seized the lapels of my dinner jacket and asked me for money. 'I'm English,' I said stupidly and that seemed enough reason for him to look for someone more affluent.

To judge from the audience I got a feeling that *Song of Norway* was not going to be another *Sound of Music*. Those of us who were members of the cast sat in the circle behind the row which contained the critics. When it came to the dinner party scene at Ibsen's house where Grieg suddenly says 'I must go back to my wife', and Ibsen stands up and says 'But not before you have played our new national anthem', a critic sitting in front of me put his head in his hands and groaned, 'Oh my God.'

Then I was *certain* that we were on to a loser.

When I arrived at Heathrow the following day, I was greeted by my manager Bob Kennedy with the sad news that my father had died. We had been expecting it to happen for some time. He had slowly become senile and we had been forced to put him in a nursing home in Ealing, near my brother's vicarage in Hanwell, and he had suddenly developed the pneumonia from which he died.

Even though I had come to terms with the fact that he could go at any time, it didn't really soften the blow when it happened. In his last days he didn't really recognize any of us, and so deeply embedded in his brain were the terrible experiences he had suffered during the First World War, that he believed he was back in the trenches.

He had been a good father to Fred, Carol and myself and when my mother was alive he was full of jokes and anecdotes about his life as a commercial traveller. His talent as an artist proved very handy as a supplement to his income, because he frequently drew cartoons for the South Wales *Evening Post*. After Mam died, he was like a lost soul. He spent his time visiting our families, and the sparkle had gone out of him.

The only 'Doctor' film I was ever in was also the only one of the series which did not make a profit. But my memory of the filming is clouded by tragedy. In the film, I played the part of a Pools winner who took a cruise on the strength of his winnings and became a target for the predatory Irene Handl who was looking for a rich husband for her daughter, Janet Mahoney. Leslie Phillips got into all kinds of trouble as the ship's doctor, and Robert Morley was the captain.

On the day that I was having a costume fitting for the film,

I had an urgent phone call from Bob Kennedy to tell me that Myra's mother had died suddenly.

It was a very dramatic scene that awaited me when I arrived home. At the time, Myra's parents, Flo and Jim, who lived in Swansea, were staying with us to help look after the kids, and I had received a request from the features editor of the *London Evening News* for Flo to be interviewed for a new series about comics' mothers-in-law. She had an angina condition for which she had to take tablets, and Myra was worried that the strain of being interviewed might be too much for her, but Flo said she would be all right.

When the reporter and photographer arrived at the house, Myra showed them into the lounge and introduced them to her mother. She then left the room and Flo sat down on the piano stool for the interview. The reporter had only asked her a couple of questions when she said 'Oh dear' and fell to the floor. Myra rushed in straight away and sent David to get Dr Unger-Hamilton who lived a few doors away. When he arrived, it was too late to do anything except place her in my study which adjoined the lounge, to await the coming of the undertaker.

There was not much that I could do to help except to offer comfort to Myra and poor old Jim who was stricken with grief. David was in a bit of a state – he was only a boy, and the shock of running for the doctor and then finding that it was too late to save his beloved grandmother remains with him.

Jim now came to live with us after the funeral was over and I'm glad to say that he lived on quite a few years after Flo. He was a lovely old fellow who was liked by everybody who knew him.

Life on a Main Road

For over thirty years we lived in a house on Cheam Road, between Cheam village and the town of Sutton. Our house stood in about an acre of ground between two side roads – York Road and Derby Road. A sturdy, detached house, the story goes that it was built in the 1920s by theatre owner and impresario Sir Oswald Stoll for his son. The front door faced a bus stop on the opposite side of the street and, after we had become established in the area, that particular bus stop became known as ' 'Arry's Corner' or 'Harry's House', depending on the social background of the conductor. From the top deck of a passing double decker it was possible to see right into our bedroom window, and I understand that the colour of my underwear became a general topic of conversation amongst those prurient passengers who happened to be sitting on the left hand side of the bus as it travelled past our house on the way from Sutton to Cheam. The name 'Flash Harry' was frequently mentioned, I believe, and I was not averse to a friendly wave.

The fact that everybody seemed to know where I lived in Cheam sometimes made us the target for eccentric behaviour. On one memorable occasion the household woke to find that someone had spray-painted the legend 'Harry Secombe is a wanker' on the wall outside the house. Between finding the graffiti and arranging to have it removed my knighthood was announced. The next day the artist added to his handiwork, which now read '*Sir* Harry Secombe is a wanker'. At least it showed he had some style.

One Saturday morning I decided to transfer a whole pile of books from my over-flowing library in the house to a mini-library I was setting up in what had been a garage alongside the property. This meant that I had to carry them out of the backdoor into the garden and through the door of their new home.

I had carried out two or three piles of books before I became aware of a girl's singing voice. At first I thought it was a radio somewhere, until I realized that the hidden singer would sing a phrase as I went from the back door to the garage door and, when I did the return journey, she would pick up from exactly where she'd left off. 'If I ruled the world every day would be the first day of spring . . .' accompanied one trip, and then on the way back, 'Every heart would have a new song to sing . . .' It occurred to me that at this rate, considering the length of the song, I could have removed half of Sutton Public Library before she had got to the reprise.

So, when I got back into the house, at the end of 'My world would be a beautiful place . . .', I tiptoed out through the French windows in the lounge, crept around to the front gate and peeped out towards the source of the singing. A young girl was crouched just below the wall, preparing to launch herself into 'Where we would dream such wonderful dreams . . .' as soon as I reappeared. She took a furtive peep over the wall, waiting for her cue, but, seeing me watching her from the gate, she gave a stifled scream and ran off. The poor girl was obviously auditioning for me, but I never found out what for.

*

For as long as I can remember, I wanted to be a writer. I was only good at two subjects in school, English and art, and I never, ever, unlocked the mysteries of mathematics.

My essays were much appreciated by one particular master, Mr Corfield, who taught English at St Thomas Elementary School. He used to make me stand up in front of the class and read my work out loud. This caused some jealousy among my fellow pupils and as a result I was often forced to defend myself in the playground. I found that the best way to do this was to try to get out of their way, and I spent many a playtime halfway up a drainpipe.

After I had left school I kept in touch with Mr Corfield, and maintained the contact through the war years, until our correspondence dried up. Then one day in 1956, when I went home to Swansea for a weekend during my first Palladium show, my mother told me that Mr Corfield was ill.

I went along to see him at his home just outside Swansea. By this time I had acquired some veneer of success, a big car, gold watch and suede shoes. As I entered his house I found him sitting by the fire in his armchair with a blanket over his knees. 'Hello Mr Corfield,' I boomed, a long way now from the spotty lad up a drainpipe.

Mr Corfield looked at me for quite a long time and then said, 'Harry, what went wrong?'

He stirred my conscience, though, and not long after I was invited to write something for a school magazine and I got the taste for writing all over again.

I had some short stories published in *Argosy* magazine and Spike asked me to do a foreword for a book he had written called *A Dustbin of Milligan*. The publisher was very pleased with what I had written and suggested that I should write a novel about show business. I replied that I was not sure whether I could do so, but promised that I would have a go at writing a first chapter and, if he approved, I would go ahead with the rest of it. His reply was most favourable and I resolved to finish the novel. Unfortunately a lot of other commitments got in the way and that first hand-written chapter lay forgotten in a drawer.

When Jennifer found it, years later, she said that I ought to finish it. I was afraid that it might not be a good idea, and anyway the man who had suggested that I wrote it in the first place was now with another publisher – Jane's Fighting Ships. My daughter has never been one for taking no for an answer and, without my knowledge, sent the material to Jeremy Robson who was just starting his own publishing company. He thought that it had the makings of a good book and offered me an advance and a deadline.

Faced with the incentive to work to a finishing date I went to Majorca and began writing. I had decided on a title, *Twice Brightly*, summarizing the content of the book which was about a comic's first week in Variety, having just been demobbed from the Army. I think I did most of the writing in three weeks, in longhand – the way I am doing this book – and Jennifer took it home to type.

By this time I was an occasional contributor to *Punch* magazine. The editor, William Davis, got Miles Kington, who was then the literary editor, to ask Prince Charles to review my book – the first time he had ever been asked to do such a thing. HRH complied and gave it a very flattering reception. His review began: ' "We would be delighted if you would write a review of Harry Secombe's first novel, *Twice Brightly*," was what the man from *Punch* said. "It doesn't have to be a comic masterpiece" (what does he mean, it doesn't have to be a comic masterpiece? People have wandered feet first into the Tower for less than that . . .)' But it went on to say, 'I was shaken with spasms of helpless mirth at frequent intervals.' And you can't get much better than that.

Other critics were pretty kind to me as well. Dennis Potter said that the novel was 'Very warm, very funny' and *The Times* called it 'a bright little novel'. For a week or two it was in the top ten bestseller list, which pleased both me and my publisher.

My next novel, *Welsh Fargo*, caused quite a stir not because of a Royal connection but in court circles of a different character.

The novel was all about a small bus company in South Wales run by a man called Dai Fargo whose bus is hijacked by an amateur gang of crooks. The title came from an ad lib by Paddy O'Neill on stage in the Palladium pantomime *Humpty Dumpty*. She suddenly pointed to me and cried, 'It's Welsh Fargo!'

It had no relation to anything that was going on in the scene and yet it got a laugh from the audience.

Thinking about it afterwards I had the idea of writing a book bearing that title, and I sort of worked backwards from there. Because I have the gestation period of a herd of elephants, it was many years later that the book eventually got written although I had mentioned the fact that I was in the process of working on it several times on various radio and television chat shows.

It came as a surprise therefore, that a solicitor's letter was sent to Robson Books complaining that a firm called Welsh Fargo Car and Van Hire in Bridgend, South Wales, was 'falsely and maliciously maligned' in my book.

I explained to my publisher that I had announced the title long before the plaintiffs had registered their business name. However, I offered to meet these people and to be photographed with one of their vans as a publicity stunt. They refused to do this and a writ was issued.

I was very sad that the case had to go to law, because we could all have benefited from a bit of good natured publicity over the affair. My publishers took legal advice, resisted the proceedings, and the plaintiffs withdrew.

Like most dilettante writers I sometimes feel uneasy in the company of those who do it for a living, although I had a good laugh at a telegram which Alan Coren sent to me from *Punch* on the occasion of the publishing of *Twice Brightly*.

'DEAR SECOMBE' it read. 'THIS IS A BLACK DAY FOR THE DEMARCATION INDUSTRY STOP WHERE DO YOU GET OFF TAKING THE BREAD OUT OF HUMORISTS' MOUTHS? IS THIS ALL THE THANKS WE GET FOR PUBLISHING YOU IN THE FIRST PLACE JUST TO KEEP YOU FROM SINGING AT LUNCH? OUR ADVICE IS TO STICK TO YOUR LAST ON THE GROUNDS THAT OLD COBBLERS NEVER DIE.

The *Punch* luncheons held at their offices in Tudor Street, just off Fleet Street, were always hilarious affairs and I was privileged to be a guest on many occasions. Some of the finest humorists in the country would swap anecdotes and insults around the famous *Punch* table. Clive James, Keith Waterhouse, Frank Muir, Alan Coren, William Davis, along with cartoonists like Geoffrey Dickinson, Wally Fawkes and David Langdon would submit famous political figures to good natured interrogation. I remember Edward Heath's shoulders heaving away, and, on another occasion, Jim Callaghan's robust laughter. After that particular luncheon I was pleased to give Jim, who was then in Opposition, a lift back to the House of Commons in my Rolls-Royce. The man at the gate gave me a startled salute. The next time I met him was when Myra and I were invited on board a Royal Naval frigate in Bridgetown Harbour, Barbados for cocktails. He was then Prime Minister and had been to a high-powered summit conference in Jamaica. It was the time when he returned home to turmoil and said, 'Crisis? What crisis?'

Incidentally, Ted Heath was also on board that evening and some of the press wanted a photograph of the two of them together. Jim was willing, but Ted demurred. Funny old world isn't it?

The eccentric behaviour outside the house was more than matched by what sometimes went on *inside* 129 Cheam Road, where we had four out of the ordinary children growing up.

Jennifer, our eldest, had an invisible alter-ego who was called Hellie Morgan. Heaven knows where Jennifer got the name from, but that's what she wanted to be called when she grew up. Jennifer used to tour with Myra and myself in my early pantomime and Variety days and mixed freely at parties. When she was four, Myra found her emptying all the glasses of wine when our guests had departed. It was a great way of getting her to sleep that night, but we discouraged her from doing it again. 'That's daddy's job,' explained Myra, looking at me in a knowing way. Jennifer has gone on to make her mark in Public Relations and now manages the Entertainment publicity team at BBC television.

Andrew was born at my parents-in-law's house in Swansea in April 1953. I was staying at the Averard Hotel in Lancaster Gate at the time he was born, and I was thrilled when Myra's Aunt Elsie phoned me with the news in the early hours of the morning. It was his arrival that spurred me into house hunting because, with two children to bring up, Myra and I decided that we had to have a place of our own. Which is why we finished up in Cheam.

He grew up to be a boy who was always wanting to be acting a part. At one time he thought he was Superman, and Myra found him on the garden wall with a towel pinned to the back of his shirt, holding the ends of the towel in his outstretched arms as makeshift wings. He was convinced he could fly and only Myra's intervention saved him from disaster. He developed a passion for playing the drums, which he used to practise in his bedroom, and his long-suffering mother used to have to take him and his percussion gear in her car whenever he had a gig at a friend's house.

He also had – still has – a dry sense of humour. One Sunday morning I decided to have a barbecue in the back garden. I had just bought all the equipment and was dying to try it out.

The barbecue consisted of a grill and spit mounted on four legs, and I set it up close to the kitchen window, filling it with charcoal. I had decided against using paraffin to get the fire going because I wanted to avoid setting the roof on fire, having once seen such a thing happen at a Sydney 'barbie' at which I was a guest. It had been an exciting evening and the presence of the Fire Brigade made the whole event 'go like a house on fire', as another guest wittily remarked.

Not having Sydney Harbour as a nearby source of water, I cleverly organized an electric poker with which to get the charcoal alight. The poker had to be passed to me through the kitchen window by Andrew and, when he plugged it in, I said 'OK, son, switch it on.'

Now, there just happened to be a loose wire in the handle of the poker, through which the house current passed on its way to my nervous system. The force of the electricity pulsed through me, making me jerk about like a marionette. I found that I could not let the damned thing go and, in between convulsions, I tried to tell Andrew to switch it off. He watched me leap about like a lunatic, thoroughly enjoying my antics, until, eventually, he got the message.

'That was very funny, Dad,' he said as he came out into the garden, still laughing. I showed him my burned hand, unable to speak after the shock. 'That's nasty,' he said. 'How did you manage to do that?'

He is now an actor.

Our youngest boy, David, was born in February 1962,

when I was at the Palladium in a revue *Let Yourself Go*, a title that raised ribald laughter backstage when the news of his birth came out. He was the first English-born child in the family, having been born in Sutton Nursing Home.

His particular peculiarity as a child was his insistence on wearing a German helmet at all times – until he was persuaded that we had not lost the war. He started collecting antiques at the age of nine, and was rarely seen without a camera round his neck. At his prep school his headmaster declared him to be a gifted child. He happened to be right, because David has turned out to be a very fine photographer and has taken photographs for many publications, including the commemorative book, *Elizabeth R*, which involved him travelling around with Her Majesty. He also has photographs in the archive of the National Portrait Gallery. To ask him to take a family photograph for our Christmas card is like using a sledge-hammer to crack a nut.

Katherine Sian arrived on 12 December 1967, just seven days after *The Four Musketeers* opened at Drury Lane. Myra was forty-three at the time Katy was born. She had to go into St Helier Hospital for the delivery and, the morning after, the gynaecologist said to her, 'Congratulations! You had the only natural birth in the hospital last night.' Myra preened herself. Then the tweedy lady doctor said, 'We old ones can show 'em a thing or two, can't we?'

David was pretty miffed when Katy arrived. For weeks before the event, he had convinced himself that the baby would be a boy. He knew that the baby was in his mother's tummy and he used to get Myra to open her mouth so that he could shout down messages – things like 'You can have the Action Man with the leg off,' or 'There's a German helmet you can have when you come out.' He managed to work up a smile when he saw Katy for the first time, but it was some while before he forgave her for being a girl.

Katy was very aware from an early age that she was a girl

and played her feminine charm for all it was worth – even on the Almighty. When Myra noticed that Katy was not cleaning her teeth, she said, 'God will know that you haven't brushed them.' Katy went straight to the bathroom and attacked her teeth with vigour. When she came out on to the landing, she turned her face up to heaven, opened her mouth wide and proclaimed, 'Look God, I've cleaned 'em!'

Once, when I had arrived home after a trip to America, I went upstairs to have a snooze before supper and was soon flat out on the bed. Some time later, Myra asked Katy to go upstairs to see if Daddy was awake. She came into the bedroom, looked at my prostrate form and called down, 'I think he's dead.'

It was Katy who inspired me to write my first children's book one year when we were in Majorca. It was a very hot night and we were all sitting around on the patio fanning ourselves. Young Katy was on my lap, refusing to go to sleep until I told her a story. I was drinking in those days, and a couple of brandies after supper had loosened my imagination. I began to tell her about a monster who lived in the sea near the house and how Katy refused to be frightened by him – the *real* Katy wouldn't either – and they became great friends. Katy was asleep after about five minutes, but the rest of the family kept prodding me to finish the story. The following morning Jennifer said that I ought to write down the story and send it to my publisher. Eventually I did just that, and *Katy and the Nurgla* was born.

She used to spend a lot of time on her own, walking around the garden talking happily to her dolls, or conducting long conversations with invisible friends. It was obvious to me that she would want to be an actress, and so it proved.

There comes a time in a performer's life when he has to face the fact that his children will want to follow in his footsteps. The first thing that I said to Andrew – and to Katy when she got older – was that my profession was a tough one, that over ninety per cent of all actors were out of work at any one time and that the comfortable lifestyle that we had was because I had been very lucky.

In Andy's case, he listened to what I had to say and then invited me to see him in the school play. This was the moment of truth for me – if he was not very good, how could I tell him? I'd be doing him a disservice if I pretended that I'd liked his performance.

It was with fear and trembling that I went to see him in *The Boyfriend* at the City of London Freeman's School Hall. Myra and I sat holding hands tightly, waiting for Andrew's first appearance. I looked through the programme and whispered, 'At least they've spelled his name right.'

'Shhh!' said Myra.

My mouth was dry and my heart was pounding before our son made his first entrance. 'Please God, make him good,' I prayed silently. And to my great relief he was. The stage lit up as he came on, and from then on I kept turning round in my seat, proudly mouthing, 'That's my lad up there.'

When it came to Katy's turn to show what her potential might be, it was also in a school play. I could not be there for her theatrical début, but Myra said she could see straight away that Katy had star quality – even though she was wearing a papier mâché donkey's head.

Katy went on to Manchester University, where she got a 2 i degree in drama. From there she auditioned for the Bristol Old Vic Drama School and passed. At the end of her time there she won the Peter Ackerman Comedy Prize. She then joined Harrogate Repertory Company for a season and, to my great pride and pleasure, she shared the stage with me in *Pickwick* at the Chichester Festival Theatre in 1993.

There are two friends who played such big parts in my life that they almost became family. The first was Bob Kennedy, who I met many years ago when I played the Dudley Hippodrome, which he owned with his brother Maurice. It was a fine theatre with a very good reputation in the Midlands, but along with many Variety theatres it suffered when television took hold of the nation's entertainment needs.

The next time I met Bob was in 1960 when he was the company manager for the summer show I did at the Palace Theatre in Blackpool for George and Alfred Black. He had had to give up the Hippodrome because of lack of business, and was then living with his second wife Beryl and their baby daughter Sarah in digs in the town.

As it happened, Len Lightowler, who was my personal manager at the time, had some domestic problems and had decided to leave, so I asked Bob if he would like the job. He was delighted to accept and after the show finished in Blackpool he and his little family came down to live in Sutton.

They had been in Sutton for about a year when it was discovered that Bob had a brain tumour. It was operated on and, one day when he was still in hospital, Beryl brought little Sarah in to see him. He thought the baby was looking pale and suggested that perhaps she might be anaemic. Unfortunately it turned out that Sarah had leukaemia and, in spite of everything that modern medicine could do at that time, Sarah died. It was a terrible blow to them both, especially when it seemed that the tide was turning for them.

After his operation, Bob was left with a limp but he never let it get in the way of his work for me. His experience as a theatre owner made him invaluable to me as a personal manager and he was never at any time a 'yes' man.

We had a lot of laughs together and Beryl and Myra became great friends. Beryl had been a fine principal boy in pantomime and was full of funny stories about the business. She had also been in ENSA during the war, and the ship taking them to North Africa was attacked and sunk by a German U-boat off Algiers.

Bob travelled with me wherever I went and I particularly

remember a time at Los Angeles airport when his limp was getting more pronounced and we had a connecting plane to catch. We had very little time to spare to make the connection, so I bunged him in a wheelchair and raced through the airport, yelling like a banshee. He enjoyed every minute of it.

When we moved down to Willinghurst, Bob and Beryl came to live near us until, at the age of eighty, he died quite suddenly. He was still working for me until the day he passed on, and a kinder, more honest man I have yet to meet. After Bob's death, my secretary Julie Stephens managed my affairs for a while.

Another great friend for many years was Johnny Franz, who was the recording manager for Philips. I met Johnny as a result of changing recording companies after my contract with HMV was not taken up. I got an offer from Philips, and the first 78 rpm record I made was 'On With the Motley', with 'Recondita Armonia' from *Tosca* on the other side. To my surprise – but not to Johnny's – the record found its way into the charts.

I stayed with Philips for twenty-five years and through Johnny's choice of songs and some great orchestrations by Wally Stott and the great Peter Knight, I managed to pick up several golden discs and a couple of platinums.

With Johnny's help I made several albums abroad, one in Paris, another in Milan and a most memorable one in Vienna. It was recorded in the Mozart Concert Hall with the Viennese Concert Orchestra and featured a compilation of Tauber songs.

When I first entered the Hall I was very impressed by the place and the size of the orchestra. Johnny Franz was also nervous and so was Wally Stott, who was to conduct. I was introduced to the musicians with much formal heel clicking, and the first number to be recorded was 'Girls Were Made to Love and Kiss' by Franz Lehár. Wally tapped his music stand with his baton and off we went. After a few bars I lost my place in the music and automatically did what I always did at home when I made a mistake at a session: I blew a raspberry.

The orchestra skidded to a halt and there were questioning looks all around. For an awful moment I thought that I had really gone too far this time – desecrating this Mecca of Viennese music and ruining my own credibility as a singer. Then suddenly the lead trombonist blew a mighty raspberry-like beast on his instrument and the whole orchestra joined in the fun. It seemed as if they had been waiting to do that for years and the whole formal atmosphere changed. As I said to Johnny later, 'Welsh culture came to Vienna.'

One day Johnny rang me to tell me that he had a great song that he wanted me to record as soon as possible. I went along to see him and ran through the song with him. 'I don't think much of it, mate,' I said. 'But let's do it anyway.' And that was how I got to number one in the Hit Parade with 'This Is My Song'. Petula Clark got there first with the same song and for a while we were both in the top ten at the same time. This meant that I had to go on *Top of the Pops* with all the trendy groups. As I said at the time, it was like Ben Hur winning the Grand Prix.

When Johnny suddenly died of a heart attack, it was not long before Philips decided that we should part company. It was a pity because I had always enjoyed making records for the label, but it seemed that middle-of-the-road singers were on the way out. Ah well!

Life at Cheam Road was always eventful and, to add to the human menagerie, we also had a wonderfully eccentric cast of canine characters – one of which, our boxer Jim, only *thought* he was human.

I had bought Jim as a companion for Myra and the children when I was on tour and they were alone in the house. There was a kennels near to where I was playing in pantomime, and I went along to see some boxer puppies. I couldn't make up my mind which one to have, until we went into the farmhouse for a cup of tea and there, snoozing by the fire and surrounded by kittens, was this clown of a puppy.

'That's the one for me,' I said. 'He's obviously a character. What's his name?'

'Jim – just Jim,' said the lady, picking him up and handing him to me. He yawned sleepily and drew blood from my nose with his sharp little teeth. I had to buy him then – if only to get my own back when he got a bit older.

Of course, when I got him home he was immediately spoiled by the whole family, but, as he got older, his character began to assert itself in peculiar little ways. The back door, for example, he would protect against all comers – including us – but *anybody* could come in through the front door; if ever we wanted to move his great bulk from in front of the fire, we only had to say 'cats!' and he was off like a shot to the top of the garden, barking his head off at nothing. It didn't matter how many times we did this, he never cottoned on, though after three times in succession one cold winter's night his bark lost some of its conviction third time round and he gave me a harsh look when he trotted back in and slumped under the table.

When he was about a year old, I decided it was time to have him trained. He kept jumping up at people and licking them all over as they prostrate between his paws. This boisterous behaviour was costing us friends, so I took him along to a place where they sort out animal eccentrics.

As I left, a kennel boy was being dragged off his feet by Jim as he went for a startled retriever. 'They'll soon cure him of that,' I thought. 'When he gets home he'll be using a knife and fork.'

After the first week, we rang the kennels, as we were told to. 'He's quite a character, your Jim,' said a voice. 'We haven't been able to put him with the other dogs yet . . . but he is settling down.'

The next week we were told that he was still on his own and that he had killed a chicken. Four days later, we were asked to remove him because he was a bad influence on the other dogs.

I drove out to collect him and was expecting to find the place besieged by Jim leading a pack of savage hounds. It wasn't as bad as that. When the kennel boy brought him out he was pulled flat on his face by Jim's sudden joyous burst of speed on seeing me. I opened the car door, let Jim in and drove away with one hand, fighting off a happy, slobbering boxer with the other.

Although that was the end of his education, some of the commands he learned lingered on in a shadowy corner of his brain. Sometimes, when I said 'Lie down,' he might do just that. But he then would not get up until the next command unlocked his reflexes. 'Up!' I'd shout. No. 'Get up!' No. It was as if he was waiting for a password – sometimes in the middle of the road. 'Here boy!' Ah, that's it, and he would get to his feet and saunter on, exhausted with the mental effort of it all.

When he was eight the vet told us that Jim had a rare kidney complaint and had not long to live. This was terrible news, and in an effort to soften the blow of his passing, I went out and bought another boxer puppy – this time a bitch.

At first, we thought he would eat her. Having been master of the house for so long he resented the intrusion and nearly went mad with rage. Then he twigged that she was a lady and a new look came into his eye, he suddenly began to quite like the idea after all.

Cindy, the newcomer, was a born flirt and soon had him eating out of her paws. He looked like a big, stupid oaf, following her around the garden, his jowls drooling in fervent anticipation. Soon there was no sign of the old Jim – his coat was shining, his nose was wet and in six months he was the father of half a dozen puppies. We kept the puppy with the most laid-back personality, and Bella became a much-loved member of the family.

Dear old Jim lived on for several years, happy with his lot, until his kidney complaint eventually got the better of him.

Some years after Jim and Cindy died, Jennifer presented Myra with a little Yorkshire terrier called Pudding, which made up in character for what he lacked in size. He never wanted to be treated as a lap dog and always adopted a pained expression when he was petted and fondled. However, he was determined to make his presence felt and was forever trying to attract attention to himself. Sometimes, if Myra was looking out of the bedroom window, he would growl to be picked up so that he could see for himself what was happening. If ignored, he would seize one of Myra's slippers in his mouth and shake it as if he was killing a rabbit. This was his party piece. Another favourite trick was to go into my father-in-law Jim's bedroom in the morning and grab his false teeth – which for some reason Jim kept in one of his slippers. This was always guaranteed to get Jim out of bed to let Pudding out to run in the back garden, where he had a secret rendezvous with a large rubber ball to which he was strangely attracted.

He could always tell when one of the family was coming home before the car entered the drive. When Andrew had a motor bike, Pudding could recognize the sound of its engine when it was at least a hundred yards away down Cheam Road, and would start up a high-pitched barking which differed in intensity from any other of the sounds he made.

Pudding never really got on with Schippel, a cocker spaniel which was another gift from Jennifer, who was obviously trying to set up an animal sanctuary in the house. Schippel was named after the character I played in the film *The Plumber's Progress*, but he was generally called 'Skip' by my father-in-law, who could never manage the German 'schi'. Not that the dog ever noticed. Having been born on Hitler's birthday, he had the same propensity for ignoring what people said.

The two dogs had some kind of tacit agreement: Pudding ruled the area of the house above the stairs and Schippel was in charge of the ground floor. The funny thing was that whereas Schippel would grudgingly allow Pudding to come *down* the stairs, there was no possible way that Pudding would let Schippel *up* the stairs. Despite the fact that the spaniel was at least three times as big as the Yorkie, he was very careful not to upset him.

Every Summer for twenty-three years when we lived in Cheam, I used to recruit an all-star cricket team to play against the local eleven. The ground was just across from our house and, after the match, we held an open house party for both sides.

It was a thrill for me as captain to toss the ball to such great cricketers as Fred Rumsey or Eric Bedser and ask them to bowl. Sutton had a strong side and it was always fixed for them to bat first. They would knock up a reasonable score without losing too many wickets and when it got near to four o'clock, Ken Barrington would sidle up to me and say, 'I think it's time to get them out, maestro.' And suddenly there would be an extra bit of effort from the bowlers and, miraculously, the score would go from 200 for 3 to 220 all out by five past four.

When my side came in to bat, we would sometimes open with Peter May and Colin Cowdrey, who would produce some wonderful stroke play until it was time to let other batsmen come in, at which point they would give their wickets away like the great sportsmen they were.

My turn at the crease used to be about eighth wicket down and it was always arranged so that I scored the winning run. Sometimes it took a couple of cries of 'No ball' from the umpire as my wicket was flattened and a considerable amount of dropped catches by slip fielders who had suddenly developed butter fingers, before I managed to hit the ball that gave my side the victory.

The matches were always played in a great spirit of fun and the subsequent celebrations went on into the early hours of the Monday morning. Myra and her mother made sure that everyone had plenty to eat, while it was my job to tend the bar, a task I thoroughly enjoyed in those days. It was a tribute to the Sutton players that they accepted their yearly defeat with good grace.

During the time that I was president of the Lords Taverners, I was frequently asked to be Captain at cricket matches for charity events, and one such occasion took us to Bickley Park Cricket Ground in Kent. My team was called the Prime Minister's Eleven (Harold Macmillan being the Prime Minister in question) and we were playing against Len Hutton's side. The players included some show business stars, but the majority of players were top notch cricketers, including the likes of Colin Cowdrey and **Fred Trueman**.

On my way out to bat, I passed the Prime Minister sitting in a deck chair outside the pavilion. 'I'll do my best for you, sir,' I said. He nodded affably enough, but his 'sleeping tiger' eyes widened at my sartorial get-up. My woollen sweater had shrunk in the wash and clung to my very ample frame and my once white flannel trousers bore the marks of many diving attempts to catch the ball in the outfield. I was told later that Macmillan put his hat over his eyes as I waddled towards the crease.

At the opposite end of the pitch fellow batsman Colin Milburn, who was about the same size as me, but infinitely more athletic, gave me a cheery wave with his bat. He was at the receiving end, thank God, because the batsman I was replacing had been dismissed by the last ball of the over.

'Olly', as Colin was called by everyone who knew him,

faced the bowler with a grin. He could see that I was nervous because I had gone to join the umpire – I felt safer there. He whacked the ball through the covers and I was forced to run. Spectators later said that our running between the wickets registered seven on the Richter scale. Fortunately for me, Colin kept the strike for a couple of overs, by which time my spectacles had misted over and the plastic protector had slipped out of my jock strap to nestle against my left knee.

But, inevitably, it came my turn to face the music. Len Hutton, who was playing wicket keeper, threw the ball to Fred Trueman to start the new over. He then called all the fielders to get behind the wicket, leaving the whole pitch in front of me free, except for Olly. The crowd laughed as Fred strode purposefully to the boundary, rubbing the ball on his trousers as he went. He turned to start his run, pawing the ground like a Spanish bull. I could only just make him out in the distance and I turned round to Len Hutton and asked him what Fred was doing.

'Don't worry,' he said. 'Just stay where you are – Fred likes to have a bit of fun at the charity matches. He'll not hurt you, lad.'

Emboldened by this advice, I did a bit of play acting myself, taking up an elaborate attitude of waiting, tapping the bat on the crease. Meanwhile, Fred had launched himself into his run up, as the crowd roared in anticipation. I began to lose my confidence as his chunky figure powered towards the wicket.

'I've known old Fred for years,' I reasoned. 'He won't bowl the ball at me. He'll drop it as he gets to the wicket.' I was still praying that this would be the outcome when Fred bowled a full toss which hit me on my instep and shot off my boot over the boundary for four runs.

I hopped about on one leg a few times before dropping to the ground 'like a felled ox', as my manager Bob Kennedy later remarked in the pavilion.

They had to carry me off the field.

'That'll teach thee, lad,' said a grinning **Fred Trueman**.

There was no answer to that.

I noticed as I was carried past the Prime Minister that he had his hat over his face. I suppose it was the most diplomatic gesture Macmillan could make.

That wasn't the only time that Lords Taverners' events have got me into trouble. I once blotted my copy book when, as President, I made Margaret Thatcher the first Lady Taverner. The Lords Taverners had always been an all-male preserve and so at the reception on the Martini Terrace I referred to her as the 'thin edge of a delectable wedge'.

She completely misconstrued what I had said and went very red, saying 'I never considered myself to be a wedge.'

I think she must have thought I was referring to her shape. Afterwards I had to pin a diamond Lords Taverners' emblem to that formidable bosom under her eagle eye. I had the absurd notion that if the pin slipped there would be a huge bang and the Prime Minister would fly around the room like a pricked balloon. However, my trembling fingers did the job and I received a gracious smile, but for a moment there I thought I would have to hand back my CBE.

I have been Captain of the Lords Taverners' Golf Society for over twenty-five years, although I'm probably the most unsuccessful player of all time. The exception to this, however, was the occasion when I partnered Christy O'Connor Snr to victory, along with the gifted amateur Jack Cannon, in the first two-day Sean Connery pro-am tournament held in Troon in the early 1970s. The other two golfers didn't need me much until, by some fluke, I happened to hole out from a bunker for a net two on a par four and, for the first time in my life, I got a cheer from the crowd around the green. It helped our combined score to victory, even though I was out of contention for the last two holes. However, that was to be my only fleeting brush with golfing glory.

In all the times I have played in the Lords Taverners and *Sunday Express* Harry Secombe Classic, which is usually held at Effingham Golf Course in Surrey, I have never turned in a decent card at the end of the day.

I did make headlines one year though, an event I prefer not to remember.

It was on the first tee at Effingham. The Taverners Golf Committee are always very careful to put a warning notice in the programme of the day's play to the effect that spectators must keep their eyes on the ball when a player is driving off, to avoid serious injury to themselves. Some people who come to see the stars making fools of themselves on the golf course are not aware of the perils of the game – especially the children who come along with their parents.

On this particular occasion, I made great play of moving spectators away from both sides of the tee. 'I think you'll all be better off behind me,' I joked as I took a couple of practice swings at the starter.

I settled down and addressed the ball, then I somehow managed to slice the brand-new Dunlop 65 at such an acute angle that a lady who had heeded my jocular warning and positioned herself behind me, was struck on the head by the ball. The poor woman fell to the ground, bleeding profusely, and was taken off to hospital. I couldn't stop shaking all the way round the course, turned in a card that was even worse than usual and phoned the hospital as soon as I got back to the clubhouse. Fortunately, she had gained consciousness and was able to tell me not to worry, although she had to have eighteen micro-stitches in the wound. The least I could do was send her some flowers and my abject apologies.

The following day my photograph was plastered over the front page of the *Daily Express*, the picture having been taken by one of the staff photographers who just happened to be there waiting for me to do something stupid. He was right, I suppose.

The following year I invited the lady I had struck to attend the event as my guest. I made absolutely sure that she stood well away from the tee when I drove off this time.

Two years later, on the eighteenth green, retribution came when I was struck on the forehead by a bunker shot played by Air Vice Marshall Ramsey Rae – and a nicer fellow you couldn't wish to meet. I was too busy lining up a twenty-foot putt to notice that he still had to play a bunker shot. I saw double for a while and was made to lie down in the clubhouse. Everyone had a good laugh, of course, and the following year's programme carried a picture of me with my bump.

You will be pleased to hear that my younger son, David, is carrying on in the true Secombe sporting tradition. He once fractured his wrist in a school cricket match.

He was umpiring at the time.

When the buff envelope with the words 'From the office of the Prime Minister' came through the letter-box addressed to me in early May 1981, I opened it with trembling hands. The last time I had received one of these was when I was asked if I would accept the honour of a CBE. What if they wanted it back?

Then I read the words 'The Prime Minister has it in mind to put your name forward for the honour of a Knighthood in the Birthday Honours.' I let out a yell, the dogs started barking and soon the whole household was jumping up and down with excitement. Myra was in tears and David and Katy whooped with delight.

I then realized that I would be in Australia when the news came out and Myra would be unable to accompany me on the trip – she had to stay home to look after the kids. The other problem was that we had to keep the news to ourselves until it was announced on the date of the Queen's official birthday, and poor old Myra would have to keep the lid on the children's natural excitement for five weeks.

I was in Sydney the week of the announcement, and was due to open at the Parramatta Workers' Club on that very day. It would have been nicer perhaps and even grander to have been performing at the Opera House and I wasn't sure how to spell 'Parramatta' if I was asked to by some reporter on the phone from England. But new Knights have to put up with these matters – *noblesse oblige* and all that jazz.

The night before the news was released I went out with Jimmy Grafton and my Australian agent, Dennis Smith, for a celebration. I had already fielded a couple of phone calls from England that evening, in case I spilled the beans, forgetting that Sydney was eleven hours ahead of London. I was paranoid about having my title taken away by jumping the gun. The kids would never have forgiven me.

Having wined and dined unwisely the night before, I was woken in my hotel room by the room service waiter with my breakfast. As he stepped over the copy of the Sydney *Morning Herald* which had been pushed under the door, he looked down at my photograph on the front page alongside the news story of my Knighthood. 'What do I call yer now, mate?' he asked, dumping my breakfast tray on the bed.

I had a matinée at the Club that day, and the caterers prepared a huge spread of delicious seafood and a couple of bottles of champagne in celebration of the event. Jimmy Grafton arranged a press call and I felt I was walking on air when I went out on the stage for the first performance to the grand announcement of 'Ladies and Gentlemen – *Sir* Harry Secombe.' They were a great audience, they laughed at everything – especially when I sang – and I can't remember anything I said on stage. Despite my elation, I deeply regretted that Myra was not there to share the day with me.

She had troubles of her own at home. The day before the news came out she and Jennifer decided to prepare our housekeeper for the news. When she came in to work,

Jennifer sat her down in a chair and said, 'Now you mustn't say a word about this, but tomorrow Mum and Dad won't be Mr and Mrs Secombe any more.'

'Jesus!' she said, crossing herself. 'They're getting divorced.'

'No,' said Myra. 'Harry will be Sir Harry and I'll be Lady Secombe.'

The poor lady nearly keeled over and it took a large brandy to settle her down. When I eventually returned home, she dropped me a curtsey and called me 'My lord'.

It took Myra a long time before she got used to answering to 'Lady Secombe', referring to herself on the phone as 'Sir Harry's wife'. Then one day the man from Harrods, who was used to dealing with much more dignified titles than ours, came to clean the chandeliers in the lounge. He 'my ladyed' her so often she got quite used to the idea.

Some weeks before I was due to meet the Queen and receive the accolade, I was sent a letter from Buckingham Palace. It said, in effect, that some persons had difficulty in kneeling on these occasions and I was to answer the following question: 'Can you kneel?' I replied 'Yes' – refraining from adding 'but I can't get up again' in case I would have the honour withdrawn for impertinence. It worried me though, because I was at my heaviest at that time. 'Nineteen stone and two pounds' my bathroom scales indicated before expiring. Not *me*, the scales. Although I would have to lose some weight before *I* did.

The day before I was due to go to the Palace to receive the tap on the shoulder from Her Majesty, Myra and I were in the kitchen preparing lunch. Myra had the carving knife in her hand ready to carve the roast lamb, when she said 'How about a dress rehearsal?'

'OK,' I said, getting up from my chair.

'Kneel down, then.'

I knelt with some difficulty, and in the process of doing so, my trousers split from crutch to knee. I looked up at Myra, ashen-faced. 'What if this happens tomorrow?'

When Myra had finished laughing she said 'We can't have you making a "pubic" performance. Let's ring your tailor and get him to reinforce your morning dress trousers.'

He did, and as I walked forward to kneel before the Queen I had my fingers firmly crossed that John's strengthened stitches would survive. They held up beautifully, but I knelt so carefully that when I arose to have the badge of Knighthood put around my neck I could have sworn there was a twinkle in the Queen's eye.

When we first moved in to 129 Cheam Road it had the grand name of 'Chatsworth' on the front gate and I often wondered if the Duke of Devonshire ever received any of our mail by mistake. The fact that the house was in Cheam was a source of amusement for some of my show business acquaintances because of Tony Hancock's fictitious address – 23 Railway Cuttings, East Cheam. It proved to be a very happy house for us and, as my career advanced, we added to the property. We strengthened the fence around the garden and had a stone wall built in front of the house. The builder was Stan Wright, the husband of our first housekeeper, and the construction of the wall caused quite a bit of local interest. The stone came from the old Waterloo Bridge and proved to be extremely durable. The crossroads formed by the junction of Cheam Road and York Road on the right of us and its continuation into Gander Green Lane, meant that sometimes, particularly at night, the odd car coming out onto the main road would overshoot and collide with another vehicle passing in front of it . . . The result was that one or other of the cars would finish up against our wall.

Around Christmas time, when the roads were icy and some drivers had taken a drop too much, our house had the appearance of a casualty clearing station. Myra said she was seriously thinking of putting up a Red Cross flag in the front garden. However, the wall stood up well to all the bashing it took, and I'm glad to say that it is still there today – even though the house has gone. We sold it in 1983 because, although we had been very happy there, the traffic noise was getting worse and Myra, who is at heart a country girl, longed to get away to where the grass was greener and the fumes were fewer. All our offspring were growing up: Jennifer had married and sadly divorced; Andrew had a bachelor pad; David was twenty-one and already standing on the edge of the nest flapping his wings; and Katy, at sixteen, was the only one still at school.

I was reluctant to leave the area when we had been so contented there – especially when the Secombe Centre in Sutton had been named after me and, in addition, I had been made President of St Helier Hospital's League of Friends. But, we were determined to make a move. We accepted an offer on our house, believing that it might be turned into a nursing home, and were given a year to find another abode. Now, that might seem enough time for anybody to spend looking for somewhere to live – but believe me it is not.

One thing we were sure about was that we did not want to move out of Surrey. It had become our home county for the past thirty-two years and we had no intention of looking elsewhere. That should have narrowed our choice down a bit, but it still took nearly twelve months before we eventually discovered what we were after.

Myra and Jennifer did most of the searching and I was only called upon for a second opinion if they were quite sure of a place. They looked at dozens of houses but there always seemed to be a drawback – either the place was in the wrong area, or a motorway was going to be built nearby, or it just didn't feel right – and we went off for a summer break still not having made a choice.

Then, out of the blue, we received a brochure on a house that seemed to have all the right requirements – in the countryside, with eight and a half acres of grounds and magnificent views across the Weald of Sussex to the South Downs. Those intrepid vetters of the estate agents' claims, Myra and Jennifer – this time with Katy – set out to see if this house would be what we wanted.

Fortunately – I say that because we were two weeks away from being homeless – they were ecstatic about what they found. I went along for a look myself and, while tramping around other people's houses looking at faults while at the same time nodding and smiling in apparent appreciation of what has obviously been a coal cellar airily described as a potential 'den' is not my idea of fun, I was really bowled over when I saw the place for myself. It was a listed house because of its architectural significance, having been designed by Philip Webb, a famous Victorian architect who was a great mate of William Morris and one of the Pre-Raphaelites, though I have to confess that I had no idea who he was until I looked him up in a reference book.

The deal was struck on the occasion of our second visit and we have never regretted it. To wake up every morning and see the view from our bedroom window is in itself well worth the price we paid for the house. Not a high rise building or an electricity pylon in sight all the way to the blue outline of the South Downs 'where every prospect pleases and only Man is vile', to quote somebody or other. We have great neighbours and have made many friends in the village, and we are determined that, God willing, we shall end our days here on the hill.

Pickwick and Other Musicals

I was relaxing on the beach in front of the Coral Reef Club in Barbados in 1962, thinking of nothing in particular, when Myra called me. 'Hey, look at this,' she said, waving a copy of the *TV Times*. 'Jimmy Grafton sent it for you to see.'

I took it from her and smudged a thumbprint of suntan oil on the cover photograph of myself dressed as Father Christmas. The shot had been taken during a photo call for an ATV Christmas Special I had starred in, which had featured the American singer Jo Stafford and was produced by Bill Ward. In the show I had played Father Christmas in one sketch and a Dickensian-type inn-keeper in another.

I lay back on the sun lounger and let my thoughts drift. I remembered fancying myself in the early nineteenth-century costume with the half-boots and John Bull-type hat. Someone had said 'You look just like Mr Pickwick.'

'Not a bad idea,' I thought as I slurped down another rum punch. *Oliver!* had opened in the West End and was proving to be a big hit. 'What's wrong with me doing Pickwick as a musical?'

By one of those fortunate coincidences, the playwright and author Wolf Mankowitz was coming to have lunch with us that day. He had just moved out to Barbados and he had not yet furnished his house. As he was an old friend, we had invited him to eat with us. 'We've got real chairs and tables in our hotel,' I said. 'It'll make a change from sitting on upturned crates.'

And so it was that over lunch I mentioned the idea I had for doing *The Pickwick Papers* as a musical. 'Great,' said Wolf. 'I'll do the adaptation.' Just like that.

When I got back to England, I told my agents, Jimmy Grafton and Frank Barnard, what I had in mind. They thought it was a good vehicle for me and got in touch straight away with Bernard Delfont. In no time at all Bernie had spoken to Leslie Bricusse about writing the lyrics and Cyril Ornadel about the music and *Pickwick The Musical*, began to take shape.

The Pickwick Papers is such an episodic novel – having originally been written by Dickens on a weekly basis for a magazine – that it was difficult to know how to whittle it down to a two-hour show. Eventually it was decided by the three collaborators to hang the central plot on the breach of promise action that Mrs Bardell took out against Samuel Pickwick.

Peter Coe, who had directed *Oliver!* was considered by Bernard Delfont to be the ideal man to provide the magic touch for our production. The casting was terribly important, and Peter had a great reputation for picking the right people. The eventual line-up proved that he had not lost his touch.

The three members of the Pickwick Club were to be Julian Orchard as Snodgrass, Gerald James as Tupman and Oscar Quitak as Winkle. Jessie Evans was to be my leading lady, Mrs Bardell, with Peter Bull as Buzfuz, Teddy Green as Sam Weller and a young, slim Anton Rodgers as Alfred Jingle.

Among the other members of the cast was Christopher Wray, playing the Fat Boy, who later became famous for his lighting emporium.

This was the first time that I had ever stepped out of my Variety character – no raspberries, no ad libbing – in other words, I had to concentrate on creating a Samuel Willoughby Pickwick who was as close to the role as Dickens and his illustrators had portrayed him. Fortunately I had the right build and with the aid of a bald wig and the brilliant costume designed by Roger Furze I managed to look very much like the old chap. I looked the part – now I had to prove that I could act it.

The rehearsals were an exciting time for all of us – and there was so much to be done. Marcus Dodds, the musical director, helped us learn the music. He had a great way with him, achieving the results he wanted with great good humour and patience, nursing the cast through Leslie's lyrics and Cyril's sometimes intricate music. From the start 'If I Ruled the World' appeared to be a big show-stopper, and so it proved on the opening night, but there were many other tunes which merited wider acclaim. 'There's Something About You' for one, which was sung in the ballroom scene, and 'Look Into Your Heart', a duet between Mrs Bardell and Mr Pickwick, which was played for comedy, but was worthy of a better fate.

The sets were by Sean Kenny who had created those for the stage version of *Oliver!* They were entirely different from anything we had worked with before and required quite a bit of getting used to. Every scene change was done in full view of the audience, with stage-hands in costume manipulating large wooden set pieces on wheels. The outside of the Fleet Prison became the inside of the prison and then metamorphosed into the George and Vulture without a curtain rising or falling. Some of us used to refer to it as 'open-cast acting' because of the stark nature of some of the sets – but it all worked magnificently. Peter Coe and Sean Kenny had collaborated on *Oliver!* – they knew exactly what they were doing and between them changed forever the old concept of stage design in the musical theatre.

The one thing which had me worried in those first days of rehearsals was the skating scene. I had never learned to skate, and as we were using a proper ice rink at the end of the first half, Peter Coe said that it was time I was given some lessons. I was duly sent off to Richmond Ice Rink with a pair of double-bladed skates, which did give me a bit more stability than the normal ones.

After a few lessons I was able to manage a couple of twirls around the stage ice rink, but I had a harder job learning how to jump off the ice on to a square of jabolite which concealed a padded trap cut in the stage into which I disappeared at the finale of the first act. Eventually I mastered the jump, but I don't think I ever landed in the trap without bruising some part of my anatomy. What with that leap and the cartwheel at the end of my duet with Sam Weller which came before it, I had Jimmy Grafton and Bob Kennedy searching the small print of my contract for a personal injury clause.

We opened at the Palace Theatre, Manchester – a venue which I knew well and where I felt comfortable – for a two-week try-out on 3 June 1963. I shall never forget the day that we heard the orchestra for the first time. We had rehearsed for weeks with just a piano, with all the usual stops and starts, and the choreographer, Leo Kharibian, shouting out the rhythms. 'Come on, come on – one, two, *three*, four.' After a while the music begins to take second place to the action in one's mind. Then came the time for the orchestra to take over. We all sat in the stalls crossing our legs and our fingers in an agony of anticipation.

When the music started up there was a collective sigh of relief as the tunes we were getting rather fed up with began to take on a new life. Brian Fahey's arrangements breathed the very spirit of the times of Dickens. No strings, plenty of brass and percussion for the jaunty pieces, and muted for the prison scenes. By the time that first full band call had finished some of us were in tears and some of us were laughing but all of us were delighted with what we had heard. I think we all knew then that we were involved in something big.

The first night Manchester audience loved the show. The performance was for the Variety Club of Great Britain and quite a few fellow actors were out front. When they came backstage afterwards the verdict seemed to be that I had passed my acting test.

By the end of the Manchester run, most of the rough edges of the show had been polished and Sean Kenny's sets weaved in and out of the action with amazing precision. Peter Coe had given us all copious notes on our shortcomings, Leslie Bricusse and Cyril Ornadel were very supportive throughout rehearsals and Marcus Dodds's equanimity remained firmly in place. Bernard Delfont pronounced himself pleased with our efforts. All we had to do now was face the ordeal of the West End first night.

The London theatre we were to occupy was the Saville, which though not in Shaftesbury Avenue, was a venue with a good reputation. The opening night was, to our relief, a huge success for all of us. As Julian Orchard said to me after the curtain came down, 'I think we can safely send our laundry.'

The press reviews the following day were generally highly favourable. 'A miraculous *Pickwick*', announced Milton Shulman in the London *Evening Standard*, going on to say, 'I think that the book by Wolf Mankowitz has made a reasonable stab at retaining the spirit and feeling of this comic masterpiece.' He had some favourable words to say about Sean Kenny's sets too: 'Manipulating a number of wooden units as if they were part of a series of gigantic jigsaw puzzles, he can transform the Fleet Prison into the

George and Vulture Tavern during the singing of a few bars of music and the tavern can become a frozen pond fit for ice-skating during the speaking of a few snatches of dialogue.'

Of my performance, Shulman was very kind indeed

It was pretty obvious by the second and third weeks of the run that we were in for a pretty long spell at the Saville, and so it proved. The Saville Theatre became my home from July 1963 until February 1965 and a very happy home it turned out to be. We all got on very well together as a company and every month I would hold a 'Harry's Happy' party in the downstairs bar. I happened to have a 16 mm projector complete with sound, and the week before the party I'd circulate catalogues of films for hire and we'd all vote for the one to be shown on the night. Most of the films chosen were either musicals or those with a showbiz theme and they were all greeted with cheers and applause as if we were watching them live. In the time taken to change reels we'd all have another glass of red wine or a chicken leg from the buffet laid out on the bar counter. I have never since enjoyed films as much as I did then.

Julian Orchard was a particular pal of mine. He was over six feet two and when he wore his top hat he simply towered over me. The character of Snodgrass ideally suited him; it allowed him to employ wonderfully exaggerated gestures as he attempted to woo the Wardle daughter, Isabella, with his execrable poetry, and his attempts at dancing in the ballroom scene were a joy to behold. We had a lot of laughs together during the run.

All the cast, without exception, were the Seymour illustrations brought to life – Oscar Quitak was the perfect Winkle, the timid sportsman; Gerald James as Tupman, the romantic middle-aged suitor to the spinster Aunt Rachel Wardle could not have been bettered, and Anton Rodgers was the personification of the loveable rogue Jingle. Perhaps

the most terrifying character of all, Mr Buzfuz, was played
by an actor who was the living image of the man in the
original drawings and yet was the gentlest and nicest person
one could hope to meet, Peter Bull. He looked so fierce that
sometimes at matinées children would cry out in fear as he
delivered his speech in the courtroom, but I could reduce him
to a giggling wreck with no bother at all. Teddy Green, a fine
dancer and singer, was the first of three Sam Wellers in this
particular production. We had a great rapport both on and
off stage and I was sorry when he left the show to join
another musical called *Baker Street*. He was succeeded by his
understudy, Norman Warwick, who did a very good job for
the last few weeks of the London run.

There were, of course, hitches in the show during such a
long run – the scenery would sometimes become snarled up
as the various trucks collided with each other in the dark. On
one particular occasion about four weeks after we had
opened, I had a rather nasty shock myself.

Right from the start of the show, I was always afraid that I
would forget the first two verses of the introduction to the
song 'If I Ruled the World'. The words were tricky because
they had to be sung with a sense of urgency. In the scene just
after the opening of the second half, Pickwick becomes
caught up between the rival factions in the Eatanswill
election. He is mistaken for Mr Slumkey, one of the
candidates, because he happens to look like the picture of
him, as depicted on a banner being carried by a Slumkey
supporter. Despite Pickwick's protestations, he is lifted on to
a balcony, while the crowd – who assume he is Slumkey –
demand that he makes a speech. Pickwick reluctantly
launches into, 'Friends, dear friends, may I say I'm not a
politician, A simple minded, silver-tongued magician, Whose
words, fine words, could charm the very birds from the trees
with ease. Please, dear friends, though I may not be the
world's physician, By nature I'm of modest disposition,

Suppose you chose, instead of men like those, Men like these
– and these. Men who want a world that's fine and free. Men
like Nelson, Wellington and Drake and me. We want a world
our children will be proud to see. And if I had the chance, I
know just how it would be . . . If I ruled the world . . .' etc.

I had always had difficulty in remembering the words,
as a precaution, just before the dress rehearsal I wrote the
first two verses in biro on the plain wooden bar on the
balcony upon which I stood to deliver the song. After a week
or two I didn't really need the words, except as a safety net to
glance down and check they were there. One Monday night,
I could smell fresh paint as I entered the theatre and was
told that the scenery had been freshened up over the
weekend. I thought no more about it until the moment came
when I was thrust up on to the balcony for 'If I Ruled the
World'.

'Please, dear friends,' I began, waving my arms at
the company, who were now in front of me facing upstage.
'May I say ...' I looked down, as was my habit, to check the
words only to find that they had been completely obliterated
by the painting.

My mind went blank as the relentless bolero rhythm
commenced in the orchestra pit. I knew that I had to say
something vaguely political, so I gabbled away insanely over
the music, speaking utter rubbish.

Below me the cast were in hysterics at my antics, knowing
that the audience could only see their backs. Fortunately the
music for the verses was soon over and the tune came to the
'If I Ruled the World' part, which the company joined in
singing to help me out.

I was still shaking at the end of the performance, and when
I was told that an old army mate was at the stage door, I was
half inclined not to see him. 'Oh, all right, let him come in,' I
said, preparing my excuses for cocking up my big number.

'Great show, boy,' said Emrys Evans, ex-Bombardier.

'That "If I Ruled the World" was magnificent. I had a lump in my throat when you started singing that, very moving.'

I could only bow my head in thanks, not trusting myself to speak.

'That first bit was very political, though. I didn't know you were a socialist.'

'Neither did I,' I said.

Later in the run, that same balcony was the setting for a far more poignant moment in my life. For some weeks I had been aware that my mother was losing her battle with cancer of the bowel and Myra and I had driven down to Swansea to see her every Sunday. On the last Sunday before she died we were all at her home, sitting around her bedside laughing and joking about the fun we used to have in the old days. Talking about the way Dad had to take a chair on stage whenever he had to do his party piece, 'The Wreck of the 11.69', a parody of a railway accident. He was so nervous that he used to grip the back of the chair like grim death during his performance. And that was the cue for the story of how I used to entertain the family on a Sunday evening after church at Gran's terraced house in Danygraig. My nervous disposition would only allow me to sing if I could not be seen, and so I would sit on the outside toilet with the door open, surrounded by squares of newspaper stuck on a nail, and from that uncomfortable wooden seat I would belt out my favourite hymns while the rest of the family gathered in the nearby kitchen to listen. Mam always used to love telling that story.

We all knew that she did not have long to go and there were tears mingled with the laughter as evening came. When we left for London the following morning, there were lingering good-byes and a tacit acceptance that this would be the last time we would see her. My sister Carol had been wonderful throughout Mam's illness and was staying with her to nurse her until the end. Brother Fred was, of course, on hand with comforting words, but poor old Dad seemed bewildered and lost.

It was agreed between us before we left that I was to stay up in London if anything happened before the next weekend, but I would fly down for the funeral.

When the news came that Mam had died, I had to go on stage as usual, and managed not to let my grief show until the time came for me to get up on that balcony to sing 'If I Ruled the World'. As I climbed up the steps I was thinking that if I *did* rule the world my mother would still be alive, and I began to shake as I started to sing the first couple of lines. Before me, the whole cast – who knew what had happened – willed me with their eyes and gestures of encouragement to get through the song. Thanks to that wonderful bunch of people, I did, but I was grateful that I had ten minutes to myself before I had to get back on stage for my next scene.

As arranged, Myra and I flew down to Swansea for the funeral in a chartered aircraft, landing at Fairwood Common – a small airstrip quite near where Myra's parents lived. The service was held at St Peter's Church in Cockett, where my brother Fred was the vicar. The church was packed with family and friends, and there were quite a few people outside the church, genuinely sympathetic for the family's bereavement and not out of a morbid desire to see Harry Secombe's mother's funeral. Mam was such a well-loved figure in the community that she was mourned for the person she had been and for the good that she did in her life, not for having a son in show business.

After the burial ceremony we all went back to the house for tea and sandwiches and the conversation was all about the joy that Mam had brought to us and the fun we had shared as a family. Everyone knew how much pain she had been suffering and the phrase 'a happy release' was the verdict of the day.

On the plane trip back to London I felt much calmer now that the service was over, and though I dreaded the evening performance, I got through it without too much trouble. The sensation of my mother being somewhere around me was most comforting and the combination of that feeling together with great support from the company made 'If I Ruled the World' less of a minefield for me.

Towards the end of the run at the Saville, Jimmy Grafton told me that Bernard Delfont was negotiating with the American impresario David Merrick for a tour of the United States, with a view to a Broadway presentation. This was exciting news for the company when Peter Coe gave out the news on stage. Thanks to the influence of Equity, we were going to be able to take quite a few of the cast. Of the Pickwickians, Julian Orchard and Oscar Quitak were coming. Peter Bull as Buzfuz was to join us later and Anton Rodgers was to rejoin the company to play Jingle. Also included were Tony Sympson and Michael Derbyshire, who played Dodson and Fogg, and Michael Logan who took the part of Wardle. Gerald James had already left to join Olivier's National Theatre company. We were to have a new Sam Weller – a young lad called Davy Jones who was already over in America having just finished playing the Artful Dodger in *Oliver!* on Broadway. But, before *Pickwick* reached Broadway, Davy was replaced by my old mate, Roy Castle.

David Merrick came over to London to see the show and to see for himself what he was going to be promoting. A slim gentleman with a dark moustache and the air of a man who was serious about money, his reputation went before him, and those of us who had been advised of it were pretty wary in his presence.

At one time, after some bad critiques of one of his Broadway productions, Merrick had banned all critics from seeing any of his shows. Instead, he found individuals who happened to share the same names as some of the 'Butchers of Broadway' – as the New York theatre critics were called –

and got them to make complimentary remarks about the show. These quotes were then displayed outside the theatre to the amusement of the whole of show business and the chagrin of the critics, who could only grind their teeth in frustration when they read the sweet congratulatory words contributed by their namesake reviewers.

Merrick was also reported to have a low opinion of actors, although I have to say that he seemed to like me and always came backstage to my dressing-room when we were on tour in the States. Before he left the theatre the night he came to see *Pickwick* for the first time at the Saville, he put his arm around my shoulders and said that I was the 'eighth wonder of the world'. I wondered at the time whether I came before the Pyramids or after the Hanging Gardens of Babylon, but I didn't think I ought to ask.

After the show closed in London, it was decided that I would spend a few weeks on holiday in Barbados before we opened again in San Francisco, which meant that I would arrive after the other members of the company, who were to start rehearsals with the American cast.

Myra and I arrived along with our younger son, David, and Bob and Beryl Kennedy at San Francisco Airport full of excitement about the forthcoming opening night. At least the others were – I was quietly dreading the moment.

We booked into a Hawaiian style hotel on Clay Street and I remember standing outside our room that night looking at the lights of the big city and wondering what the hell I was doing there. Myra came and joined me. She took hold of my arm and said, 'Hey, you're shivering. Are you cold?'

'No,' I replied. 'I'm frightened.'

'You'll be all right, love,' she said. 'You wait and see.'

'God, I hope so.' I looked up at the stars, addressing him directly.

The following morning was the time for me to meet the whole cast and orchestra for our first orchestral run-through.

Bob and I went along to the Hertz Rent-a-Car office to pick up the Cadillac I was hiring for our seven-week stay in San Francisco. It was an enormous yellow convertible and I sat in the driver's seat with some trepidation. From what I had seen of the lay-out of the city's streets, it was not going to be an easy first drive to the theatre. It took me ten minutes before I could find the 'hand' brake – it was one of those pedals that you release with your foot. Bob and I were both too proud to go back into the garage and ask the Hertz representative how it worked, as I had airily assured him that I knew how to drive the car, not realizing that there was no handbrake as I knew it. Eventually, after going through the driver's handbook, Bob discovered the secret.

To make matters worse, I decided to take what the map called 'the scenic route'. This was a great mistake. I found myself unable to turn off the freeway out of the city and was forced to drive across the Golden Gate Bridge in the opposite direction to where we were supposed to be headed. Eventually I found a place to turn around, but by this time we were already half an hour late for the band call.

I have always prided myself on being early for appointments, especially when meeting people for the first time. And now, here I was, pulling up outside the Curran Theater over an hour late. Bob went off to park the car – I never expected to see him again – and I went in to face the music, and the musicians, to say nothing of the new members of the company, some of whom adopted elaborate attitudes of waiting, looking at their watches and heaving sighs.

My abject apologies were readily accepted by the English production members who were getting fed up with making excuses for me . . . 'He's never late . . . Perhaps he's been kidnapped', etc. As I was introduced to all the new actors, I noticed a wariness in their manner, something I had come across some years before when I had met the orchestra for the first time at the band call for an Ed Sullivan television show in New York. It seems that until you have proved yourself, until you have shown them what you can do, American showbiz folk reserve their judgement. I don't think it's really a bad attitude – it certainly puts you on your mettle. And so, when the time came for me to sing the Christmas number in the opening, I gave it all I had. My voice was in pretty good shape after the holiday in Barbados and it was a great feeling to be back in harness again. The musicians in the orchestra nodded approvingly and my lovely Saville cast members turned to their new American colleagues to smile knowingly as if to say 'We told you he wasn't too bad'.

Fortunately the conductor, Ian Fraser, was a Scotsman, and he too seemed to heave a big sigh of relief as he brought his baton down at the end of the number. 'Well done, mate,' he said with a grin and I knew then that I had a friend in the orchestra pit. My fears of a potential disaster on the opening night were at least lessened. All I had to worry about now was where Bob had managed to park the car.

The new Mrs Bardell was Charlotte Rae, who was known to American television audiences as the wife of the policeman in the comedy series *Car 54 Where Are You?*, and the American Tupman was John Call. Davy Jones as Sam Weller was always full of life and we got on like a house on fire. I never quite knew what he was going to get up to on stage, which made a change because I was the one with the reputation of being somewhat unpredictable.

There was another member of the team I was glad to see. Gillian Lynne, with whom I had worked in the pantomime *Puss in Boots* in Coventry, had joined the company as choreographer. She was already building a tremendous track record in her field and had a great reputation for getting good results.

Rehearsals started in earnest and the newcomers soon got into the swing of things under the combined direction of

Peter Coe and Gillian. David Merrick insisted on some new scenes being added and new songs were also tried out. This happened all the way through the tour across America and was a constant source of friction between Peter and Merrick. I was on Peter's side – going along with the principle of 'if it ain't broke, don't fix it'.

Bernie Delfont sent over to England for Keith Waterhouse and Willis Hall to provide some extra material. They stayed for a couple of weeks, but in the end very little of what they had written was used. Leslie Bricusse was staying at the same hotel as ourselves, and every day he sat around the pool scribbling away on a writing pad, trying to keep up with Merrick's demands.

The Curran Theater was an old fashioned building, not unlike those in the West End, and I felt quite at home after the first couple of rehearsals there. The theatre had an intimate atmosphere and the acoustics were good, something which was always of concern to me.

The dress rehearsal went very well, or so I thought, until the theatre manager came into my dressing-room afterwards and said 'Great, Harry – but what the hell were you saying? You were talking so quickly I couldn't understand a word.'

I should have realized that whereas a British audience understands most of the dialogue spoken by American actors due to years of watching American movies, the reverse did not apply. The majority of UK films only played the art house cinemas in the States and the only English accents the American cinemagoers recognized were the mid-Atlantic speech of the likes of Ronald Colman, C Aubrey Smith, David Niven and Greer Garson – British actors who lived in Hollywood. Any other British accent was difficult for them to pick up. My own version of the character Pickwick was a hint of Bloodnock from the *Goon Show* with strong overtones of my Welsh upbringing. In addition, I have always had a habit of speaking rather quickly.

I took the manager's advice and slowed down my dialogue so much that I put about ten minutes on the show. (It made me laugh later when one critic referred to Davy Jones's 'Cockney' accent. Davy hails from Manchester and never attempted to speak anything other than pure Mancunian.)

When opening night came, I remember sitting in the Curtain Call Bar across the street from the theatre about two hours before the show having a drink with Bernie Delfont, Jimmy Grafton and Bob Kennedy. It was too late to do anything more to the production and, as Jimmy said, 'It's all in the lap of the Gods . . .'

'And, of course, the stalls and the circle,' added Bernie, who was more practical.

My career was on the line and Bernie's trust in me to succeed was also going to be tested. We all shook hands quietly and, as we crossed the street back to the theatre where my name was now in lights, I thought of my usual reminder to myself on these occasions. 'Don't forget there are a hundred million Chinese who neither know nor care that you are going out front tonight.' Then I remembered that San Francisco had about the biggest Chinese population of any city outside China.

When I entered my dressing-room it was full of flowers and cables wishing me well from Myra and the kids, members of the company and all my mates back home. My Scottish dresser, David, was in the kilt and sporran he always wore on first nights and he too was in a fine old state of excitement. He had been in the chorus of many West End musicals as a young man and was always very nervous on first nights. There was a cup of tea waiting for me and he had already begun to arrange the flowers I had received.

The 'half-hour call' came over the tannoy system and I started to climb into my costume. As I did so, a calm came over me and I began to look forward to the performance.

Myra was the last one in the dressing-room to wish me good
luck and I think she was more nervous than I was now that I
had settled down. She knew more than anyone else what was
at stake for both of us, and the knowledge that she would be
out there in the audience rooting for me gave me added
strength.

For the last fifteen minutes I had the dressing-room to
myself. David knew that I liked to be quiet before I went on
stage and discreetly left the room to be on hand side-stage. I
paced up and down like a caged lion for about five minutes,
psyching myself up for my entrance, until the 'overture and
beginners' announcement came over the speaker. 'It's too
late to go home now, Harry,' I told myself, and walked down
the steps to the stage.

'Break a leg, folks,' I said to the assembled company, all set
for the opening. Then the curtain rose and we were off . . .

To my great relief – not to mention that of Bernie, Jimmy,
Bob, the theatre management and, last but by no means least,
Myra – the first night performance of *Pickwick* in America
was a huge success. After the final curtain, Jimmy, Bob,
Myra and I huddled together in my dressing-room, crying
unashamedly, so strong was our collective emotion. I can
say, quite honestly, that I have never cried like that before or
since.

The reviews were pretty good for the show, although one
Oakland newspaper referred to the author as 'Chuck
Dickens'.

As a family we had great fun driving around Northern
California at weekends, although the streets of San Francisco
were quite frighteningly steep. I remember one particular time
when I stopped at a traffic signal and was unable to see over
the bonnet.

I found the people of San Francisco very hospitable and
one resident in particular became quite a chum. His name

was Lou Luhrie, a great theatre buff and a man of considerable influence in the city. His life was a typical 'rags to riches' story. As a boy he had sold papers on a Chicago street corner outside a large building which he swore that he would one day own. He made his money during the Klondike gold rush – not by digging for the precious metal, but by selling the miners the tools with which to prise it out of the ground. Consequently he made a fortune and acquired a lot of real estate in San Francisco as well as the building in Chicago he had promised himself he would buy.

Lou used to host a lunch party once a week at Jack's Club to which many of the most influential politicians in the city were invited. I had an open invitation from him because he loved *Pickwick* so much. As it happened, I had a couple of Dickens' original letters with me which I had brought to the States for publicity purposes. I gave him one of them and he was overwhelmed by my gesture. This was probably because Lou was more used to giving than receiving, a trait that I have found in many wealthy Americans – great givers but somewhat bewildered recipients.

Myra, Jennifer, Andrew and David saw quite a bit of San Francisco while I was working. It was the 'flower power' era and there were some rather weird looking people wandering abroad in those days. A few weeks into the run Myra and the children had to go back home so that Jennifer and Andrew could return to school. It was very lonely without them and weekends saw me driving the big Cadillac up to the Yosemite Valley or down to the Big Sur country with my faithful manager Bob beside me, covering his eyes as I manoeuvred the hairpin bends.

Pickwick's next venue was the Los Angeles Music Center where ours was only the second show to be staged. It was a wonderful theatre with a huge auditorium and a stage that was so large that our sets were dwarfed. When the manager showed me around on the first day of rehearsal I said 'If we get the bird here, at least it'll be a peacock.' He looked at me strangely, crossing himself at the thought. There was little chance of *Pickwick* being a financial flop because most of the seats had been booked well in advance, but we were still an unknown quantity as far as Los Angeles' audiences were concerned.

On the first night, before the curtain went up, I spent my quiet moments in my capacious dressing-room reading some of the first night telegrams, and was delighted to find one from Bob Hope saying 'Welcome to Piccadilly West'. That cheered me up no end, and I went down to the stage for my entrance feeling a little less nervous because of his kind gesture.

The show went very well – perhaps not quite as well as San Francisco because we all felt a bit inhibited by the size of the stage and the number of film stars in the audience, but we had good reviews from most of the critics and settled in quite comfortably for the eight week run.

During this run Myra and the children came back out to join me. We stayed at the Hollywood Hawaiian Hotel – a nice little motel on Grace and Yucca, not far from Sunset Boulevard. The hotel pool was very welcome in the hot climate, and the fact that the children could splash around in the water took a lot of the pressure off Myra. There was a supermarket quite close to the motel where Myra used to shop. I'll never forget one afternoon when she returned from a shopping trip looking quite upset. She is dark-haired and brown-eyed and with her vivacious personality and lilting Welsh accent she has often been mistaken on our travels as a native of Spain, Italy, Greece – and even Fiji! As she was paying at the supermarket check-out for her purchases – which included a large melon – the man at the till enquired, 'Persian?'

'No,' replied my wife, dimpling prettily. 'I'm Welsh.'

'Not you, lady, the melon,' replied the man tersely.

There was a Lions Club International Convention being held in Hollywood at the time and we were all surprised one morning to find the pool full of Eskimos. It was no surprise to me, though, that they assumed Myra was one of their ilk.

Our younger son, David, was just four years old at this time. He had watched so many Westerns on American television that he had taken to wearing one of my suede trilby hats and had affected a limp in a fair impression of Walter Brennan. He also made a firm friend of the hotel's short order chef, imitating his cries of 'two eggs over easy' or 'two eggs looking at you', and became a great favourite with the staff at the hotel – at least, that was what they claimed.

At weekends we went on many sightseeing trips to places like Santa Monica, Carmel, Palm Springs, San Diego – all places I had seen in American films or read about in movie magazines as a boy and was determined to visit while I had the chance. It was an exciting time in the theatre, too. Stars of the calibre of Jack Benny, Jim Backus and Claire Trevor came backstage to meet me and the great film director Mervyn LeRoy asked me to meet him at Universal Pictures Studio to discuss a project in which he thought I might be interested.

It was a good idea. LeRoy wanted to produce a re-make of *Ruggles of Red Gap* with me playing the Charles Laughton role. He even went to the trouble of hiring the original picture for me to watch. His office was in one of the bungalows on the studio lot and as I was drinking a cup of tea he had provided before viewing the film, Cary Grant entered the room. He had seen me in *Humpty Dumpty* at the Palladium in 1959 and, hearing that I was visiting Mervyn LeRoy, he had come over specially to say hello.

I was flattered by all this attention, but by this time I'd been in show business long enough to know that Robbie Burns was right when he wrote 'the best laid schemes of mice and men gang aft agley'. And so it was with *Ruggles of Red*

Gap. Correspondence went to and fro for some time, then gradually ceased. But it made me feel marvellous at the time.

The *Pickwick* company left Los Angeles as the Watts riots were beginning, and we could see the fires burning as we took off from the airport. It was a sad time to be leaving and it brought home to me the great divide that exists in American society.

Our next port of call, Cleveland, was memorable for a couple of events. The first occurred when we discovered after our Sunday off that the machinery which provided the ice for the rink in the skating scene had failed and we were ankle-deep in water when we reported for the show on the Monday.

The second event I remember was that our eldest son, Andrew, finally learned how to swim in the pool of the hotel we were staying in on Euclid Avenue.

The show received good notices, including one in the *Cleveland Plain Dealer* which referred to me as 'the nearest thing to Ionescu's bald soprano' that the reviewer had ever heard. Meanwhile we continued to rehearse extra scenes which were all eventually thrown out. One of them had a memorable lyric, 'You'll always find a chap who'll slap your back and slip you ten.' Very Dickensian, that.

Detroit was our next stop. What can I say about the city except that it was hot and humid and that Myra was refused entry to a restaurant because she was wearing a trouser suit? But this was where Roy Castle joined us with his lovely wife Fiona. It was great to have him playing Sam Weller in the show, although we were all sorry to say goodbye to Davy Jones. He went on to fame and fortune as a member of The Monkees pop group.

Detroit was not the greatest place to be staying at that time. There was growing unrest in the city and many muggings. Our stage manager was attacked and robbed under the canopy of his hotel, and our hotel receptionist used to take a taxi home every night – even though she only lived two blocks away. I had a cousin, Margaret, who, during the war, had married a Canadian airman and emigrated to toronto, so Myra and the children spent a couple of weeks with her and at weekends I would drive over the border to see them – which made a welcome change.

Washington, our next venue, was something of a contrast with elegant architecture and interesting historic sites and monuments to visit. At first we rented an apartment in the district of Alexandria – but after Jennifer and Andrew returned home to school we moved out to stay in a picturesque log cabin in the Shenandoah National Park. It meant a journey of about eighty miles each way to and from the theatre, but the air was so pure and the scenery so beautiful that the travelling was well worth the effort.

Pickwick was a critical success in Washington, and with Broadway as our next stop we all felt that the show was in good shape – or as good as it would ever be after the months of touring. It was impressed on us all by Peter Coe that the audiences we were about to play to in New York were not going to be push-overs, that the audiences in the places we had already appeared were softer and not as cynical as those in the Big Apple. Peter was preparing us for the worst, but praying for the best, because there was so much at stake for everybody concerned.

There couldn't have been a more inauspicious time to première a new Broadway musical – not only was a news-paper strike underway, but also the Pope was making an official visit to New York.

The charity preview audiences were, like most of their kind, pretty subdued. They had paid a fortune for their seats so the women were determined to show off their finery and were more interested in each other's outfits than the action on stage, while their husbands, having been dragged along, were consequently rather resentful and unappreciative of the performance.

The official opening night, however, went very well, except for one mishap when a piece of scenery fell down in the middle of the ballroom sequence – luckily without hurting anybody.

We were all in a pretty high state of expectancy as we trooped along to Sardi's Restaurant for the traditional after-show party. It is a custom on Broadway for the early editions of the morning newspapers to be brought into the restaurant and the notices to be read out. Due to the strike there were only two reviews printed. One was bad and the other was good. There were cries of outrage from the cast and murmurs of sympathy from friends as they slowly drifted away into the night. I had a sick feeling in the pit of my stomach as I shook hands with a grim-faced Peter Coe before Myra and I headed back to our penthouse apartment in the Berkshire Hotel. It was now obvious to me that *Pickwick* lacked the sharp edge which the sophisticated Broadway public wanted.

I should have smelled a rat when David Merrick chose to visit the Far East with a production of *Hello Dolly* rather than stay in New York for our opening. Bernard Delfont, I believe, had a feeling after San Francisco that Broadway might be a tougher proposition. I remember him saying 'Make the most of it, Harry,' as we shook hands before he left for England.

In spite of the poor review, the business at the box-office wasn't bad at all. The trade papers always carry the returns of every Broadway show, revealing whether a production is making a profit or a loss, and at no time during our run did we ever go into the red.

However, as fate would have it, I developed mumps – of all things – which at my time of life could be rather dangerous, and was forced to take to my bed. Myra had gone back to England with David, not thinking for one moment that there was any trouble with the show. In fact, I had asked her to arrange to ship over my Rolls-Royce as I thought it would be a good publicity gimmick.

At the end of my first week off from the show, I was lying in my hotel bed watching television. Bob Kennedy had come round for the evening to keep me company. The TV picture was quite fuzzy and Bob tried to tune it in to get a better reception to no avail. 'I'll fix the blasted thing,' I said, rising painfully from my bed. The frustration of being confined to my room and being unable to visit the theatre had made me irritable. I waddled over to the set and applied my patent method of 'fixing' television sets. I kicked it.

I swear that at that very moment the screen went black and all the room lights went off. 'I've fused the bloody lights now,' I said.

Bob looked out of the window and said, quite calmly, 'You've fused New York.'

Unbeknown to us this was the beginning of the great black-out of the city. The only lights we could see from the hotel room were the headlights and tail-lights of the cars down below in the street.

My penthouse suite was right at the top of the building and it dawned on us that Bob – who had a severe limp – was going to have to climb down dozens of flights of stairs in the pitch darkness because the elevators would be out of order. A bellboy arrived with some candles and we set about looking for the toy space-gun that young David had left behind. The gun had a red light that went on and off when the trigger was pressed. However, if you kept your finger on the trigger, it produced a steady beam of light. The drawback was that this action also produced a loud 'Whee-whee-whee' sound. Bob's progress back to his own hotel must have been an amusing sight.

I had a little transistor radio set at my bedside so that I could listen to the BBC World Service. I switched over the

FM stations to find out what had happened to the New York power supply and heard the announcement that 'all our forces are on red alert!' and that the public was 'not to panic'. Hundreds of people all over the city were trapped in lifts. It was quite gripping to lie there listening to the drama unfolding and I stopped feeling sorry for myself. 'At least,' I thought, 'there'll be no performance tonight.'

The next day when my doctor arrived to see me, the electricity supply had been restored, but he apologized for being late because so many of his elderly patients had suffered heart attacks from having to scale the stairs to their apartments at the top of skyscrapers. As he left, the doctor gave me his newspaper which I fell upon greedily. I wanted to read all the news about the black-out, but first I turned to the page containing the theatre advertisements. And there I read the customary little box with the heading '46th Street Theatre – *Pickwick*'. Underneath, below the press quote 'Should run for years', was the announcement 'Last two weeks'.

I couldn't believe it. I rang Bob immediately and asked him if what I had read was true. He had no idea and said he would ring Biff Liff, the company manager. Biff, an affable man who was genuinely fond of the show and its company, had to admit that *Pickwick* was coming off. No reason was forthcoming except that David Merrick didn't want to lose any money.

That was enough for me. I crawled out of bed and got dressed. I rang Bob again and told him that even if my wedding tackle was to hit the ground I was going back into the production to finish the last two weeks on Broadway.

I was welcomed back by the cast and by my understudy – a man even bigger than me who had found my costume too tight and 'If I Ruled the World' too high. During my absence the whole company had demanded to have innoculations against the mumps virus, a precaution that had proved very costly for Mr Merrick.

On the Tuesday of the final week, Bob came to my

dressing-room and said 'Before you get changed for the show, come to the front of the theatre for a minute.' I followed him, a bit annoyed to have my quiet time before the show interrupted. But there, in the rain, surrounded by a knot of admiring passers-by, was my grand old Rolls-Royce Silver Cloud, gleaming and fresh from its trans-Atlantic journey.

I had a lump in my throat as I patted its bonnet. 'At least we can fly the flag for the old country before we go back,' I said to Bob. And for the last few days I drove around New York in style, before watching the Rolls being loaded back on board ship for its return journey home.

The Saturday night that *Pickwick* closed found the stage door besieged by people demanding to know why such a good musical was coming off and the theatre was packed for both performances. It was a great way to finish, but I was heartbroken that all the hard work that the talented cast had put in over the months we had toured across the country had not achieved the end result we had all desired — a Broadway triumph.

And yet it was not a complete disaster, because, apart from all the money the show had made on tour — which was considerable — there was to be a pleasant postscript the following year when the Tony nominations (the Broadway equivalent of Hollywood's Oscars) were announced.

By that time *Pickwick* was long gone from Broadway and I was back in the number one dressing-room at the London Palladium. Jimmy Grafton came backstage to tell me that both Roy Castle and I had been nominated for awards for the best lead and best supporting actor in a musical respectively. Charlotte had also received a nomination for best supporting actress. There were only four nominations in each category, and although none of us was awarded the final accolade, it was a pretty good effort when one considers how very many shows come and go on Broadway in a year.

*

Four years after *Pickwick*, it was with high hopes and the same production team that the musical version of *The Four Musketeers* began to take shape. Peter Coe was to direct, Sean Kenny was the set designer and Bernard Delfont was producing. The music was by Laurie Johnson and the lyrics by Herbie Kretzmer.

When rehearsals began, Myra was expecting Katy and it was a toss up as to which production would happen first. *The Four Musketeers* won by seven days when it opened on 5 December 1967, and our lovely daughter arrived on the twelfth.

A lot of money was spent on the elaborate sets and, for the first time since the war, full use was made of the vast area of the Drury Lane stage, with all the huge stage machinery that in the past had made possible such spectacular scenes as a boat race, an avalanche, a snow storm, even an earthquake.

The costumes – which were truly magnificent – were designed by Loudon Sainthill and the cast that Peter Coe assembled promised well.

Kenneth Connor played the King; Aubrey Woods was the Cardinal; Joyce Blackham was to play Milady Clara, but did not eventually get around to doing so, and her place was taken at short notice by Elizabeth Larner; Stephanie Voss was Constance, my girlfriend; Porthos, Aramis and Athos were played by Jeremy Lloyd, John Junkin and Glyn Owen respectively, though they gave a month's notice in before the show actually opened; Jan Brinker, who was to be the Queen, also left before opening night and was replaced by Sheena Marsh; Sidney Tafler was supposed to play the Sergeant-at-Arms, but he took sick and Bill Owen took over the part. He also left the show.

As you can imagine, all this to-ing and fro-ing caused a constant draught across the stage as different members of the cast exited through the stage door. Bernie Delfont became so alarmed at what was happening that he decided to take over some of the directing himself, believing that Peter Coe had somehow lost his celebrated gift of finding the perfect cast.

I had my own problems. I had just returned from a trip to Aden for the army and, as a result of singing in the open air three or four times a day, the searing heat had damaged my vocal chords. As a precaution I pre-recorded the two big numbers in the show – 'A Little Bit of Glory' and 'The Masquerade' – with just a piano accompaniment, so that if my voice was seriously affected, I could mime to the track while the orchestra played live. Also, because Joyce Blackham had to pull out, I had very little time to rehearse with the lovely Liz Larner, and, indeed, on the first night I spent our scenes together gently guiding her to her positions on stage. I have to say that she gave a fantastic performance in spite of everything. Stephanie Voss also gave me a lot of support that night.

The massive sets presented many problems for the cast. They consisted of a complex central revolve which included four sets of stairs, each of which swivelled, integrated with great blocks, slabs and towering shapes, plus two side units that could move out on five horizontal tracks to link up to the central unit by means of flying drawbridges. In addition, there were other large units that were let down from the flies. These included arches, columns and heraldic emblems – one of which clobbered me one night. All this mechanical wizardry was worked electronically and moved while supporting members of the cast.

I remember at one dress rehearsal when, every time I was about to sing, the stairs I was standing on began to go into reverse. 'You don't want an actor!' I cried to the unfeeling moguls in the stalls. 'You want a bleeding singing goat!'

The two people responsible for setting everything in motion were the stage manager, Peter Roberts, and his very young assistant, Stella Richards. Stella was so competent at her very complex job that when the show finished I employed her as my secretary – and she was great at that job, too.

One further complication as far as I was concerned was the fact that I had to make my first act finale entrance on a horse. Now, I am not a very competent rider, and the nag I was given to ride stood nearly eighteen hands. He knew from the moment he saw me that 'here was a berk', and he devised all sorts of ways to unseat me at rehearsals. It was not until I found out from his trainer that he loved carrots that I began to make friends with him. Every performance, before I got on board the beast, I would feed him a couple of juicy carrots and on we would trot. Once, because I had run out of carrots, I gave him an apple, and he flew on stage, practically stood on his hind legs and deposited a message to me at the feet of Kenneth Connor – who was not too pleased. From then on, my dresser arranged for a constant supply of carrots with a bloke who worked at Covent Garden Market.

For the most part, the critics were not very kind about the show, but in spite of the notices, *The Four Musketeers* ran for about fourteen months. After a while, it began to get a cult following, partly because I decided that the only way to get the show going was to be even more outrageous than ever.

One night my voice was so bad that it was decided that I would have to use the tape that I had pre-recorded. I said that we should let the audience know what had happened and tell them that I would be miming to the big numbers in the show by making an announcement to that effect, and George Hoare, the manager of Drury Lane, was elected to make the announcement. The first time he did it, George was a little nervous because, when he came on, there was a murmuring from the audience as if they were expecting calamitous news. When he said I was indisposed there was quite an angry reaction, but the fact that I would be appearing, albeit hoarse, seemed to satisfy them.

When it came time for me to mime the big song 'The Masquerade', I started off perfectly seriously and in perfect synchronization with the tape. Suddenly, the bizarre nature of what I was doing got the better of me and I began to stuff a handkerchief in my mouth as my recorded voice went on. then I took a glass of water – specially set out in case I needed it to soothe my throat – and drank it slowly as the song progressed. By this time the audience, bless them, were in convulsions and at the end of the song I had more applause than I had ever had when I sang it live.

After the show, I had a chat with Jimmy Grafton and Bob Kennedy, and it was agreed that I would keep it in. The show was desperately short of laughs, and what I had just done seemed to provide the answer.

So it was that from then on, throughout the production, George Hoare made his announcement before the opening. By the time the show finished, George must have made over 300 appearances. He reckoned that it must have been some kind of theatrical record.

One night Her Majesty came to see the show from the stalls and, on her way out, she remarked to George that it would be a shame when my voice came back – a back-handed compliment, but one of which I was very proud and one which served to vindicate my decision to take a chance on sending up a good song.

It's amazing how many people have come up to me since the *Musketeer* days and said, 'I was in the audience on the night you lost your voice.' And I nod and smile, and never let on that my voice came back as strong as ever two weeks after that first announcement by George Hoare – the record breaker.

The Plumber's Progress started life as *Schippel*, written before the First World War by a German playwright called Carl Sternheim, the author of *The Mask of Virtue*, a 1935 vehicle for Vivien Leigh. *Schippel* was adapted in 1974 by C P Taylor for the Traverse Theatre Company in Edinburgh. Set in Germany in 1913, the piece told the tale of a quartet of class-conscious Meister Singers who, with the demise of their tenor, are forced – against their better social instincts – to recruit the local plumber, a gifted singer, in his place.

Jimmy Grafton saw the play and decided that it would be perfect for me for a West End comeback. I went to see it at the Open Space Theatre and I was captivated by the concept.

When I saw it, the leading part of the tenor, Schippel, was played by Roy Marsden. He gave a great performance and I felt somewhat embarrassed about taking over the role from him. It says a lot for Roy's breadth of spirit that he stayed with the production in a lesser part and agreed to act as my understudy.

Bernard Delfont who had produced all my shows for as long as I could remember, thought that it would be a good vehicle for me at the Prince of Wales Theatre, although he wanted to change the name. He thought *Schippel* sounded too much like the Dutch airport and didn't want audiences to come to the show thinking that they were going to see me playing a singing air steward. So the title was altered to *The Plumber's Progress*, which caused a certain amount of controversy among the purists.

The cast was particularly strong. Priscilla Morgan (Clive Dunn's wife) and Patricia Heneghan played the sister and wife respectively of Tilman Hiketier, the goldsmith and leader of the quartet, who was played by Roger Kemp. Roy Marsden and Gordon Clyde portrayed the other members of the singing group and Simon Callow was Crown Prince Maximilian. The director was Mike Ockrent, who has since made quite a name for himself in the theatre.

Mike was extremely kind to me at rehearsals, teaching me how to control my wilder moments and how to change the mood without jarring the whole production. I was determined to play the part straight and not indulge myself in ad libbing, which I had been forced to do in *The Four Musketeers* out of sheer desperation. As the singing all came naturally out of the context of the play – for example when Schippel auditioned for Hiketier – I did not have the awkward transition from dialogue to song. When we sang as a quartet we were accompanied by a piano on stage played by Gordon Clyde, one of the members of the quartet.

I found the rehearsals invigorating, working as an ensemble player throughout the piece, learning how to blend with the other actors. All the music was sung in German, which could have been a bit of a turn-off for some members of the audience, but it was true to the piece.

In September 1975, we opened in Manchester for a two-week try-out at the Opera House. The play was received pretty well and took just over £7,000 for five performances in the first week. However, I sensed that there might be trouble ahead when I overheard a lady's comment as she passed under my dressing-room window after one of the performances. 'I'm not paying good money to hear Harry Secombe say "bollocks",' she said firmly.

When we opened at the Prince of Wales with a charity performance for the Variety Club of Great Britain, exception was taken to the singing of 'Deutschland Uber Alles' at the final curtain. This was deliberate – the song emphasized the resurgence of German militarism as portrayed by the fanaticism of Hiketier, the quartet's leader. It was meant to be ironic but I suppose it could have been taken the wrong way by certain sections of the audience. The decision was taken to change the final song to 'Stille Nacht', which somehow emasculated the effect that Sternheim and C P Taylor had originally desired.

The reviews after the first night were nearly all good. Sheridan Morley wrote 'the result is a broad comedy with, at its centre, the resolutely unchanging Schippel, unflinchingly working class and deaf to all entreaties to improve himself or his station. It is a comic performance I shall long treasure and I see no reason why Mr Secombe should not now start thinking about *The Good Soldier Schweik*, maybe even *Peer Gynt*.'

Michael Billington's review went 'Snobs will be upset that *The Plumber's Progress* has found its way from the Traverse Theatre Club to the Prince of Wales, but personally I'm delighted to see the commanding heights of the West End falling one by one to the subsidized companies and Mike Ockrent's production of this anti-bourgeois satire of 1912 has undergone physical expansion without sacrificing its precision.'

The Plumber's Progress was a fruitful experience as far as I was concerned because I learned so much from working with the other actors. They were all very generous to me on stage and off and I have watched the subsequent rise to fame of Simon Callow and Roy Marsden with a great deal of satisfaction. I was very upset when I had to leave the show with a viral pneumonia, and though Roy carried on for a few performances as Schippel, he developed a throat infection and the show had to come off. It was never a huge box-office success, but it was mounted at a time when all the West End theatres were suffering a listless period. Perhaps if the production had been in a smaller theatre we might have run longer, but there is no point in looking for excuses in our profession. If the public like what you have to offer they will come and see it, and if they don't, well, they won't.

There are so many excuses made for badly attended shows, but the most priceless I have ever heard was Arthur Askey's. He always used to say, 'There'll be nobody in tonight – there's pearl diving at Oldham.'

A Wanderlust

Ever since I was a small boy, I have longed to find out what lies over the next horizon. I used to sit on the front gate of our council house at 7 St Leger Crescent, St Thomas, Swansea, South Wales, Great Britain, Europe, The World, and gaze longingly in the direction of Town Hill, because my dad told me that that was where the West was and that America was over there somewhere. As far as I was concerned, buffalo roamed on the other side of that hill and you could get scalped in Llansamlet.

As I grew older, my horizons got wider and my desire to travel grew proportionately. My army service took me to North Africa, Sicily and Italy via troop ships, landing craft, bren carriers and three-ton trucks – which was not exactly the way that Thomas Cook would have planned it, but was enough to whet my appetite for further excursions, without, of course, the necessity of having to persuade the Germans in front to keep moving.

When I became more affluent, obscure places beckoned and I would set off with Myra and our two children, Jennifer and Andrew, on holiday trips to what were in those days fairly remote Caribbean islands like Trinidad and Tobago. It was an adventure to travel by plane then and we would all be togged up in brand new outfits for the journey and both sets of parents would come to the airport to see us off. Then we would pose for photographs at the foot of the airline steps before boarding the plane. The reason for this was twofold: one, to show the general public that we were brave enough to fly BOAC; two, if anything happened to the plane, Associated Press would have a scoop on their hands – 'Comedian and Family Before Fateful Flight'.

Nowadays, travel is much more sophisticated and the world has shrunk. There is even a Hilton International hotel at Llansamlet, where you won't get scalped but you might get a decent haircut.

Africa never ceased to fascinate me. As a child I was always off hunting lions or cutting my way through the dense undergrowth of our local park and when, some years later, I was invited on a safari, I was off like a shot to the Army & Navy Stores to be fitted for shorts and several pairs of unsoiled white duck.

It was thus attired that I strode out on to the verandah of my hotel in Nairobi, showing a full inch of leg between the bottom of my shorts and the tops of my khaki stockings. On my head I wore a bush hat, and a pair of suede boots completed my white hunter ensemble. Across the hotel gardens a parrot chained to a stand sent up a raucous screeching, and an American couple having an early breakfast paused abruptly in mid-kedgeree. I went back to my room and changed. If I was ready for Africa, Africa was not quite ready for me.

My spirits lightened as we headed for Nairobi National Park, where giraffe, lion and all sorts of other wild life go about their business with complete disregard for the planes roaring over their heads as they fly to and from the airport.

We had only just got inside the Park when a large baboon jumped on the bonnet and performed a disgustingly human act, after which it bowed politely and held out its hand for a nut. It was like that all the way: lions rolled playfully on their backs like cats wanting to be tickled, giraffes nibbled disdainfully at the tops of thorn bushes and ignored us completely.

Disillusionment set in. Where was my Africa? The Africa of my boyhood imaginings? This was Longleat with flies.

Our next stop was Murchison Falls and, after a dusty but fairly uneventful journey into Uganda, we arrived some days later on the banks of the White Nile just in time to catch the last ferry to the camp. During our short stay at Murchison, we were able to observe hippos and elephants without the slightest danger – a fact that began to irk me after a while. I was still in search of the real, unspoiled Africa.

My chance came a few days later when I was invited to accompany a game warden on one of his regular trips in search of poachers. Our base was a permanent camp near the Ugandan border with the Congo. We were going to sleep in sleeping bags and really rough it. At last, I thought, this is it.

On the way to the camp, I heard two of the native boys who were travelling with us referring to me several times in what I took to be Swahili. When we got there, I mentioned this to the warden.

'That's good,' he said. 'If they have a special name for you it means they respect you. Try to find out what it is.'

The camp consisted of one round metal hut with a straw roof and a wooden table. It was getting late, so the boys built a big fire and set tin plates on the table. Beer was produced and, as a Tilley lamp pumped a brilliant circle of light around the table, dinner began.

Somewhere an animal snuffled and, flushed with beer, I smiled to myself. I was Mungo Park, Livingstone and Chaka the Zulu chief all rolled into one. This was how I had always imagined it – the camp fire, the animal noises and the convivial chat around the table. Soon it will be time to slip into our sleeping bags while the native boys keep the fire going and ward off the animals, I thought.

The table was cleared and the boys, to my amazement, retired into the metal hut and shut the door.

'Time for bed,' said the warden, stretching. 'If you want to go to the toilet, there's one over there.' He pointed vaguely into the blackness. ' 'Night.'

I sat for a while drinking beer and keeping the fire going until, with the last piece of wood gone, I struggled into my sleeping bag, whistling tunelessly and staring uneasily about me. There was the whole Aardvark to Zebra of African wildlife out there, and here I was lying on the ground in this open air supermarket, two hundred and twenty pounds of human flesh, fresh and ready wrapped.

I eventually fell asleep, but dawn was never as welcome as the next morning. I was up and sluicing my naked body as the native boys emerged from the safety of their hut.

One of them laughed and pointed at me. 'Tumbo Mkubwa,' he said.

I turned proudly to the game warden who was now awake and regarding me with some amusement.

'There, that's the name they called me yesterday. What does it mean?'

He scratched his head and stretched his arms out wide, taking his time. 'Big Belly,' he said.

Somehow, it was the final indignity.

As a family we have travelled many times around the world on the way to concert tours in Australia and New Zealand, dropping off at Hong Kong or Singapore on the outward flight and Fiji or Hawaii on the return journey. The very names of these exotic places are still fascinating to me and the fact that I've had prickly heat in all of them still does not put me off. Even the fact that I have never had a suit that fitted made in twenty-four hours by a Hong Kong tailor is no deterrent to my urge to travel. Myra had one of these suits made into seat covers for her car and still had enough left over for a table cloth. The fly buttons that adorned it were always a good topic of conversation with visitors who came to tea in Cheam.

We have had a place in Majorca since 1963. Myra and I had holidayed there a couple of times previously and had taken a liking to the island. Jimmy Grafton had a villa in Paguera, which he sold in favour of an apartment in a new development called Costa de los Pinos which was on the other side of the island, and one day he suggested to me that perhaps we would like to go out there and see if we too would like to invest in property in the same complex.

It didn't take us long to decide that we would indeed fancy one of the houses there. We chose one on the hillside on which the collection of villas and apartments had been built, a promontory jutting out into the sea and forming the north end of a beautiful bay encompassing miles of golden sand.

I was still doing *Pickwick* at the Saville Theatre when we moved into the villa, and it provided the perfect bolt-hole for the family. In the summer, Myra would go over with her parents and Andrew, Jennifer and David, who was then still a babe in arms. I would join them at weekends, catching a late-night flight from Gatwick – usually by the skin of my teeth – and returning on the Monday morning plane from Palma. It might seem like a lot of trouble for twenty-four hours in the sun, but to me it was well worth the effort. To be able to enjoy the view from our balcony and smell the pine-scented air more than compensated for the time taken up by travelling.

The nearby village of Son Servera was where we did our shopping and the locals soon got used to the fat foreigner with the pretty little dark wife – who they all thought was

Spanish. My knowledge of Spanish was very rudimentary and I soon became a source of entertainment for the customers at the butcher's shop as I had to order what I wanted in mime. For example, for a shoulder of lamb, I would pat my own shoulder and bleat baa-baa. For a leg of the same animal I would, obviously, indicate my leg. A chicken was dead easy as I've always been able to cluck. A rump steak was always a tap on the behind accompanied by a mooing sound. I never really got around to ordering sausages.

As the years went by and Katy came along and the other three got bigger, the little villa seemed to shrink in size. Myra was finding the place a bit claustrophobic and the journey she had to make down to the little cove below us and back again up the many steep steps to the house, which happened about three times a day, was beginning to get her down. So it was either sell up and leave Majorca, or find another place not too far away.

Jimmy Grafton came to the rescue. He had seen a villa for sale about a mile down the coast, right on the sea. It was newly built and could be exactly what we wanted. He was dead right, as usual, and the whole family fell in love with it. The entrance to the house was through an archway into a little courtyard, where an ornamental fountain played away. Inside, there were two bedrooms on the ground floor with toilets and bathrooms en suite, and a large dining and living room combined, while upstairs there was a master bedroom with French windows that led on to a patio facing the sea, with stunning views of the pine-clad hills of Costa de los Pinos on our left and the sea at our back garden gate.

I was in Australia at the time, and Myra moved in as soon as she was able without telling me. After the long journey back to Palma via Los Angeles, New York and Madrid, I was met at the airport by Myra and Jennifer. Feeling pretty jet-lagged, after the excitement of seeing the family again, all

I wanted was to get into bed. But, as we headed for where I thought we still lived, Myra insisted that we paid a visit to the new villa so that I could see how it was getting on. 'Can't I see it later?' I yawned, desperate for a kip. Of course, when we turned into the new address, the rest of the family were all waiting to welcome me. It was a wonderful surprise and my tiredness vanished immediately, only to return hours later when my head fell in the gazpacho at dinner.

'Don't worry,' said Myra. 'It was cold anyway.'

That was twenty-two years ago and we're still in love with the place. In recent years, Majorca has suffered from the bad reputation it has received from reports in the tabloid press about the behaviour of 'lager louts' in the fleshpots of Arenal and Magaluf. But there are still little-known corners of the island where the tourist in search of beautiful scenery allied with peace and tranquillity can find what he is looking for: where honeysuckle grows in profusion and blackberries ripen unseen; where eagles ride the thermals above rock-clad mountain peaks and shepherds tend flocks of wiry sheep whilst listening to their personal stereos. Well, you can't get away from everything.

It was only when we had been living there for about ten years that we began to understand the Majorcan people and the workings of the Majorcan mind. Shopkeepers will say yes out of politeness. We had half an iron gate for four years, and it was considerably longer before we could get rid of the string that held the shutters open. Every six months the local blacksmith calls around for a sherry and a look at the jobs he hasn't yet finished. He nods, promises, asks after the family, then we ask after his and that's it for another six months.

We had a hole in the ground for two years before it underwent its metamorphosis into a swimming pool. Strange-looking weeds grew out of it, the kids kept falling into it and every time we came out for a holiday we went through the ritual of pleas and promises with the builder.

Then, suddenly one Easter, it was practically finished . . . and it stayed practically finished until we went back in August.

Majorcans have a very keen sense of humour, which they conceal beneath an outward appearance of dourness. When I went to pay the plumber's bill one day in Son Servera, his wife searched through the files for it to no avail. I repeated my name with the Spanish pronunciation I had become used to – (SEC-OM-BEE) – but she still couldn't find it. Then her husband came in and took over the search. He found it easily, and when I asked him why his wife had been unable to do so, he grinned and showed me the name under which it had been filed: 'El Gordo' – 'The Fat One'. Later on, I discovered that I was also known as 'El Tenor' (The Tenor) or 'El Cantante' (The Singer). This came about because, in a rash moment, I gave a café owner one of my records. It was a mistake because for weeks after, whenever I entered his café he put the damned thing on at full volume. He seemed to think that that was the reason I had given it to him – I had it on authority that it was never played at any other time. There's only so much of my own voice that I can stand listening to and in the end I had to plead with him not to play the record. He agreed reluctantly, or so it seemed until out of the corner of my eye I caught him winking at his waiter. There is subtlety in abundance in the Majorcan character.

Majorca is my second home, but if I could afford a *third* house it would definitely be in Australia. I love the place.

The first time I went there was in 1961 when I was booked to appear in a television show and a concert in the Sydney Town Hall. I was enchanted by the place and the people and for the first time I began to realize how popular the *Goon Show* had become outside the UK. I was constantly being greeted by cries of 'Hello Ned,' or 'How's Eccles?' by people in the street. The programmes had been going out on ABC Radio for some time and had become something of a cult.

I did not exactly take the place by storm, but I was sufficiently taken by my reception to want to return there as soon as I was able. However, it was not until 1969 that I was free to make another trip to Australia. This time I was booked to appear for four weeks at St George's Club in Sydney. This was a huge Taj Mahal-type building run by the Returned Servicemen's League. Inside there was every type of gambling including a host of one-armed bandit machines from which came most of the club's revenue.

It was a time when many English and American artists were looking for new venues to play outside their own countries. For some who were well past their sell-by dates, Australia was a welcome source of income although they could be given a hard time by club audiences if their acts were not up to scratch. Having been disillusioned by a succession of self-proclaimed Las Vegas or Palladium 'top-liners', I found the audiences were determined to assess the worth of my performance for themselves and one had to earn their approval. They were not prepared to give a big hand when the act was introduced, but if they liked what they saw, they were unstinting in their applause at the end. So I was pleasantly surprised on the Saturday night of my first week at St George's, to receive a standing ovation – my first ever. My first thought was that it might be mass cramp considering the age of some members of the audience, but it was for real and my heart leaped. Of course there were many ex-pats out front who had come to cheer, but there were plenty of home-grown Aussies too and from them it was a genuine seal of approval.

I have been back many times over the years – sometimes twice a year – and I have travelled all over that continent and both North and South Islands of New Zealand. There was one memorable show in Kalgoorlie that sticks in my mind. I flew in on a private jet along with Jimmy Grafton and Bob Kennedy to be met by a civic reception. At the time I was wearing a blue and white striped blazer prompting the mayor to remark, somewhat acidly, that if he had known I was going to be wearing a butcher's apron he would not have bothered to put on his chain of office.

The concert was held in a football stadium on a specially built stage and the promoter had borrowed a brand new baby grand piano from the mayor's parlour. Kalgoorlie is a gold-mining town in the heart of the desert and, at the time of my arrival, had been without rain for many months.

The show had only been going for about twenty minutes when the previously starry night sky began to cloud over and ominous distant rumbles of thunder were heard.

'Don't worry, Harry,' said the promoter. 'It never rains here.'

A few minutes later, just as I had started to sing 'Bless This House', lightning flashed and the heavens opened. As the rain poured down, the audience rose to its feet and cheered – not me but the rain. The shower lasted long enough to ruin the mayor's piano and my dinner suit but there were no complaints from a soaking wet public. 'Good on yer, mate!' was the cry as I paddled damply off stage and for the rest of the tour I was known as the 'Rain Maker'.

At the beginning of the 1970s, Stan Mars, an associate of Jimmy Grafton's, was inspired to write the screenplay for a film based on a poster he had seen advertising for teachers in Australia. The poster had depicted a schoolmaster in mortar board and gown and wearing a pair of shorts, posing in brilliant sunshine on Bondi Beach, and thus the film *Sunstruck* was born.

The story was about a middle-aged school teacher in South Wales who, having been rejected by his girlfriend, sees the poster and decides to emigrate to Australia. He fancies himself as a sun-tanned figure standing on the golden sands of a spectacular beach under a cloudless blue sky, living an idyllic life in some fancy Sydney suburb.

Instead, he finds himself in the outback, miles from the sea and having to teach a bunch of recalcitrant youngsters who live in a small farming community. He gets into all sort of trouble as he tries to fit in with the locals and falls out with the landlord of the only pub in the area, played by that fine actor John Meillon. Eventually, he wins over the community and forms a school choir which goes to Sydney and is successful in a choral competition. Along the way he becomes romantically involved with a lady played by Maggie Fitzgibbon, who runs a farm and, of course, it all ends happily. A slight story indeed.

James Gilbert, an old friend from BBC Television, directed the film, which incidentally was the only one being made in Australia at that time. Impresario Jack Neary, who had originally brought me out to Sydney, was executive producer along with Jimmy Grafton. The first scenes, showing the school in South Wales, had to be shot in the worst possible weather so that it would be a tremendous contrast to the brilliance of Bondi Beach – but things did not work out too well to begin with. The location of the school was set in Treharris, where my mother was born, and Donald Houston took the part of the sports master who was my rival for the affection of the girl teacher we both fancied.

It seemed that everybody in the town had known my mother and I was constantly being introduced to aunts and uncles and distant cousins. I was awash with tea and Welsh cakes. The attention I was attracting did not interfere with the filming because we were waiting for the bright sunlight overhead to change to the overcast sky we wanted for the contrast with Bondi Beach. I was having a great time meeting my long-lost relations but poor old Jimmy Gilbert was getting desperate about going over budget as we waited for rain. In the end we got what we wanted and it was 'Australia here we come'. When we turned up at Bondi about a week later, it was overcast and raining and we had to wait a day or two before we could get those sparkling sunlit shots we needed. I got the feeling somebody was trying to tell us something.

The main location for the shooting was a place called Parkes in Western New South Wales and the film unit took over the whole of a motel outside the town. It was a typical little outback community consisting of one main street in which verandahed shops sold agricultural implements, clothing and fast food and in every one we entered we were asked if we were the film people. We caused quite a stir amongst the very hospitable citizens.

The family had all come out to join me. Jennifer was working as an assistant publicity officer for the film company, and David and Katy, because they were away from school, had to have private tuition while we were filming.

The heat was quite like that which I had experienced in North Africa, dry and dusty, and it took some getting used to. As we drove the long journey from Sydney to Parkes, Myra and Jennifer began to have grave doubts about the smart evening wear they had brought with them for cocktail and dinner parties. 'I think we'll have to settle for a couple of sheep-shearers' vests,' said Myra as the dusty road unwound before us. As it turned out, after a couple of days' filming, the ladies of the unit began to make an effort to dress up for the evening meal and my two soon joined in. One member of the cast, Norman Erskine, a very large tough-looking actor with a wry sense of humour was moved to say to Myra, 'For an old Sheila you don't look too bad.'

The one big problems about filming was the presence of the flies. They were not like our English ones who have the decency to fly off after being swatted away – these Aussie ones kept coming back, clinging to the corners of one's eyes and mouth with great tenacity. They can also bite. Much time was wasted trying to get 'flyless shots', especially close-ups. One way to keep them at bay was to use a fly spray but sometimes it could cause a sneezing bout amongst actors and crew, and filming would be held up even longer. When the refreshment van drove up to the location you could follow its progress on the horizon by the swarm of accompanying winged insects. When the van finally arrived it was a battle to get a mouthful of tea before the flies got to it. 'Every biscuit a Garibaldi' as Norman Erskine remarked, removing a couple of the cursed creatures from his tongue. We all developed what is called Down Under the 'Bush Salute' – a waving motion of the hand before the face which became automatic as soon as we left the cool sanctuary of our hotel for the heat of the day.

Another thing to worry about was the snake population. When the prop men were renovating an old tumbledown house to turn it into a pub, four brown snakes fell on them from the rafters above. When it came time for me to do my scenes in there I made sure that I was word-perfect because I had no intention of hanging about. Night filming was also hazardous. The moment that the powerful lights were switched on, every living, flying creature for miles around descended on us. Kamikaze beetles threw themselves at the lamps and huge moths flew sorties in the arc light's beam only to sizzle bravely as they hit their target. We managed to complete the filming by the miracle of Jimmy Gilbert's patience and the complete dedication of cast and crew. In spite of all the trouble, everyone seemed to enjoy themselves. As a family we had a great time and David and Katy came away having learned an entirely new vocabulary of quaint Australian expressions from the crew – some of which upset their teachers when they got back to school.

Sunstruck was the last family film to be made in Australia before a flood of productions of a more adult nature overtook it, and I'm afraid it sank almost without trace. It was a pity really because there were some good performances from Maggie Fitzgibbon and John Meillon, and Jimmy Gilbert did an excellent job as director. It can be found occasionally in the early dawn programmes for insomniacs, but it's still good for a chuckle or two. Incidentally, Hal McElroy, who was on the production side, went on with his brother to produce the acclaimed *Picnic at Hanging Rock*.

One traumatic incident in my life that I will always associate with Australia – even though it only really started there – was the first time I had been seriously ill since childhood.

It was late 1980, about halfway through the last week of my Australian tour. I was performing at the Twin Towns RSL Club, right on the border between New South Wales and Queensland. As a matter of fact, the hotel I was staying at was in Queensland and the club, just across the road, was in New South Wales.

A niggly pain started low down in my left side, and because I knew that appendicitis affected the right side, I put it down to indigestion – and, anyway, I was going to Barbados to join Myra and the kids for Christmas. *Nothing* was going to stop me from getting on that plane.

When I woke up on the Sunday morning the pain had got worse and I had a terrible headache which no aspirin could touch. Dennis Smith, my Australian agent and a very good friend, was most concerned. 'Are you sure you can make the journey?' he asked, going on to outline the route. 'You've got to go on your own from the airport here at Surfer's Paradise to Sydney, wait three hours, then on to Los Angeles via Honolulu. There's a five hour wait in Los Angeles where you have to change planes. Then it's on to New York for another five hour wait and another change of planes to Barbados. You don't look as if you can make it up the road to Coolangatta, let alone fly all those miles to Barbados, mate.'

I convinced him that it was a recurrence of some old stomach trouble and that I would be OK.

The journey was a nightmare. The flight attendants wanted to put me off the plane in Hawaii, but I insisted it was a touch of flu. By the time I got to Los Angeles I was hallucinating. I sat in the terminal for four hours and witnessed all sorts of weird happenings. Mind you, Los Angeles Airport lounges can be like that at the best of times. I managed to make the change of planes and was again questioned about my health, but my determination to get to Barbados and my waiting family helped me to persuade the purser that I just had an upset stomach. All the time I was airborne I was unable to eat – all I could do was drink soda water.

The change of planes at New York was the worst. It was snowing and I was only wearing a blazer and flannels. I didn't realize that I had to go to another terminal which entailed getting on to a bus outside the airport with all my luggage.

I am not going to pile on the agony, but to cut a long story short, I eventually landed in Barbados on the Monday afternoon. Myra, David and Katy were in the reception area at the airport. They waved to me through the glass and I put on a big grin and waved back. 'Be right with you,' I mouthed, not knowing that my luggage – which had travelled all the way from Surfer's Paradise – had been left behind in New York. After reporting the loss to officials and filling in forms, it was another hour before I was at last reunited with my family.

I managed to play down my pain all that afternoon and evening, until at about two o'clock in the morning it got the better of me. Myra managed to get a doctor on the phone but when she had described my symptoms to him he sleepily declared that he was on the other side of the island and that anyway it sounded like colic to him. 'Give him a couple of aspirins,' he said. 'I'll see him in the morning.'

The pain became more intense and by the time he eventually turned up to see me I felt pretty rough. 'My word, you're in a bad state,' was his first bright remark. 'I'll come and see you again this afternoon,' he said after a somewhat perfunctory examination. He handed some tablets to Myra and went off to play golf.

A couple of hours later he was prised away from the golf course by a frantic call from Myra. This time he could see that I was in desperate trouble. He sent for an ambulance and after a rocky ride I arrived at the Queen Elizabeth Hospital in Bridgetown. The attendants put my stretcher down on the floor at reception while the necessary paperwork was transacted. 'Oh look!' said a couple of passing tourists. 'It's Harry Secombe.' And so strong is the 'ham' in me that I managed a deprecating grin and a wiggle of the fingers.

I was now safely in the hands of a very competent medical staff who soon whipped me into a ward where I was examined by Mr Irving Smith, a Barbadian surgeon who had been a lecturer in surgery at Edinburgh University. He immediately sent me to the x-ray department and when he had seen the results he said, 'I'm afraid I've got to go in there.' He sounded a bit like the US Fifth Cavalry. 'It looks very nasty,' he said to Myra. 'I think he's got peritonitis.'

She turned to David and said, 'That's what his sister Joan died of.'

One thought flashed into my mind as I lay on the stretcher. A couple of years before, Arthur Dickson Wright, a famous surgeon and wit, had told me that if he had to operate on me he would wear bathing trunks and a pair of Wellingtons and open me up with a six-foot scalpel.

I don't remember much about what happened next, except the pain and saying to a gowned operation theatre assistant, 'I've played many theatres in my life, but this is the first Operating Theatre.' Not very witty, but apposite, I thought, before going to sleep.

I woke up about six hours later in the recovery room, to

find that I had all sorts of tubes poking out of various parts of my anatomy, and that the intolerable pain had been reduced to a dull throb. 'At least I'm alive,' I thought and went back to sleep.

When I came to again a tearful Myra and a very serious David were at my bedside. 'The surgeon told me you only had a fifty-fifty chance of coming out of the operation the right side up,' she said, squeezing my hand. 'You had a perforated colon.'

I tried to make a joke about suffering from 'punctuation', but the tube up my nose spoiled my delivery. David smiled anyway.

Irving Smith came to see how I was feeling. I thanked him profusely for saving my life. 'Don't thank me,' he said. 'Thank Him.' And he pointed his finger heavenwards.

He told me that he had also removed my appendix – as an encore I suppose – and that a blood test before the actual operation had revealed that I was suffering from diabetes. 'Nothing to worry about as long as you look after yourself,' he said with a smile and a parting wave of the hand.

The nurses were great to me – especially one very large lady who was as strong as an ox. She used to lift me up on her own while another nurse straightened the sheet beneath me, and would let me down as lightly as a feather.

I'll never forget one Sunday morning, just before Christmas Day, when an old ward maid came in at about five o'clock to open the windows wider and tidy up the ward.

I was feeling particularly sorry for myself that morning. The stitches were beginning to hurt, my backside was numb and I had a thumping headache. Not even the sounds of a Barbadian early morning – the cooing of the pigeons and the first throaty cock crows – or the perfume of the frangipani and hibiscus outside the window could lift my spirits.

The old lady, sensing my mood, came and stood beside my

bed. She had no idea who I was – just some poor soul in pain. She gave me a lovely smile and, holding my hand, she said a little prayer for me. Then she went on her way.

From then on I began to feel better.

Convalescence was slow, partly because my diabetic condition slowed down the healing process, although I could not have been in a better place in which to get well. The after-care at the Queen Elizabeth Hospital was excellent, but I was anxious to get back to the hotel with Myra and the kids. They had to take a taxi across the island to see me every day and, naturally, the Christmas festivities were spoiled for them. So it was a great relief when I was allowed out of hospital for New Year's Eve.

Budge and Cynthia O'Hara who ran the Settlers Beach Hotel have been friends of ours for many years. They treated Myra and myself like royalty, and the house we were staying in was always full of fruit and flowers.

Day by day I took longer walks along the sands with Myra steadying me until I was able to toddle along unaided. Together we would sit on the beach and watch for the green flash which was said to come just the second before the sun went down into the sea. We never actually saw it, but it was fun looking for it.

I was very moved by the letters and phone messages wishing me well. Danny La Rue, God bless him, rang from Australia to enquire about me and I had a cable from Spike and Peter which read 'Get a second opinion from a witch doctor.'

As I said, this was the first time that I had been seriously ill since I was a child, and as I lay in bed I began to come to terms with the fact that I would have to start taking care of myself. I remember looking at my arms and thinking 'These are an old man's arms.' They were flaccid and wrinkled, not plump and firm as they once were. I realized they hadn't got that way overnight, the process had begun gradually, but I was not in the habit of checking myself out for signs of old age. Now, lying around with nothing to do, I was able to take stock of myself. My girth was considerably reduced as an effect of the operation and the scar which ran from my navel downwards was not a pretty sight, but the rest of me could do with an overhaul. The diabetes would have to be controlled for a start, and Myra had a look in her eye that said that I would diet whether I liked it or not. And so I did, at least for a while.

My principal worry was that the operation might have weakened the muscles around the diaphragm, making singing more difficult. I could still do comedy, but without the odd song or two my act would be a bit weak. Man cannot live on raspberries alone. Another worry was the fact that I was very constipated and I was afraid of the stitches bursting if I tried to relieve myself. I toyed with the idea of singing a couple of notes to see if everything was all right down there, but kept saying to myself 'Have a go tomorrow.' Eventually I managed to summon up the courage when I was in the toilet to let rip with a couple of top Cs. People ran from all over Settlers Beach to find out where the loud sound was coming from.

Myra was the first one into the house. She had been on the beach sunbathing at the time. She burst into the loo to discover me with my trousers around my ankles and a beatific smile on my face.

'I can do it!' I cried. 'I can do it!'

'I can see that,' she said. 'But what was all the noise about?'

Fortunately I had taken out an insurance policy before I left for the tour because I had to stay on at the hotel in Barbados for another four weeks before I was allowed to fly home. I needed all that time to get my strength back.

While we were waiting for the plane to take us home, a lady approached Myra and asked 'What's the matter with the old man?' That set me firmly on the way back to recovery. After all, I was only fifty-nine.

During my early visits to Australia it was interesting to see how the building of the new Opera House in Sydney Harbour was progressing. Opinions about its design were mixed and the architects came in for some heavy criticism from the national press. Some said that it looked as if it had been doodled on the back of an old envelope.

To my untutored eye I thought it looked very impressive and added to the beauty of the harbour, so when I was invited to perform in the inaugural concert on the day after its ceremonial opening by the Queen, I was extremely flattered and even muted my raspberry blowing in deference to the occasion.

It was generally accepted that of the two main theatres which comprised the Opera House, the one which was supposed to be for operatic productions did not have an orchestra pit big enough to contain the musicians required for grand opera performances, while the other hall, designed for concert performances, *did* have enough space for a large orchestra. So the opera theatre became the concert hall, and vice versa. Anyway, it was a great thrill to be performing in such pristine conditions, although there was some trouble with the sound system to start with.

I have played there many times since, but one particular concert sticks out in my memory. It was a year after my operation and although I knew that I was diabetic I was not really taking my condition seriously. I had been performing once again at the Twin Towns RSL Club, for a week before coming down to Sydney for the Opera House show. At that time I was still much heavier than was healthy for me, about seventeen and a half stone, and I had not given up drinking.

It was a special concert that Dennis Smith had arranged:

the Sydney Welsh male voice choir – about 100 of them – was backing me and I was accompanied by the Australian pop orchestra which consisted of sixty-odd musicians. Normally on such occasions with such magnificent support I came off stage on a high, but this particular night, even though the audience gave me a standing ovation, it was all I could do to walk off to my dressing-room where I lay down on a settee. All around me my usual Aussie mates Billy Rowe, my road manager, Peter Worram, my accompanist, and Dennis Smith, along with Jimmy Grafton, were bustling about dispensing drinks to the management and other members of the cast, while Myra, who could see that I was in a bad way, sat alongside me on the settee holding my hand. She called Dennis over and said 'Harry's not at all well. He said he nearly passed out on stage.'

I didn't want any fuss that night but agreed to see a doctor the following morning in his surgery in the Rocks area. When I turned up there I was accompanied by a whole retinue of concerned people: Dennis, Billy, Jimmy, Peter and of course Myra. The doctor was a large burly Greek Australian called Nick Paphos, to whom Dennis took any of his artistes who were taken ill. 'Which one of you is the patient?' he said, winking at me. I gave him a sickly grin because I was not in the mood for jokes, and he waved the others into his waiting room, taking just Myra and me into his surgery.

He gave me a thorough examination, even the dreaded prostate exploration. My voice went up an octave at the sight of the rubber glove, and my strained attempts at casual conversation from the very undignified position in which he placed me, set Myra giggling. 'Lovely place to sing in the OPERA HOUSE!!' was the observation I made which nearly sent my wife into hysterics. After he had finished probing and prodding and paying the Barbadian surgeon's work a nice compliment, he told me to get dressed. Then he sat down at his desk and wrote down some notes on his pad, which Myra, sitting opposite, tried to read upside down.

When I was finished dressing, he addressed me very seriously. 'Harry, your blood sugar level is sky high, your blood pressure is through the roof, you've got an infected throat, and to top it all, mate, you're five stone too heavy. I'll give you two years at the most if you don't look after yourself. Go on a diet, cut out the booze, and you've got a chance.' He turned to Myra, 'You'd better make sure that he looks after himself.'

'Don't worry,' she said very firmly. 'I'll see that he does.'

And believe me, she did. From then on, I was on a strict diet and from that day to this, I have never touched a drop of alcohol. I needed his straight talking and Myra's determination to make sure that I followed his instructions, to jolt me into the realization that I was in mortal danger if I didn't change my eating and drinking habits. In a way, Nick Paphos saved my life and I shall be eternally grateful to him.

Several years later I received a newspaper cutting in a letter from Dennis Smith. It was from a Sydney paper and told of Nick Paphos being jailed for drug smuggling. Apparently he and a couple of others had purchased an old tramp steamer in Piraeus harbour, loaded it with cannabis and had a crew sail it to a point off Darwin on the North Australian coast. It was unloaded into small boats and the cargo brought ashore. The crew was paid off and the ship scuttled. The cannabis was then transported in lorries from Darwin down to Sydney. However, the authorities had been tipped off and the cargo came under police surveillance from the moment it left Darwin. Nick and his accomplices were arrested red-handed with the drugs in Sydney and were all sent down for several years apiece.

He was a fine doctor and now that he has paid his debt to society, I hope he has been accepted back into the mainstream of life and found happiness. I wrote to him several times when he was in prison but had no reply. Perhaps one day we'll meet up again and I can thank him for what he did for me.

It is said that everyone remembers where they were when President Kennedy was assassinated and when John Lennon was shot. I was making up as Samuel Pickwick in my dressing-room at the Saville Theatre when Kennedy was killed and I heard the news about John Lennon in my room on the leisure complex on Lizard Island on the Great Barrier Reef off Cairns in Northern Queensland. It was my third visit to the island having first set foot there when it was completely undeveloped except for a rough landing strip, a tractor and a wooden toilet. We had flown in as a family by courtesy of Syd Williams, the chairman of Bush Pilot Airways, who we had met at a hotel in Cairns. It turned out that he and his wife had been hosts to Prince Charles when he had been on holiday from his boarding school.

We told them that we were going on to Dunk Island for a holiday and Syd suggested that we might like to pay a flying visit to another island which he and others were going to develop as a leisure complex for big game fishermen and wealthy tourists. It was a little jewel of an island set in the sparkling waters of the Coral Sea, uninhabited except for a couple of workmen and quite a number of large monitor-type lizards.

We were taken out fishing on the cabin cruiser which was moored off a beautiful sandy beach and almost as soon as we dropped our hand lines over the side the bait was taken by coral trout. There were several hooks on each of our lines and they were all occupied – if that is the right word – by these large fish. A barbecue had been set up on shore and it was soon grilling our catches, gutted and wrapped in tin-foil. They tasted absolutely delicious and we washed them down with a very smooth Australian claret. Andrew and Jennifer went snorkelling, safe in the knowledge that the outer reef protected them from sharks. Myra, David and Katy went looking for shells and I just lay in the sand like a beached whale soaking up the sun, claret oozing from every pore. A day like that will linger long in the memory and even longer in the liver.

The next time I visited Lizard Island was to perform at the newly finished, very exclusive leisure complex into which it had been transformed. I had promised Syd Williams – now Sir Sydney – that I would bring a show along, complete with orchestra, to mark the opening. We decided between us that it would be a black-tie affair and that it should be televised. After that it began to take on the appearance of a national event. A Royal Australian Navy frigate turned up and its ratings formed a guard of honour for the Premier of Queensland Jo Bjelke Peterson who flew in to the brand new airstrip for the occasion. Guests came in from all over the place, some by air and some by boat, and champagne flowed like water. A somewhat bizarre occasion considering we were in the middle of nowhere, but everyone had a good time and the rising sun found several dinner-jacketed guests asleep on the sand.

A lot of good things happened to me in Australia, including my silver wedding anniversary and the announcement of my knighthood, and I have accumulated many, many friends. I made a farewell tour three years ago, but I have promised to return with Myra on our golden wedding anniversary in 1998 just to visit my old Aussie mates and Beryl Kennedy, Bob's widow, who is now living there with her son.

Many of my tours Down Under have included side trips to New Zealand where there are some fine concert halls. Christchurch Town Hall in particular has magnificent acoustics. In comparison, the first time I played the old

Wellington Town Hall about twenty-five years ago, there were cries of 'We can't hear you, mate', from certain parts of the auditorium. Normally I don't get that kind of reaction because my voice has the piercing quality of a laser beam when I'm in full throttle. Apparently there were dead spots in the hall where the cheaper seats were. There was nothing I could do about it apart from going around to those who couldn't hear me and singing to them individually which would have probably deafened them. However, the last time I played Wellington I performed in a new concert hall with a great sound system and an audience to match.

New Zealand folk are more reserved than the Aussies and a little more formal. I remember playing an open air theatre in South Island which had an ornamental pond between the front of the stage and the first rows of seats. The audience had come prepared with blankets and thermos flasks which surprised me when I saw them settling themselves down before the show began. The day had been reasonably warm and I wondered why the public were muffled up. It was still daylight when the show started, then as the sun went down a mist began to rise above the little lake in front of the stage. By the time it was my turn to go on, moths and other flying creatures fluttered about in the spotlight just as they had done in Parkes when we did a night shoot, and it was difficult to make out the audience through the miasma before me. Fortunately the sound system was in good order thanks to Billy Rowe my road manager, and though my facial expressions were lost in the fuzzy, moth-ridden stage lighting, my voice was coming through loud and strong. I sang my heart out that night and in spite of the fact that most of my gags were greeted with polite applause, the songs went down very well and people stamped their feet at the end of each ballad. I commented on this to Billy Rowe after the show. 'Don't fool yourself, Harry,' he said. 'They were trying to keep their feet warm.' Mind you, he was grinning when he said it.

During my tours in New Zealand we covered a lot of territory, visiting places like Dunedin, Invercargill, Nelson, New Plymouth, Auckland and everywhere we went we were made very welcome, especially by the ex-pats to whom we brought a touch of home. It's a long way to go and I have to confess that when Myra and the kids were not with me I often felt very alone. I would sometimes stand on some lonely beach surrounded by every kind of tropical beauty and look yearningly across the sea, wishing that I were back in noisy old Cheam Road with the bus stop opposite and the bus conductor calling out 'Harry's corner!'

Entertaining the Services

There is a saying amongst old Royal Artillerymen which goes, 'once a gunner, always a gunner', and there's a lot of truth in that. I don't mean that every ex-gunner should keep a twenty-five pound artillery piece in his garden – there's enough trouble about hand guns in private ownership as it is. What the saying refers to is that the comradeship forged in battle lasts one's whole life.

That is why I have always had a soft spot for the Army, and so whenever I have been asked to entertain the Services I have gone willingly, with the result that I have been to nearly every trouble spot that our soldiers have been involved in.

Together with Eric Sykes I visited Kenya in 1952 when the Mau Mau uprising was on. The hairiest part of that trip was after our outbound plane had landed at Rome for refuelling and took off again for Nairobi. The starboard engine of our South African Airways DC7 feathered itself and blew up. This meant that we had to go back to Rome, but before we could do so, the fuel we had taken on board had to be jettisoned.

As we circled above the Eternal City with all the plane's

lights switched off because of the danger of St Elmo's fire, Eric and I opened a bottle of Italian brandy I had bought at the airport and, as the aircraft ditched its load of aviation spirit, we were taking on board quite a large amount of another liquid. Eric had his guitar with him and we regaled our fellow passengers with what I suppose could be called a 'spirited' rendition of 'The Banana Boat Song', about the only tune Eric was able to play.

By the time we had landed back at Rome there were fire engines and ambulances waiting for us, but my friend and I tripped down the landing steps without a care in the world – until the next day when we both had terrible hangovers. We were stranded in Rome for two days while we waited for a spare engine to be sent up from South Africa, but the rest of our journey was nothing like as eventful, thank God.

I took another trip to Kenya a year or two later with Norman Vaughan and Harry Worth – two of my best mates. The only thing that bugged me about my companions at the time was their apparent indifference to what was going on around them. They spent a lot of their spare time reminiscing about old Variety performers with whom they had worked, while I was wide-eyed with wonder and fascination at the sights and sounds around us. In Cyprus, the first stop on our tour, I was always looking for subjects for my ever-present camera. Harry and Norman would give me a cheery wave, declining my offer of a trip out to some exciting archaeological dig, preferring the comfort of the sergeants' mess.

When we got to Kenya, we did a show at the Bell Inn on the shore of Lake Naivasha, where we were staying. It was the most beautiful spot, and the flamingos on the lake shone pinkly in the setting sun as I wandered down to the lakeside in the early evening before the show was due to start. To my surprise, Harry and Norman had beaten me to it and were sitting on a bench facing this spectacular scene.

'They've got the message at last,' I thought happily as I crept up behind them.

'Now, Sandy Powell,' Harry was saying. 'There was a funny man . . .' I left them to it.

I have done many shows in Nissen huts, on rickety, temporary stages – even from the backs of Army trucks – from Northern Ireland to the Far East, with some excellent travelling companions – people like Anita Harris, who came with me on several CSE trips and was always great company; and an excellent comic called Kenny Cantor, who has worked with me both here and in Australia and, incidentally, was responsible for me becoming a member of the Grand Order of Water Rats, a show business charity – but there are two outstanding occasions which I want particularly to mention. The first one was the time I went down to visit the Services in the Falklands.

When the war in the Falklands was over, I was asked to head a British Forces Broadcasting Services concert party to entertain the lads down there. I agreed immediately – after all, we had won the war and I was keen to see what the place looked like. The party consisted of Jack Honeyborne, my accompanist, Bryan Marshall, a very good young comic, Joan Hinde, who can play the trumpet like the Archangel Gabriel himself, and two pretty, young singers. Tony Boyd, Jimmy Grafton's assistant, also came with us to help with the staging of the show. Derek Agutter, Jenny's father and an old friend from previous tours, was in charge of the operation.

The first part of the journey was fine. We boarded a VC-10 at RAF Brize Norton and left for Ascension Island, arriving there in the middle of the night. I sat up front for the landing, marvelling at how the pilot and navigator could find this tiny speck in the Atlantic, and feeling extremely relieved when they did.

After we went through the usual formalities, I was driven by the station Commander up to his house on the hill, where

I was to be his guest for the night. It was pitch black dark and I couldn't see a thing on the way, but my host insisted on pointing out various beauty spots which I could look out for in the morning. When we got to his place we sat and chatted for quite a while over a cup of tea. He explained that the flight down to Port Stanley would be by a Hercules air transport plane, which would have to be refuelled in mid-air because it could not carry enough fuel to make the journey.

The tanker plane was a Vulcan bomber which had been adapted for the purpose. If we missed the rendezvous somewhere over the South Atlantic, or the weather was bad over Port Stanley, we would have to go back to Ascension Island and start again. He also told me that the last flight that had gone, a couple of days previously, had made two attempts before it eventually landed in Port Stanley. I thanked him for the information and went to bed where I lay rigid and sleepless until daybreak.

We made our rendezvous with no problems, thank God, and I joined the crew on the flight deck for the refuelling. The pilot explained that the top speed of the Hercules was stalling speed for the Vulcan, so the operation had to be performed in a dive.

The Vulcan circled us and released a fuel line from under its fuselage. At the end of the hose was a device into which the probe on the nose of our aircraft had to fit to take the fuel on board. It was a complicated operation, relying on the fine expertise of both pilots, but it was completed with no bother at all, and everybody on board cheered when it was over.

The Hercules, by the way, is essentially a transport plane, and passenger comfort is a low priority. We sat where we could, on whatever piece of equipment looked most comfortable, but no one complained, although we were all glad to disembark at Port Stanley airport, where our welcome was warm and everybody was looking forward to the shows.

Memories of the battle were still fresh and we were told some hair raising stories of the ill-treatment of the young and inexperienced Argentine soldiers by their officers. Towards the end of the conflict, some of these youngsters were starving while their officers had a stockpile of rations which they kept to themselves.

Rex Hunt, who was the Governor at the time of the invasion, showed me around Government House, pointing out the bullet holes in the walls from the first attack. Then he produced something quite remarkable. The official Government visitor's book had been signed by all the high-ranking Argentine officers. Rex left for England before we did our first show. Perhaps he'd had enough trouble.

We did shows in all sorts of places – in hangars, sheds – in fact wherever Jack Honeyborne could plug in his electric piano. We performed on Merchant ships and Royal Navy vessels, and our audiences were more than kind. The final show was at Port Stanley Town Hall, the first time that the local population had seen any kind of entertainment since the occupation.

The mines that the Argentines had laid so indiscriminately made travelling anywhere on the main island very hazardous and new mine maps were issued at regular intervals, and for this reason we had to travel by helicopter quite often.

I have to say that I was very proud of the way the members of the show put up with the rigours of battling against a constant wind and having such primitive conditions in which to work. Joan Hinde was particularly stoical and never complained. Neither did Jack Honeyborne. A very droll man at the best of times, he didn't make too much fuss when he fell off an improvised stage one night when I was singing a top note. When he came back up again he was wearing ear protectors.

At the time we were there, in May 1983, quite a few soldiers were billeted with the locals, and we heard tales of some of the lads lighting fires first thing in the morning and generally being helpful in the home. After a while though, to avoid the inevitable friction between the younger members of the community and the more sophisticated servicemen, a huge complex was built around the airport at Mount Pleasant which could accommodate the servicemen and provide them with television and more of the comforts of home, leaving the local inhabitants to get on with their lives. When I returned in 1986 with *Highway*, the new complex had already been completed, apparently, in record time.

I was struck by the very British lifestyles of the Falklanders. I remember being entertained to tea at a farmhouse in Goose Green. It was just like being back in 1930s England, with an Aga stove in the kitchen and a little boy in flannel pyjamas and a woollen dressing-gown, with little carpet slippers on his feet, sitting on the fender in front of the fire, watching his mother, in a flowered pinafore, busying herself making the tea and arranging home-made scones on decorated plates. It brought back memories of the times when I was home from school with a cold and watching my mother getting the table ready for tea.

Other things which had not changed were the stink of cordite and the sight of empty shell cases and old field-dressing bandages littering green, windswept fields. As the song goes, 'When will they ever learn?'

The second outstanding tour I was involved in came about after I received a letter from the man in charge of Forces Entertainment. The letter said that I was invited to go out to the Gulf to meet some of the servicemen and try to spread some Christmas cheer, even though the Christmas season was a few weeks off. Apparently the lads were sitting around down there in Saudi Arabia waiting to have a go at Saddam Hussein and needed to see a familiar face from home. I thought at first that the army had the idea that if I sang a few choruses of 'We'll Keep a Welcome' within earshot of

Saddam's front line troops, they might think twice about hanging around in Kuwait. But when Julie Stephens, my secretary at the time, made a few discreet enquiries, she was told that I was not expected to sing because not even the combined efforts of myself and Des O'Connor would shift Saddam in his present unpredictable mood.

And so it was that I presented myself at RAF Brize Norton with just an overnight bag for the flight down to Riyadh. I also met up with the gentleman from British Forces Broadcasting who was to accompany me.

When I presented my passport at the flight desk, there was some consternation at the fact that it included an Israeli visa, due to the fact that I had been out there to record three *Highway* programmes. Saudi Arabia does not admit anyone with an Israeli visa. Messages whizzed to and fro between Brize Norton and Riyadh and eventually I was given some kind of diplomatic immunity.

The next thing was the briefing, which took place in the lounge at the RAF airport. I'm pretty used to this sort of thing, having made many trips abroad for the services, but this briefing had a chilling message. The officer instructing us told us that due to the possibility that Saddam might decide to launch a nerve gas attack, we all had to try on the protective suits and masks with which we were provided and which had to be carried around with us at all times. The equipment was duly produced, and I had some difficulty struggling into mine. The gas mask was the most important item. Apparently one had only about ten seconds to get it on before one became contaminated. This put something of a damper on the previously light-hearted atmosphere in the lounge, and I began to wonder if I'd been a bit hasty in agreeing to make the trip. I even had the idea of ringing Bob Kennedy to tell him to check the small print in my insurance policy. I knew that there was something in it about an 'Act of God', and I hoped that Saddam did not come under that category, even if *he* thought he did.

We were given plenty of time to practise getting in and out of the decontamination suits and, having realized how essential they were to life preservation, I would have made Robert Nesbitt proud at the speed with which I made the quick change.

Eventually we were escorted to the aircraft and made welcome by the RAF flight attendants who were jolly but firm about the procedures that were to be undertaken in the event of something unexpected happening during the flight. The other passengers, being mostly air crew – pilots, navigators, etc. – took it all in their stride, while I sat, a 71-year-old ex-gunner, veteran of a war light-years removed from this new one which might happen at any time, pondering on the reception I might receive from the young soldiers who were out in the desert preparing to face Saddam with every conceivable kind of modern weapons system which made our old 25-pounder guns seem as antiquated as bows and arrows.

On the plane, a young navigator approached me and asked if I remembered him from Barbados. As a matter of fact I did, just. The last time I had seen him he was a little lad who used to play football with my kids on the beach at Settlers Beach on the St James's Coast. He was then known as Tiger, and he was David Coleman's son.

I wished him well and he grinned and gave me the thumbs up as he went back to his seat. I suddenly felt very old and sad, and tears welled up in my eyes.

The flight was a long one because we were flying in a military aircraft and had to keep to a flight plan which kept us from flying over certain countries. When we landed I was amazed at the amount of military aircraft around us, but I was given no time to linger, and was whisked off the plane and into a car which took me and my companion from BFBS straight to the Embassy, where we were to spend what was left of the night.

I was given a very comfortable room in which cold drinks and fruit awaited me, along with a welcoming note from the Ambassador inviting me to have breakfast with him before I left for the next leg of the journey up to the area where I was to start meeting the lads.

I seemed only to have slept for a few moments before I was woken with a cup of tea and the news that breakfast would be ready in half an hour. I changed into the light clothes I had brought over and trotted downstairs to meet the Ambassador. He was a charming man and we got on like a house on fire. He even loaned me a floppy hat to protect my bald spot from the sun which, he warned me, was going to be very fierce.

The next flight was by Hercules aircraft to Al Jubayl, where there was more evidence of the tremendous build-up of planes and equipment, and a greater sense of urgency, which always deepens the nearer you get to where the action might be. I remembered this very well from the battles I had been involved in and I began to get the same old churning in the stomach, together with a sort of suppressed excitement.

Time now to meet the servicemen at my first port of call and try to raise a smile or two. There was a bit of embarrassed shuffling for a few moments as I was introduced to them, but to my relief we all had a laugh together as they got used to me. I posed for photographs and signed various pieces of paper – 'it's not for me, it's for my mum' – and then a cheery wave, and off to the next place.

It all became a kaleidoscope picture of shaking hands, asking where the lads came from – 'anyone here from Wales?'

'I've got an auntie who lived next door to you in Maesteg.' I never lived there, but smile and nod anyway.

'My mum always watches you on *Songs of Praise*.' I resist

the temptation to say 'No, I'm on *Highway*,' glad at least that they know me from somewhere, they're too young for the Goons.

Then a welcome cry of 'Ying tong iddle I po' from the older blokes, and 'Give my regards to Spike' – they all know him.

'What are you doing out here, mate?' No answer to that one.

'Saw you when you came out to Cyprus or Belfast, or Port Stanley . . .' Shoulders back a bit at that.

'Like a brew-up, bombardier?' Ah, that's more like it.

Brigadier Cordingley, the man in command of 7th Armoured Brigade, escorted me personally around the heavy gun artillery positions further up in the desert towards where the front line would be when the fireworks began. He was the antithesis of the common concept of a brigadier. For a start, he volunteered to carry my heavy camera and asked me seriously what it was like to be in action. Having often been under fire during my service in the war, I could speak from experience, although only in the capacity of a walk-on part. I answered, 'How's your sphincter muscle?'

There was a lot of compassion in the man and he was obviously a favourite with those who served under him. We chatted about opera, about which he was far more knowledgeable than I, and when we parted, after a ride in one of his tanks, I thought to myself that I would have been very happy to have been under his command. Not *now*, of course, but when I was a soldier.

Later, when the balloon went up, he acquitted himself very well indeed, and is now Major-General Patrick Cordingley, DSO, and deservedly so.

The idea was for me to visit all three services, and after being with the 7th Armoured Brigade, I was taken by helicopter out to HMS *Cardiff*, which was on duty off Kuwait. By this time I had a couple of minders and the BFBS man with me, and away we went to land on the ship while it was cruising along – a most interesting experience, to say the least.

I was shown around the ship – which was then on some kind of constant alert – and I managed to meet most of the ship's company. Below decks there was a bewildering array of computer equipment, which I was only allowed a brief look at, and then we all had tea in the Captain's cabin. Like most of the officers in all three services with whom I came into contact, he seemed remarkably young for such a high command, but there was no doubt about his ability.

We piled back into the helicopter for the return journey feeling pretty good about things and looking forward to lunch ashore. Then, out of the blue, all hell broke loose in the cockpit and the easygoing crew suddenly became terrifyingly efficient and our helicopter descended towards sea level as the pilot issued terse commands into his headset.

We jigged about over the sea for a while, until he seemed to get some reassurance that all was well and we returned to our previous height. I was just about getting my heart back to where it was supposed to be, when the same thing happened all over again. The pilot followed the same procedure and down we went to sea level. The first time it happened I had a faint suspicion that it might have been a bit of a 'send-up', to give me something to talk about when I got home, but there was no denying the seriousness of the pilot's behaviour the second time.

After we had returned to our proper height again, the pilot told us that a missile had locked on to us twice and he had had to drop down to sea level in order to confuse the missile's homing in mechanism.

'So that's what it was,' I remarked calmly as I disentangled myself from the navigator's lap, wondering where I could change my underwear.

Months later, I found out what the fuss was about when I

was invited to lunch at Chequers by the Prime Minister. I was on the same table as General Sir Peter de la Billière, and he explained that a Saudi naval frigate had not been alerted that a helicopter was leaving HMS *Cardiff* and had prepared a missile launch when said helicopter appeared on its radar screen. So, thanks to the quick thinking of the pilot, an international incident was avoided.

If you think I'm kidding, this is all noted by the general in his book.

After I had finished what the Army had referred to as a 'grip and grin' visit, I went back to Riyadh for a barbecue with a lot of service personnel at the staff military attaché's house. As it was getting near to Christmas, we all sang carols in his garden. I was delighted to see the Ambassador again and return his hat. To my surprise, he had a fine baritone voice and together we belted out the old favourite carols until we were hoarse.

It was a night to remember in many ways. There we were, celebrating a Christian festival in the heart of an Arab country under a sky studded with stars – just as it might have looked from that stable in Bethlehem. There we were, singing songs about peace on earth and goodwill to mankind, and yet, not far away, young men were readying themselves for a war which could come at any time.

Later that night, as we flew back to Brize Norton, my head was crowded with the events of the past twenty-four hours, and I remember saying a silent prayer for the safety of all the people I had met. Sadly, the young Lancashire Fusilier who had driven us around Riyadh was killed by 'friendly fire' when the battle for Kuwait began, some weeks after my visit.

I worry sometimes that these overseas trips for the services are regarded as self-publicity exercises which do little to lift the morale for the rank and file, and I begin to question my motives. And then I get a letter from a lad's parents, saying how much their son enjoyed meeting me – and I feel better about it.

I was to get more involved with the Army when, one evening in my dressing-room at the Palladium, I happened to remark to one of my regular visitors, Arthur Watson, that I seemed to be getting quite a lot of requests to perform at midnight matinées for the RAF Benevolent Fund. Arthur, along with George Brightwell, had run Combined Services Entertainment.

'Is there an Army Benevolent Fund?' I asked him. 'If so, I'm sure that a lot of performers who had served in khaki would be delighted to help it earn a few bob.'

In no time I was knee-deep in generals, all of them connected with the ABF and ready to listen to any ideas I might have. They were really splendid chaps and not in any way like some senior officers I had met in my period in the services.

In due course, the idea was born of a Sunday concert in a West End theatre with contributions from as many ex-Army performers as we could get, with all the proceeds going to the ABF. The show was to be called 'Fall in the Stars' and the venue was the Victoria Palace. Billy Chappell, an ex-captain and a brilliant choreographer and director of ballets and West End revues, was to be the producer. I had met Billy when he came backstage to see me after an Army show in Rome in which I was the lead comedian. He said then that the next time he'd see me would be in the West End. When he turned up to see me at the Palladium ten years later I said 'Where have you been till now?'

The show was a great success and was the forerunner of many more. One particular senior officer, Brigadier Gerry Landy, became a great personal friend. He really should have been in the theatre – he has a genius for organization and always gets what he wants without ever raising his voice.

Mind you, so does Myra.

It was always a secret thrill for me to be able to call these generals by their first names, and the first time I was invited to an Army Council dinner I felt quite chuffed as I dressed for the occasion, proud of my cluster of medals and the emblem of a Commander of the British Empire around my neck.

When I arrived, the first person I met was Field Marshal Lord Templar, who had so many medals and decorations that there was hardly enough room for them all. I was glad to retire to a corner of the room with my pathetic collection. My humiliation was complete when my brand new CBE became unstuck and dropped into the soup, which happened to be Brown Windsor – somehow making the incident doubly *lèse-majesté*.

On the Highway

One day in 1983, I received a letter which led to a big change in my career. It was from Bill Ward, who I had worked with in television for many years, and who had been responsible for wooing me away from the BBC to the newly established Associated Television Company when Independent Television first started. In the letter, he asked if he could take me to lunch to talk about an idea he had for a television series.

We met for lunch in the restaurant of the Stafford Hotel, which is conveniently situated around the corner from my office in St James's Place. There were only the two of us and, after we had spent some time chatting about mutual acquaintances and shared reminiscences, Bill came out with the reason for our meeting. He told me that there was a plan to put out a series of programmes of a religious nature, to be broadcast on a Sunday evening in what was known as the 'God Slot'. The content of these programmes was to include plenty of music and interviews with interesting people, and they were to come from a different region of the country every week. 'And we want you to present the programme,' said Bill, leaning back in his chair and looking me straight in the eye.

I was, to say the least of it, flabbergasted. I had sung lots of hymns and sacred songs on *Stars on Sunday*, and I had once presented a children's programme about Easter called *The Cross on the Donkey's Back*, but I was not a heavily religious person myself. I also thought that my long association with the *Goon Shows* was not quite the right background for a presenter of the kind of programme he had in mind. Bill didn't agree.

'You don't have to be a "guru",' he said. 'We'd just like you to sing a couple of hymns and interview interesting people who have done good things for those around them. Turning the spotlight on the unsung saints in the community, if you like. It will be more about caring than about religion and we see it as inter-faith and inter-denominational.'

I was intrigued by the suggestion and said that I would think about it. The one thing that worried me was that I did not want to be seen as a 'holier than thou' kind of presenter. What I thought was that I would act as a 'Mr Everyman', asking questions which the average viewer would like answered. I certainly would not be blowing raspberries, but at the same time I would still be myself as the viewing public knew me.

It was eventually agreed that I would give it a try, and Jimmy Grafton arranged a contract for six programmes, with a view to extending them if all went well. I was delighted to find that my old mate, Ronnie Cass, a fellow Welshman from Llanelli, was going to be the musical associate on *Highway*. I had worked with Ronnie on many television shows, mostly the *Secombe With Music* programmes with Peter Knight and his orchestra from Yorkshire Television. He knows my voice better than I do and coaxes performances from me that I never thought I could possibly achieve.

The first two programmes came from the Tyne Tees Television area, primarily because that was the station from which the show was to be administered. The first show was a Remembrance Sunday *Highway* from Durham Cathedral and the chief guest was Wendy Craig, who was to appear several times during the life of the programme.

In the beginning I found it strange to be the interviewer and not the interviewee, though chatting to Wendy, an old friend, made things easier. Another strange thing was having to speak into the camera lens and address the viewing audience directly. The only way I could do this without freezing up was to imagine that I was just talking to one particular family, and I gradually got used to the idea. Obviously, I was no stranger to the camera lens, but I had previously been Harry Secombe the comic and though I wanted to retain some of that identity, I would also have to be taken seriously when the occasion demanded. In addition, I had to learn all the links within the programme by heart, something I did not always manage to do, as my frequent appearances on Denis Norden's *It'll Be All Right On the Night* will testify.

One thing I did learn early on was to put at ease the person I was going to interview, and the best way to do this was to have a cup of tea and a chat beforehand. This was most important as the majority of people were terrified of the prospect of going before the television cameras. They all had a good story to tell and it was in their interest and the interest of the programme that they were presented in the best possible light. This was much easier when, after we had done a few series, a mobile caravan was provided for me, in which I had a place where I could be made up and where I could meet the folk I was going to interview. It was good to be able to go over what they were going to say and gradually calm them down. I would have all the information about the interviewees from the researchers in the region in which we were working, and I'd know from the director what area he would like the interview to cover. Naturally, as time went by

I became used to the technique, but in those first programmes I was usually more nervous than those I was attempting to settle down.

The first six programmes went very well indeed and more were commissioned, until *Highway* became firmly established and began to give *Songs of Praise*, which went out at the same time on Sunday evening on BBC 1, some healthy competition.

Highway was a unique programme because it came from eleven different regions – Tyne Tees, Border, Grampian, Scottish Television, HTV Wales, HTV Bristol, Anglia, Channel, Ulster, TV South and TSW. Each region provided its own director, researchers, wardrobe and make-up, camera crew, lighting and sound people. The Central Unit, which was based in London at the Tyne Tees Television offices, consisted of Bill Ward as executive producer, Ronnie Cass as musical associate and script writer, a secretary and myself. To ensure that no two programmes contained the same ingredients, the scripts were sent to us in advance, often accompanied by the director. Ronnie would then consult with each regional musical director about what hymns or sacred songs were to be recorded.

Once *Highway* had been going for a couple of years, the music was always recorded at CTS Studios in Wembley. We had the finest session musicians in the country to play for us under the baton of Ted Brennan who, with Ronnie, did all the arrangements, apart from those done by the incomparable Peter Knight in the early days of the programme.

Perhaps I should explain why the music had to be pre-recorded. First of all, it would be rather difficult to conceal an eighteen-piece orchestra behind a couple of trees when I sang a ballad in a sylvan setting, or to have a male voice choir following me down the street as I belted out 'Onward Christian Soldiers', and so, in order to achieve a balanced sound, the music had to be recorded under studio conditions. Secondly, for the same reasons, I had to sing in the studio, too. This meant that I had to mime to the pre-recorded sound relayed by speakers strategically placed out of sight of the cameras. Now, it looks a bit phoney when the singer just opens and closes his mouth in synchronization with the words, without making a sound. Under normal circumstances, for example, I go a funny colour when I hit a top C, so if I appear to sing a high note with no apparent effort, the viewers will automatically say 'Hey up! He's not singing – he's miming', and they think they're being cheated. It has always been done that way in film musicals and has been accepted by the general public, but on television, for some reason, one cannot always get away with it. That's why I take great care that my lip movements coincide as near as possible with those I made in the studio, and I can do this by actually singing along with the recorded sound, so at least I can be seen making an effort.

I remember one snowy day somewhere in Dorset when I had to sing 'Trees' alongside a fast-flowing stream, the sound of which almost drowned out the music being played through the concealed speakers. When I had finished – after about half a dozen goes at it – I climbed wearily up the bank, encrusted with snow, to be confronted by a large lady, with an almost equally large dog, who had been watching the filming. 'Why are you not singing properly?' she said, pointing an accusing finger at me. 'You're doing it the easy way.'

I straightened up indignantly, preparing to discuss the pros and cons of singing unaccompanied in a snowstorm, when I lost my balance and slipped backwards down the bank.

'Serves you right!' she cried and marched off.

I think she must have seen *Song of Norway*.

Highway soon became a new way of life for me. I met so many fine people – ordinary folk who had done extraordinary things – that I began to realize that, contrary to what the tabloid headlines seem to indicate, there is a tremendous amount of good being done, quietly and without thought of reward, throughout the country. Previously, when I had toured the provincial theatres, I rarely came into contact with the people who lived in the towns because the nature of our profession confines one to the journey from the digs to the theatre and back again, with the occasional round of golf thrown in. One never gets to meet the audience individually, except for the autograph hunters at the stage door, and one leaves a town without getting to know anything about it or those who live in it.

It was different with *Highway*. I got to learn a lot about towns and cities at grassroots level, and listened to stories of triumph in the face of dreadful adversity. Like the experiences of Cantor Ernest Levy of Glasgow, who had been in eleven different concentration camps in Germany during the war and yet felt no bitterness for those who had treated him so harshly. As he told his story, simply and with no histrionics, all those of us involved in the recording were in tears. There was a shining sincerity in the man that transcended all the evil that had been done to him, adding a new dimension to what tolerance and forgiveness really mean.

I had the privilege of interviewing and presenting many inspirational characters during the ten years of *Highway*, but here are a few extra special ones that I will always remember.

I first met Evelyn Glennie in a programme we recorded for Grampian Television in Royal Deeside. She was introduced to me as a musician who was profoundly deaf, but who had an amazing facility to lip read. Her lip reading was so good that if she was addressed as 'Eevelyn', with a long 'ee', and not 'Evelyn', with a short 'e', she would politely correct one's pronunciation. She has the most attractive and vibrant personality and, after a chat with me in the church at Balmoral, she played the piano for us. She said in the interview that her ambition was to teach music to deaf children. She also mentioned that she was a percussionist, and in later programmes we found out what a superb percussion and xylophone player she was. She went on to become a regular member of the *Highway* orchestra and from there became an internationally renowned musician and won the 'Scots Woman of the Decade' award. She is now in constant demand around the world, but she is still the modest girl we met in Deeside.

Another remarkable lady who appeared on a *Highway* from Edinburgh was Carolyn James who, after being partially sighted for many years, became completely blind. The amazing thing about Carolyn is that she is a very accomplished watercolourist with many exhibitions to her credit. In addition, she has developed a talent for lyric writing and, in association with Ronnie Cass, who has written the music to her lyrics, she has had many of her songs performed by Dana, Ian Wallace and myself.

In a *Highway* from Gloucester we introduced a Mrs Denise Cole who had a miraculous story to tell. She had been suffering from MS for some years and was confined to a wheelchair. One day she went to a local church service and became a born again Christian. Some time later, she joined a group of fellow worshippers who were going on a trip to the Holy Land, sponsored by her church. She was determined that when they got to Jerusalem she would walk, with a walking frame, the length of the Via Dolorosa, the route taken by Jesus on his way to be crucified. For her it was going to be an act of faith, purely and simply.

But something truly miraculous happened to her that day. She told me that she suffered excruciating pain as she struggled along the narrow road and, by the time she reached her goal, she was about to pass out. Then, quite suddenly, the pain left her completely and she found that she could walk unaided. The shock of this happening to her made her afraid to tell anyone about it in case it was a temporary remission. However, she began to realize that she really had recovered the use of her legs and she told the others around her of her miracle.

She has completely recovered from her MS and has since dedicated her life to helping others with the same condition. There seems to be no medical explanation for her sudden recovery. Temporary remissions do occur in some cases of multiple sclerosis, but Denise's recovery has long outgrown the period of other remissions.

In the programme we were both sitting down during the interview, only to realize after the show had been transmitted that we had not taken the opportunity to show Denise's ability to walk about. So it was decided that when we recorded our special Christmas show I would introduce her and the two of us would waltz around the studio together, just to prove that we had not been telling 'fibs'. Ronnie Cass had written a 'Mrs Cole's Waltz' especially for the occasion.

Then there was the lovely Laura Morris of Caerphilly, who beat off lymph cancer, became an air hostess and now devotes all her spare time to raising money for the hospital that helped to cure her.

Two doctors, from different parts of the country but both blessed with the same gift of compassion, made a big impression on me in two separate programmes.

The first was Dr Peter Griffiths, who was featured in a *Highway* from HTV Wales. He had given up a lucrative practice in south London to found and maintain a hospice in Tŷ Olwen near Swansea. I always felt like an intruder when we filmed patients in hospitals, especially when they were terminally ill, so I was prepared for a hushed atmosphere and long faces when we went along to Tŷ Olwen. The scene that met us could not have been more different. There was laughter in the wards and dogs wandered in and out between the beds, as Dr Griffiths believed that his patients could have anything that they wanted, within reason, to ease their last days, and had no objection to well-loved pets being brought into the hospital so that their owners could wish them farewell.

Dr Griffiths spoke of his 'little triumphs', such as allowing a patient to go home to attend a wedding even though he knew that he only had a couple of days left. Like a lot of doctors who tend to the terminally ill, he believed in counselling the family about how to cope with the coming bereavement and, although he had to administer pain-killing medicine, he was determined that his patients would die with dignity and not in a drug-induced coma.

The other doctor, Dr Lloyd, runs a premature baby unit in an Aberdeen hospital. His charges are so tiny that at first sight it is hard to believe that they are human, they look just like little dolls as they lie in their incubators. When I said this to Dr Lloyd, he smiled and said, 'That's why we dress them in dolls' outfits, to give the little souls some kind of dignity when the parents come in to see them.'

He takes a keen interest in the babies after they leave his care and is proud of every one of them. When you see photographs of some of these wee scraps of humanity just after their birth and then compare them with the sturdy boys and girls of a couple of years later, you realize that he and his staff have every reason to be proud.

Jenny Rees-Larcombe was a lady we met in a programme from Tunbridge Wells. She was a patient at Burswood, a centre which combines spiritual healing with orthodox medicine and comes under the aegis of the Archbishop of Canterbury. At that time she was suffering from encephalitis and was confined to a wheelchair. When I interviewed her, she had refused to take any pain-killing drugs that day so that she could speak coherently. She told me that she had come to Burswood hoping for a miracle but had, instead, settled for the lesser miracle of coming to terms with what had happened to her. She spoke of how angry and frustrated she had been when she was first stricken by her illness, how her attitude had changed during her stay at the centre, and how she had found an inner peace. It was a most moving interview and one that remained with me long after the programme went out.

Then, several months later, the *Highway* office received a letter from Jenny telling us that she had been completely cured of her encephalitis.

Apparently, she had gone to a Christian meeting where prayers were being offered for the sick and a young girl asked Jenny whether she minded if she prayed for her. Jenny said she had no objection, and this young girl then said a prayer for Jenny to be cured. To her great surprise, Jenny felt her illness leave her to such an extent that she found that she could walk home unaided. Her recovery was complete and has remained so.

There is one other lady I have to mention. No miracles happened to her, but, instead, by sheer strength of character and faith in God, she overcame tremendous physical handicap. She is Hilary MacDowell from an Ulster Television *Highway*. Hilary was born severely disabled and seemed doomed to spend her life in a wheelchair. Her parents were told that she would never be able to walk and that she could never go to school. Hilary was so determined to beat these odds against her, that she got the other members of her family to teach her what they learned at school and then set about teaching herself to walk. She succeeded so brilliantly that she now has a PhD from the Open University, is a deacon of her local church and runs a street theatre group in Donaghadee.

There are so many other *Highway* stories of people who have demonstrated the power of faith over seemingly insurmountable adversity, that it would be impossible to list them all. Remember, we did over 365 programmes in the ten years that *Highway* was on the air.

We shed a lot of tears during the making of some of those shows, but we also had plenty of laughs along the way. I have never believed that religion should be a grimly serious affair, after all, it is natural to assume that as Christ and his disciples spent so much time together, as well as praying together, they must have laughed together.

There is a traditional prayer that is always heard at the annual Clowns' Service and it was recited on a *Highway* from Monmouth by little Luke Mumford.

Dear Lord, I thank you for calling me to share with others your precious gift of laughter.

May I never forget that it is your gift and my privilege.

As your children are rebuked in their self-importance and cheered in their sadness, let me remember that your foolishness is wiser than men's wisdom.

We covered around 25,000 miles a year during the time *Highway* was going, and there were plenty of things which should not have gone wrong but which, of course, did.

We went to Rome with Border Television for two *Highway*s, one of which was to be a special Easter programme in which I was to try to get an Easter message from the Pope.

I found it great fun to be filming in some of the famous Roman places of interest, like the Fountain of Trevi and the Castel di Sant Angelo, where I sang 'E lucevan le stelle' – 'The Stars Are Brightly Shining' – from Puccini's *Tosca* from the very cell in which the scene was set in the opera.

It was 'nostalgia time' for me because I had spent some time in Rome after I had finished playing walk-on parts in the Italian campaign in 1944. Now I was able to see the city in a different light. I remembered entering St Peter's Cathedral, looking in awe at the magnificence around me, as my army boots rang out on the marble floor. This time I was there to sing, with the Vatican choir backing me, the lovely 'Agnus Dei'. We had pre-recorded the music, as we always did, and I was glad we had done so, because inside the Cathedral there was an echo that seemed to go on and on, making it quite difficult to mime. However, Aled Jones seemed to have no trouble with it when he sang his solo, once again proving what a great musician he is.

The interview with His Holiness had been set up in the auditorium of the Vatican and I had been allotted a seat in the front row. The camera had been sited so that as the Pope walked along he would be in sharp focus when he got to me. A microphone, powerful enough to pick up both our voices, had been fixed to the front of my jacket. In the background, by the camera, Bill Ward stood with Bill Cartner, the Border Television director, ready to give me the signal that the camera was running.

The auditorium was packed with people from all over the world and the atmosphere was more like that of a Wembley Cup Final, with banners waving and lots of chanting going on.

Those in the front pews, who were given the honour of actually shaking hands with His Holiness, had senior members of the Catholic Church sitting beside them to effect the introduction. Unfortunately, the Monsignor who was to look after me had not turned up. We found out later that the poor man had flu. As the Pope got nearer to me, Bill Ward began waving his arms about to give me the signal that the camera was now recording the action. By this time, I was going over in my mind what I was going to say. 'I am from British television, Your Holiness. Could you please give us a special Easter message?' I made up my mind to speak slowly because I knew that the Pope did not speak perfect English and, as he got nearer and I got more nervous, I realized that neither did I.

Then, there he was, standing in front of me accompanied

by his retinue. He raised his eyebrows questioningly and I stuck out my hand. As he gently shook it, I blurted out 'I'm from British television.'

'Good luck,' said His Holiness with a smile, and moved on to the person next to me who had someone to introduce him. Bill Ward, never a man to admit defeat, motioned for me to get as close as possible to the man with whom the Pope was chatting and pretend that I was joining in the conversation. This I managed to do, nodding away in the direction of the Pope's back. Fortunately, it did not turn out to be too bad and, although we did not get our Easter message, we got away with it.

We had started filming in bright sunshine, with blue skies over the city producing sparkling pictures for the first couple of days. Then one morning we woke to find that there had been a snow storm in the night and Rome was under a foot or so of snow. The temperature had dropped and it was now bitterly cold. This made things difficult for me because I was only wearing a blazer and flannels and, as I had already conducted a couple of interviews dressed that way, for the sake of continuity I had to continue to wear them, shivering my way through the rest of the songs while cameraman Tom Ritchie had to shoot everything from underneath so that the snow didn't appear on the pictures.

One lunchtime when we were filming near St Peter's Square, we all piled into a little restaurant that had been recommended to us by Monsignor Bill Purdie, an Englishman who was then the Press Officer at the Vatican. He came with us to make sure we would get a good meal. Myra was there, and Ronnie Cass and his wife Valerie, along with Bill Ward and the rest of the crew. During the first course, Monsignor Bill and I were discussing opera and he started singing a snatch of the duet between Rudolfo and Mimi in the first act of *La Bohème*. I started humming along with him, and soon we were doing the whole duet between us.

'We can't both be Rudolfo,' he said. 'I'll have a go at Mimi's part.'

There were very few customers apart from ourselves, so I didn't feel too embarrassed. Then the proprietor came to our table and encouraged us to sing some more. Bill Purdie opted out and suggested that I should sing something on my own.

'If you sing "Cantari" for me,' said the owner, 'I will give you a bottle of a very special wine which I only keep for myself.'

'Go on,' said Myra. 'We can take it home with us.'

And so I sang it, slightly higher than I would normally have done, and Ronnie was beginning to worry about me bursting a blood vessel. However, I finished with a couple of ringing top notes and everyone applauded generously.

'Grazie, signor,' said the proprietor, producing the very special bottle of wine he had promised me. To Myra's chagrin, he proceeded to open it there and then and poured it out for everyone. As a non-drinker, I had to be satisfied with a Diet Coke, but I had a good laugh and so did Myra, who claimed the empty wine bottle. 'If we come back tomorrow can we have a refill?' she said, jokingly.

'Yes of course!' said the proprietor, his eyes lighting up. 'We can arrange a special price for you.'

'No thanks,' I said, looking at the remains of my Diet Coke.

We managed to get both programmes finished on time and when they went out there was not a trace of snow anywhere, but some viewers did wonder why my nose had gone blue halfway through the Easter *Highway*.

Our travels during the making of *Highway* took us to many places outside the British Isles. We did three programmes from the Holy Land, two from the Falklands, a Christmas special from Orlando, Florida, one from Malta, a Remembrance Sunday programme from Caen, one from

Majorca, in which I tried to show viewers my own view of the island that has been my second home for over thirty years, and one from Lapland, when we flew up to the Arctic Circle with a plane-load of underprivileged children for a visit to Father Christmas. Roy Castle came along on that trip and won the hearts of everyone on board.

He had worked out a little dance on skis, which he was going to perform in the snow. There was great consternation when we kept getting reports that there had not been a snowfall for quite a while. Then, the night before we were due to fly from Gatwick, we got the news that the flakes were coming down at last. Someone up there loved Roy.

The whole trip was organized by the staff at Gatwick Airport, who paid for the chartering of the plane and presents for the children – all of whom had a really wonderful time.

Incidentally, it was a *Highway* from Gatwick Airport itself that produced the highest ratings we ever had – eleven million viewers tuned in to watch that programme, on which Barry Sheen was the principal guest – although it says a lot about the show that our average viewing figure was eight million.

One of the things I enjoyed most about *Highway* was the recording of the music. There was always a great atmosphere in the studios at Wembley CTS and the musicians were nearly all old friends of mine – some from pit orchestras in the theatres I had played, some from Wally Stott's orchestra, who provided the background music for the *Goon Show*, others, like the great trombonist Don Lusher, from my days with Philips.

We usually fixed the band call to start at ten o'clock in the morning, which meant my leaving home at seven o'clock to get to the studio in time for a run-through with Ronnie and Ted Brennan, who was the conductor for all the *Highway* music sessions. After we had got all the banter out of the way, we would then decide the tempos of the songs I was to record and discuss the interpretation of them. Most of the material consisted of hymns I already knew – I reckon I have sung my way through *Hymns Ancient and Modern* with only a few exceptions, and I'm no stranger to the Methodist Hymn Book either. But there were also new songs to record and I welcomed the challenge they presented.

By ten o'clock the orchestra would be in place with their parts set on the stands by Ted who, with Ronnie, had arranged the music. I never ceased to be amazed at the ability of the session players to play the music at first sight. After going through the first piece a couple of times, the recording engineer Dick Lewzey would ask me to sing a few bars with the orchestra to get the right sound balance and then we would put down the track. Sometimes I would record up to eight songs in two sessions and, when you consider that each song had to be sung three or four times to get it right, it could be a bit of a strain.

Apart from the very popular hymns like 'The Old Rugged Cross', 'Abide With Me', 'How Great Thou Art' and 'Onward Christian Soldiers', the greatest number of requests came for a song, the lyric of which was sent in by a viewer and set to music by Ronnie Cass. The song was called 'Cover Me With Roses' and the lady stipulated that she was to remain anonymous and that any royalties her words earned were to go to the Musicians' Union Benevolent Fund to repay the pleasure musicians had brought into her life.

One of the pleasures that *Highway* brought to me was the privilege of singing with some of the greatest musical talents in the country, Sir Geraint Evans and I sang the big duet from *The Pearl Fishers* on his boat in the marina at Aberayron. Unfortunately for me, on the trip out to his boat I managed to get my trousers very wet. I bet that was the first time that duet had been sung with one of the singers having a wet bum.

In a *Highway* from Portmeirion, the fantastic brainchild

of William Clough Ellis, I sang the same duet with that brilliant young baritone Bryn Terfel – this time with dry trousers. Helen Field, the little Welsh soprano with a terrific voice, joined me in the first duet from *La Bohème* – the same one that I did with Monsignor Bill Purdie in that restaurant in Rome – in a programme from Merthyr. Delme Bryn-Jones and I sang another duet from that same opera, 'O Mimi Tu Più Non Torno' in the magnificent setting of Sherbourne Castle. Ian Wallace was once brave enough to join me in 'The Gendarme's Duet', and Cleo Laine and I sang a duet from her and John Dankworth's lovely home outside Milton Keynes.

Apart from the music on *Highway*, some of the readings became very popular with our viewers. One was 'Death Is Nothing At All', which was beautifully read by Bernard Cribbins on the 1985 Remembrance Day programme from the beaches of Normandy. The words were written by Canon Henry Scott Holland (1847–1918) and had been sent in by Mr L A Maxim of Sudbury, Suffolk, who told us that they had been read at his wife's funeral service. He hoped that they might bring comfort to others. Well, they certainly did. We had so many requests for the piece that eventually we had the text printed in the *TV Times*. I think it's well worth seeing it once again in print.

> Death is nothing at all – I have only slipped away into the next room – I am I and you are you – whatever we were to each other, that we are still. Call me by my old familiar name, speak to me in the easy way which you always used. Put no difference into your tone, wear no forced air of solemnity or sorrow. Laugh as we always laughed at the little jokes we enjoyed together. Play, smile, think of me, pray for me.
>
> Let my name be ever the household word that it always was. Let it be spoken without effect, without the

ghost of a shadow on it. Life means all that it ever meant. It is the same as it ever was, there is absolutely unbroken continuity. What is this death but a negligible accident? Why should I be out of mind because I am out of sight? I am just waiting for you, for an interval, somewhere very near, just around the corner . . . All is well.

I was very sad when *Highway* was eventually taken off the air because it had become an oasis of calm on a Sunday evening, giving viewers a chance to reflect, to revisit, from the comfort of their armchairs, places they may have been to in the past, the opportunity to hear good music and perhaps find comfort and inspiration in the tales of fortitude in adversity and the selflessness of those who spend their lives helping others.

Apparently the reason given for closing down the programme was because it was not attracting the kind of audience that the commercials were being aimed at – a case of God versus Mammon. We had a tremendous amount of mail from viewers who were highly indignant that the show was no longer going to be the high-point of their Sunday evenings, and quite a number of letters were written to the newspapers expressing anger at the decision.

After *Highway*, I went on with another religious programme called *Sunday With Secombe*, a two-hour Sunday morning show that I co-hosted with Kay Adams. It was a Scottish Television production, directed by one of the nicest men I have ever known, John MacDonald, and lasted for thirteen very happy weeks. It went out live, which meant that we were provided with an autocue – a device that fits over the camera and brings up the words on a screen in front of the lens. It is worked by an operator who feeds the words through the screen at the speed of the presenter's voice. There's nothing to it, once you get used to it. Unless it breaks down. That's when the viewer at home becomes aware that the presenter is looking blankly into the camera with nothing to say, until galvanized into action by a command in his ear-piece from the director to get on with the next item in his script.

This happened to Kay and me in a show from Scotland. About ten seconds before we were due to go live, the autocue broke down and, when the red light on the camera came on, we were both smiling inanely with nothing to read. Fortunately, Kay grabbed a script from an assistant standing nearby and handed it to me. 'Ah yes,' I said, breathing a huge sigh of relief and tried to read it upside down until Kay turned it the right way up. A very resourceful girl, Miss Adams! Between us we carried on with the programme, alternately reading from our scripts, and nobody seemed to notice that there was anything wrong.

And now I have come full circle again. Last year I was asked by BBC television if I would like to present half a dozen *Songs of Praise* programmes. I was very flattered because, although we had been opposing each other during the life of *Highway*, we always had great respect for each other's work. After all, we said, we're working for the same Boss.

It was a standing joke when we were filming on location for *Highway*, that if a plane flew over or a lorry went past during a critical point in the action, the cry would go up, 'There goes the *Songs of Praise* plane', or 'Thora's driving that lorry'.

Although I have changed jerseys, so to speak, I am very happy to be associated with our old rival and comforted by the fact that I still have Ronnie Cass and the Ted Brennan boys playing on my side.

Pickwick Again

It was sometime in 1992, when *Highway* had finished and I was contemplating semi-retirement, that I received a phone call from Leslie Bricusse asking me if I was interested in doing *Pickwick* again. I had never really given it a thought, and said that perhaps it might be a retrogressive step — afterall, it was twenty-nine years after we had first opened at the Saville Theatre. 'I'll think about it, Leslie,' I said, and put the phone down.

Myra was not too keen on the idea at first. 'You're seventy-one now, and you're a diabetic, remember.' She was worried that my voice would not be able to stand the strain. I belted out a couple of verses of 'If I Ruled the World' in the kitchen, making all the cups on the table rattle and sending Vincent the cat running for cover. 'All right, you've made your point,' said Myra. 'Ask the kids what they think.'

Jennifer was all for it because she had grown up with the music, and so had Andrew, who also urged me to have a go. David, who only vaguely remembered the show from touring with us in America, was equally enthusiastic. Katy, who had not been born when it was done the first time and was slightly jealous because the other three had, threw her weight behind the decision that the old war-horse should have one more gallop into battle.

Jennifer said that since I had been doing *Highway* for ten years, a lot of people would have forgotten that I was an actor and comedian before I became a presenter of religious programmes.

I was secretly pleased at the offer, and asked Tony Boyd, who had taken over Jimmy Grafton's agency after Jimmy's death, to contact Leslie Bricusse and find out what his idea was. Since dear old Bob Kennedy had died too, I was missing his friendly advice, although I still maintained my office in St James's Place, manned now by my secretary Ruth Levine and Egon Painz, my business manager.

Ronnie Cass, whose opinion I have always valued, advised me to have a go, assuring me that, vocally at least, I would have no problems.

To cut a long story short, a meeting was arranged between Leslie, Tony Boyd and a couple of Leslie's associates and it was agreed in principle that I would star once again in *Pickwick the Musical*. There were several meetings after that, some at our house, where I met Patrick Garland, who was to be the producer. We had met once before when I interviewed him in Chichester for a *Highway* programme. He was the artistic director of the renowned Chichester Festival and, as 1993 was to be his last year in the job, the idea was to have *Pickwick the Musical* as his crowning achievement if I would agree to do it.

'In for a penny, in for a pound,' I thought. And, in truth, I knew I would be getting more pennies than pounds if I took the job, because everyone playing in the Festival had to settle for a salary far less than they would normally receive. But it was a challenge I was determined to take – after all, how many other actors had the opportunity to recreate a musical role thirty years after he had first performed it?

The deal was struck and it was now time to cast the show. After the débâcle on *The Four Musketeers*, I wanted to have some say in the casting, or at least have the chance to approve the choice of cast.

Patrick and I got on very well together and obviously, because of his well-deserved reputation in the theatre, I was prepared to accept his word on actors of whose work I had no knowledge. When he suggested Ruth Madoc for Mrs Bardell I was delighted because I have known Ruth since she had written to me as a young girl asking for advice about how to get into show business. I passed her letter on to Frank Barnard, my agent at the time, and he was a considerable help to her.

Glyn Houston, Donald's brother and a very fine actor, was my own choice for Tupman, but Patrick rightly thought that Glyn would make a great Buzfuz, doubling the part with that of Wardle, the brother of Rachel Wardle who runs off with Jingle, and the father of the two daughters for whom Snodgrass and Winkle fall hook, line and sinker.

The part I was most anxious to see played by someone with whom I could establish a rapport was that of Sam Weller, the boy who becomes Pickwick's valet. It was very important that he should be a person with whom I could get on, both on and off stage, because our relationship was essential to the success of the whole production.

'I know just the man for the role,' said Patrick. 'He's very versatile and he has a marvellous sense of comedy. His name is David Cardy.'

I took Patrick's word for it and crossed my fingers that when I met David the chemistry between us would work. I need not have worried, because he was the best possible man for the part. He has a great sense of comic timing, which is about the rarest thing to find outside the old variety performers and, as a bloke, he was very easy to get on with – the nearest choice to the great Roy Castle, who had played Sam

Weller on Broadway all those years ago.

The part of Sam Weller's father, Tony Weller, was a tricky one to cast at first, until Leslie and Patrick suggested that perhaps Roy Castle would play him. I was delighted at the thought that my old mate might be able to do it, but we all knew that he had been diagnosed as having lung cancer. In fact I was one of the first to know of his illness when he phoned me on the day his doctors told him. However, at that stage the news on his condition was more hopeful, and he had just successfully gone through his first bout of chemotherapy.

When he agreed to play the part of Tony Weller my joy was complete. The whole country was aware of his battle with cancer, and his appearance in *Pickwick* would give him a goal to focus on.

Michael Howe was a new name to me, but when Patrick told me that Gillian Lynne, who was going to be the choreographer, had highly recommended him for the part of Jingle, I accepted her choice with alacrity. I was feeling very happy about the prospect of working with Gillie again because, since she had been responsible for *Pickwick* in America, she had enjoyed fabulous successes with *Cats* and *Phantom of the Opera*, and travelled the world supervising and choreographing ballets and operas. We were going to be lucky to get her to stay still long enough to get the show into production.

The cast that finally assembled in Chichester for the first rehearsal was as good as the one that had been such a success thirty years before. There was one member of the chorus of whom I was particularly proud: Katy had been determined to work with me and had auditioned for the Bird Seller and as understudy to Ruth Madoc. She got the job – and a free lift down to Chichester with the star of the show.

Kevin Ranson, who played Tupman, also understudied my part and at our first musical run-through, I was relieved to find that he was more than capable of singing all my songs. Peter Land was a flamboyant Snodgrass and Robert Meadmore, a tall, handsome baritone, played against type as the timid Winkle. Everybody in the company could sing well, and the choral work was better than it had been the first time – and that's saying something.

Any doubts I had about my voice being able to cope with the demands of the show soon vanished after the first band call. I managed the top C in the number that closed the court scene with no bother at all and earned a round of applause from the cast who, if the truth were known, were also wondering whether I could make it.

The rehearsals were pretty gruelling, especially for the dancers, and Katy declared that she was aching in muscles she didn't even know she possessed. Gillian was a hard task master, but no one could complain because she never asked any dancer to do something that she herself could not. Even though she was well into her sixties, she could out-dance the lot of them – and there were some extremely good ballerinas in the company.

The stage at the Festival Theatre is of a modern design, being almost a theatre in the round, with the audience at very close proximity to the action because there is no orchestra pit. We all made our entrances and exits through the gangways used by the public to get to their seats, and quite often the odd latecomer was surprised to find Mr Pickwick himself lurking in the shadows as they climbed the stairs to the auditorium. There was no curtain and no overture; there was also a kind of show within a show which began about a quarter of an hour before the printed show time, when various members of the cast would wander around in the auditorium in full costume, chatting up the customers in lusty Dickensian fashion. Katy yelled herself hoarse trying to sell birdcages, and one of the girls who had apples in a basket actually sold them on the first night to the people in the front row – which caused some consternation with the property master who needed them for the first scene.

It was strange at first getting back into the Pickwick outfit, which bore a very close resemblance to the one I wore back in 1963. I had kept the original flat-topped hat that I had worn in the Broadway production and I clung to it as my lucky mascot. I had written the words of 'If I Ruled the World' on the inside of the lining, along with odd cues that I was anxious not to miss.

What I found somewhat terrifying on the first night was the fact that the only way I could see the conductor was on two small television screens mounted over the front gangways. Fortunately for me, the conductor, Ted Brennan, my faithful friend from *Highway* days, knew how nervous I was about missing my music cues even when his baton was practically up my nose, let alone fifteen feet away on a television screen, and he armed himself with a baton with a light at the end of it and all went well.

The advance bookings for *Pickwick* were quite phenomenal and everybody from the cast to the usherettes was hoping for a good first-night audience. I had heard that the Chichester lot could be sticky on the opening show, so there were plenty of 'Break a leg' and '*merde*' salutations among the cast, and a very special wish for success for dear Roy.

Myra, Jennifer and the grandchildren had filled my dressing-room with so many floral arrangements and pot plants that I thought I might catch greenfly. Incidentally, I shared my dressing-room with Prunella Scales, who was appearing in *The Matchmaker* on the nights we had off. We left many messages for each other, each vowing to see the other's performance, but unfortunately we never actually managed to do so.

I made my first entrance from the gangway in front of the stage, with my knees beating a tattoo as I walked and the lenses of my wire spectacles clouding over. David Cardy,

God bless him, whispered 'Good luck, guv'nor', and I got a round of applause before I even opened my mouth. My nervousness vanished, and I was back as 'Samuel Willoughby Pickwick' once again.

The set, by Poppy Mitchell, who had designed the *Plumber's Progress* set, was not as complicated as the original Sean Kenny one, but was very effective, with stage-hands dressed in black manoeuvring the trucks into their different positions to become the outside of Fleet Prison, then the inside, and then, in a burst of light, transforming into the George and Vulture at Christmas time.

Everything seemed to go well that night. We had done a couple of preview performances, but nothing can compare or be as important as the first night. The critics are out there, and nothing concentrates an actor's mind better than that fact. Although these days – unlike in the past – a critic can no longer be the cause of the closing of a production, their notices, if they are very bad, can have an effect on the box-office.

At the finale there was generous applause for all of us, Roy Castle getting an especially warm reception and, as we sang the reprise of 'If I Ruled the World', the company received a standing ovation, the first at the theatre for many years.

At the reception in the foyer after the show everyone was very complimentary. Patrick Garland gave me a big hug and thanked me for a great performance, as did Gillian Lynne. Cyril Ornadel, who had written the music for the original show, made the journey from his home in Israel to be there on the first night and Wolf Mankowitz, who also remembered the first opening night thirty years back almost to the day, gave me a thumbs-up sign. Like Roy, Wolf was undergoing chemotherapy and had made a special effort to attend the performance.

I slept well that night.

When the reviews came out, I was 'Tinkered', 'Spensered'

and 'de Jonged' in the *Daily Mail*, the *Sunday Times* and the *Evening Standard*, but the local press were ecstatic. There was a time when a bad notice would have sent me straight to bed with my head under the pillows, but those days have gone and I'm more philosophical. I remember the occasion during the North African campaign when, in the process of obeying a call of nature, a neat hole suddenly appeared in a cactus leaf above my head. My first instinct was to straighten up and shout 'Hey, watch it! You could kill somebody like that!', and then I realized that that was exactly what the enemy rifleman had in mind. I was a legitimate target – and so I am when I brave an audience. The only consolation is that firearms are forbidden in the theatre.

We had a wonderful season at Chichester and the idea was to play five weeks in a London theatre before going on to Birmingham's Alexandra Theatre for the Christmas season.

For reasons I'm not too sure about, the publicity for Sadlers Wells was late going out and we played to poor houses most of the time. It was a period that I called the Valley of the Shadow, because there is nothing more dispiriting than trying to squeeze laughter from a sparse audience. I was glad that Roy was not with us for those five weeks, because it would have been very hard work for him. At the end of the Chichester season he had begun to look very ill again and though he was contracted for Birmingham I had grave doubts about him being able to make it.

The company was very supportive during the time we were at Sadlers Wells and David Cardy and I began to think up ways that we could liven up our comedy scenes together. I'm afraid that I became rather outrageous again in the bedroom scene, but Ruth, like the good trouper she is, joined in with the ad libbing and we found laughs between us that Dickens had never intended.

Throughout the five weeks at the Wells, we were sustained by the news that the advance box-office in Birmingham had topped a million pounds. We couldn't wait to get there.

After we had finished in London, I took a couple of weeks off at our home in Majorca to prepare for the season at the Alex, and when I returned to the company we were all set for a successful time. Roy was back, looking better than he had in the last week at Chichester, and, naturally, everyone was glad to see him.

We opened to full houses and the production took on a new sparkle after the pessimism of the previous five-week season. Then, after the Wednesday matinée of the week before we were due to finish, with notice-boards outside the front of the theatre proudly announcing 'House full for second performance', we were all summoned back on to the stage to be told that the theatre had to close there and then. There was to be no evening performance and there was no money available to pay any of the cast.

It was a tremendous shock to everybody, and we all sat in the stalls afterwards while it was explained that the theatre was now in liquidation on the orders of the City Council. Even the theatre staff were being sacked. We were asked not to 'rock the boat' by commenting adversely to the media about the closure in case there was some last minute miracle that would save the situation. Most of the kids in the show were in tears, and poor Roy, who was being sustained by working in the production, looked absolutely shattered, worse than I had ever seen him. Ruth and I went on television later that afternoon to talk about the closure, choosing our words carefully because we did not want the public at large to think that *Pickwick* was coming off because business was bad.

Outside the theatre, the audience was starting to arrive for the evening performance and finding that the tickets they had bought in advance could not be honoured. People were milling around in the street complaining about the cancellation.

I do not know the exact reason for the closure, but there was talk that our advance booking money had been used to shore up other productions and, when the management went to the corporation for yet another grant, they were turned down.

It seemed that the rest of the tour that was planned for the show was now in jeopardy. We were supposed to return to Birmingham for a further two weeks after the end of the Christmas run, and then go on to Woking, Sheffield and Norwich. Obviously, the fortnight in Birmingham was now out of the question, but the managements of the other three venues had such good advance bookings that they formed a company between them, called P W Productions, and put the show on themselves.

Patrick Garland and Gillian Lynne were in the same boat as the rest of us as far as not receiving any money for the last two weeks at the Alex was concerned, and were prepared to go along with the new company. It was a gamble that paid off, and the two weeks in each theatre proved profitable for us all.

Sadly, Roy, who had been delighted when the tour had gone ahead and struggled on with his role, was to make his last appearance at Norwich. By this time, he was failing again – although his grin never wavered and no one could have guessed from his performance that there was anything wrong with him. But, backstage, in the dressing-room he shared with David Cardy, Roy had to lie flat on his back all the time he was off stage. At the finale of the show, I used to bring him forward for a special bow and every night without fail, the audience would rise to its feet and give him a standing ovation. There was such a tremendous wave of love and affection for him that those who were privileged to work alongside him were engulfed by it and the tears flowed freely from us all. He was a constant source of inspiration and he always had time for other people. Even in the last week at

Norwich, when the weather was very cold, he would stand outside the stage door with his woolly hat hiding his now bald head, signing autographs and chatting with his fans.

He made the decision, along with his wife Fiona and his family, to meet his cancer head-on and in full view of the public, so that others could benefit from his illness through the Roy Castle Cause for Hope Foundation and the International Centre for Lung Cancer Research, the first of its kind in the world.

Before he died, Roy rang me in Majorca to wish me goodbye. He knew that his fight was over, and he just wanted me to know that the drugs he was taking would soon make it impossible for him to talk coherently. I found it extremely difficult to speak, leaving unsaid all the things I really wanted to say.

'I've seen the other side,' he said, 'and it's beautiful. I'll see you there.'

Three days later, Fiona rang me to say that Roy had passed away, and suddenly the world was a sadder place. He epitomized everything that is decent and good in the profession he had enhanced with a boundless talent and the courage of a lion. I still miss him.

Pickwick is still alive and kicking, having toured for a couple of years with Christmas seasons in Bristol and Manchester. This year, we'll be in Oxford for Christmas and then – who knows? – perhaps it will be time to put the old fellow to bed. And yet, and yet . . .

Grand Finale

The trouble with writing an autobiography is that with such a broad canvas to fill, it is inevitable that a lot of people and events will be left out. Things one always meant to include but forgot . . .

. . . Like the time Myra was presented with a beautiful bouquet of flowers on our arrival at Bermuda airport, only to have to hand them back when it was realized that the flowers were meant for someone else . . .

. . . Like the time when, during a week's variety at Cleethorpes, a young comic had to use a caravan in the car park of the theatre as a dressing-room, and consequently had to trek through the mud to get to the stage door. I had the number one dressing-room all to myself, so I invited the lad to share it with me, and that was the first time that Bruce Forsyth had a star on his door . . .

. . . Like the time that Mario Lanza and myself were on the same Command Performance bill and he was miffed because I was singing opera in the first half of the show. His minders had to lock him in his room to stop him getting drunk, but we shook hands on the stairs of the Palladium foyer as we waited for the Queen to greet us . . .

. . . When Myra and the Crown Princess of Japan had a long chat at the Buckingham Palace reception before the wedding of Prince Charles and Lady Diana. In a room full of very tall people, they were the only two who could see eye to eye . . .

. . . When I had to make a speech at a Variety Club luncheon to honour Lord Louis Mountbatten, and I opened with 'My Lords, distinguished guests, fellow barkers and,' turning to his lordship, 'Hello sailor!' He laughed . . .

. . . When, after the first time I had ever performed for an hour alone on stage at the Blackpool Opera House, I had come off feeling ten feet tall and Bob Kennedy, my faithful manager, came towards me with his hand outstretched. 'Good old Bob,' I thought. 'He's overwhelmed.'

He came up to me and said, 'Give me the keys to the car, you're blocking the stage door.'

. . . When Tommy Cooper told me the story of when he was in the Welsh Guards, on duty one night outside Windsor Castle. He had dropped off to sleep standing up in front of his sentry box. Suddenly he became aware of a light shining in his face as the duty officer approached. With his head still bowed, Tommy said a loud 'Amen.' And straightened up to attention.

. . . When the manager of the Garrick Theatre in Southport, after making an unsuccessful attempt to remove me from the bill, actually growled at me like a dog whenever he passed me back stage.

. . . Like the day when Johnny Franz discovered he had vertigo. He was driving in the Alps at the time.

. . . When I was told the story of an actor playing the part of Baron Hardup in a pantomime up north who tragically died of a heart attack in his dressing-room in the middle of the first half. The manager went on stage in the interval to announce the fact that 'Baron Hardup is unfortunately dead.' Back came the reply, 'Oh no he isn't!' And he said, 'Oh yes he is!'

. . . Like the most hilarious luncheon I ever had. Billy Connolly and me finished directing traffic outside the restaurant.

. . . When Eric Sykes and I were on safari in the middle of Uganda amongst a very primitive tribe called the Karamojong, who wore nothing but a long strip of cotton with a hole in the middle through which they put their heads, Eric got out of his bed, without a stitch of clothing on, and said, 'Give me my spear, I'm going shopping.'

. . . When I did a concert at Pentonville Prison and finished by singing 'Bless This House', which had the prisoners in hysterics.

. . . When Lionel Bart came up to me at a reception at 10 Downing Street in Harold Wilson's time in residence and said, 'Your flies are undone.'

'Come off it, Lionel,' I said, not bothering to check and walking in to the next room, where I became involved in a conversation with the Governor of the Bank of England and two Cabinet ministers. I thought I had them enthralled as they listened open mouthed to my views on the European Monetary System, until a waiter whispered in my ear, 'Your flies are open, sir.' And they were.

. . . When, along with Dame Vera Lynn and Sir Cliff Richard, I was invited to lead the community singing outside Buckingham Palace as part of the 50th anniversary of VE Day celebrations. At the reception in the Palace after a truly moving and inspiring concert, the Queen came over to talk to me. Noticing that my bar of medals had come adrift, Her Majesty fixed them back in position. 'There,' she said, giving them a pat. Then she smiled – and at that moment I would have climbed Everest for her.

This is the time, I suppose, at nearly the end of what has been known in the family as THE BOOK, originally referred to with a kind of reverence and, as time dragged on, gradually recognized as 'the sword of Damocles over Dad's head', that I should sum up the seventy-five years that I have trodden this earth. The best way to do this is in the form of an obituary I have prepared for myself.

He was born in 1921 in Swansea, South Wales, to a Mr and Mrs Secombe, from whom he took his name. The first sign of Secombe the creative artist appeared when his parents acquired a gramophone. He took to leaping about the house to the music, wearing the boots the doctor had suggested as a support for his weak ankles. He also took to wearing lampshades and his mother's hats. His parents exchanged worried looks, and one day his father presented him with a pair of boxing gloves. He put them on his head.

His scholastic achievements were few. Overshadowed by a brilliant elder brother and a clever four-year-old sister, he turned instead to sport. He was caught carving his initials on his desk during a maths lesson, and was told by the master that he was for the high jump. He won the event easily and followed it up with a superb win in the three-legged race, from which he was subsequently disqualified when it was realized that he was running alone.

Perhaps the turning point in his life came when he joined the church choir. He revelled in the old hymns, forever trying to sing higher and louder than anyone else. In this he succeeded so well that his solos in the church concert were performed from behind locked doors in the vestry, in order to protect the stained glass windows.

He was forced to practise hymn singing alone on the hill behind his house and even then, with a following wind, his top notes played havoc with the glass houses on the allotment a mile away. This made him very unpopular with the neighbours.

World War Two arrived in time to save the situation. He was called up with the TA, to the delight of the rest of the council estate who formed the first ever Adolf Hitler fan club in wartime Britain.

His Army career was undistinguished until he was sent out to North Africa in 1942, an event which changed the whole course of the war.

'I was at a troop concert in Tunisia in December 1942,' said Major-General Sir Brian Cobblers from his home last night, 'when this little fat Lance Bombardier came on stage. He did some unfunny impressions and then he began to sing. My God, I've never heard anything like it. Windows shattered and men dived for cover as his top notes broke the glasses in the officers' mess. I sat there deafened by the noise and then, quite suddenly, it came to me: why not harness this terrible power, turn it against the enemy and get myself a KBE?

'That night, we drove Secombe out into the desert and placed him in a large round hole, immediately in front of an Italian division, with instructions to begin singing "O Sole Mio" at 4.30 am precisely.

'For two or three minutes there was no reaction at all from the other side. Then pandemonium broke out. White flags waved; men reeled about, clutching their heads and sobbing piteously. "Please-a stop," cried the Italian commander, brokenly. "We give-a in."

'My strategy had worked. Secombe the Sonic Songster Mark One was born, and, under conditions of great secrecy, we used him again and again throughout Europe. Believe me, if he had not developed laryngitis at Arnhem, we would have been in Berlin in 1944!'

After the end of the war, Secombe drifted into show business, managing to control his voice to a reasonable level, though at one performance at Blackpool Opera House, he managed to unleash a top C that opened the swing bridge at Warrington.

His subsequent appearances on television were always recorded in the presence of an ear surgeon and a glazier. The Rose Window at York Minster had to be boarded up when he sang there.

Success of a sort came his way – he acquired a wife, an agent and four children,. though not necessarily in that order. He was written up in the popular papers and written down in the intellectual ones. He suffered fools gladly because he was one of them and, like all performers, he was basically insecure. This was to be expected from someone who once said of his career that it was built on such shaky foundations as a high-pitched giggle, a raspberry and a sprinkling of top Cs.

PS. We are now settled up on the hill, with Jennifer living close by with her three children, Harriet, Emily and Sam; Katy, at present a member of the National Theatre Company, has a house nearby; David is married to Judy, a brilliant young publisher, and they have a lovely little daughter called Florence; and Andrew is married to the actress Caroline Bliss and they will have had their first child by the time this comes out.

My cup runneth over.

Family Memories

This mock obituary was written by Sir Harry Secombe in January 2001. It appeared in the *Daily Mail*.

Born Swansea, 1921. Left school 1936. Colliery clerk 1937–8. Soldier 1938–46 (North Africa, Sicily, Italy, concert party). Met Spike Milligan 1944 when his howitzer fell over a cliff. Met girl by pretending to be Canadian, 1946; married 1948. Professional debut Windmill Theatre, 1946; followed by touring variety, pantomime and radio. Met Tony Hancock, Mike Bentine, Peter Sellers. *Goon Show*, 1951–60 and forever thereafter. Singing lessons, four kids, Palladium, *Pickwick*, Broadway, *Oliver!*, records, books, telly, West End, hymns, peritonitis, diabetes, Knighthood, *Songs of Praise*, *Pickwick* again, six grandchildren, devoted wife, prostate cancer, stroke, malaria expected soon, wind slight to variable.

Best Mates

By Lady Secombe

My life changed irrevocably one Saturday night in the spring of 1948. I had gone to the Mumbles Pier dance with a group of girlfriends and had told my parents that if I didn't catch the 10.45 pm bus to Gower I'd be staying with one of them in Swansea. It was a dreadful evening, and after a couple of hours I decided to go home and set off to collect my coat. One of my friends stopped me on the way. 'Don't go home, Myra,' she said. 'Stay a bit longer.'

I allowed her to persuade me to stay and walked back to the dance floor. The next minute a young man in a check shirt came over and in a Canadian accent asked, 'Can I have this dance, please?' He was a good dancer, so when he asked me for another dance I accepted. After a while he took me over to meet his friends and I remember being very impressed that one of them – the only officer in the group – offered me a cigarette from a silver case.

It turned out that my 'Canadian' was the Swansea born and bred Harry Secombe, newly demobbed, and on a night out with his army pals from the same battery. I spent the rest of the evening dancing with him before he asked to see me home. I explained that I was staying at a friend's house, but he still insisted on accompanying me on the Mumbles train

to Swansea, with my girlfriends sitting in the seats behind us.
'Do you always have a bodyguard with you?' he asked.

He wanted to see me the next day, but as it was a Sunday
I suggested that instead we meet on Monday outside the
Plaza Cinema. When Monday rolled around I'd forgotten
what he looked like. I told my aunt, who worked with me in
Sutherland's dress shop, 'I don't think I'll go tonight.' She
played pop with me – 'You must go. That boy has been
fighting for his king and country – you can't disappoint him,
you have to go.'

So I went. But I positioned myself behind a pillar so that I
could see him before he could see me. I hadn't bargained for
him pulling the same stunt. We both laughed like hell when
we realised what we'd done. From then on we went out
together regularly. We'd go to the cinema or The Grand
Theatre and he'd make me laugh so much in the queue that
I thought I'd be sick; we'd take picnics to the beach and feed
our left-over lamb sandwiches to the sheep; he'd shout such
outrageous remarks after me as I got on the bus to go home
that I'd sit red-faced all the way from Swansea to Gower;
we'd walk down to The Slip and have stale doughnuts and
coffee and he'd tell me that one day he would drip me in
'mink and diamonds'.

I was soon invited round to tea to meet all his family, and
then he came home to meet my Mum and Dad and
grandmother. My grandmother hadn't been very impressed
when I'd told her that the boy I was seeing wanted to be on
the stage. 'Don't you bring any actors home here in shiny
suits,' were her exact words. I needn't have worried, Harry
charmed her from the word go.

It was on a bus on the way back from a visit to see Harry's
brother Fred, then a curate in Machen, that Harry proposed.
No, actually, he didn't propose – he *told* me that we would
be getting married in a few months' time. Throughout our
courtship Harry would be going to London to audition, and
it was on the strength of his engagement at the Windmill
Theatre and a concert party tour of Germany that he saved

enough money to spend £40 on a diamond engagement ring. I still have the bill for that ring and the one for £9 10s. for my wedding ring.

From day one he made me laugh and I tried to make him happy. There can be so many disappointments in show business and I always tried to encourage him when the going was tough. He worked so hard to give us all a good life. We always did everything together and we were always best mates. It's so hard without him in my life.

Harry always used to say that in the end 'You and I will jump off the roof together.' I wish we could have.

A Wonderful Father

By Jenny Secombe

My father should have been writing this endpiece for his two volumes of autobiography, but sadly it was not to be. He died on my 52nd birthday, 11 April 2001, after a long battle with cancer and suffering the cruel aftermath of a series of strokes.

The last years of his life, which should have been a golden time of relaxation spent with my mother, Myra, were instead a constant struggle for him. But it was typical that he bounced back, achieved so much and hung on to life for as long as he possibly could. He loved life and he loved Mum and he didn't want to leave this world without putting up a fight.

Dad was diagnosed with prostate cancer in the summer of 1998. In December of that year he wrote a piece for the *Daily Mail* about his diagnosis because he felt it would highlight this 'Cinderella' disease and encourage men to seek help if they showed any symptoms. This is what he said:

I have been tremendously moved by all the phone calls and messages of good will that have been pouring in. I have had calls from old mates like Spike Milligan, Norman Vaughan, Tony Snowdon and Jimmy Tarbuck. Nothing from Saddam Hussein as yet, though.

My sons and daughters and my grandchildren regularly ring to cheer me up. People I have never met send me 'get well' cards, many of them fellow cancer sufferers and I have the feeling that if I don't get well they'll never forgive me.

I'm not going to lie back and wait for the Grim Reaper to give me the 'red card' – I have a long way to go yet and the loving care of Myra, my family and friends and my faith will sustain me for however long the journey takes.

Compared with the battles against cancer bravely fought by my old friends Roy Castle and Mike Bentine, mine is a mere skirmish – but I think it is important for men to know that an early diagnosis of prostate cancer is very important, and to get a check-up as soon as they suspect something is wrong. So if my experience can take some of the fear out of this enemy which lurks within so many of us, at least some good may come of it.

My GP who, as well as being a fine doctor is also my very good friend, will forgive the slight exaggerations in my story...

It all started in my GP's surgery with a 'flu jab. He had informed me that as a 77-year-old diabetic it would be a good idea to have one before the winter set in. It would last for a year.

After he had performed the necessary inoculation he said matter of factly, 'How's the old water works?'

'Fine,' I lied, with my hand on the door handle.

'Perhaps we'd better have a look anyway.' He proceeded to put on the dreaded rubber glove, upon which I reacted like any other red-blooded male would have done. I made a dash for the open window.

'You've got a lovely view from up here,' I cried.

'Don't be silly. Come down from that window ledge,' he admonished. Back on his couch, in the required foetal position, with my knees practically under my chin, he probed around my nether regions with a rubber-clad finger. I tried to carry on as normal a conversation as possible under the circumstances but my voice kept jumping an octave or two. Outside in the street, a dog howled in sympathy.

'You can get dressed now,' he said. In thirty seconds I was fully clothed. 'Your prostate seems quite firm,' he informed me as he returned to his desk. 'And, by the way, your trousers are on back to front.'

'Is that a good sign?' I asked, readjusting my dress.

'As far as your trousers are concerned I've no idea, unless you're a Mason, but the firmness of the prostate is significant. We'll have to do some tests.' He removed some blood from a recalcitrant vein, fixed an appointment with a specialist and led me to the door. 'Even if you have got prostate cancer you'll probably die from something else,' he said, reassuringly.

On the way home I had visions of leprosy and black water fever rampaging through Guildford and got so absorbed in my thoughts I was nearly knocked down by a passing bus. 'He's got a point,' I breathed nervously.

Four days later he rang to tell me that it was cancer and that I had to see the specialist as soon as possible to decide on the treatment. I said 'If anything happens to me before the year is out will Myra get a rebate on the 'flu jab?'

He thought for a moment. 'I'm afraid not,' he replied.

'Ah well – easy come easy go,' I said, somewhat inappropriately.

When I met up with the specialist, who happened to come from my home town, he explained that he was going to take some tissue samples for a biopsy. 'I'm afraid you'll be impotent for a while,' he said diplomatically. Myra was with me and she raised an eyebrow and smiled a little secret smile. I suppose that knowing that the urologist came from Swansea somehow kept the conversation flowing a bit more freely; we discussed the beauty of the Gower coast as he removed several pieces of tissue from my prostate gland with what felt like a machete.

I was getting so used to being attacked from the rear

that two days later, on a visit to the diabetic doctor, I automatically dropped my trousers and adopted the knees up position on his couch. He rapped me on the shoulder. 'I just want to take some blood from your finger.'

The days waiting for the result of the biopsy caused some concern in my family, and even the cat presented me with a mouse. It appears that the cancer I have is of the liveliest type and therefore I had to have a bone scan. This fortunately revealed nothing abnormal and the pelvic scan which followed showed, to our great relief, that the cancer had not spread.

Before the pelvic scan I was taken to a dressing room and told to strip off completely. I was given a green surgical gown that was open all the way down the back, giving me the appearance of a decadent druid. A jolly young lady then inserted some metal object into my long-suffering fundament and I was off on the greatest adventure of my life.

The pelvic scan was most bizarre – it meant being carried inexorably at a snail's pace on one's back through a large tunnel-like machine while X-ray pictures were taken of the suspect area of my anatomy. It was like a journey through the Channel Tunnel without the consolation of duty-free shopping. I've got some nice photos though.

I have now to wait until next month while the hormone treatment I am having reduces the tumour to a size that can be targeted by radiotherapy. In my ignorance, before I became a reluctant 'expert' in prostate cancer, I vaguely imagined that 'radiotherapy' meant being forced to listen to endless repeats of *The Archers*.

It is, in reality, a highly technical machine which zones in with great accuracy onto the site of the tumour and for just a couple of minutes a day, for six weeks a high-energy radiation beam 'zaps' the cancer until it waves the white flag.

That is what the future holds for me in mid-January and

we all hope that it will do the job.

Finally, it would be hypocritical of me not to confess that, in spite of my decision to take a positive attitude towards my cancer, sometimes in bed at night there creep unbidden into my mind those 'what if?' and 'why me?' thoughts. I lie awake desperately wanting to clutch the present to my bosom and never let it go. I want the mornings to last longer and the twilights to linger and I resent the tyranny of the bedside clock draining away the time.

'Nothing lasts for ever' the rational side of me says, but I refuse to accept it. Self-pity rolls over me like a black tide.

At my side, Myra, who can read my thoughts even in the dark – because after all this is our Golden Wedding year – reaches for my hand and squeezes it.

'Don't worry love,' she whispers. 'It's going to be all right.'

And suddenly, I know that it *will* be.

In a cruel twist of fate, the week before Dad was due to undergo the radiotherapy treatment he collapsed at home having suffered a brain stem stroke. The effect of a stroke is devastating. Not only did it paralyse the left side of his body, but also initially caused him to slur his speech. Literally, at one stroke, he was rendered immobile, dependent and unable to communicate fully. The father I loved for his independent spirit, vitality, energy, humour, quick wit, optimism and ebullience became dependent, trapped by a body that no longer obeyed his commands, unable to communicate fully, his razor sharp brain temporarily dulled and his emotions seesawing.

It was so hard for him to come to terms with the limitations inflicted by the stroke but even at this terrible time he wanted something positive to come out of his experience. He had suggested to the BBC that it would be a good idea to make a programme about prostate cancer to help others in the same predicament and he volunteered that they should chart his treatment and document his experience. The stroke changed all that – the cancer was 'put on the back burner' and, instead, he decided that the film should follow his progress from the early days of the stroke, through his long rehabilitation. Anyone who watched the resulting programme, *The Trouble With Harry*, has witnessed the frustration he suffered and the determination and good humour with which he fought back. He had to relearn to walk, to talk and to do the simple actions that able-bodied people take for granted. The man whose thrilling tenor voice had been trained by a top Italian maestro was reduced to taking singing lessons from a young therapist to improve his speech. He applied all the determination that he had used to climb the ladder of success to push himself to the limits to walk again with the aid of a stick. He really was an inspiration. I had always been proud of my dad, but I was never so proud of him as during this agonising learning curve he had to negotiate. Although he mourned the 'old Harry' he realised that it was futile to regret all the things he could no longer do and that he had to get on with the present. He sold the big Jeep he used to love driving and bought a special scooter that he could ride round the grounds of the house. A stair lift was fitted to the beautiful sweeping staircase to enable him to continue sleeping upstairs and other adjustments were made to the house to help him adapt to his disability. Eventually he managed to come to terms with his new, limited lifestyle and, as was always his way, he turned negative experiences into positive ones.

The stroke had impaired his vision, so reading – which had always been a passion – became very difficult. His reaction was that if he could no longer read then he would have to write another book instead. *The Zoo Loo Book* of his limericks, illustrated by Bill Tidy, was duly written and published by Jeremy Robson.

The stroke had destroyed his beautiful singing voice. This

was a deep source of sadness to him and he couldn't bear to listen to his old recordings because they reminded him of a gift he no longer possessed. Yet he collaborated with his friend and musical director Ronnie Cass on an album that brought together all the best songs from the *Highway* and *Songs of Praise* programmes that he had performed over the years. Although stricken by illness, he continued his charity work for Diabetes UK and added The Stroke Association and The Prostate Cancer Charity to the causes that he supported.

His bravery at this time of trial was not a surprise to his nearest and dearest because Dad had always been a fighter. According to his sister, Carol, he used to fall out of the vestry after church services scrapping with his fellow choirboys. I loved to hear these stories about him when he was little. Whenever my grandmother used to stay with us I would climb into bed with her in the morning and ask her: 'Tell me the one about when Dad went camping up Kilvey Hill and he burnt your new frying pan', or, 'Tell me the story about when he was dressed up in a cat costume and flushed his paws down the lavatory before the school concert.' And off Gran would go, laughing at her recollections of the son who was the apple of her eye.

I am sure that he was a brave soldier too. During World War II he had served in North Africa, Italy and Sicily and seen heavy action with his artillery regiment. He would often regale us with wonderfully funny stories about his exploits as a 'walk on' in the war but he never dwelt on the tragic events he witnessed during battle. He was the same age as my teenage son, Sam, when he joined up. It's hard to imagine how he must have felt leaving home to fight the enemy in a strange land. When he was in Italy near the end of the war he made a short gramophone recording to post home to his parents. His voice sounds so painfully young and his message, typically, was intended to dispel their fears and make them laugh.

It was after the war that the newly demobbed Harry

Secombe met the love of his life, Myra Atherton, at a dance on the Mumbles Pier. This was truly a marriage made in heaven. My mother was to be his rock throughout his life and their love and devotion to one another was constant. They were never happier than when they were together. Their partnership was founded on a shared set of values and sense of humour and my father always said that Mum made him laugh more than anybody else in the world. Even at the end of his life when Dad was struggling against all his afflictions and Mum was taking care of him single-handed they still managed to have a giggle together. Their deep love for each other never ever wavered.

Initially it must have been very strange for my mother to leave the stability of her respectable Swansea home and lead a gypsy life on tour while her husband served his apprentice-ship in show business. To her great credit she took it all in her stride. She is the kind of person who is completely at ease in any company. You can take her anywhere and everywhere – and my father certainly liked to do that. She has, in the nicest way, remained the same lovely woman that my father fell in love with all those years ago.

Mine was an idyllic childhood. Despite the fact that my first four years of life were spent on the road staying in theatrical digs that were often less than salubrious, I always felt secure and loved. My early days were a kaleidoscope of summer seasons and pantomimes. Chorus girls would adopt me as their 'mascot' and I would be whisked off to their dressing rooms. I remember gathering up the brightly coloured sequins off the floor where they had fallen from their glamorous costumes and being plonked in front of the light-studded mirrors while they applied lipstick and rouge to my face before returning me to my father's dressing room. If I was very good I was allowed to stand side stage to watch my Dad do his act. This was the bit I liked best. Watching him from the wings as he stood centre stage in the spotlight always made me feel so proud. He shone and I basked in the reflected limelight. The stage was his natural environment where his boundless energy and huge personality were completely at home. I would listen to the roars of laughter as he clowned around and then wait for the audience to fall quiet as he started to sing. Soaring top Cs would be followed by rapturous applause. Then he would rush off stage, sweating profusely and on a high of adrenalin. 'How was it, Jen?' he would always ask as I mopped his brow. And I would always reply with complete honesty that he was the best.

Later on in his career the variety theatres would be replaced by television studios and film sets and the summers spent riding donkeys on the beach at Blackpool would be replaced by holidays in exotic locations. We were always included in everything that he did, not only because he enjoyed sharing the good times with all the family, but also because he felt it was important that we should appreciate what he did for a living. It wasn't all glamour, there was a lot of hard slog involved and he wanted us to respect his profession. We were never allowed to take our privileged lives for granted. Every Christmas he bought boxes full of toys for the local hospital and I remember accompanying him on one of his visits round the children's ward to distribute them. I was all decked out in my Christmas finery in a new coat, hat and little fur muff. It was humbling to see some of the very sick children and how they were spending their Christmas. The roast turkey dinner with all the trimmings and the presents under the tree that were waiting for us when we returned home seemed all the more special after that experience. Dad never forgot where he came from nor how fortunate he was to be 'a round peg in a round hole' doing a job he loved and being paid handsomely for it – and he wanted us to understand that too.

There are so many happy memories. Lots of star dressing rooms for him to pace in before going on stage, lots of trailers where he would rest in between takes, lots of countries to tour and lots of people to meet. I remember lazy, sunny days at our house in Mallorca, winter holidays in the

West Indies, long Sunday lunches at home in Cheam – all punctuated with lots of laughs. He was such fun to be with and had led such an interesting life that he was always great company. I think though that sometimes people underestimated him – they saw an ebullient clown but didn't see beyond that to his intelligence and wisdom. He had so many talents apart from his comedy and acting skills and his brilliant voice. He was a really great writer who wrote two best-selling novels, two children's books and two collections of short essays as well as being a regular contributor to *Punch* magazine. He was a gifted cartoonist and artist, and as a photographer he had pictures exhibited at the Royal Academy. He spoke Italian and French and schoolboy German, he completed *The Times* and *Telegraph* crosswords every day and never lost his love of learning.

He never baulked at a new challenge, and his career had been a whole series of new challenges. There can't be many performers who began their career as 'an angry young man of comedy' and ended up a pillar of society presenting religious TV programmes. There were, in between, detours into variety and musicals and films. He topped the bill at the London Palladium and starred in *Pickwick* on Broadway and made a very memorable Bumble in the film version of *Oliver!*. He had an appetite for new ventures and was always thinking about what he was going to do next. 'Follow that with the sea lions!' as they say in variety.

After such a thrilling career it was with great sadness that he announced his retirement from public life in September 1999. He chose to do this at his charity golf match, The Harry Secombe Classic held annually in aid of The Lords' Taverners, at the Effingham Golf Course in Surrey. Playing golf was another thing that the 'new Harry' missed.

He realised that the time had come for him to stop carrying on as he had done when he was in good health. It was never going to be possible for him to perform again and he had to admit that his charity commitments were taking too much of a toll on his health. He missed the buzz of performing, he missed the laughter and applause of an audience, but most of all he missed being able to sing. He was first and foremost a comedian, and this gift of making people laugh would continue until the end. But because he had worked so hard honing his singing talent and derived such pleasure from belting out songs, the loss of his voice was probably the most difficult thing for him to accept. When he was in hospital recovering from the first stroke we took in one of his CDs to play for him and he was reduced to tears.

He became much more emotional after he suffered the stroke. The right side of the brain – which was affected in my father's case – not only governs the mobility of the left-hand side of the body but also the emotions. The 'new Harry' was often moved to tears as well as laughter. There was a positive side to this as Dad was essentially a shy man but now seemed more able to express his feelings verbally. We always knew that he loved us, but now he told us regularly how much we meant to him.

Don't get me wrong, he never became over-sentimental – his sense of the ridiculous was still as highly tuned as ever and his wit never deserted him. Even on his deathbed he managed to make the nurses and doctors laugh. He always wanted people around him to have a good time and as a natural performer he was not about to change the habit of a lifetime.

By the beginning of 2001 the cancer, which had gone into remission while he had been recovering from the first stroke, had spread to his bones and he was in constant pain. It was terrible to see him suffer – even though he always tried to hide the pain from us, sometimes we were able to glimpse his despair.

A couple of months before he died, Dad and I were sitting alone together while Mum was in the kitchen. I asked him how he was feeling and he said, 'I know I haven't got long left. I want you to know that I'm prepared.' I started to protest and tell him that he was going to be around for a lot longer, but I could see that he was telling the truth. He had spoken to his doctor and he knew that if he was lucky he would live long enough to see his eightieth birthday in September. I asked him if he had told anybody else and he said, 'No, this is our secret. Don't tell your mother.' With tears in my eyes I promised I'd keep quiet and knowing how worried he was about Mum I also promised him that I would look after her although I would never be able to do it as well as he did. It was quite clear to me that although he had put himself in God's hands, he certainly didn't want to die, but if that was going to happen sooner rather than later then he was prepared to meet his Maker. He had a strong, unostentatious faith that was a great source of strength to him during his final years.

In February he collapsed at home and was taken into Mount Alvernia Hospital in Guildford. After a week he was allowed home but the next month his health deteriorated rapidly and he was rushed into hospital again. This time he would never return home. He went downhill fast, he lost his appetite and we had to coax him to eat. We even smuggled fish and chips into the hospital one night as a treat for him.

Dad hated being away from the home he loved. All the family and his close friends were constant visitors to his bedside and he was very uplifted by a telephone call from Prince Charles. But he desperately wanted to be back at home and in the middle of one night when he was at his lowest ebb and I was sitting with him he said quite firmly 'Get me out of this bed, Jennifer, I've got to get dressed and go home.' If only it had been possible, I would have hitched his bed to the back of my car and driven him home then and there.

The care that Dad received in hospital was exceptional. The doctors and nursing staff were incredibly sensitive – they genuinely cared for him. Dad was always telling them 'just call me Harry' when they tried to use his title, and they warmed to this gentle, funny man with no airs and graces. When he died they felt that they had lost a friend.

The hospital also had a number of nursing sisters who

provided palliative care and would call in to see Dad each day and say a prayer at his bedside. One of them, Sister Maria, told us that the last sense to go is hearing and advised us to keep talking to Dad even if he didn't respond. We didn't need any encouragement and chattered away non-stop. This was when Dad made his final comic gesture. In the middle of one of our conversations, we became aware that he was trying to attract our attention. With an almighty effort he pulled his bed sheet right over his head. One of his old gags was to put a handkerchief over his head and then put his glasses on over the top, and it was as if he was trying to do the same thing with the sheet. He looked so comical that Mum and I burst out laughing. We pulled the sheet back from his face, but with perfect comic timing Dad looked at us and yanked the sheet over his head again. We were giggling hysterically by now and our hilarity was only heightened when a nurse came in and tried to comfort us because she thought we were crying.

A lot of crying went on that last week of Dad's life. He was surrounded by all the family – my brothers Andy and David and sister Katy were at the hospital every day – even his six grandchildren were able to see him before he completely lost consciousness. Aunty Carol came down from Sheffield for the day, Uncle Fred was on the phone from Cardiff regularly and my mother and I spent every day and night at Dad's bedside, taking it in turns to sleep. It was a harrowing time yet an incredibly precious time. Nothing seemed to exist outside that hospital room.

Dad was drifting in and out of consciousness at this time, but there was a very tender moment when he opened his eyes, looked straight into mine and smiled and then made a supreme effort to turn to my mother and give her a kiss. Each night that Easter week we didn't expect him to survive till the next morning – but his strong heart kept beating, and his lungs kept going like a great pair of bellows. He was still fighting. But by now all we wanted was for him to be out of pain and at rest. I never thought that I would pray for my father to be released from life, but I asked God for a very special birthday present. On the night of 10 April my mother poignantly gave me my birthday present and a card that she had signed from 'Mum and Dad' – 'because tomorrow I may not be able to give it to you from both of us.' The following afternoon as I sat holding his hand, he opened his blue eyes and looked straight at me, but I could see that he was looking beyond me to some other place. I rushed out to fetch my mother and she ran to his bedside and cradled him in her arms as he drew his last breath.

I still find it difficult to believe that my father is no longer here. Every time I go home I half expect him to be sitting in his chair and I want to pick up the phone and talk to him. I miss him so much and yet I feel his presence every day. The grief that we all feel is great and still very raw. He was a huge presence in our lives and leaves a gaping void. Our mourning seems to have been shared by so many people all over the world. News bulletins and tribute programmes were broadcast on radio and television. The national newspapers devoted acres of space to reports of his death. His face beamed from all the front pages and a rare and genuine sense of affection was expressed in the obituaries and leaders. The Prince of Wales and The Archbishop of Canterbury paid public tributes to him and we have been inundated with letters from the great and the good. We have also heard from thousands of people who never even met Dad but whose lives he had touched in some way.

There were two anonymous cards we received that seemed to sum up Dad's very special qualities. One was from a man in Wales who wrote to tell us that he had just heard one of Dad's records played on the radio and 'here I am, a 76-year-old, six foot, ex-Welsh Guardsman and I'm sitting in my kitchen listening to his voice and crying like a baby.' And the other contained the simple message 'To Neddy Seagoon – thank you for making a schoolboy laugh.'

What a wonderful testament.

What a wonderful father.

That's My Dad

By Andy Secombe

I must have been about five or six when I first realised that my father was a national treasure. During my early school years, teachers and older pupils would often address me as 'Neddy' or 'Seagoon', and in those days I didn't have a clue what they were talking about. It was only when I first visited the London Palladium where he was appearing in one of a run of summer seasons, that I began to realise. My daddy didn't just belong to me – he was public property. But seeing him on stage swept away any misgivings I might have had about sharing him with the world. When he came on, he lit up the house, and that's not just filial pride speaking – it was obvious the rest of the audience also basked in the sun of his presence.

I went to see him many times after that, and never lost the thrill of watching him from the wings and hanging out in his dressing room. During the early sixties, the Palladium became a second home, in fact so comfortable a place did the theatre become, that I later became an actor.

He was not a big man – being a modest five foot eight – but he was 'larger than life'. When he came into the room his sheer vitality and the benevolence that radiated from him never failed to turn heads and draw smiles. He made people feel good; it was evident from the many functions I attended with him that people just liked to be near him. Often I would be pinned to the wall by a well meaning and usually inebriated party guest and told how lucky I was to have such a man as my father. I didn't really mind, after all it was true. No matter the drawbacks of being the child of a celebrity – and they are many – I was more than happy to be the son of one who was so deeply loved.

He filled the sky of my young world. So vital was he that I thought he was indestructible. When he was first diagnosed with cancer, and then suffered the ignominy of a stroke, it was a terrible shock. It was heartbreaking to see the god of my childhood, shrunken and slightly stooping, leaning for support on a stick.

For one so long in the public eye, his inability to perform was a dreadful blow, cruelly compounded by the loss of his fabulous voice. But with Mum beside him, he never lost his good humour and the will to live. Right up to the end he kept cracking jokes. His first words to Denis, the house-keeper's husband, coming to his aid when he collapsed at home for the final time, were: 'I can see right up your nose...'

Most people remember him today as the presenter of religious programmes like *Songs of Praise* and *Highway* – a role which, despite initial misgivings, he came to relish; meeting ordinary people with extraordinary stories was a humbling experience that he said helped him to keep a sense of perspective.

But I shall always remember him in his prime – on stage at the Palladium. While I watched from the wings as he turned cartwheels and hit top Cs; bestriding the stage like a colossus, I would turn to one of the stage hands and, glowing with pride, would say – 'That's my dad, that is.'

The Real Man

By David Secombe

I once asked my father if life had taught him anything. This was, uncharacteristically, a serious question. He was silent for a moment and considered his answer carefully before replying. 'Never play peek-a-boo with a small child at the start of an international flight.'

Most performers create a public persona behind which they can remain uniquely themselves. In Harry's case, he owned more than one public image and people knew and loved him for different and often contrasting reasons; indeed, it is fair to say that his appeal was so diverse that it was sometimes difficult for him to balance the varying expectations of his public. But he was a professional, a true 'pro's pro', and an extremely versatile one at that.

If I were to pick just two pieces of hard evidence to illustrate his character, I would start with a *Goon Show*; let's say 'The Histories of Pliny the Elder'. I particularly like this one because he is obviously having a great time, and it is his genuine laughter that we hear. I also have a photograph that I took of Dad at a recording session in 1980. He is in full flow, and completely inside the music. In both cases, you get the real man.

Dad

By Katy Secombe

Warm, funny, generous, talented, he was all these things; but most importantly, he was Dad.

My Lovely, Warm, Funny Brother

By Carol Williams (née Secombe)

Well! Where to start? So many memories. Life with Harry as a boy was never dull. You learned to expect the unexpected.

There was one time while on holiday in Cardigan when he miaowed his way across a barn roof on all fours and purred his way around the chimney pots.

Then he would be a ventriloquist's dummy perched on brother Fred's knee, answering his questions with a jerky head and fixed smile and squeaky voice.

Then he would be Stan Laurel. Off would come his garter (we all wore garters to keep our socks and stockings up – as my varicose veins will now testify) and it would be twisted round his head until his hair stood up straight. His face would contort into a half-crying Stan Laurel and he would rub his hand through his hair. He was such a good mimic and could 'do' any of the radio voices then. But, put him on stage with an audience and he would be petrified with nerves and inaudible beyond the front row.

My father became responsible for organising concert parties for church socials and local functions. Half of Wales seemed to be entertaining the other half in those unsophisticated times. Dad's family were already involved

– sister Margie was a pianist, her husband George was a tap dancer and drummer, and brother Cyril played the ukulele, sang and also played the saw – with a hammer!

I had always been a little show-off ready to perform at any time. Then Mam got hold of a record made by Ted and Mae Hopkins, a Welsh brother and sister who must have toured the music halls and then made a record – in those days quite something. I don't know where or why Mam got it but at the time we only had one record. It had 'In a monastery garden' on one side and 'A miner's dream of home' on the other, so the Hopkins record was a welcome relief.

Mam thought I could learn the Mae Hopkins monologue about being an old Welsh maid. These were the days of Shirley Temple so audiences were generous to precocious little girls. Then Mam thought Harry and I could learn the flip side with Ted and Mae conducting a Welsh courtship. Whether it was because he was working with somebody or whether it would have happened anyway, Harry began to lose his shyness and kept putting things in – reducing me to giggles. He also realised that if he took off his specs he couldn't see anyone anyway! We had lots of fun together and were well paid with loads of ham sandwiches and cakes served by women in pinnies – and always a hat – as they 'manned' the tea urn.

Then came the war, and Harry was called up and everything stopped. But there was no escape. I remember he once came to accompany me as I was going to work. The bus stop was opposite a post box in the wall. We had only recently moved to the 'posher' end of Swansea and didn't know anybody. The queue was quite large and as we walked past the post box he did a quick turn and put his ear to it and shouted: 'You'll have to speak up! What? Been in there since 1 pm?' He looked at the collection time on the front and said, 'Not till 6.15 pm, I'm afraid!' Fortunately the bus came and he said cheerio and went home – leaving me giggling and blushing with the queue furtively eyeing me all the way into town. No, life was never dull.

But I also remember a time when I was alone with Mam and she had a slight stroke. Dad was in hospital having a hernia operation. So I was alone and feeling the responsibility. We had no phone then but I'd managed to nip to a neighbour's to get the doctor. He came and said he'd be back in the morning. So there I was worrying and suddenly there was Harry at the door – just like the cavalry. He was on tour and had just come home. Anyway we could see Mam was recovering and we crept downstairs and stayed up all night drinking endless cups of tea and Harry started talking about his war experiences. About being stuck in a slit trench with a dead German for about a week (he must only have been about twenty at the time), about how it felt to be in the invasion force in North Africa and about his feelings when his friend was mown down in the Italian invasion and he didn't know whether he was still alive (he was). It all poured out and I felt very privileged to have been there for him. I still do, as he never ever mentioned it again.

It was ironic that Harry and his best friend at school would sit on Kilvey Hill looking at the ships in the docks and dream of going to Africa to shoot the lions and tigers. He never dreamed that he would go there in army uniform with a gun in his hand to shoot more dangerous game. He did go to Africa in more peaceful times – but armed with a camera – he'd 'had his fill of killing', he said.

He had so much talent – apart from his beautiful singing voice – photography, caricature drawing (we'd fire him a name – Mario, hairdresser – and quick as a flash there he was. Or Mr Bloggs, bank manager, and there he was – all plump cheeks and little moustache) and in later years writing. But greatest of all was his inventive sense of humour. He always made you feel better – no matter how he was feeling. He told me that he'd had so many flowers that he was afraid that he'd get greenfly! This was when he had just had a stroke.

I remember too when Mam was dying of cancer and Harry had made a dash home and he and brother Fred and Dad were talking in the living room. I was tending to Mam in the bedroom when there came a burst of laughter from the other room. Mam's face lit up and she whispered, 'Listen to them laughing' and she smiled a big smile.

That was Harry, my lovely, warm, funny brother and he leaves a big hole in my life.

A Good Man

By The Reverend Prebendary Fred Secombe

Who would have thought my brother, that the shy little boy, born in the back room in Swansea, devoted to his jockey cap to the extent of wearing it in bed, would have ended his life as front page news on every newspaper from *The Times* to the *Sun*. What is more, he had the undiluted respect of the whole entertainment world.

He was a good man, good in the best Christian sense of the word. No one spoke ill of him. He was kind and generous. His sense of humour was a supreme factor in his life, devoid of that cynicism which compels some comics to raise laughs nowadays.

We were raised in a council house overlooking Swansea Bay with the parish church at the bottom of the street. That church was to play a big part in our lives. It led to my ordination and to Harry's love of singing and the stage. When he was just seventeen he acted the role of beggar in Mansfield's *Good Friday* in the church hall. I am just two years and eight months older than my brother and before I went to college to prepare for ordination he was called up to serve in the Royal Artillery, having signed forms for the Territorial Army, hoping to get some spare pay and holidays from office work. It was a long holiday – six years!

When at last we were reunited, we went for a walk in Swansea's Singleton Park, I in my clerical garb and he in his demob suit. He said, 'Do you think it possible for me to have a vocation to the stage, just as you have to the church?' I told him that of course he could be called to the stage as much as I was to the church. I believe he worked on that basis all through his professional career. I know that the amount of time he had for church worship was limited (especially in his earlier days) when he had to work on a Sunday. However, he was delighted to be able to catch up with his religious programmes on television.

Down through the years we have been in touch with each other either in person at all his great occasions or else by telephone. Always his sense of humour would leave me the better for the contact. For example, when I began writing novels about the life of a curate in the Welsh valleys, the publishers were at a loss for a title. 'What about *How Green Was My Curate?*' he suggested. Problem solved! Even in his last days he managed to squeeze some humour out of his dying. 'I've had everything now, Fred,' he said, 'except malaria!'

In the eternal realms above, Mum and Dad, Roy Castle, Mike Bentine and his many friends will have welcomed him into their midst with the greatest of joy.

Rest eternal, grant unto him, O Lord, and let light perpetual shine upon him.

Growing Older

By Harry Secombe

I want the mornings to last longer
And the twilight to linger.
I want to clutch the present to my bosom
And never let it go.
I resent the tyranny of the clock on the wall,
Nagging me to get on with my day.
I am a time traveller,
But a traveller who would rather walk than fly
And yet it's joyous growing older,
The major battles of life are over.
There is an armistice of the heart
And a truce is signed with passion.
To forgive becomes easier
And reason takes the place of strife.
There's one more hurdle left for crossing
Though you're reluctant to approach it.
If you have lived your life with love
There will be nothing at all to fear,
Because a warm welcome awaits you on the other side.